AMANDA
BEVAN

University of London Legal Series

under the auspices of
The Institute of Advanced Legal Studies

X

LAW REPORTING IN ENGLAND

1485–1585

This volume is published with the help of
a grant from the late Miss Isobel Thornley's
Bequest to the University of London

Law Reporting in England 1485-1585

by

L. W. ABBOTT

UNIVERSITY OF LONDON
THE ATHLONE PRESS
1973

Published by
THE ATHLONE PRESS
UNIVERSITY OF LONDON
at 4 Gower Street, London WC1

Distributed by Tiptree Book Services Ltd
Tiptree, Essex

U.S.A.
Humanities Press Inc
New York

ISBN 0 485 13410 1

Printed in Great Britain by
WILLIAM CLOWES & SONS, LIMITED
LONDON, BECCLES AND COLCHESTER

PREFACE

THIS BOOK is a revised and abridged version of a thesis approved for the degree of Ph.D of the University of London in 1969. For its appearance in its present form I have to thank, first the University's Board of Studies in Law for recommending its inclusion in the Legal Series and, second, the Committee of the Isobel Thornley Bequest for a grant towards the cost of its publication. The studies which over the last six years have gone into its preparation were made possible by generous assistance from the Canada Council and the Province of Quebec.

The book is principally concerned with the period between 1535 and 1585, that is to say, between the year to which the last of the printed Yearbooks is devoted and that which saw the death of the greatest of the sixteenth-century reporters, Edmund Plowden. The half-century before 1535 is the subject of the first two chapters, which treat of the close of the Yearbook era and the beginning of 'Private' reports, and the development of reporting from 1585 until the end of the century is sketched in a concluding chapter. I hope to deal fully with this next phase of the subject, and in particular with the work of Sir Edward Coke, in a future volume.

Although the history of law reporting in the early modern period has lacked comprehensive study, I have profited much from the work of earlier scholars, notably Wallace, Maitland, Holdsworth and Plucknett. To their most distinguished living successor, Mr A. W. B. Simpson, I owe not only the benefit of his published work but great personal help and kindness throughout my own apprenticeship. In particular Mr Simpson has led the way in the elucidation of the problems posed by manuscript reports, a body of largely unused material which constitutes a major source for the present study, and as such is catalogued in the first Appendix.

Among the bodies and persons to which I am also indebted stands first the History of Parliament Trust: permission to utilize its biographies of law reporters who sat in the House of Commons spared me much labour in tracing their careers. I must also thank the custodians of books and manuscripts at the British Museum, Lincoln's Inn, the Inner and Middle Temple, Cambridge University Library, and the Bodleian Library, the Record Offices of Hertfordshire, Kent and Essex, and the libraries of Guildhall, University College London, the Harvard University Law School and the Congress of the United States. Private owners of manuscripts who allowed me to consult these include the Duke of Northumberland, the Marquess of Bath, Sir John Neale and Professor S. E. Thorne. In common with all its members I owe an immense debt to the Institute of Historical Research, where there is not only an extensive collection of printed books on legal history but a convivial scholarly environment: at the Institute of Advanced Legal Studies I enjoyed the use of its facilities and received advice and help from its librarian, Mr W. Steiner. Among many friends and colleagues who have helped me I should like to mention Dr Marjorie Blatcher, Professor J. P. Collas, Dr J. H. Baker, Dr Louis A. Knafla, Professor S. F. C. Milsom, and not least Mrs D. H. Easterling who had the skill and strength to type the manuscript on two occasions.

I owe a special debt of gratitude to Professor S. T. Bindoff, whose unselfish interest and efforts on my behalf have extended from the time the research commenced up to and including the reading of proofs and preparation of an index.

L. W. A.

CONTENTS

LIST OF PLATES

TABLE OF CASES

This table includes all cases, printed and in MS, cited in the text, footnotes and appendices.

TABLE OF STATUTES

ABBREVIATIONS

Add. MS	Additional Manuscript
Adm. Reg.	*Register of Admission*
And.	Anderson's *Reports*
A.J.L.H.	*American Journal of Legal History*
A.P.C.	*Acts of the Privy Council of England*
A.S.	Ames Society
Barr. MS	Barrington Manuscript
Bendl.	Bendlowes' *Reports*
Bodl.	Bodleian Library
B.M.	British Museum
Brooke	Brooke's *Abridgement*
Bull. John Rylands Lib.	*Bulletin of the John Rylands Library*
Bulstrode	Bulstrode's *Reports*
Cal. I.T. Recs.	*Calendar of Inner Temple Records*
Cal. M.T. Recs.	*Calendar of Middle Temple Records*
Camd.	Camden Society
C.L.J.	*Cambridge Law Journal*
Co. Litt.	Coke's *Institutes*, Part I
Co. Rep.	Coke's *Reports*
C.P.R.	*Calendar of Patent Rolls*
C.P.	Court of Common Pleas
Croke Car., Jac., Eliz.	Croke's *Reports*, Vols. 1, 2, 3
C.S.P. Dom.	*Calendar of State Papers, Domestic*
C.U.L.	Cambridge University Library
Dal.	Dalison's *Reports*
D.N.B.	*Dictionary of National Biography*
Dyer	Dyer's *Reports*
E., East.	Easter Term
Econ. Hist. Rev.	*Economic History Review*
E.E.T.S.	Early English Text Society
E.H.R.	*English Historical Review*
Exch.	Court of Exchequer

F.N.B.	Fitzherbert's *New Natura Brevium*
Fitzh.	Fitzherbert's *Abridgement*
Foss	Edward Foss, *The Judges of England*
G.I.	Gray's Inn
Gould.	Gouldesborough's *Reports*
H., Hil.	Hilary Term
Harg. MS	Hargrave Manuscript
Harl. MS	Harleian Manuscript
H.E.L.	W. S. Holdsworth, *A History of English Law*
Herts. R.O.	Hertfordshire Record Office
Hist. Parl.	History of Parliament Trust
H.L.R.	*Harvard Law Review*
H.L.S. MS	Harvard Law School Manuscript
H.M.C.	*Historical Manuscripts Commission*
Inst.	Coke's *Institutes*
I.T.	Inner Temple
Jenkins	Jenkins' *Centuries*
Keble	Keble's *Reports*
Keil.	Keilwey's *Relationes*
K.B.	Court of King's Bench
Lansd. MS	Lansdowne Manuscript
L. & P. Hen. VIII	*Calendar of Letters and Papers, Foreign and Domestic, Henry VIII*
L.Q.R.	*Law Quarterly Review*
Leon.	Leonard's *Reports*
Lib. of Congress MS	Library of Congress Manuscript
L.I.	Lincoln's Inn
Longleat MS	Manuscript of the Marquess of Bath preserved at Longleat
M., Mich.	Michaelmas Term
Mayn. MS	Maynard Manuscript
Moore	Moore's *Reports*
M.T.	Middle Temple
Official Returns	*Returns of the Name of Every Member of the Lower House* . . . 1213–1874
Owen	Owen's *Reports*
Palmer	Palmer's *Reports*
P.C.C.	Prerogative Court of Canterbury
Plow.	Plowden's *Commentaries*

Poph.	Popham's *Reports*
Rawl. MS	Rawlinson Manuscript
Rec. Soc.	Record Society
R.S.	Rolls Society
Salisbury	*Manuscripts of the Marquess of Salisbury preserved at Hatfield*
Savile	Savile's *Reports*
Shower	Shower's *Reports*
S.I.	Serjeants' Inn
S.S.	Selden Society
S.T.C.	*Short Title Catalogue*
T., Trin.	Trinity Term
Trans. R.H.S.	*Transactions of the Royal Historical Society*
YB	Yearbook
Yorks. Arch. Jour.	*Yorkshire Archeological Journal*

INTRODUCTION

THE sixteenth century was, in Sir John Neale's phrase, 'a law-ridden age' in which litigation bred lawyers and lawyers litigation. It is appropriate that attention should be given to the literature which was spawned by this natural, if all too prolific, union. In common with so many other features of English government and society, law-reporting in the sixteenth century underwent changes which were inextricably bound up with the status of the legal profession and the juridical system it served. The present study is an attempt to survey the work of reporters in relation to both.

Edward Coke, that self-appointed apostle of the common law, defined a report as

> a publike relation, or a bringing againe to memory cases judicially argued, debated, resolved, or adjudged in any of the king's courts of justice, together with such causes and reasons as were delivered by the judges of the same.[1]

In other respects adequate, this definition omits to state that it was advocates themselves who compiled reports, although this is their most distinctive feature. On an earlier occasion, however, Coke did assert that no man could effectively report on a subject with which he was not entirely familiar.[2] Certainly outsiders such as monastic chroniclers, law clerks and prothonotaries are known to have recorded court decisions during the medieval and early modern period but, like the *State Trials*, collections of this sort are not in the mainstream of sixteenth-century reporting.[3] By the same token a few volumes of cases taken exclusively from the conciliar courts and Chancery turn up at the end of Elizabeth's

[1] Co. Litt. 293a. [2] 3 Co. Rep. Pref. va.

[3] Coke warned his colleagues, 'beware of chronicle law reported in our annals'; 3 Co. Rep. Pref. va.

reign, but again, these were not the work of common lawyers and are distinctly inferior to the regular reports.[4] For the most part, conscientious barristers preferred to compile decisions from the three common law courts although these might well be interspersed with notable cases taken from rival tribunals. Until the end of the sixteenth century, the Court of Common Pleas commanded the major share of business and consequently most of the attention of lawyers and law-reporters. A corollary to this is the fact that disputes relating to criminal law receive considerably less attention than those concerned with civil matters. Irrespective of where a case was heard it was not so much the facts that interested practitioners as issues of law arising from those facts. The principal function of the justices in Westminster Hall was to resolve these issues: since many of the known sixteenth-century reporters were also judges it was their method of noting cases which set the general pattern.

These considerations notwithstanding, the work of the legal profession itself does not constitute the only significant source of our knowledge of litigious proceedings. The non-legal records of the central government, as made accessible in print through the Calendars, contain much material connected with the judicial process. Again, Tudor lawyers frequently cited precedents from their printed books of entries, registers of writs, the 'Old' *Natura Brevium*, Fitzherbert's *Natura Brevium*, *Novae Narrationes*, and, in fact, practically any text which might supply guidance in resolving a dispute. But, undoubtedly, the principal counterweight to the explicitly unofficial compilations of the lawyers is the vast repository of case-law contained in the official plea rolls. Each type of legal material was indispensable to the effective operation of the central courts yet each represented a distinct sphere of influence amongst the personnel who operated within the precincts of Westminster Hall.

The plea rolls enshrine irrebuttable evidence that a dispute did in fact take place, the identity of the litigants, the final judgment and the liability for any damages assessed. The record, in

[4] W. J. Jones, *The Elizabethan Court of Chancery* (1967), pp. 1–6.

Chief Justice Dyer's phrase, 'is a witness of the truth'. It was also the monopoly of those court officials who prepared the rolls and thus, whereas the attornies who filed the pleadings are invariably named, the advocates who argued the case are ignored. Conversely, the lawyers who compiled reports rarely bothered to recognize the existence of attornies but concerned themselves with the speeches of their colleagues on the bench or at the bar. For centuries after Bracton had taken upon himself to copy out decisions from the plea rolls, record and report were segregated, although by the sixteenth century it was not uncommon for an advocate to corroborate his notes of a case by referring to the official version. In any event, he was mainly concerned with what his colleagues actually said, how a particular legal issue was handled and the grounds upon which the judges based their decision. In the words of Maitland:

> The object of the record is a decent finality . . . The object of the report . . . is science, jurisprudence, the advancement of learning.[5]

This cleavage between record and report has had its repercussions in modern scholarship. Legal historians have tended to take sides when assessing the respective merits of law reports and plea rolls as source material. The Selden and Ames Societies, led by Maitland, Turner, Plucknett and their successors, have opened the Yearbooks to the scholar, and in doing so have extolled the virtues of these diverse, rambling, highly instructive, medieval compilations while tacitly belittling 'the chilly record'. To be sure, when modern editions of the Yearbooks are prepared the rolls are consulted as a matter of course and relevant sections of the record usually given along with the cases concerned. Nevertheless, there has been a tendency in the past to dismiss the rolls, with their massive bulk and anachronistic formulae, as fit only for statistical analyses. In recent years, however, there have been notable attempts to harness their vast potential and to place the Yearbooks and law reports in their proper juxtaposition. Professor Hastings' study of the Common Pleas in the fifteenth cen-

[5] *Year Books 1 & 2 Edward II* (S.S.), p. x.

tury and Professor Kiralfy's *Source Book of English Law* and *Action on the Case* are examples of how the plea rolls have been made to yield valuable information, while Dr Marjorie Blatcher is pursuing a similar course with respect to the Court of King's Bench. As a result, it appears that a better balance is being struck whereby the two great bodies of source material are becoming complementary in the advancement of English legal history.

It is nonetheless appropriate to recognize some of the particular advantages enjoyed in working amongst law reports. Professor Galbraith concedes in his *Guide to the Public Records* that in tracing the growth of law the Yearbooks are more important than the rolls. He reminds his readers that the very bulk of the latter and the absence of any form of reference present serious obstacles to the researcher. It is also difficult to follow the course of a particular dispute which may range over several widely-separated terms. Again, as Professor Hastings points out, the official record can be misleading, as for instance in describing the purely civil off-shoots of trespass in language which harks back to its ancient role as a remedy against crimes of violence. On the other hand, violent upheavals in society as a whole, or other momentous changes, invariably pass unnoticed.[6] But the lawyers, in collecting what was deemed relevant in their practice, were more attuned to the world about them. In theory the law did not change, but in six centuries of reporting it can be seen that the growth of legal thought was directly related to the evolution of the society it served. The emphasis was naturally on the forms of action involved and their applicability to given circumstances. In the sixteenth century this meant the proliferation of actions on the case in general, and assumpsit and trover in particular,[7] the conversion of the action of ejectment into a means of trying title, the recognition in law of copyholders and the use of fictitious recoveries to destroy estates tail; in short, a shift from reliance on status to fuller recognition of the rights of the individual. It also

[6] Hastings, *The Court of Common Pleas in Fifteenth Century England* (1947), p. 8.

[7] These are forms of action which derived initially from the writ of trespass but came to be applied as a means of enforcing contractual obligations.

meant a more subtle approach to the interpretation of statutes which, under the Tudors, assumed far greater influence within the body politic. Some of these developments could, and eventually may, be illustrated from the plea rolls, but, until such time, recourse to the reports as a form of selective index remains the only practical option.

The reports of the sixteenth century, concerned as they are with specialized subjects and couched in a technical, if corrupt, jargon, might seem to have little appeal to the layman. For the general historian such collections may appear narrow in scope and of minimal value as source material. They were, nevertheless, the product of inquiring, flexible minds trained to consider any manifestation of human endeavour or human nature which came for adjudication before the courts. Subjects as diverse as the authenticity of Henry VIII's sign manual and the impounding of a copyholder's livestock, Queen Mary's 'pregnancy' and the depredations of mice upon court records, and Queen Elizabeth's use of 'etc.' in the royal title and whether peacocks were classifiable as domestic animals—all basked equally in the light of judicial scrutiny. While practitioner-reporters tended to concentrate on the finer points of the land law (which still accounted for the bulk of business in the Common Pleas), leading cases of parliamentary privilege, the majority principle of election and the royal supremacy are examples of issues which commanded wider interest. Their enterprise also throws light upon the problems of the workaday world: the operation of markets, the export and import of various commodities, the types of food consumed, the regulation of usurious contracts, the effects of plague, and the attitude of Englishmen towards aliens. These, and a multitude of other subjects of dispute, can contribute to a picture of a society emerging from a neo-feudal towards a competitive economy.

The aim of the present study is two-fold: first, to present a survey of sixteenth-century law-reporting and to assess its role within the profession; and, secondly, to examine certain subsidiary topics associated with the reports themselves. The bulk of this study deals with the period between 1535 and 1585 since this was when the practice of reporting passed through one of its more critical phases. It is also a period which has not been examined in recent years although useful studies have been made of conditions at the beginning and at the end of the century.

The most comprehensive work on the subject is J. W. Wallace's *The Reporters Arranged and Characterized*, the last and fullest edition of which appeared in 1882. It has been the standard guide to English reporters for successive generations of historians,[8] and despite its discursiveness and archaisms it has weathered the twentieth century remarkably well. The author's preliminary remarks form a valuable introduction. What is, in effect, a summary of Wallace's survey was published by V. V. Veeder as a lengthy article under the title 'The English Reports, 1292–1865'.[9] Yet neither Wallace nor Veeder, in attempting to cover practically the entire history of English law-reporting, has succeeded in doing full justice to the early 'private' collections of the sixteenth and early seventeenth centuries. Holdsworth, on the other hand, in the fifth volume of the *History of English Law*, did survey this period with the aid of a useful table of reporters and some prudent generalizations. But Holdsworth, like Wallace and Veeder, confined his observations to the printed reports, a natural yet, for the sixteenth century, very misleading approach. One of the principal aims of the present study is to emphasize the importance of reports which circulated in manuscript.

T. F. T. Plucknett's monograph on Coke's Reports, which appeared in 1942,[10] surveyed with admirable thoroughness the background and preparation of this most famous set of reports from the period. The most recent studies on early law-reporting are four articles by A. W. B. Simpson which examine conditions

[8] For an appreciation of Wallace's book see W. L. Friend, *Anglo-American Bibliographies* (1944), pp. 18–22.

[9] *H.L.R.* xv (1901), 1–21, 109–57.

[10] 'The Genesis of Coke's Reports', *Cornell Law Quarterly*, xxvii (1942), 190–213; *cf.* J.H.Baker, 'Coke's Notebooks and the Sources of His Reports', *C.L.J.* 30 (1972), 59–86.

at the beginning of the sixteenth century and in the process revealed that 'private' collections were being compiled concurrently with Yearbooks.[11]

The first two chapters of the present work really constitute an introduction to the subject: Chapter I reviews the much-discussed problem of the Yearbooks and their disappearance as the standard vehicle of reporting, while Chapter II goes on to examine the first generation of 'private' reporters with the aid of evidence adduced by Simpson. Chapters III to VI are concerned with the second generation of reporters—those of the immediate post-Yearbook period—with particular attention being given to William Bendlowes, William Dalison, Richard Harper, James Dyer and Edmund Plowden; Chapter V also contains some remarks on the judicial process as revealed from a cross-section of case collections, and Chapter VI reviews the subject of statutory interpretation, in the light of information adduced from both printed and manuscript reports, as an adjunct to the main discussion of Plowden's *Commentaries*. The study concludes with an attempt to summarize developments in reporting in the last eighteen years of Queen Elizabeth's reign, and, in particular, to assess the part played by Sir Edward Coke.

The material used in this book has, of necessity, been extracted about equally from printed and manuscript sources. The notes of the most able reporters, Plowden, Dyer and Coke, were put into print during their respective lifetimes or—in the case of Dyer—shortly afterwards: consequently the published volumes form the basis of study when dealing with these men although, wherever possible, the printed word is amplified by recourse to manuscripts. The great majority of sixteenth-century reports were either never printed or were brought out long after their authors had died: for this group, manuscripts are relied upon in large measure but are supplemented by reference to the printed volumes where such exist.

[11] 'The Reports of John Spelman', *L.Q.R.* lxxii (1956), 334–8; 'Keilwey's Reports, Temp. Henry VII and Henry VIII', *L.Q.R.* lxxiii (1957), 89–105; 'The Circulation of the Yearbooks in the Fifteenth Century', *L.Q.R.* lxxiii (1957), 492–505; 'The Source and Function of the Later Year Books', *L.Q.R.* lxxxvii (1971), 94–118.

The number of manuscript law reports extant for the period under consideration runs to approximately 300. The main concentration of this material is found in the British Museum, where it is scattered through the Additional, Hargrave, Lansdowne and Harleian collections. Sizeable collections also survive at the Inns of Court, especially Lincoln's Inn and the Inner Temple. Outside London, the Bodleian Library and the Cambridge University Library contain many valuable manuscripts; a few legal compilations have also been traced to individual college libraries and the County Record Offices of Essex, Hertfordshire and Kent. Reports now the property of the Library of Congress and the Harvard Law School Library have likewise been utilized. The task of examining and appraising manuscript sources has consumed the greatest amount of time but cannot be regarded as complete. It is hoped that the appendices will be of some value as bearing witness to the wealth of material available for further study.

CHAPTER I

The Last of the Yearbooks

THE sixteenth century was a time when to become a recognized law-reporter was the mark of the successful practitioner, when a lawyer's reputation usually governed the value attached to any cases he collected. Yet no survey of these men and their work can be properly undertaken without preliminary consideration of the Tudor Yearbooks which lasted intermittently until 1535. In common with those of previous reigns, these tattered remnants of a great medieval tradition stand as a monument to the articulate, if nameless, reporters of the early common law. So much has been written over the last hundred years by so many eminent scholars on the origins, maturity and decline of the Yearbooks that further comment may seem sterile, if not presumptuous. Nonetheless, it is hardly possible to appreciate the development of 'private' reporting without endeavouring to place it against the background of the Yearbook tradition. The picture which emerges is not so much that of one system ending and another taking its place; rather, what we see is the slow decline of the one and the parallel growth of the other, both unpremeditated and probably unrelated.

The Yearbooks of Henry VII and Henry VIII have attracted little attention. Apart from the traditional preference shown by legal historians for the medieval period, the later volumes have been regarded as somewhat inferior specimens lacking the youthful exuberance which characterizes the Yearbooks of Edward II.[1] (Yet it is worth recalling that in the seventeenth century Francis North commended to every student the Yearbooks of Henry VII

[1] Neither the Selden nor the Ames Society has ventured beyond the reign of Edward IV, if we except Dr M. Hemmant's edition of *Select Cases in the Exchequer Chamber* (S.S.), vol. ii.

because 'much of the common law, which had fluctuated before, received a settlement in that time'.[2]) This neglect is the more unfortunate since only when a modern edition of the last generation of Yearbooks is available will it be possible to evaluate the entire series and to speak more confidently about its demise.[3] From the outset of the sixteenth century, however, it is evident that reporting of law-cases for circulation within the profession became noticeably more haphazard. The Yearbooks as a consecutive series extend no further than 1500, although a further nine scattered volumes from between 1501 and 1535 were to find their way into print.[4] It is symptomatic of the problem facing the modern student that the lawyers of the time were either ignorant of or unconcerned with the subject themselves. The earliest allusion to the mode of production does not occur until 1571. In the Preface to Part I of his *Commentaries* Plowden inserted a much-discussed reference to 'four reporters of our cases in law' and their 'yearly stipend from the King'.[5] Shortly afterwards, William Fleetwood took up what was really only a parenthetical observation and propounded the theory that these supposedly official reporters had ceased work on the death of Henry VII,[6] a view which was later adopted by Coke.[7] Despite the resourceful attempts of two Yearbook editors to rationalize Plowden's remark, the arguments marshalled by Maitland and Holdsworth tell heavily against the existence of royal patronage in the production of law reports before the seventeenth century.[8] The Yearbooks, we may be sure, were from beginning to end purely the

[2] *Lives of the Norths* (1826), i, 28.

[3] *H.E.L.* ii, 527–8; cf. A.W.B. Simpson, 'The Source and Function of the Later Year Books', *L.Q.R.* lxxxvii (1971), 94–118.

[4] J.H. Beale, *Bibliography of Early English Law Books* (1926), pp. 98–104.

[5] Plow. Pref. iv.

[6] *Annalium tam Edwardi quinti . . . Titulorum Ordine Alphabetico digestorum Elenchus* (1679), Dedication (written September 1579).

[7] 3 Co. Rep. Pref. xvia; he seems to have had second thoughts, however; cf. 4 Inst. 3–4.

[8] L.O. Pike, *Year Book 20 Edw. III* (R.S.), ii, pp. lxv–lxxvii; G.J. Turner, *Year Books 4 Edw. II* (S.S.), pp. ix–xxviii; cf. F.W. Maitland, *Year Books 1 & 2 Edw. II* (S.S.), pp. xi–xvii; *H.E.L.* ii, 532–41.

result of initiative within the legal profession and it is in this light that they are examined below.

Certain commentators have assumed that some of the mystery surrounding the Yearbooks might be dispelled by a scrutiny of relevant manuscripts of the late fifteenth and early sixteenth centuries.[9] Such a belief depends for its validity on the survival of sufficient material from which to draw meaningful conclusions. The number of legal manuscripts in circulation at this time must have been considerable. Printed Yearbooks were still comparatively rare and lagged somewhat behind current law terms. Yet while contemporary readings, commonplace books and pleadings survive in substantial numbers, reports proper are conspicuously scarce.[10] Although a number of abridged collections based on later printed editions are extant,[11] only three volumes of manuscript Yearbooks for the reigns of Henry VII and Henry VIII have been traced which can reasonably be regarded as contemporaneous.[12] While furnishing a valuable basis of comparison with the corresponding printed editions, these volumes are themselves incomplete and raise as many problems as they solve.

So meagre a residue from such an eventful period in the history of English law does not seem to be related to any external pressures which might have affected business in the courts. From the investigations of Holdsworth and the more recent researches of Dr Marjorie Blatcher it appears that litigation in the courts at Westminster began rising in volume at the beginning of Henry VII's

[9] J. W. Wallace, *The Reporters* (1882), p. 640; *H.E.L.* ii, 527–8.

[10] B. H. Putnam, *Early Treatises on the Practice of the Justices of the Peace* (1924), pp. 175–6, 184–7.

[11] I. T. Barr. MS 56, ff. 5–87 contains a summary of printed entries for 1–14 Hen. VII and 12–14, 18–19, 26 & 27 Hen. VIII; B.M. Add. MS 35938 (224 ff.) includes extracts from all the Yearbooks printed between 1485 and 1505; H.L.S. MS 8 (66 ff.) comprises YBB 5–8 Henry VII (with two cases from 12 Hen. VII) translated into English, probably prepared in the late sixteenth century.

[12] Bodl. MS Lat. misc. C.55, B.M. Harg. MS 105, and Lib. of Congress, Gell MS (see *H.M.C. Ninth Rep., App.* p. 385). Details of the contents of these MSS are set out in Appendix I, pp. 256, 267.

reign.[13] Although this trend was punctuated by periodical contradictions, the only short-term disruptions which seem to have affected the production of law-reports were outbreaks of pestilence.[14] The scarcity of manuscript Yearbooks must thus be ascribed either to a lack of demand on the part of the profession or to wholesale destruction.

It was Stubbs' belief that while people wrote and printed more under the early Tudors they also destroyed more: he gave the neat, if oversimplified, explanation that Catholics destroyed all that was new and Protestants all that was old.[15] Undoubtedly, many valuable and important manuscripts of all types were lost as a result of book-burning and iconoclasm, but these can hardly account for the shortage of early-sixteenth century law reports. Clearly, more immediate and specific causes were at work. For one thing, paper was being used in place of parchment for the later Yearbooks and this must have resulted in more rapid deterioration. For another, whereas it is assumed that the initial time-unit of reporting and distribution was a year, most of the surviving collections from Edward IV to Henry VII combine several years together: presumably the original yearly pamphlets had perished, had been recopied several times, and were eventually consolidated into larger groups.[16] The only full collection of Yearbooks for Henry VII which has survived, Hargrave MS 105, was probably compiled at about the time when the first printed editions were in course of production. The printing of Yearbooks, although slow by comparison with that of the statutes, was fairly prompt when compared with the fate of most private reports later in the century. As far as the Henrician Yearbooks are concerned, the need for producing fresh manuscript

[13] *H.E.L.* iv, 252–8; Dr Blatcher is studying the volume of litigation in the courts as revealed by an analysis of sealing fees recorded in the Hanaper accounts.

[14] The effect of plague in London is discussed further in Chap. III, pp. 62–4.

[15] William Stubbs, *Seventeen Lectures on Medieval and Modern History* (1886–7), p. 384.

[16] A. W. B. Simpson, 'The Circulation of Yearbooks in the Fifteenth Century', *L.Q.R.* lxxiii (1957), 492–3.

copies was, for the most part, rendered superfluous by the 1540s;[17] after that, most of the existing manuscripts are likely to have been lost or destroyed.

Such considerations cannot, however, wholly account for the dearth of later Yearbook manuscripts. It was formerly suggested that these had always had limited circulation, perhaps being restricted to the order of serjeants,[18] but a more recent study has shown that many surviving copies of fifteenth-century Yearbooks were originally prepared for practitioners below that rank.[19] There is, moreover, evidence that fewer reports of all sorts were being compiled in the early sixteenth century and that many were to remain in private hands until long after the last of the Yearbooks was published.[20] Between 1501 and 1519 the system by which annual reports were produced, if such a system ever existed, broke down almost completely: the only cases ever to appear in print from that period were the Yearbooks 20 and 21 Henry VII.[21] This was the first break in the series since 1447. More important, there is a strong presumption that Yearbooks did not circulate in manuscript during this twenty-year period. It seems unlikely that Fitzherbert or his collaborators would have neglected to make use of them, had they been available, when compiling the *Graunde Abridgement*; as it is, he includes no cases later than 16 Henry VII (1500–1).[22] Similarly, Robert Brooke, who began practising about 1530, has no reference to court decisions during the years 1501–3 and 1506–8, and a solitary entry from the period between 1 and 11 Henry VIII (1509–20).[23]

[17] By then only YBB 10, 11 & 13 Hen. VII remained to be printed; these were brought out by Tottel in 1555.

[18] T. F. T. Plucknett, 'The Place of the Legal Profession in the History of English Law', *L.Q.R.* xlviii (1932), 337.

[19] Simpson, 'Circulation of Yearbooks', pp. 495–505.

[20] See below, pp. 18–19, 29–31.

[21] These were published in erratic fashion, appearing respectively in 1555 and circa 1530–9; see Putnam, p. 135, n. 3.

[22] Fitzherbert does, in fact, include one entry dated 19 Hen. VII (1503), but this is a personal note taken verbally from Justice Frowick and not an orthodox report; see tit. 'Bastardie', no. 33.

[23] Brooke, tit. 'Fine levy', no. 111, 'Count', no. 87, 'Saver de default', no. 50.

It was not until late in Elizabeth's reign that these 'missing' years began to turn up in the hitherto private case-books of judges and barristers. It is still a matter of conjecture whether such isolated productions can be considered embryonic Yearbooks or merely a substitute for them.[24]

On the present evidence, there appear to be only two possible explanations: either traditional methods of production were faltering or the profession no longer required a continuous flow of new reports for its work; each factor was undoubtedly dependent on the other, but in what order is difficult to determine. In any case it is obvious that the introduction of printing into England in the fourteen-seventies was a decisive event which was to alter drastically both the preparation and the style of Yearbook reports in the early sixteenth century.[25] The first volumes were published during the fourteen-eighties by William Machlinia and John Lettou;[26] but the key-figure during the critical period between 1500 and 1530 was Richard Pynson, the first printer to bring out Yearbooks in any quantity. Pynson had learnt his trade at Rouen and he set up shop in St Clement's parish about 1490. In the course of the next forty years he was to bring out over ninety volumes of Yearbooks from 1363 to 1522, and of the forty-seven years between 1 Edward IV and 14 Henry VIII for which they were made he was responsible for the initial publication of thirty-two.[27] In 1508 Pynson was appointed King's Printer and during the next twenty years he had a virtual monopoly of the production of Yearbooks. Whatever their fate he must have been closely involved.[28]

From the outset there was a noticeable gap between the year reported and that of its emergence from the press. Machlinia and

[24] They are examined in more detail below, Chap. II, pp. 37–58.

[25] *H.E.L.* ii, 542–3; Simpson, 'Source and Function of the Later Year Books', pp. 94–118.

[26] Beale, pp. 182–3.

[27] Ibid. pp. 187–90 and entry nos. R.-223 to R.-454; Soule, 'Year Book Bibliography', *H.L.R.* xiv (1901), 564.

[28] The only other printers to bring out Yearbooks in this period were John Rastell (YBB 17, 18 Edw. III, 10 Edw. IV, 1 Edw. V and 1 Ric. III) and Robert Redmond who mostly issued reprints of Pynson's work.

Lettou chose to go back fifty years and publish reports from 33 to 37 Henry VI.[29] If the reason for their choice could be discovered a great deal more might be known about the preparation of Yearbooks in the courtroom, but it probably related to the availability of manuscripts, a circumstance which may also account for the lack of chronological sequence in Pynson's output.[30] It has been suggested that the gap between preparation and publication arose from some sort of restrictive practice exercised by the scriveners and reporters.[31] If so, it was not enforced consistently: the break might be as much as thirty years or as little as ten, and in one case it was only a year or two.[32] It is to be inferred, moreover, that had such an arrangement been in force more manuscript reports would have survived. The suggestion also presupposes a fairly sophisticated organization for the production of Yearbooks, whereas by the time Pynson gained ascendancy the dissemination of reports seems to have rested entirely in his hands, and the only response from the scriveners was to offer lawyers a larger collection of years in one volume than did their rivals. Both scribes and printers, it appears, were obliged to seek out material wherever and whenever it could be found.

The reluctance of Pynson and his colleagues to bring out current cases may also have reflected apathy on the part of the lawyers. Plucknett has contended that while the older Yearbooks were popular as material for study they played little part in the barristers' professional work.[33] This view, however, does not seem to take sufficiently into account the changing function of Yearbooks and law-reports in the Tudor period. It was during the reign of Edward IV that written pleadings first came into use.[34] This innovation not only caused the style of reporting to alter but

[29] Beale, pp. 182–3. [30] Ibid. pp. 188–90.

[31] Soule, p. 564; P.H. Winfield, *The Chief Sources of English Legal History* (1925), p. 174.

[32] Pynson published three contemporaneous volumes: 9 Hen. VII—[1508], 12 Hen. VII—[1508], 14 Hen. VIII—[1525].

[33] T.F.T. Plucknett, *Early English Legal Literature* (1958), pp. 111–13; cf. *H.E.L.* ii, 543.

[34] *H.E.L.* iii, 650–8; Hastings, pp. 186–7.

probably encouraged the use of Yearbooks as a source of authority as well as learning.[35] Under the older system of oral pleading, reports had served as manuals of instruction in the technique of formulating the essential issues necessary if the court was to pass judgment.[36] As Maitland pointed out, more often than not medieval reporters neglected to record final judgment in a case under consideration;[37] their job was to instruct both barristers and students in the art of pleading. With the advent of 'paper pleadings' the Yearbooks continued to stress the arguments of bench and bar, but the emphasis was now directed towards the issues of law already formulated.[38] In addition, new forms of action were being introduced to cope with problems engendered by a society moving from a neo-feudal to a commercial economy; subject-matter no less than technique was now the concern of the profession and the first thing every new student was required to study were writs and the remedies they gave.[39] This emphasis on results is also demonstrated by the evident appeal of printed abridgments. On the other hand, while judicial consistency was a recognized principle in the courts, the time had not yet arrived when up-to-date decisions were essential. Case citation in the later Yearbooks was infrequent and vague,[40] and in the circumstances a case from Edward IV might be as persuasive to a Tudor judge as one from Henry VII: even in Coke's *Reports* Yearbook decisions are cited more frequently than those of Dyer and Plowden. Finally, from the point of view of an entrepreneur like Pynson, it was probably more economical to publish several volumes at a time, regardless of how 'out-of-date' they had become.[41]

When the Yearbooks of Henry VII are examined more closely in relation to the few remaining manuscripts a number of problems arise. Because he rarely dated his work, it is difficult to estab-

[35] Turner, pp. xv, xxix. [36] *H.E.L.* ii, 553–6; iii, 654–5.

[37] *Year Book 3 Edw. II* (S.S.), p. lxxi. [38] *H.E.L.* iii, 654–5.

[39] Sir John Fortescue, *De Laudibus Legum Angliae* (1952), pp. 117–19.

[40] Turner, p. xxix; T.E. Lewis, 'The History of Judicial Precedent', *L.Q.R.* xlvii (1931), 411; but see C.K. Allen, *Law in the Making* (1964), pp. 190, 203.

[41] Beale, pp. 188–90.

lish with any precision the chronology of Pynson's printed editions for this reign. He waited until the first decade or so of the sixteenth century before starting and then proceeded to publish years 1–8 Henry VII (1485–93) in one volume.[42] This in itself was a novelty, perhaps prompted by competition from the scriveners. The number of cases for each year is somewhat smaller than in previous volumes. If Pynson had difficulty in collecting sufficient material he may have deemed it more economical to prepare the entire eight years in one impression. The edition follows closely the version transcribed in Hargrave MS 105, although there are sufficient discrepancies to make it clear that this particular manuscript did not serve as Pynson's model;[43] moreover, Hargrave 105 is part of a fuller collection which could not have been copied until after 1505. Both versions, however, obviously emanated from a common source. Thirty years later Robert Redmond reissued Yearbooks 1–8 Henry VII using Pynson as his model. He added a number of new cases, particularly for 1–4 Henry VII, which he noted were 'hucusque deficientibus':[44] the additions are fairly substantial, amounting to almost one hundred entries in all.[45] The source of these new entries cannot be traced, but it was presumably a distinct collection 'discovered' by Redmond. Some of them concern matters of constitutional significance such as the problem of attainders hanging over from Richard III's time.[46] Doubts have been cast upon the authenticity of this case which took the form of a reference to the Exchequer Chamber;[47]

[42] Ibid. p. 188, gives 1502 as the likeliest date; Soule, p. 565, estimates 1505; the *S.T.C.* omits any reference to the Pynson edition but generally chooses 1525 as the date for other printings by Pynson from this period; *S.T.C.* nos. 9913, 9930–1. This edition is now rare: one copy is owned by the Harvard Law School Library and a second by the Huntington Library, while a third (incomplete) is in private hands, the owner being Mr John R. Hetherington, Vernon House, Edgbaston.

[43] R. V. Rogers, *Year Books 9–10 Henry V* (1948), p. xxi n. 8.

[44] Redmond's edition came out sometime in the 1530's; Beale, p. 285.

[45] Twenty new cases in 1 Hen. VII, thirty-one each in 2 and 3 Hen. VII, twelve in 4 Hen. VII and two in 5 Hen. VII.

[46] Printed in Redmond as YB T. 1 Hen. VII, 20b.

[47] *C.S.P. Spanish*, 1485–1509, intro. l; Hemmant, i, App. 1; Rogers, *Year Books 9–10 Hen. V*, p. xxi; cf. Fitzh. tit. 'Parliament', no. 2.

but, given the troubled times, such questions were bound to arise, and indeed did, on several occasions in 1485.[48] Much of Redmond's material concerns criminal matters and, in general, gives more attention to proceedings in the King's Bench.

Yet a third version of the Yearbooks for 1 to 8 Henry VII was issued. In 1555 Richard Tottel put out a large volume containing all the known Yearbooks for the reign of Henry VII.[49] Most of the cases from the Pynson–Redmond series were included although the order is quite changed and some entries are considerably fuller. For the years 1 and 2 Henry VII a further selection of 'new' cases was added: Tottel refers to these as coming 'de nova at valde bona collatione'. Many of the earlier cases, it seems, had never circulated among the lawyers since both Dyer and Brooke specifically cite some of these for the first time shortly after 1555.[50] On the other hand, Tottel also published, in the same volume, the first edition of Yearbooks 10, 11, 13, 16 and 20 Henry VII (1494–6, 1497–8, 1500–1, 1504–5).[51] All the above years, except 11 Henry VII, had long been in circulation, as is proved by their inclusion in Hargrave 105 and Fitzherbert's *Abridgement*. Either Pynson neglected to print them or his volumes have since perished,[52] but if he had brought them out, Redmond would probably have reprinted them. As it is, there are no Pynson editions of reports beyond 1496 in the Henry VII series, although he did publish Yearbook 14 Henry VIII. Yet Thomas Berthelet brought out editions of 14 and 15 Henry VII in 1529 and Redmond is credited with the earliest printing of 21 Henry VII.[53] From such a tangled situation the only conclusion to be reached is that no coherent organization existed to produce

[48] P. Vinogradoff, 'Constitutional History and the Year Books', *L.Q.R.* xxix (1913), 273–84.

[49] Beale, p. 285, R.-409.

[50] Dyer, 105a; Brooke, tit. 'Sanctuarie', no. 18, 'Pape', no. 1, 'Patentes', no. 109.

[51] Beale, pp. 98–9.

[52] Some printed Yearbooks seem to have been lost: Simpson suggests that a pre-1536 edition of YB 12 Hen. VIII was printed but has not survived; 'Circulation of Yearbooks', p. 493.

[53] Beale, p. 285.

manuscripts for publication; rather, the printers were obliged to glean whatever material they could from individual students or practitioners. Towards the end of Pynson's career the same sort of competition seems to have existed as prevailed in the first half of the seventeenth century with respect to 'private' reports.[54]

The foregoing observations must be tempered by what has been described as the 'almost hopeless chronological chaos' within the printed Yearbooks.[55] The division into terms, especially among the reports for Henry VII, seems to have been an arbitrary affair. Except for 5, 20 and 21 Henry VII, neither Pynson nor the copyist of Hargrave MS 105 makes any reference to terms, while because both Redmond and Tottel employed different sources, the arrangement of terms in 1 and 2 Henry VII in their respective editions is quite distinct.[56] Moreover, the numerous entries found under Michaelmas 20 Henry VII in Tottel's edition are divided into five separate terms taken from 20 and 21 Henry VII in the Hargrave manuscript.[57] It also appears that the cases printed under 9 Henry VII in the 1555 edition really belong to the following year, as tabulated in the manuscript version; this is corroborated by the fact that the call of serjeants referred to in one entry did not occur until 1495.[58] Undoubtedly, some of the confusion arose from the nature of the cases themselves. If, as often happened, a dispute extended over more than one hearing, the reporter might either scatter parts of the case in different terms or wait and write up his report after it had been settled. In the circumstances, mistakes regarding years and terms were bound to be made.[59] For early Tudor lawyers there was really no need for precision; it was usually sufficient for a barrister to refer simply to 'nostres livers' when citing a case in court. It is worth noting

[54] Wallace, pp. 10–12; see below, Chap. III, pp. 85–6.

[55] Putnam, p. 131 n. 9.

[56] The division of terms in Bodl. MS Lat. Misc. C. 55 is at variance with the other collections covering Hen. VII.

[57] Noted by Putnam, p. 135 n. 3.

[58] Ibid. p. 131 n. 9; see B.M. Harg. MS 105, f. 23.

[59] Hemmant ii, p. xlviii; cf. YBB T. 12 Hen. VIII, pl. 2; T. 13 Hen. VIII, pl. 1; T. 27 Hen. VIII, pl. 2.

that the practice of numbering cases in both the Yearbooks and Fitzherbert's *Abridgement* was first introduced by Tottel in the second half of the century. Brooke's *Abridgement*, which was compiled before 1558, contains virtually no references to terms.[60]

The early Yearbooks of Henry VII present other problems. Why, for instance, are some cases written in Latin instead of the usual law-French? The use of Latin begins at Michaelmas term 2 Richard III and persists for the ensuing thirty-three entries; the final twenty cases, however, are in French, as are those for Edward V. A similarly irregular pattern emerges in the reports between 1485 and 1487, where Latin reports are to be found in random blocs throughout. Using the Pynson edition as model, in 1 Henry VII there are twenty-five out of a total of thirty-eight entries, in 2 Henry VII eight out of twenty-eight, and in 3 Henry VII eleven out of thirty-four.[61] A further four Latin reports turn up in 21 Henry VII.[62] The reprints of Redmond and Tottel include some Latin cases, although in Tottel's version the number is noticeably fewer.[63] These entries are not writs or extracts from the plea rolls but summaries of arguments taken in court such as were customarily prepared in law-French.[64]

The problem is to determine at what stage in the reporting process Latin was introduced. If cases were put into Latin by the original reporter, there is the possibility that a clerk or prothonotary was involved, as has been suggested by Pike in connection with earlier Yearbooks.[65] But it appears from the rather stilted syntax employed that the Latin is a translation from the original.[66] Moreover, the retention of certain traditional French phrases

[60] The second edition of Fitzherbert was issued by Tottel in 1565 and of Brooke in 1573; Beale, p. 287.

[61] There are the same number of Latin reports in Harg. MS 105 but four additional cases in law-French.

[62] Found in both the Redmond and Tottel editions but not in B.M. Harg. MS 105.

[63] In 1 Hen. VII, 12 out of 64; 2 Hen. VII, 2 out of 55; 3 Hen. VII, 10 out of 66,

[64] For a discussion of French as the medium of expression see below, Chap. III. pp. 86–9.

[65] *Year Book 20 Edw. III* (R.S.), ii, lxxi–lxxvii.

[66] Cf. Hemmant, ii, p. xvi.

indicates that the reports were initially made in that language, a conclusion which is reinforced by the fact that versions of certain cases survive in both Latin and French, sometimes in the same Yearbook; one of these cases concerns the attainder of Humphrey Stafford in 1486, of which the earliest copy is located, in French in the Bodleian manuscript, Lat. Misc. C.55.[67] The very fact that the Latin entries are found as scattered items suggests that they became assimilated with contemporary French manuscripts prior to publication. It is hardly conceivable that members of a profession which so jealously guarded its use of law-French would have prepared reports in Latin; it is much more likely that some reformist clerk prepared a translation. Such an undertaking would have been an interesting prelude to the call for greater use of Latin within the profession which arose as a by-product of the New Learning.[68] While there is no way of making a positive identification, the author must have been associated with both the legal and clerical branches of the law. One person who falls into this category was John Jenour, who rose from being a Clerk of Assize to become, under Henry VIII, Prothonotary of the Common Pleas.[69] Jenour's opinions carried great weight with the serjeants-at-law when cases were being pleaded in court; he is often mentioned as citing 'presidents' or discussing legal points in the Yearbooks.[70] In addition, Jenour was a prominent member of the Middle Temple where he held the office of Treasurer between 1517 and 1520. He also compiled a large Book of Entries which, though never printed, was in use during the sixteenth century and survives to this day.[71] Perhaps Jenour, or someone like him,

67 Cf. Harg. MS 105, ff. 101–102; Tottel edition (1555) 22b–24a; see also C.H. Williams, 'The Rebellion of Humphrey Stafford in 1486', *E.H.R.* xliii (1928), 186–7.

68 See below, Chap. III, p. 88.

69 E.W. Ives, 'Some Aspects of the Legal Profession in the Late Fifteenth and Early Sixteenth Centuries', unpublished Ph.D. thesis (London, 1955), p. 110.

70 YBB E. 27 Hen. VIII, pls. 2, 14; T. 26 Hen. VIII, pls. 13, 25.

71 *Middle Temple Bench Book*, i, 4; Dyer, 172a, 189a; in his will (P.C.C. 10 Spert) he bequeathed his 'bok of Entries' to his son Richard; the manuscript (in Latin) is in the Library of Congress, MS. Ac. 1093–4.

decided that his colleagues at the bar would benefit from a set of Yearbooks rendered into Latin from that 'barbarouse tong' so dear to the fraternity.

Whether the compilers of Tudor Yearbooks acted on their own initiative or in accordance with some arrangement with the printing trade, both their status and proficiency rose during the late fifteenth and early sixteenth centuries. Even by the reign of Richard II that 'eager, adventurous spirit' which had characterized the earlier Yearbooks was fading. The various undisciplined pamphlet-reports compiled by students in the 'crib' had shrunk to a single definitive text.[72] Reports were less discursive and more orderly in the presentation of issues. While exchanges between bench and bar formed the basis of most entries and the use of hypothetical analogies continued, there was an effort to formulate principles of substantive law. This can be accounted for, in part, by the fact that by the fifteenth century the legislation of Edward I dealing with the holding of land had been assimilated into the common law. At the same time, new statutes had been enacted which removed numerous areas of discretionary justice.[73] The evident grasp which successive reporters of the fifteenth century had of their material shows that they were accomplished apprentices in the full professional sense. Under Henry VI and Edward IV their art matured thoroughly. Yearbooks were fuller and more accurate with the arguments between serjeants and judges more formalized. The 'Long Quinto' marks, perhaps, the most ambitious example of reporting in the fifteenth century. This is a separate volume of cases for 5 Edward IV, probably compiled from various first-hand accounts. Besides being a far larger volume than any other individual Yearbook, it contains an immense number of long, impersonal entries which summarize, rather than report, specific cases.[74] We must remember, however, that the Long Quinto was not printed until sometime between

[72] T.F.T. Plucknett, *Year Book 13 Rich. II* (A.S.), p. xvi; Turner, p. xxiv.

[73] Plucknett, *Year Book 13 Rich. II*, p. xvii.

[74] *H.E.L.* ii, 537; Beale, R.-370, p. 187; Simpson, 'Source and Function of Later Year Books', p. 94.

1547 and 1553 and that there is no evidence to show that it ever circulated among the lawyers prior to publication.[75]

The Yearbooks of Henry VII, although apparently drawn from a number of sources, display a fairly uniform method of reporting cases. Most entries are highly condensed, with any superfluous material covered by the lawyers' customary shorthand, '&c'. A thorough grasp of the law was required on the part of the reader as well as the reporter. Some cases are dealt with in a two- or three-line 'nota'; on the other hand, the reports of a number of conferences in the Exchequer Chamber record in considerable detail the opinions of senior jurists. Occasionally, hearings in Chancery are noted, as well as an increasing number of King's Bench cases.[76] The majority of reports begin with a recital of facts and a description of the nature of the action; an increasing proportion include the names of the litigants involved. Practically all deal with one or more clear-cut issues of law, and while judgments are occasionally recorded, the main object of the report is to discern a consensus among the various arguments.[77]

While they remain anonymous, and apparently stood 'outside' the trials they were recording, compilers of Tudor Yearbooks began to display greater personal involvement with their subject-matter. They tended to interject their own remarks and 'quaeres'. These had been common enough in earlier Yearbooks, but now they frequently took the form of commentaries upon judicial opinions, conversations with court officials and, occasionally, lengthy dissents from rulings of the court.[78] Reporters were sometimes in a position to mix with serjeants and judges and note 'off-the-record' statements.[79] They seem, indeed, to have dis-

[75] This also seems to be true of Rastell's *Book of Assizes* printed in 1516.

[76] For instance, YBB H. 1 Hen. VII, pl. 25; E. 1 Hen. VII, pls. 5, 6; H. 2 Hen. VII, pl. 14; T. 2 Hen. VII, pl. 3.

[77] For a discussion of the decision-making process see below, Chap. V, pp. 177–97.

[78] For instance, YBB T. 2 Hen. VII, p. 10a (Redmond edition); H. 8 Hen. VII, pl. 3; M. 10 Hen. VII, pl. 19; H. 10 Hen. VII, pl. 14; M. 21 Hen. VII, pl. 45; see Hemmant, ii, p. xvii; *H.E.L.*, ii, 552.

[79] YBB T. 15 Hen. VII, pl. 9; M. 20 Hen. VII, pl. 18; E. 26 Hen. VIII, pl. 7; M. 27 Hen. VIII, pl. 5; E. 27 Hen. VIII, pl. 24.

played an ambivalent attitude towards their work. On the one hand, there is an obvious subjective element in the form of queries and comments which might be expected in a lawyer's private casebook;[80] on the other, there appears to be an awareness that various eyes would see their reports. An effort was made to present a balanced account of debate in the more weighty disputes. The fact that it was deemed necessary to account for the omission of two judges' opinions in a particular case strengthens the impression that such reports were not intended solely for personal use.[81] There also appears to have been a conscious choice of disputes to be covered so as to include both important litigants and important litigation.[82] Half a century later, Plowden was to carry this process much further, but he was probably influenced by the method employed in the later Yearbooks.[83]

Plowden's own comment on the status of Yearbook reporters does not indicate at what point they stopped work. Coke, declaring it to have been on the death of Henry VII, contends that the ensuing volumes from Henry VIII reveal 'no small difference'.[84] While the existence of official reporters may be discounted, little has been said on the subject of these final scattered Yearbooks.[85] There is no doubt that Coke considered them inferior to their predecessors. He was probably influenced in this judgment by William Fleetwood, who purposely compiled a separate table for the cases of Henry VIII because in his view they were not fit for inclusion among the 'official' reports.[86] It has been suggested that the reason for this denigration is the intrusion of personal comments by the reporters concerned.[87] Yet such comments are no more numerous than those occurring in the Yearbooks of Henry VII,[88] while in other respects the later cases

[80] See below, Chap. V, pp. 169–70. [81] YB H. 21 Hen. VII, pl. 2.
[82] Hemmant, i, p. lxxvi. [83] See below, Chap. VI, pp. 207–10.
[84] 3 Co. Rep. Pref. xvia.
[85] J. G. Marvin, *Legal Bibliography*, p. 755; Turner, p. xiii.
[86] *Annalium*, Dedication. [87] Turner, p. xiii.
[88] For example, YBB. E. 13 Hen. VIII, pl. 1; M. 26 Hen. VIII, pl. 4; T. 26 Hen. VIII, pls. 9, 13.

are as well reported as, if not better than, the earlier; the names of parties are included more often and case citations, though rare, are more precise.[89]

The ground of Coke's and Fleetwood's disapproval is more likely to have been the small number of terms which eventually got into print. There is simply a lack of useful material. The first volume to be published was 14 Henry VIII, which Pynson brought out sometime between 1523 and 1528.[90] It is the fullest Yearbook of the reign although it contains only three terms. In the corpus of Pynson's Yearbook publications this seems rather out of context, being the only one for Henry VIII that he produced. Its late appearance is also rather surprising since he had not printed a Yearbook since 1520.[91] He probably acted in response to the recent incursion into the field by Robert Redmond, who was in the process of reprinting several of Pynson's earlier volumes.[92] In 1540 Redmond reissued 14 Henry VIII with a few minor additions but still bereft of Trinity term. This probably formed a companion volume to the composite edition of 12–13 Henry VIII which he prepared about this time.[93] The latter was decidedly inferior to previous Yearbooks: only ten cases are reported and these are distributed over four terms, disappointingly meagre fare even in a slack period for reporting. Presumably by the late 1530s manuscript material was scarce, or perhaps Redmond did not retain the close links with the profession which Pynson must have had.

Taken as a whole, the cases reported for the years 1520 to 1522,

[89] For instance, YB T. 27 Hen. VIII, pl. 21.

[90] Both Beale (pp. 189, 285) and Dr Jennifer Nicholson [*Register of Manuscripts of Year Books Extant* (S.S. 1956), p. 26] have erroneously dated this edition 1508. The only known copies are in the B.M. and the Library of Lincoln's Inn.

[91] Beale, pp. 189–90.

[92] Ibid. p. 192; cf. H.S. Bennett, *English Books and Readers 1475–1557* (1969), p. 78.

[93] This Yearbook is tentatively dated 1540 (Beale, p. 285) but William Rastell sold his copy to Ranulph Cholmeley in March 1539 as part of a large volume of reports; hence it was probably printed sometime in 1538. The volume in question is part of the Cholmeley Bequest at Lincoln's Inn Library.

though few in number, are quite lengthy, sometimes running to three or more pages. By contrast, Yearbooks 18 and 19 Henry VIII (1526–7) consist principally of short entries, summary comments on a specific point of law. The only notable exceptions are three 'Exchequer Chamber' cases, two of which were adjudicated at Serjeants' Inn, Fleet Street.[94] Again, neither year is fully reported; only Michaelmas 18 Henry VIII and Trinity and Michaelmas 19 Henry VIII are represented, a total of fourteen folios. The printer was William Myddelton, who succeeded Redmond at his shop in Fleet Street and carried on trade between 1541 and 1547. During that time he published eighteen Yearbooks, most of them reprints from Henry VI and Edward IV.[95] Like his predecessor, Myddelton apparently found it difficult to obtain material for Henry VIII. He did print what are assumed to be the first editions of the Yearbooks for 1534–6 (26 and 27 Henry VIII), the final volumes of the whole series. In style they closely resemble 18 and 19 Henry VIII, and appear to be abridged from a fuller collection. But, in contrast to the earlier cases, each year has been compiled separately, although 26 Henry VIII's four terms cover a mere dozen folios. The last of the printed Yearbooks, 27 Henry VIII, is the largest of the reign, running to thirty-six folios;[96] even so, it contains only three terms.[97]

These terminal divisions, however, are probably no more trustworthy than those for Henry VII. When the printed version is collated with the same reports still to be found in manuscript[98] considerable discrepancy is found, both with respect to law-terms and regnal years. This is probably explained by the fact that Henry's reign began in Easter term 1509. Those cases printed as of Easter 27 Henry VIII have been copied into the manuscript under

[94] YBB. T. 19 Hen. VIII, pls. 4, 10 and 11; cf. Dyer, 3a–3b.

[95] Beale, pp. 184–5.

[96] Each year is printed in a separate volume, concluding with the colophon, '. . . noviter impressus'.

[97] Easter, Trinity and Michaelmas 27 Hen. VIII.

[98] A set of surviving Yearbook reports for 18 and 26–27 Henry VIII is deposited in the Library of Congress as the Gell MS (ff. 1–55); cf. *H.M.C. Ninth Rep., App.* p. 385.

Easter 26 Henry VIII.[99] The former allocation is probably correct for that particular year (1535), although the term, being based on a moveable feast, of course varied from year to year. If a modern edition were to be made the most sensible arrangement would be to label this term with both regnal years since they frequently overlap.[100]

The Yearbooks of Henry VIII are in some ways reminiscent of those of Edward II two centuries earlier. Whether because of the calibre of the men at the bar or the style of reporting, many spirited exchanges between judges and counsel are recorded. Typical is an extract from Yearbook 14 Henry VIII just after Serjeant Spelman had put a case concerning the performance of certain conditions in a lease:

Brudnel a Spelman: Avez vos melieure matier? Spelman: Ouy sir, car le retorne ne fuit avere come jeo enten. Brudnel: Donq ne faits vos matier in Ley de ce, jeo vos conseil. Et tantum dixit Fitzherbert. Spelman: Bien Sir, jeo parlerai ove mon Client ce que il veut faire etc.[101]

The formalities of pleading had changed but the underlying conflict between the judge applying law as he saw fit and the barrister attempting to represent his client's interests remained unchanged.

This reference to Fitzherbert was one of the first since his appointment as justice of the Common Pleas that term.[102] The reign of Henry VIII is not remembered for its judges. Perhaps the one exception is Anthony Fitzherbert, the greatest legal scholar of his day and as dominating a figure on the bench in the fifteen-thirties as Chief Justice Beresford, so prominent in the reports of Edward II, had been in the early thirteen-hundreds. The Yearbooks of 26 and 27 Henry VIII abound with his opinions and although only a puisne justice he clearly guided the court in

[99] Lib. of Congress Gell MS, ff. 16*v*–34; for an explanation of the rather involved means of calculating law terms see C.R. Cheney, *Handbook of Dates* (1961), p. 65; Hastings, pp. 22–4.

[100] Cf. Dyer, pp. 32a–34b. [101] YB E. 14 Hen. VIII, pl. 4.

[102] A description of his elevation to the bench is found in B.M. Harg. MS 388, f. 22*v*; cf. YB E. 14 Hen. VIII, pl. 7.

many of the reported decisions. His advice was frequently sought by counsel at the bar and on occasion he was summoned to the Chancery to join with Audley and Cromwell in adjudicating a particularly pressing issue.[103] Much of the conversational content of the reports relates to Fitzherbert's pronouncements and the manner in which he dealt with dissenters. For instance, in one action, *Prior of Holey v. Fulbert* (1534), he clashed with Serjeant Humphrey Browne over the efficacy of his chosen writ. Fitzherbert 'marvelled' that he moved the case at all. Browne contended that he could 'monstre un livre . . . que est come iay dit'. 'Jeo ne force de votre livre', the judge countered, adding that 'les livres sont comen encounter cel, per que le plee ne vault sans doubt'.[104] Apparently doubts did not obtrude in Fitzherbert's deliberations, although he could on occasion change his mind and admit it.[105] To judge from Yearbook reports, it was the precedents cited by counsel which most frequently aroused his critical faculties. Fitzherbert, like Coke, commanded a comprehensive knowledge of decided cases. When his brother-justice William Shelley cited a point from Edward III, Fitzherbert contended that there was no such case in Edward III, 'ne en nul auters livers . . .'.[106] On another occasion, a report from Yearbook 12 Henry VIII was brought to his attention. He replied by urging counsel to 'put that case out of your books, for it is not law without doubt'. His authority in this instance was the fact that he had represented the plaintiff in the decision cited.[107] If necessary, Fitzherbert would resort to more fundamental doctrine to counter his opponents. When James Hales had recourse to 'nostre leivres' in a dispute over the sale of property held in trust he denied the law to be as claimed, ' & prove per reason si le matter fuit destre'.[108] If Fitzherbert did distrust an excessive reliance on prece-

[103] YB T. 27 Hen. VIII, pl. 6; cf. *H.E.L.* iv, 277.

[104] YB E. 26 Hen. VIII, pl. 2.

[105] For example, YB H. 14 Hen. VIII, pl. 7.

[106] YB E. 27 Hen. VIII, pl. 32.

[107] YB T. 27 Hen. VIII, pl. 21; translated and discussed in Plowden's *Commentaries* (1816), p. 182.

[108] YB E. 27 Hen. VIII, pl. 16.

dents, he was probably fighting a rearguard action. In one of the few reports in which he does not figure for this period, a problem arose relating to certain lands in wardship; Shelley objected that the majority opinion was 'encontre reason', but Chief Justice Norwich admitted, 'si nostre lievres ne fuissint issint, que il est dure pur prover per reason'.[109] Fitzherbert did, in fact, make effective use of decided cases when necessary, not only from the Yearbooks but from material which he probably collected himself.[110] By the time he died in 1538, the practice of citing decisions was gaining ground.[111]

One of the more recondite, yet relevant, problems concerning sixteenth-century law-reports is whether there was such a thing as an unprinted Yearbook. It is unlikely that an Elizabethan lawyer would have thought so. By the time Brooke's *Abridgement* was published in 1573 the Yearbooks were invariably cited from the printed editions of Tottel; Coke, it appears, used nothing else.[112] By contrast, modern commentators have been prone to designate certain manuscript reports 'Yearbooks' when in fact they can be traced to the casebook of some eminent practitioner.[113] From a comprehensive survey of available material it is fairly certain that anonymous, 'objective' reports in the Yearbook mould do not extend beyond the reign of Henry VIII.

Only one volume has survived which may plausibly be held to fit the above description. It consists of reports from 33 to 36 Henry VIII and forms a section of the Gell manuscript.[114] It occupies forty-six out of the total of 145 folios and is written in the

[109] YB M. 26 Hen. VIII, pl. 5.

[110] YBB T. 26 Hen. VIII, pl. 8; M. 27 Hen. VIII, pl. 14.

[111] His will is found in P.C.C. 20 Dyngeley (1538).

[112] Coke omitted references to Ric. II and extracted his material for Edw. I from Fitzherbert.

[113] Hemmant, ii, p. xviii; Miss Nicholson's *Register of Manuscripts* (S.S.) lists a number of 'Yearbooks' which in fact were the work of known practitioners such as William Bendlowes, the subject of Chapter III, pp. 91–4.

[114] This MS, now held by the Lib. of Congress, was originally owned by Anthony Gell (adm. I. T. 1547) who appears to have collected material from a wide variety of sources; *H.M.C. Ninth Rep., App.* pp. 384–5, and below Appendix I, p. 267.

same neat, scrivener's hand as the preceding Yearbooks 18, 26 and 27 Henry VIII. The fact that it has a separate foliation, and its omission of cases from the years 1537 to 1540, are immaterial in view of the erratic nature of all Henrician Yearbooks.[115] More significant is the fact that in point of style and subject-matter its entries closely resemble the printed reports for 1535–6. The reporter remains a knowledgeable observer, but contributes if anything even more outspoken commentaries on judicial pronouncements. In one entry, an action on the case for words, he challenges the court's interpretation of the evidence, examining at length contrary authority from other 'books'.[116] The same vigorous interplay between bench and bar which marked the later Yearbooks is found in this series, except that the firm hand of Anthony Fitzherbert is absent. It was Justice William Shelley who now assumed the leading, if less authoritarian, role in the Common Pleas.[117] A considerable proportion of the decisions emanate from the King's Bench, however, with the consequent appearance of many up-and-coming barristers: men such as James Dyer, Nicholas Hare, Edward Saunders and John Pollard are frequently reported as pleading in this court while still apprentices-at-law. There are also occasional trials from the Chancery, Exchequer and Exchequer Chamber and one decision argued at Serjeants' Inn.[118] The reporter admitted in two instances his failure to note an opinion because he was unable to hear what was said:[119] presumably, therefore, these cases were compiled for circulation, if not publication. Although this is the only manuscript of its kind to survive, an identical copy of one leading case is found in another volume.[120] Both collections are

115 As it is, the reports in the Gell MS for YB 18 Hen. VIII are in a separate foliation from those for YBB 26 & 27 Hen. VIII.

116 T. 36 Hen. VIII; Gell MS. f. 91*v*.

117 For example, ff. 70*v*, 73, 104, 104*v*; Shelley vigorously maintained, however, that the claims of copyholders could not be entertained in the King's courts; see, for example, ff. 74*v*, 103.

118 Ff. 75, 89, 104, 107–11.

119 Ff. 104, 104*v*.

120 The case in question is *Wimblish v. Tailbois*, M. 36 Hen. VIII, Gell MS ff. 107–11; cf. B.M. Harl. MS 1691, f. 167; it is also noted in Brooke, tit. 'Collusion', no. 46; see below, Appendix III, p. 315.

associated with members of the Inner Temple, a fact which may have some bearing on their circulation and that of reports in general. But whoever compiled these 'unprinted Yearbooks' may well have been the author of the printed Yearbooks for 26 and 27 Henry VIII.

It would be futile to speculate on the identity of any of the reporters in question, but it may be feasible to consider their position in the legal profession and the reasons which led them to compile reports. Pleaders at the bar below the rank of serjeant enjoyed a dual status. One related to their rank in the profession as a whole, the other reflected their attainment within their respective Inns. Thus the terms 'apprentice-at-law' and 'utter-barrister' are roughly equivalent.[121] It is with the latter capacity that the production of Yearbooks seems most intimately concerned. The importance of a practitioner's Inn to his working life cannot be overestimated.[122] Besides being places of residence in term-time and the centre of legal education for lawyers of all ranks, the Inns of Court were the clearing-houses for much of the legal literature produced. It has been suggested that Statham's Abridgment may have been the product of a joint effort at Lincoln's Inn,[123] and there is evidence to show that Richard Pynson, the printer, retained members of the Middle Temple to correct the proofs of certain legal publications.[124] The close companionship and constant interchange of information were to be essential to the compilation of private reports throughout the sixteenth century, just as the Inns had provided the necessary milieu for the preparation and circulation of Yearbooks as well. It is appropriate and significant that these two institutions represent what is most distinctive in medieval English law.[125]

[121] *H.E.L.* ii, 496–8; *Black Books L. I.* i, pp. ix–xii; *De Laudibus*, p. 117.

[122] A. W. B. Simpson has examined the relationship of the production of late-15th-century Yearbooks with learning exercises at the Inns in his recent article, 'Source and Function of the Later Year Books', pp. 96–103.

[123] Turner, pp. xxxii–xxxiv.

[124] H. R. Plomer, 'Two Lawsuits of Richard Pynson', *The Library*, New Series, x (1909), 130–3.

[125] F. W. Maitland, *English Law and the Renaissance* (1901), p. 27.

As a group, those most likely to have been involved in the collection of cases for Tudor Yearbooks were the utter-barristers. From an examination of the learning exercises carried on at the Inns of Court and Chancery it appears that these were the men who combined the proficiency and the motive for such work. Upon admission to one of the four Inns of Court a student began his career as an inner-barrister. It might take from six to nine years after this for him to qualify as an utter-barrister, during which time certain exercises must have been performed.[126] Once qualified, he was fully equipped, in theory at least, to plead at Westminster or to be called to the bench of his House.[127] In practice, it was generally another five years before a man could conduct litigation in the central courts,[128] and it was during this period that he was most capable of productive work on behalf of his Inn and of the profession as a whole. Consequently, utter-barristers played an active role in the education of junior members. During the learning vacation one of their number was designated at each session to challenge propositions in law put by the appointed reader.[129] In the evening after supper utter-barristers were expected to propound 'doubtful cases' to the reader and benchers. At the mesne vacation in the evenings moots were brought in and pleaded by students before the utter-barristers.[130] These cases, it seems, were chosen by the latter, but written up by the students and submitted again for approval.[131] Such exercises were carried on partly in French and partly in English, 'even as the Serjeants doe at the barr in the King's Courts to the Judges'.[132]

The foregoing description dates from 1540 but it doubtless

[126] *G.I. Pension Book*, i, p. xxxiii; 3 Co. Rep. Pref. xixa.

[127] *Cal. I.T. Recs.* i, pp. xxxiv, 187–8; *Black Books L.I.*, i, 100.

[128] *Cal. M.T. Recs.* i, 234; *G.I. Pension Book*, i, 43.

[129] For an invaluable description of the organization of the Inns see the report submitted to Henry VIII in 1540 by Thomas Denton, Nicholas Bacon and Robert Cary, printed by Edward Waterhous in his *Fortescutus Illustratus* (1663), pp. 543–6.

[130] *Cal. I.T. Recs.* i, 515; *Fortescutus Illustratus*, pp. 545–6; Sir Simonds D'Ewes, *Autobiography* (1845), i, 231–2.

[131] *Black Books L.I.* i, pp. xxvi, 127, 215.

[132] *Fortescutus Illustratus*, p. 545.

reflects the regime under which law was taught throughout the later Yearbook period. This was the training which produced such skilful pleaders that even unsympathetic observers like Thomas Elyot and Thomas Smith praised them.[133] The analogy between learning exercises at the Inns and litigation in the courts gives rise to the possibility that certain utter-barristers may have collected cases to assist in their duties as readers. This hypothesis is reinforced by the relationship which existed between the Inns of Court and their satellite Inns of Chancery. The function of the latter institutions has never been adequately explored and surviving records are sparse.[134] Fortescue simply noted that young men came there to learn 'the originals and something of the elements of law', before passing on to the parent Inns.[135] From other sources it appears that learning exercises were much the same as at the latter, but more elementary: particular emphasis was placed on studying and reciting the formulae of writs, attendance at readings, and the arguing of moots.[136] Once again it was the utter-barristers who played a leading role. Each year one was elected reader by the Inn of Chancery in question from a selected panel. This was an office of some responsibility and occupied the recipient during the course of both the learning vacation and term time. Besides being an important rung in the promotional ladder, the readership formed one of the chief links with the parent House.[137] The procedure involved seems to have varied somewhat from Inn to Inn. At some, the formal reading lasted three weeks and three days with a different subject covered each day,

[133] Sir Thomas Elyot, *The Boke named the Governour* (1883), i, p. 154; Maitland, *English Law and the Renaissance*, p. 28.

[134] See D. S. Bland, *A Bibliography of the Inns of Court and Chancery* (1965), pp. 12–13, 36–8.

[135] *De Laudibus*, p. 117. The 'originals' were original writs issued out of Chancery.

[136] *Fortescutus Illustratus*, pp. 527, 545; see also D. S. Bland, *Early Records of Furnival's Inn* (1957), pp. 29, 42, 50, 77; Cecil Carr, *Pension Book of Clement's Inn* (S.S.), pp. xxvii–xxviii, 220.

[137] *Fortescutus Illustratus*, pp. 544–5; John Stow, *A Survey of London* (1923), p. 72; *Black Books L.I.* i, pp. xxviii–xxix, 223, 224, 292.

such as 'jurisdiction', 'person', 'writ', etc.[138] The reader might recite certain questions or doubts on the daily topic after which students would attempt to demonstrate his conclusions unsound in law. During the learning vacation the utter-barrister, together with two colleagues, heard moots regularly.[139] In term time the appointed reader was expected to lecture three times a week and to keep moots.

The reader's regime also included what is described as 'arguing and debating cases after dinner'.[140] Whether these 'cases' sprang from current litigation is not clear, but it is worth noting that the practice of conferring on issues pending in court over the noon-time meal was becoming more frequent among the judges at Serjeants' Inn.[141] Again, the regulations governing Clement's Inn, which had their origin in the late fifteenth century, speak of those 'that shall moot or report', but without giving details of the difference, if any, between the two.[142] The statutes of Clifford's Inn, newly-written in 1528 but drafted in the reign of Henry VII, refer to fines to be levied against those pensioners who fail to attend the reading of a writ, lecture or 'reports'.[143] Without further information as to the nature of these reports, it is difficult to discuss their origin; but it is conceivable that utter-barristers from the Inns of Court, or even students in the Inns of Chancery, equipped themselves with reports of current litigation being heard at Westminster Hall,[144] and that this material, in turn, may have been prepared for distribution among the profession as a

[138] Charles Pugh, 'Origin and Progress of Barnard's Inn', *Notes & Queries*, 7th series (1887), iii, 83–4.

[139] *Pension Book of Clement's Inn*, p. 220: D'Ewes, *Autobiography*, i, 218–19.

[140] *Fortescutus Illustratus*, p. 545; *Pension Book of Clement's Inn*, pp. xxvii, 219–20; D'Ewes, *Autobiography*, i, 231–2.

[141] See below, Chap. V, pp. 195–6.

[142] *Pension Book of Clement's Inn*, p. 220.

[143] 'Statutes and Ordinances of Clifford's Inn', paragraph 40; a copy of the statutes is in the Library of the Inner Temple.

[144] It has been suggested that Coke prepared his report of *Shelley's Case* (1581) in conjunction with the course of lectures he delivered at Lyon's Inn; T.F.T. Plucknett, 'The Genesis of Coke's Reports', *Cornell Law Quarterly*, xxvii (1942), 205 n. 3.

whole in the form of Yearbooks. Alternatively, certain barristers might have been commissioned by a law printer, notably Richard Pynson, to compile cases for eventual publication.

In 1914 the view was put forward that Yearbook reports may have been compiled by, or under the supervision of, the two practitioners appointed each year to lecture at each Inn of Court.[145] Apart from a number of technical and factual flaws in this suggestion, it places the production of Yearbooks within a framework of organization which simply did not exist. By the same token, there is little likelihood that a carefully-regulated system for the collection of cases operated among Inns of Chancery readers or utter-barristers in general. It may be observed, however, that, as a group, those practitioners who had been called to the bar of their Inn but had not yet qualified to plead in the courts were admirably placed to draft the sort of reports found in the later Yearbooks. It should be remembered that a barrister who had read at an Inn of Chancery for two years became eligible to practise at the bar of the central courts, a rule which suggests that the office entailed considerable familiarity with techniques of pleading and current topics of litigation.[146]

By the end of the sixteenth century, despite the evident demand for reprints of the Yearbooks, purists like Coke and William Fulbecke found it necessary to admonish their colleagues for excessive reliance upon the Abridgments of Fitzherbert and Brooke in place of the 'books at large'.[147] Francis Bacon complained that students went to the Abridgments before they had learnt any law in an attempt 'to make a lawyer in haste'.[148] Whether the appearance of Fitzherbert's *Abridgement* or any other single event was solely or chiefly responsible for the cessation of regular reporting after 1535 is open to doubt, but it may have been one of the contributory causes. It was Coke's view that the Year-

[145] Turner, p. xxv.

[146] See *A.P.C.* 1571–5, p. 247; *Tudor Royal Proclamations*, i, no. 270.

[147] 3 Co. Rep. Pref. ivb; 4 Co. Rep. Pref. xi; 5 Co. Rep. 25.

[148] James Spedding, *The Letters and Life of Francis Bacon* (1872), vi, 70.

books came to an end because the sages of the law thought there were sufficient reports in circulation.[149] The fact that Fitzherbert, and later Brooke, compiled what were, in effect, classified statements of the law as it then existed is an indication of the widespread belief in the unchanging substance of that law. In practice, the falsity of this notion is borne out by the need for practitioners to collect their own cases on an independent basis. The few, but significant, private casebooks which survive from the first half of the sixteenth century indicate that available reports, whether in the form of Abridgements or printed Yearbooks, were not sufficient for the needs of the profession. Yet the fact remains that up-to-date law reports ceased to be printed in the 1540s and did not revive as a form of legal literature until 1571 with the publication of Plowden's *Commentaries*.

149 3 Co. Rep. Pref. xvib.

CHAPTER II

The Early Reporters

IT IS generally believed that law-reporting in the sixteenth century exhibits a simple, comprehensible pattern: the Yearbooks cease in 1535 and the first-hand reports of Dyer and Bendlowes commence in the following year. Based as it is on printed evidence the belief is quite plausible: when the surviving manuscripts are scrutinized, however, this veneer of continuity is quickly stripped away. As has already been intimated, it is probable that Yearbooks continued to circulate in manuscript until the end of Henry VIII's reign. Furthermore, it is now evident that reports were being systematically compiled on purely personal initiative by 1500, if not earlier.[1] There is thus an overlapping period of at least forty years during which two ostensibly distinct modes of reporting existed side by side. This apparent dichotomy, however, is also quite misleading, since 'Yearbook' and 'private' reporters were probably one and the same—but at different times in their careers: the utter-barristers who compiled cases which eventually went into the Yearbooks might later become the judges and serjeants whose notes were copied and published. The reports prepared by James Dyer, for instance, until his creation as serjeant in 1552, certainly bear a striking resemblance to the Yearbooks of Henry VIII.[2] From the evidence of surviving material it appears, moreover, that the earliest private collections can be ascribed to men who reached senior rank under Henry VIII. Like their

[1] Coke cited a decision purportedly out of Hengham's reports 'written in parchment, in an ancient hand of the time'; 7 Co. Rep. 9b. Hengham was Chief Justice of the King's Bench between 1273 and 1291. Walter Moyle, a justice of the Common Bench (1454–71), once cited his own reports taken while a serjeant; YB M. 5 Edw. IV, pl. 6; noted by T.E. Lewis, 'The History of Judicial Precedent', *L.Q.R.* xlvi (1930), 342.

[2] The reports of Dyer are discussed in detail below, Chap. V, pp. 162–8.

Elizabethan successors these display a wide variety in style and method. Individualism in the production of reports grew, it seems, with the reporter's rise in the profession. This somewhat neglected phase of law-reporting merits attention; not only does it furnish valuable source material for the period of the early Tudors, but it provides a glimpse of the manner in which unprinted collections circulated within the profession.

The best-known of the early private compilations was printed in 1602 as Keilwey's Reports.[3] The volume seems to have found a ready market and was reprinted in 1633 and 1688.[4] Sir Simonds D'Ewes wrote that he read Keilwey 'with more satisfaction and delight' than any other set of reports.[5] The work was edited by John Croke, who had entered the Inner Temple in 1570 and occupied the chamber of his godfather, Robert Keilwey.[6] Keilwey had for many years held the position of Surveyor-General of the Liveries and much of his career was concerned with the administrative side of government rather than with the law courts.[7] Although he was made a serjeant in 1552, his name rarely appears in contemporary reports except in connection with the Court of Wards.[8] When he died in 1581, his papers were left with Croke who eventually saw a chance of exploiting the interest created by the publication of the first part of Coke's Reports in 1600.[9] Despite the fact that Keilwey's career centred principally on Elizabeth's reign, the collection bearing his name relates exclusively to the Yearbook period. There are four distinct sections in the printed volume. Sections 1 and 4 contain, respectively, reports 12–24 Henry VII (1496–1508), and 1–11 and 21 Henry VIII (1508–19, 1529–30). The two middle sections consist of assorted material from earlier years: section 2 has a series of 'casus

[3] *S.T.C.* no. 14901; this discussion of Keilwey's Reports is based in large measure on A.W.B. Simpson, 'Keilwey's Reports, Temp. Henry VII and Henry VIII', *L.Q.R.* lxxiii (1957), 89–105.

[4] *S.T.C.* nos. 14902, K. 134.

[5] *Autobiography*, i, 224.

[6] *Cal. I.T. Recs.* i, 256, 274.

[7] H.E.Bell, *The Court of Wards and Liveries* (1953), pp. 20–2.

[8] See Dyer, 150b, 174b, 181a, 193a; Dal. 90; B.M. Lansd. MS 1095, f. 108*v*.

[9] Simpson, 'Keilwey', p. 89; Keilwey's will is registered in P.C.C. 9 Darcy.

incerti temporis' which have been identified as a selection of moot cases from the years 1480 to 1486,[10] and section 3 is made up of reports from the reign of Edward III relating primarily to writs of *quo warranto* together with a final folio from Edward I.

The cases from Henry VII and Henry VIII are of considerable interest and raise the question of Keilwey's status as owner or author of the original collection. Since he was born in 1497 and probably did not enter the Inner Temple until about 1520, he cannot be credited with reporting the entries for Henry VII.[11] It appears, in fact, that most of 'Keilwey's' Reports were prepared by John Carrell, a fellow-member of the Inner Temple who was called to the coif in 1510.[12] Carrell's status as a law-reporter was, until recently, only a matter of conjecture. Wallace noted citations in Lane's *Reports* of decisions from 12 Henry VII and 9 Henry VIII attributed to Carrell, but professed ignorance as to the latter's identity.[13] Professor Putnam drew attention to a John Carrell as the possible author of a set of reports in the Harleian collection, although the lawyer to whom she alluded was actually the eldest son of the serjeant.[14] Yet, as Simpson has pointed out, there is evidence of a connection between Carrell and Keilwey as early as 1559. In that year Dyer reports the case of *Coningesby v. Throckmorton*, pointing out that the dispute initially arose in Easter term 8 Henry VIII 'per report de R. Kayleway il appiert en son lieur del report de Seriant Carell':[15] the case in question can be identified in the printed edition of Keilwey.[16] It is apparent from this and other evidence that Robert Keilwey possessed a set of

[10] S.E.Thorne, *Readings and Moots at the Inns of Court* (S.S.), i, pp. xlvi–xlvii.

[11] The earliest reference to Keilwey in the *Calendar of Inner Temple Records* is dated 1533 and the offices which he held in the Inn at that time were fairly junior; he did not read until 1547; *Cal. I.T. Recs.* i, 105, 130, 140, 150; *D.N.B.* x, 1199; Simpson, 'Keilwey', p. 93.

[12] Simpson, 'Keilwey', p. 95.

[13] Wallace, p. 104 n. 2; the cases were cited by John Dodderidge who may well have been aware of Carrell's authorship; Simpson, 'Keilwey', p. 96.

[14] Putnam, p. 182 n. 4; the collection in question, Harl. 1691, is discussed below, pp. 41–4; Simpson, 'Keilwey', p. 100.

[15] Dyer (1585), 174b; Simpson, 'Keilwey', p. 97.

[16] Keil. 176a.

reports which included cases originally collected by Serjeant Carrell. Once such a link is established it can be inferred that other precedents cited by Keilwey came from the same source. Thus in 30 Henry VIII he submits as authority a case argued in 22 Henry VII; although he makes no reference to Carrell the entry turns up in the published collection.[17] In *Woodward v. Lord Darcy*, reported by Plowden in Trinity term 4 & 5 Philip & Mary (1558), the attention of the court was drawn to the decision of *Dive v. Langston*, 19 Henry VII, 'which (it was said) appears in a special report thereof extant'.[18] This case later appeared in Keilwey and presumably was extracted from Carrell's personal notes. It is significant that this 'special report' was worthy of being singled out from the regular series of Year-books.[19]

An examination of the reports for Henry VIII as found in Keilwey shows that they are a plausible reflection of Carrell's later career. In June 1514 he was designated King's Serjeant.[20] From this privileged position he was able to record not only 'secret' comments from the bench but also proceedings at special conferences as well. These include the debates at Baynard's Castle on the Hunne affair and a meeting of the Council with the King at Greenwich concerning certain offices claimed by the Duke of Buckingham.[21] John Carrell's authorship of the printed cases, however, is subject to certain qualification. In Keilwey, the reports for Henry VIII run in sequence from 1509 to 1519 but conclude with two cases from 1529 to 1530.[22] Serjeant Carrell died in 1523, so that these final entries must be ascribed to someone else, possibly his son John Carrell or even Keilwey himself.[23]

[17] Dyer, 41b; Simpson, 'Keilwey', p. 94; Keil. 92b.

[18] Plow. 186.

[19] Keil. 59a; there is a discrepancy in the dating; it is reported under Hil. 20 Hen. VII in Keilwey; cf. Dyer, 2a.

[20] *L. & P. Hen. VIII*, i, no. 5141.

[21] Keil, 170b–172a, 180b–185b; see Arthur Ogle, *The Tragedy of the Lollards' Tower* (1949), p. 13.

[22] Keil. 202b–203b.

[23] John Carrell Sr. died in May or June 1523; see P.C.C. 10 Bodfelde.

It is clear from remarks made by John Croke in the preface to his edition that the cases put into print were only a selection of those which the reporter initially collected. This is borne out when a comparison is made between the printed book and a collection of cases in manuscript found in the Cambridge University Library entitled 'cases in temps H. septem ex libro Roberti Kiloway'.[24] Most of the decisions in the published volume can also be found in this manuscript, but a number of entries in the manuscript, notably those for the years 1 to 11 Henry VII (1485–96), were never printed. The elder John Carrell began his legal studies about 1485 and therefore could quite plausibly have compiled these earlier cases.[25] Another interesting collection is preserved among the Harleian manuscripts.[26] This is composed of a cross-section of legal material, including moots and readings as well as reports ranging in time from 1485 to 1560, and it was probably transcribed early in the second half of the sixteenth century from the case-books of various Inner Templars. The volume contains, among other items, twenty-three leaves of reports for the years 4 to 11 Henry VII which the copyist describes as taken 'ex libro Magistri Carelle'.[27] At another point in the manuscript the same Master Carrell is described as Attorney for the Duchy of Lancaster; it is fairly certain that this reference is to Serjeant Carrell's son, who did hold this office. Thus one of the sources from which the copyist worked was owned by John Carrell Jr., but it must have included material inherited from his father (although there is no mention of this in the latter's will). It appears that when Croke was editing the material from which emerged 'Keilwey's *Reports*' he deliberately omitted cases prior to 12 Henry VII (1496) in order to avoid duplicating those reports already published *inter libros nostros*, that is, the Yearbooks 1–11 Henry VII.[28] It should also be noted that the printed volume

[24] C.U.L. MS Gg. 3.26, ff. 97–108; another copy of this collection appears to have formed part of L.I. Mayn. MS 27 although the cases in question are missing; cf. Maitland, *Year Books 1 & 2 Edw. II*, p. xxii.

[25] Simpson, 'Circulation of Yearbooks', pp. 496–7.

[26] B.M. Harl. MS 1691.

[27] Ff. 58–61; Simpson, 'Keilwey', pp. 100–103.

[28] Keil. Pref.; Simpson, 'Keilwey', p. 90.

contains no decisions from 11–20 Henry VIII (1519–29). This seems to indicate that the elder Carrell, perhaps because of increasing professional duties, discontinued his reporting activities in 1519; in any event, he died in 1523.[29]

Of the cases printed in Keilwey for Henry VIII, that is, the years 1508–19 and 1529–30, the majority also exist in manuscript in two other, virtually identical, collections, one in the British Museum, the other in the Library of Lincoln's Inn.[30] Neither supplies any clue to its source or authorship, but from collation with other reports it appears likely that both were the work of lawyers at the Inner Temple.[31] They were probably compiled in the early seventeenth century and contain material ranging from Henry VII to Elizabeth. The reports for Henry VIII as transcribed in these volumes are divided into five regnal years, 1, 6, 7, 9 and 11; all but two entries are reproduced in the printed Keilwey as 1–3 and 5–11 Henry VIII, a circumstance which indicates that while both versions originated in a common source they had diverged into separate collections and been recopied in the interim.

As has been indicated, apart from the two isolated entries for 1529 the cases reproduced in the fourth section of the printed Keilwey run consecutively from 1 to 11 Henry VIII (1509–19). Yet John Carrell the elder appears to have gone on practising until 1522.[32] It has been suggested that the reporter of those three isolated Yearbooks, 12 to 14 Henry VIII, may have been the same John Carrell; their omission from Keilwey could again be explained by Croke's wish to publish only those terms not already included in the Yearbooks, while Carrell's death in 1523 and the publication soon after it of Yearbook 14 Henry VIII by

[29] Note also that Yearbooks were eventually printed for 1521–23; see below pp. 25–6; Simpson, 'Keilwey', pp. 92, 98.

[30] B.M. Harl. MS 1624; L.I. Mayn. MS 86.

[31] Mayn. 86 was at one time apparently owned by one John Bluells; Harl. 1624 is composed of two distinct collections: the first extends to 5 Eliz. (ff. 1–85), as does Mayn. 86; see Appendix I, p. 259.

[32] He appears as a pleader in YBB M. 14 Hen. VII, pl. 6, and H. 14 Hen. VIII, pl. 7; Simpson, 'Keilwey', p. 97.

Pynson seems an interesting conjunction.[33] Unfortunately, there is no evidence to substantiate this hypothesis, while certain objections immediately come to mind. Why, for instance, did not Pynson also publish as Yearbooks Serjeant Carrell's reports for 17–19 Henry VII and 1–11 Henry VIII? More important still is the matter of style and method. Carrell's approach, especially after 1509, is quite at variance with that of the Yearbooks 12–14 Henry VIII. His output constitutes a subjective and highly selective body of cases.[34] This is particularly true after he was appointed King's Serjeant and had the opportunity of noting proceedings beyond the scope of the ordinary Yearbook reporter. He also seems to have been concerned with disputes relating to the Crown's corporate capacity and the royal prerogative.[35] Furthermore, when Keilwey is collated with one of the surviving MS versions, Harleian 1624, it is evident that the entries, as divided up in the printed version, are both misleading and artificial: there are far fewer 'cases' in the manuscript. Carrell's technique, apparently, was to jot down a series of arguments, decisions or hypothetical issues which arose in court or at extra-judicial conferences. The Yearbook reporters might intrude a personal opinion on occasion, but essentially they recorded proceedings in court as pleaded by others rather than themselves.

To judge from the material found in Harleian 1691, the younger John Carrell not only inherited his father's notebook but also reported or compiled cases for himself. Immediately following the reports from Henry VII is a section written in the same hand but separately foliated.[36] It consists of thirty-one leaves and begins with several brief entries taken from the period between 1 & 2 Philip & Mary and 2 Elizabeth (1554–60). There is no heading or other clue to indicate that John Carrell Jr. was associated with these reports. The years in question were those in which he was

[33] Pynson may also have brought out an edition of 12–13 Hen. VIII although no copy survives; Simpson, 'Keilwey', p. 92 n. 5.

[34] There is no reason to attribute this to Croke's editing since the entries correspond closely with Harl. 1624 and Mayn. 86.

[35] Keil. 194a–202b.

[36] B.M. Harl. MS 1691, ff. 90–121.

mainly engaged in administrative duties on behalf of the Crown, having evaded a call to become serjeant in 1555.[37] Yet several years later Coke was to cite a decision 'hors de report Carrell en 1 Mary';[38] as no such decision can be traced in Harleian 1691, the reference suggests that Carrell possessed a collection of cases beyond those transcribed by the copyist.

Next comes a series of entries extending from 18 to 28 Henry VIII and consisting of both court and moot cases. The copyist states specifically that these were out of Carrell's book.[39] If they represent Carrell's own work, he must have begun taking notes shortly after his admission to the Inner Temple about 1522.[40] Under Elizabeth, Carrell is known to have cited cases 'en son liver de reports' from the 1530s.[41] A final group of reports within this foliation consists mainly of entries from 21 to 33 Henry VIII, although two are dated 1 and 5 Henry VIII and were printed in Keilwey.[42] Obviously, neither of these last two cases could have been the first-hand work of Carrell, although perhaps they originated with his father. The copyist has not indicated that any of this material came from the Carrell casebook, but there is a rather fragmentary collection in the Inner Temple Library which includes many of the same decisions and specifically identifies the latter group with the younger Carrell.[43]

It is by thus bringing together various sources of information that one may hope to build up a picture of the unofficial network through which lawyers in the sixteenth century gained access to unprinted cases. The dissemination of Serjeant Carrell's original reports, as well as of those attributable to his son, illustrates the sort of cooperation which existed between members of the legal

[37] Carrell seems to have avoided the call on three occasions, in 1540, 1552 and 1555; Ives, 'Legal Profession', p. 209.

[38] B.M. Lansd. MS 1095, f. 35*v*.

[39] B.M. Harl. MS 1691, ff. 89, 111.

[40] *Cal. I.T. Recs.* i, 70.

[41] Plowden refers to a report of Carrell's from 22 Hen. VIII in B.M. Harg. MS. 373, f. 196*v*; Carrell himself put a case from 24 Hen. VIII as noted in B.M. Lansd. MS 1133, f. 140*v*.

[42] Harl. 1691, ff. 113–22*v*; the cases from 1 and 5 Hen. VIII are at ff. 116–19*v*. 120–1.

[43] I.T. Petyt MS 511, vol. 13, ff. 7–14.

profession, especially those from the same Inn. The line from the senior Carrell through his son to Robert Keilwey is clear enough. The last two entered the Inner Temple in the early 1520s, in later years they showed a common devotion to the Catholic faith and the administrative branch of law, and in his will Carrell refers to his 'assuered loving frende Mr. Robert Keyllwaye'.[44] It appears, however, that others of their colleagues had access to the same notes. Among his unpublished reports Dyer refers to an Exchequer Chamber decision in 1556 in which a case from 2 Henry VIII was cited as authority and adds that it was taken 'ex libro Bromelie per report de seriant Carrill'.[45] (This particular matter concerned forcible entry and was reproduced in the Keilwey volume.)[46] The Bromleys, like the Carrells, were a gifted and successful legal family who made their way to prominence at the Inner Temple. They included Thomas Bromley, a Chief Justice of the King's Bench who died in 1555, and his younger kinsman, another Thomas, who became Lord Chancellor in 1579.[47] The latter did not enter the Inn until 1560, but some years later Dyer describes 'Bromelie Solicitor' as putting a 'liver report' by Carrell from 26 Henry VIII.[48] If both these citations were from the same casebook it obviously included entries collected by both the Carrells. The Chancellor may have inherited a copy from his cousin the Chief Justice or even from his father, George Bromley, who had lectured at the Temple back in 1508;[49] on the other hand, he was 'a good friend' of Keilwey's and may have taken cases out of his book.[50] At all events it is evident that by mid-century the

[44] Hist. Parl., biographies of John Carrell Jr., and Robert Keilwey; Carrell died in 1567; see his will, P.C.C. 34 Stonarde.

[45] The entry is undated but probably originated from a case on circuit in the summer of 1556; I.T. Petyt MS 511, vol. 13, f. 36*v*.

[46] Keil. 159a.

[47] Foss, v. 356–8, 463–6; the entry in the *D.N.B.* (ii, 1308) for Chief Justice Bromley contains errors and must be used with caution.

[48] Bromley was Solicitor-General 1569–79; Petyt 511, vol. 13, f. 58*v*.

[49] *Cal. I.T. Recs.* i, 11, 12, 34–6; both George and Thomas Bromley the elder were contemporaries and are recorded as pleading in court about the same time; B.M. Harl. MS 5143, f. 232.

[50] Keilwey's will, P.C.C. 9 Darcy.

Carrells' collection was circulating among a number of members of the Inner Temple.

This is corroborated by a set of reports in manuscript which was owned by Nicholas Jordan, another Inner Templar who began practice in 1588.[51] The volume is a diverse collection of cases obviously put together from a number of sources. In one entry reference is made to the arraignment of Lord Dacre for treason in 1534. According to the compiler, the trial was reported by Serjeant Gawdy 'que mort en le temps le roigne Mary'; in fact, this is much the same version as the one Dyer said was extracted by Thomas Bromley, the younger, from Carrell's book.[52] The Gawdys represented yet another legal dynasty attached to the Inner Temple, perhaps the most remarkable of all. Four lawyers of that name—a father and his three sons, by three different wives—flourished in the sixteenth century, all of them named Thomas.[53] The Thomas Gawdy mentioned above was created serjeant in 1552 and was active in the courts under Mary until his death in August 1556.[54] Despite his protestant leanings Serjeant Gawdy was a member of the 1555 heresy commission in Essex. He also seems to have carried out official duties under Protector Somerset together with John Carrell, a fact which may explain how he came to have access to the latter's reports.[55]

At another point, the compiler of this volume reproduces an entry from Henry VIII relating to the Duke of Buckingham's title to the constableship of England. 'Cest report', he adds, 'fuit deliver a moy per Mr. Henry Beaumont.' The case in question is an abridged version of that reported in Keilwey for Michaelmas 6 Henry VIII.[56] The Henry Beaumont referred to began his studies at the Inner Temple in 1561. His father, John

[51] B.M. Harg. MS 373; entitled 'Jordan's Collectanea' by Edward Umfreville although this is misleading; *Cal. I.T. Recs.* i, 421.

[52] Harg. 373, ff. 134–5; cf. I.T. Petyt MS 511, vol. 13, f. 58*v*.

[53] *H.M.C. Tenth Rep.* pt. 2, *App. II*, 2–3.

[54] Foss, v, 488 and *D.N.B.* vii, 960 are inaccurate and unreliable, although they contain useful references.

[55] *H.M.C. Salisbury*, i, 55.

[56] B.M. Harg. MS 373, ff. 142–3; Keil. 170b–172a.

Beaumont, had been treasurer of the Inn and rose to be Master of the Rolls under Edward VI until his dismissal for alleged forgery.[57] There is no evidence of a direct connection between the Beaumonts and Carrells but it is worth noting that John Beaumont was a personal friend of Anthony Gell, whose own case-book contains material covering much the same period as Carrell's. Although Gell seems to have had no more than professional dealings with John Carrell Jr.,[58] and none of their reports duplicates one another, there is an indirect link between their respective volumes which illustrates further the cooperative system which apparently obtained at the Temple. Both the Gell manuscript and Harleian MS 1691 have almost identical versions of the leading case of *Wimbish v. Tailbois* (1544).[59] It is clear from the date and from internal evidence in these manuscripts that neither Carrell nor Gell was the first-hand reporter; yet it is a fair inference that someone at the Inner Temple made notes on the case and that these circulated as early as 1547.[60]

In addition to being an advocate of some ability and a highly respected administrator,[61] the younger John Carrell also sat in five parliaments between 1547 and 1559. When he was a Member for Taunton in the Parliament of 1547–52[62] his fellow Member was Nicholas Hare, who also rose to prominence through a series of crown appointments; Hare had previously represented Lancaster and this seat he may have owed to Carrell who was by then Attorney of the Duchy.[63] Like John Beaumont, Hare eventually became Master of the Rolls, an office he filled until his death in 1557. In the early stages of his career, when he was

[57] *Cal. I.T. Recs.* i, 259, 295, 306, 333; *I.T. Adm. Reg.*, p. 44; Foss, v. 290; *H.M.C. Salisbury*, i, 96.

[58] See Anthony Gell's will (1583), P.C.C. 40 Rowe.

[59] Lib. of Congress Gell MS, ff. 107–11; B.M. Harl. MS 1691, f. 167; see Appendix III, pp. 259, 267.

[60] Gell was admitted to the Inner Temple in that year; *I.T. Adm. Reg.*, p. 3.

[61] Simpson notes that Carrell was considered as a candidate for appointment as Chief Justice of the Common Pleas; 'Keilwey', p. 100.

[62] Hist. Parl., John Carrell Jr.

[63] Ibid.; J.D. Mackie, *The Earlier Tudors* (1952), p. 654.

pleading at the bar, he may have benefited from Carrell's case-book, as well as collecting material himself. In a volume from the Lansdowne manuscripts entitled 'Wray's Reports' are six separate folios containing seventy-one numbered entries.[64] Written in a late-sixteenth-century hand, these cover decisions from Henry VIII to Elizabeth; many cannot be traced to a known source but some end with the simple reference, 'liber Hare' and relate to decisions from the years 1511 to 1552. Two further entries are ascribed to the books of Serjeant Carrell and his son and are dated 11 Henry VII and 27 Henry VIII respectively. Again, there is no clear connection between the two sources, but their appearance within a select compilation of cases strengthens the impression that lawyers of the Inner Temple maintained close, if informal, ties with one another in the matter of law-reporting.

It was probably inevitable that a collection such as Carrell's, containing as it did many 'missing years' from Henry VII and Henry VIII, should find its way into the hands of outsiders. Presumably Dyer was aware of the existence of these cases as early as 1538.[65] Then in Trinity term 4 & 5 Philip & Mary another reporter recorded an argument of Dyer's in which he claims to have seen an 'especiall report' from 24 Henry VII; this appears to be an inaccurate reference to a decision later published in Keilwey under 20 Henry VII.[66] Eventually, half-a-dozen cases attributable to Serjeant Carrell found their way into Dyer's Reports. Inasmuch as they were printed together with the entries for Trinity 11 Elizabeth it seems probable that Dyer came into possession of them around 1569, perhaps through his friend Thomas Bromley, then Queen's Solicitor.[67] It may be inferred that by the latter part of the century the collection, in whole or in part, was circulating within the profession generally, but few manuscripts survive to substantiate this. Although the anti-

[64] B.M. Lansd. MS 1084, ff. 3–8; a number of the cases ascribed to Hare are also found in H.L.S. MS 1058, ff. 1–2, but none of those ascribed to Carrell.

[65] He reported a citation by Keilwey in 30 Hen. VIII; Dyer, 41b.

[66] B.M. Harl. MS 1624, f. 62*v*; Keil. 58a–59b.

[67] Dyer, 285a–286a; Vaillant, 'Life of Dyer', in his edition of Dyer's *Reports*, pp. xv–xvi.

quarian-minded John Dodderidge apparently was aware of the connection between Carrell and Keilwey, his colleague Edward Coke was not,[68] even though Coke, an Inner Templar himself, had referred to Carrell's notes as early as 1586.[69] This ignorance may not be so surprising in view of the chaotic situation prevailing among manuscript reports at the turn of the century; even Croke, it seems, was unaware of the original source of the cases he edited, although from the remarks in his preface it appears that he realized it was not Keilwey. It must be concluded that John Carrell and his son, like many later reporters, were lost sight of in the tangle of 'wandering and masterless reports' which served the profession in the reigns of Elizabeth and James I.

From what has already been said it is clear that a number of lawyers at the Inner Temple collected their own cases, either at first or second hand. A piece of further evidence is provided by an isolated reference to Thomas Audley, Henry VIII's Chancellor between 1533 and 1544. In the course of his report of *Nevil's Case* (1570) Plowden quotes a precedent which was shown to him by Edward Saunders, the Chief Baron, and which, he claims, was 'reported by Audley Lord Chancellor'.[70] The case, which concerned a grant of the shrievalty of Cheshire to William and John Brereton, is undated and does not appear in any other collection surviving from the Inner Temple. It can be dated approximately from the parties named. William Brereton was one of the gentlemen of Henry's Privy Chamber executed for treason in connection with Anne Boleyn's condemnation; this was in May 1536.[71] The question of the shrievalty must have arisen soon afterwards and the suggestion that Audley recorded the case as Chancellor raises the possibility that a unique set of reports was in circulation in Plowden's time. Audley, like Thomas More, brought to the Chancellorship a lengthy apprenticeship in the common law, having begun his studies at the Inner Temple in

68 Co. Litt. 139b, 210b; 2 Inst. 52, 403, 413, 430; Lane's *Reports*, 8–9.

69 B.M. Lansd. MS 1095, f. 35*v*.

70 *Sir Henry Nevil's Case*, E. 12 Eliz. (Exchequer), Plow. 377 at p. 381.

71 Edward, Lord Herbert, *The Life and Raigne of King Henry the Eighth* (1672), pp. 446, 448; John Stow, *Annals* (1631), p. 573.

1510. Despite numerous absences from learning exercises, he was qualified to read in 1526.[72] During his tenure as Chancellor he sought the assistance of the common law judges on several occasions.[73] Unfortunately, only the single report relating to Brereton seems to survive from Audley's eleven years in office.

Law-reporting in the early sixteenth century could not have been the exclusive prerogative of the Inner Temple. There is, however, rather less evidence that a similar combination of personal friendship and professional cooperation obtained at the other Inns, although it may well have done. The reports of John Spelman do hint at a similar pattern in Gray's Inn, as well as providing another example of cases being compiled while the Yearbooks were still in production, albeit sporadically.[74] Spelman was the first of a distinguished line of judges whose case-books represent the backbone of sixteenth-century law-reporting. He came of an old legal family from Norfolk. His father Henry had been Recorder of Norwich, while his grandson, another Henry, is best known as a legal antiquarian.[75] John Spelman probably entered Gray's Inn before the start of the sixteenth century. His name is first mentioned in a citation from 17 Henry VII and he delivered his first reading in 1514. He was created a serjeant in 1521, King's Serjeant in 1528 and a puisne justice of the King's Bench four years later.[76] Both as pleader and judge he appears frequently in the Yearbooks and the earlier reports of Dyer. His first recorded appearance in the Yearbook of 14 Henry VIII coincided, fittingly enough, with Serjeant Carrell's last.

Spelman's contribution as a law reporter was perhaps better recognized than Carrell's, but none of his cases has ever been put into print. Coke cited his decisions in his own *Reports* and

[72] *Cal. I.T. Recs.* i, 19, 84, 97–8; Foss, v, 126.

[73] For instance, YBB E. 27 Hen. VIII, pl. 22; M. 27 Hen. VIII, pl. 6.

[74] Again, the writer is indebted to A.W.B. Simpson for much of the material on Spelman; 'The Reports of John Spelman', *L.Q.R.* lxxii (1956), 334–8.

[75] Ives, 'Legal Profession', p. 183.

[76] Co. Litt. 130a; Foss, v, 234–5; Simpson, 'Spelman', p. 335; the estimate in *D.N.B.* xviii, 741, that he was born about 1495 is too late seeing that he first read in 1514; *G.I. Pension Bk.*, i, 495.

Institutes:[77] he must have come into possession of a copy of Spelman's case-book about 1607, a conclusion borne out by a reference in Croke's *Reports* for Hilary term 4 James I.[78] Spelman's authority as a reporter is also cited in the printed volume ascribed to Richard Brownlow.[79] The scope of his work, like that of so many sixteenth-century reporters, exceeded the narrow limits of common law doctrine. His description of the trial of Anne Boleyn was cited by Coke and used as a source by Burnet, while another extract attributable to Spelman describing 'the manner and attendance of the Judges at the coronation of Queen Anne' is found in the Cottonian manuscripts.[80] There are, in addition, fragments of case collections designated as Spelman's. Among a large volume of reports in the Cambridge University Library catalogued as Bendlowes' Reports are twenty-two entries entitled, 'Certaine cases in Temps H. 8 reports per Spilman justice'.[81] These span an interval of thirty years in the reign of Henry VIII and appear to be taken from a larger collection: most of the entries relate to actions on the case.[82] Another, even smaller, selection of decisions attributed to Spelman forms part of a collection compiled by Edward Fenner, a justice of the King's Bench under Elizabeth, and is found among the manuscripts preserved at Longleat. There are only nine entries, relating to the years 7, 10, 20 and 21 Henry VIII.[83] According to Dugdale, Spelman's original case-book came into the possession of Clement Spelman, the judge's great-grandson who was also a member of Gray's Inn.[84] Efforts to dis-

[77] 6 Co. Rep. 62b; Co. Litt. 146a; 2 Inst. 493, 636; 3 Inst. 9, 10, 17, 30.

[78] Croke Jac. 152; *H.E.L.* v, 369; Coke had his own MS copy of Spelman's reports; W. O. Hassall (ed.), *Catalogue of the Library of Sir Edward Coke* (1950), p. 26.

[79] Simpson, 'Spelman', p. 334; Wallace, p. 107.

[80] B.M. Cotton MS. Vesp. C. XIV, ff. 139–139*v*.

[81] C.U.L. Gg. 2. 5, ff. 29–35*v*; Simpson assigns the MS to the mid-seventeenth century; see Appendix I, p. 261.

[82] Simpson, 'Spelman', p. 336.

[83] Longleat MS 240, f. 189*v* (*H.M.C. Third Rep., App.* p. 188); most of the other entries (ff. 187–90) look like extracts from Bendlowes which Fenner may well have taken from a MS such as C.U.L. Gg. 2. 59; see Appendix I, p. 266.

[84] *Origines Juridicales* (1671), p. 137.

cover it among the most likely repositories have been unsuccessful: it may well have been destroyed along with the other legal manuscripts in the library of Gray's Inn.[85]

Simpson was able to discover, however, a volume of reports among the Hargrave collection containing a very full complement of reports which may be ascribed to Spelman.[86] There is no indication of its source or ownership. It appears to have been copied in the late sixteenth century. Of the 255 leaves, the first 216 may well be the work of Spelman.[87] These folios form a separate section (which concludes with the word 'finis') comprising cases, arguments and readings from the first forty years of the sixteenth century.[88] This section, in turn, has two distinct parts. The first, folios 1 to 107, contains reports in chronological sequence for the years 1 to 32 Henry VIII: all but three years in this period are represented and the scribe has left space for additional entries.[89] With one exception the cases occurring in the Cambridge manuscript are found here. Seven out of the nine decisions from Edward Fenner's notes can also be traced, and, in addition, the references to Spelman in Coke and Brownlow appear as cited.[90] Equally strong evidence for Spelman's authorship is found in the reports themselves; in an entry for Trinity 23 Henry VIII, 'ego Johannes Spilman' records that he was elevated to the King's Bench by Chancellor Thomas More.[91] The second part of this section of the Spelman manuscript, folios 108 to 216, is composed of what Francis Hargrave described as 'varia juridica', together with a number of entries commonplaced under titles which lean towards the criminal law and rules of interpretation.

[85] Simpson, 'Spelman', p. 337. The MSS of Gray's Inn were destroyed when the library was bombed during World War II; the *Catalogue of Ancient Manuscripts* (1869) by A.J. Horwood contains only 24 entries all dating from before the fifteenth century, only one of which related to the law.

[86] B.M. Harg. MS 388.

[87] The remaining material seems part of another collection; Simpson, 'Spelman', p. 337.

[88] Ibid. pp. 336–7.

[89] There are no reports for 9–11 Hen. VIII, but cf. Fenner's notes in Longleat MS 240, f. 189*v*.

[90] Simpson, 'Spelman', p. 337.

[91] B.M. Harg. MS 388, f. 57*v*.

It is almost equally certain that this section originated with Spelman. For one thing, much of the material concerns Gray's Inn or lawyers attached to that house: there are, for instance, notes on the execution of Edmund Dudley, opinions of Chief Justice John Fineux in Gray's Inn, and a reading delivered by Anthony Fitzherbert.[92] For another, these folios include the material on Anne Boleyn already identified as Spelman's.[93]

The arrangement of that section of the manuscript comprising the case collection is not only chronological, but on closer inspection it proves to conform to the rising career of an able and observant advocate. During the first twelve years of Henry VIII Spelman, then an apprentice-at-law, left comparatively few entries—an average of two a year. This may be the result of later editing, but it may equally well reflect the reporter's modest first years of practice. What is already clear is that Spelman was leaning towards the criminal side of law: most of the entries deal with pardon, justices of the peace, error and 'pleez del corone' generally.[94] A noticeable increase in both the number and scope of his reports occurs after his call as serjeant in 1521. During the ensuing six years there are four times as many cases recorded than during the previous twelve. These include arguments in the Courts of Common Pleas and Exchequer, as well as in the King's Bench: in addition, Spelman took part in a few Exchequer Chamber cases, including the earliest known instances of such hearings being held at the Serjeants' Inns.[95] As do the Yearbooks of the same period, he quite frequently notes the names of the parties at issue and invariably sets out a résumé of the facts before summarizing the arguments of bench and bar.

Perhaps the most historically interesting phase in Spelman's reporting career was his three years as King's Serjeant (1528–32). Like Serjeant Carrell, he had the advantage of being on the periphery of government; but whereas Carrell experienced in the Hunne case only a foretaste of the 'Tudor revolution', Spelman was to witness the thing itself. During Michaelmas term

[92] Ibid. ff. 111, 123, 146*v*; Simpson, 'Spelman', p. 337.

[93] Harg. 388, ff. 130*v*–132*v*. [94] Ff. 7–17. [95] Ff. 26*v*, 43.

1529 he noted that a praemunire was taken by bill against Cardinal Wolsey, ex-Chancellor and 'home de graund pompe et riches'.[96] Later in the term he described Wolsey's formal dismissal, More's appointment as Lord Chancellor and Audley's promotion to the chancellorship of the Duchy of Lancaster.[97] These changes set the stage for the tragedy which Spelman himself narrated as a judge six years later, when More stood before his accusers, commissioners of oyer and terminer, who included in their number Audley, the new Chancellor. In the same year John Fisher, Bishop of Rochester, and the three monks of the Charterhouse were tried for treason. Both trials are reported by Spelman in a typically dry, impersonal manner which gives the impression that these momentous events signified nothing more than some useful points of law worthy of record.[98]

The largest single bloc of reports deals with matters which arose during Spelman's thirteen years on the bench.[99] Because of its comparatively large number of entries this series supplies a valuable cross-section of the business carried on in the King's Bench during the last phase of Henry VIII's reign as well as Spelman's activities elsewhere. The celebrated public trials and Exchequer Chamber conferences have the most general interest but form a very small proportion of the whole. Much of Spelman's attention was devoted to the legal issues raised by writs of error against judgments rendered in the Common Pleas. It is indicative of the length to which legal process could run that so many appeals could be launched even after judgment had been executed. Many of the hearings involved the reversal of outlawry on some technical point.[100] Technicalities also played a part on the criminal side. The harsh punishments exacted by the law found their antidote in the insistence on strictly literal drawing and interpretation

[96] Ff. 46–46*v*. [97] F. 47*v*. [98] Ff. 97*v*–98*v*.

[99] Out of a total of 396 entries 153 relate to these years; Spelman sat on the bench from Trinity 1532 until his retirement in November 1544; Foss, v, 356; cf. Dugdale, *Chronica Series*, p. 82, and *D.N.B.* liii, 333, both of which are inaccurate as to the dates in question; Spelman died in early 1546; see his will, P.C.C. 3 Alen.

[100] B.M. Harg. MS 388, ff. 57*v*–107.

of indictments: many writs of error succeeded by reason of a missing word or wrong initial in the name of an accused. The natural desire to evade punishment also accounts for the frequent review of the issue of clergyable offences, while other forms of relief from barbarous penalties are illustrated by the numerous appeals against false imprisonment and suits against jailors for escape of prisoners.[101]

Although Spelman remained active as a judge until 1544, his reports run no further than 1540.[102] This indicates that, while Hargrave MS 388 is fuller than most collections from this period, it is probably incomplete: Coke, it seems, cited cases from Spelman which are not found in this volume, and two of the entries attributed to Spelman by Edward Fenner are also missing.[103] Conversely, it is possible that some of the cases copied into Spelman's reports are from another source. This seems the only explanation for a curious feature observable among the entries in Hargrave 388 between 21 and 26 Henry VIII.[104] Many of these conclude with the single name 'Pollarde' in bold lettering. Although the copyist made a point of adding the names of various pleaders in such fashion, the recurrence of Pollard's name at the end of set groups of cases without more ado seems to connote authorship rather than mere participation. None of the decisions in question can be traced to the two collections bearing Spelman's name.[105]

It was common for Elizabethan barristers to conflate various collections from the same period in order to achieve a fuller casebook or longer sequence of yearly reports. It was not unusual either for copyists to indicate the source of their material if they were aware of it. We may thus reasonably infer that the 'Pollarde'

101 Such actions generally took the form of debt or action on the case; see, for example, ibid. f. 230.

102 *L. & P. Hen. VIII*, xx, pt. 1, no. 622 (vi, vii); he was succeeded in November 1544 by Thomas Bromley; Foss, v, 356.

103 There are no entries in B.M. Harg. MS 388 for 10 Hen. VIII or T. 20 Hen. VIII; cf. Longleat MS 240, f. 189*v*.

104 B.M. Harg. MS 388, ff. 50–95*v*, 149–50*v*.

105 C.U.L. MS Gg. 2. 5, ff. 29–35*v*; Longleat MS 240, f. 189*v*.

in question was an advocate rather than a clerk or attorney, since the latter rarely prepared volumes of this sort.[106] But even if the reporter was a barrister, his identity cannot be established with complete certainty. The Pollards were perhaps the most prolific of legal families in Tudor England. A total of thirteen attended the Inns of Court in the sixteenth century, eight of them at the Middle Temple. It was probably here that the compiler of the cases in question studied, since five members—all kinsmen—gained admission there down to 1550.[107] The best-known was Lewis Pollard, a judge of the Common Pleas under Henry VIII,[108] but inasmuch as he died in 1526, before the period covered by the reports began, he is eliminated as their possible author.[109] Two others, Anthony and another Lewis, began their studies sometime in the 1550s;[110] they could have collected the cases, though not at first hand, and neither achieved prominence at his Inn or in the profession. Two other candidates are Richard and John Pollard. Richard is listed as being admitted to Clerks' Commons in 1519[111] but he is not mentioned in the records of the Inn.

A far stronger claim can be made for John Pollard, a kinsman of the judge with an equally distinguished career. The admission records omit his Christian name but there is little doubt that he is the Pollard who entered the Middle Temple in 1515.[112] Like so many of his colleagues he was strongly conservative in religion, but in common with Nicholas Hare and John Carrell he gained preferment under both Somerset and Northumberland. He was created a serjeant in 1547, but was discharged by letters patent in 1550 and appointed Vice-President of the Council of the Marches

[106] Brownlow and Gouldesborough were the only exceptions in the sixteenth century; cf. Pike, *Year Book 20 Edw. III*, ii, lxv.

[107] *M.T. Adm. Reg.* i, 10, 17, 40, 44, 69, 73; *Cal. M.T. Recs.* i, 59, 113, 118.

[108] Foss, v, 228; *M.T. Bench Book* (1937), p. 52.

[109] See Additions and Corrections to the *D.N.B.*, Institute of Historical Research, University of London.

[110] Both were admitted sometime between 1524 and 1550; the records of admission for that period are lost; *M.T. Adm. Reg.* i, 17.

[111] *Cal. M.T. Recs.* i, 59.

[112] *M.T. Adm. Reg.* i, 8; *Catalogue of Notable Middle Templars* (1902), p. 193.

of Wales.[113] He sat in six parliaments over a span of twenty-five years, four of them in Mary's reign. As a staunch supporter of her regime he was elected Speaker in both October 1553 and 1555. Pollard's evident skill and experience in pleading is seen to advantage in the early reports of Plowden during his short tenure as serjeant.[114] In the Commons Journal for 5 October 1553 Pollard is described as 'excellent in the laws of this realm'. Since he was almost certainly the 'Pollard apprentice' who was arguing in the courts in 1535,[115] there is reason to believe that he had been practising for many years and was thus in a position to have reported cases between 1529 and 1534. It is worth adding that he had first lectured at the Middle Temple in 1535.[116] He may have compiled a selection of cases in anticipation of just such a reading.

Spelman, who was many years Pollard's senior, cannot have extracted these particular reports from Pollard's notes; the fusion of the two collections must have taken place several years later. In all, fifty-eight entries bear the 'Pollarde' colophon.[117] They are not radically different in style or content from the rest, although they tend to be briefer and in the form of 'notas'.[118] The majority originate in the Court of Common Pleas, although some may be moot cases or extracts from readings.[119] This sort of material is particularly noticeable from the thirty entries inserted during the time Spelman was on the bench and concerned with pleas of the crown. 'Pollard's' notes, like those of the Yearbook reporters, were the work of a qualified observer who was primarily interested in recording useful points propounded by 'the sages of the law'.

Although Spelman's own reports were evidently circulating

[113] Plow. 89.

[114] Pollard's career is traced in the History of Parliament Trust biography; see also J.E. Neale, *The Elizabethan House of Commons* (1949), p. 273.

[115] YB E. 27 Hen. VIII, pl. 22.

[116] *M.T. Bench Book*, p. 61.

[117] They are divided as follows: 21 Hen. VIII—11 entries, 22–17, 23–11, 24–9, 25–5, 26–5.

[118] One was reported from the Exchequer Chamber and a few from the King's Bench including one with an opinion by Spelman J.; B.M. Harg. MS 388, f. 62*v*.

[119] Note particularly ibid. f. 50.

among his colleagues by the late sixteenth century, there is not the same impression of cooperation at Gray's Inn as is found at the Inner Temple in connection with Carrell's collection. Coke obtained one of his references to Spelman out of the case-book of Christopher Yelverton, a judge of the King's Bench and a member of Gray's Inn.[120] Yet by then the profession at large seems to have gained access.[121] Edward Fenner, of the Middle Temple, was also a justice of the King's Bench, but senior to Yelverton. He probably came across the Spelman reports about 1600. All three volumes in which they appear are part of larger compilations which are not tied to any one Inn.[122] It remains to be seen whether Spelman was following established practice at Gray's Inn. There is a tradition originating with the biographer David Lloyd that when he died in 1525 Chief Justice John Fineux left behind twenty-three volumes of notes and 3,502 case reports. No reference to such a massive collection is found in his will and no identifiable trace of his work survives,[123] but it is quite possible that Fineux could have amassed it in view of his long career. He was probably born in 1441 and thus lived to the age of eighty-four: during that time he is supposed to have pleaded for twenty-eight years at the bar and to have spent another twenty-eight on the bench.[124]

The name of Edmund Dudley has also been associated with reporting within the orbit of Gray's Inn. Unfortunately, Dudley's fame rests primarily on his later role as servant to Henry VII. In 1503, after twenty-five years as a practising lawyer, he was

[120] *Catesby's Case*, 6 Co. Rep. 62b; Yelverton left some reports in MS; see particularly B.M. Harg. MS 17; the same case is cited by his son Henry Yelverton whose collection was printed in 1661; Yelverton's *Reports*, 100.

[121] George Croke of the Inner Temple refers briefly to his book: Herts. R.O. Gorhambury MS XII. A. 6A. f. 64.

[122] The material in B.M. Harg. MS 388 at ff. 155–255 may originate in Gray's Inn but this cannot be proved; both C.U.L. Gg. 2. 5. and Longleat MS 240 are mixed up with Bendlowes', who was a member of Lincoln's Inn.

[123] David Lloyd, *State Worthies* (1665), p. 63; his will is in P.C.C. 1 Porch; one possible hint of his work may be inferred from a citation by Dyer of a precedent relating to Fineux 'extra terminum . . . anno 15 H. 8'.

[124] Foss, v, 163–4.

nominated a serjeant, but in October of that year he paid an exemption fine and in the following January was elected Speaker of the House of Commons. His ill-fated career as one of the king's leading councillors between 1504 and 1509 pre-empted what might have been a secure seat on the bench.[125] In any event, he left behind two memorials of his erudition, *The Tree of Commonwealth* (1509) and his readings at Gray's Inn.[126] A number of useful dicta from his lectures percolated into later case-books. Although readings do not constitute reports, both Fitzherbert and Brooke regarded them as a legitimate source for their Abridgments. A compilation of such material from a slightly later period includes 'cases' from Spelman's reading in 1514.[127] Dudley's Lent reading was apparently something of an event, with such prominent jurists as Chief Justices Brian and Fineux and Judges Fairfax, Ernley and John Brooke in attendance.[128] In addition to three surviving copies of the lecture itself, someone collected a series of debates arising from it and these now reside within a large volume of regular reports; although undated, they are easily identified by frequent references to 'Dudley, Reader'.[129] As late as 1601 'a case' was inserted among some orthodox court decisions specifically designated as a report from Henry VII 'per Dudley de Greys Inn'.[130]

The collections mentioned constitute virtually the total evidence of private law-reporting during the last phase of the Yearbook era. This meagre yield is sufficient, however, to demonstrate that the Yearbooks by no means made up the entire output of reported cases available to the legal profession in this period. Evidence that a tradition of reporting independent of the Year-

[125] *The Tree of Commonwealth* (1948), pp. 1–3; Putnam, pp. 132–3; R. Somerville, 'Henry VII's "Council Learned in the Law"', *E.H.R.* liv (1939), 438–42.

[126] The first in 1496 was on Westminster II, Chap. 25, the second sometime before November 1503 on Quo Warranto; Putnam, p. 183.

[127] Bodl. Rawl. MS C. 705, ff. 95–100, 128–39; this collection belonged to John Daniel, one of the many lawyers of that name; he was probably one of those of the Cheshire family; see *L.I. Adm. Reg.* i, 77.

[128] Thorne, *Readings and Moots*, p. xxii.

[129] B.M. Harl. MS 5143, ff. 223–30*v*.

[130] B.M. Add. MS 35952, ff. 162*v*–63.

books was developing also lends weight to the argument that from the later fifteenth century the Yearbooks represented not so much an organized system of collecting cases as a prescribed style imposed by and for the printing trade in the person of Richard Pynson, the King's Printer.[131] It is all the more difficult, therefore, to ascribe the cessation of new Yearbooks flowing from the presses to a lack of interest among lawyers for fresh material. Inasmuch as they persisted in collecting recent cases, not only for their own use but for the benefit of close colleagues, it is clear that they did so in order to inform themselves of recent interpretations of the law as pronounced by the judges in Westminster Hall. It appears that Pynson's successors simply found it too difficult or too expensive to collect and print up-to-date decisions in competition with the legal profession itself. Yet, given the situation with respect to printed reports that prevailed in the early sixteenth century, it is not hard to understand why prominent members of the bar such as Carrell, Spelman and Audley decided early in their careers to compile their own case-books: no reports from their period were printed until well after 1500, and then only in the most erratic fashion; and, as has already been pointed out, those manuscripts from which the Yearbooks of Henry VII and Henry VIII were published had very limited, if not restricted, circulation.[132] If the principal aim of the Yearbooks was, as is generally accepted, to instruct students and junior barristers in the fine points of pleading and oral argument, it is hardly surprising that more senior and experienced practitioners, not to mention the judges, felt the need of current decisions close at hand as the impact of decided cases began making itself felt.[133]

To conclude, not only were there at least half-a-dozen members

[131] Added weight has recently been given to this argument by A.W.B. Simpson in his article 'Source and Function of the Later Year Books', pp. 109–10.

[132] It is worth noting that, while John Carrell Sr. and his contemporaries are known to have ordered copies of MS Yearbooks for the period before Hen. VII, no evidence exists that the same practice persisted with regard to the Tudor Yearbooks; see Simpson, 'Circulation of Yearbooks', pp. 496–500.

[133] For example, Fitzherbert's citation and discussion of a decision from YB M. 12 Hen. VIII, pl. 3, as reported in YB T. 27 Hen. VIII, pl. 21.

of the bar compiling reports during the first fifty years of Tudor rule but the resulting collections fall into two distinct categories: one in the traditional Yearbook style, objective, relatively impersonal and clearly designed for the benefit of other barristers, the other more subjective and idiosyncratic, and just as clearly intended for a restricted readership if not for the exclusive use of the reporter in question. If the first category represents the work of junior (and anonymous) utter-barristers, possibly under the aegis of Richard Pynson, the second is the product of mature, acknowledged practitioners in response to more subtle, if no less compelling, pressures than those exerted on their younger colleagues. More to the point, perhaps, the older method was dying out while the newer was to attract progressively more adherents as the sixteenth century unfolded. It was to be thirty years before an enterprising printer found an adequate replacement for the Yearbooks, not only as a vehicle for instructing students but as a means of keeping the profession at large abreast of current developments at Westminster Hall. In the meantime a new generation of practitioner-reporters, who began their legal careers in the 1530s, was to maintain and strengthen a tradition which was fundamental to the common law itself. It is their work and careers which are examined in the following chapters.

CHAPTER III

William Bendlowes

On 9 July 1534 William Bendlowes, the twenty-year-old son of a well-to-do Essex yeoman, was admitted for study at Lincoln's Inn. Unlike the majority of his fellows at that time he had not 'graduated' from one of the lesser Inns of Chancery but came directly from Cambridge.[1] He was simply one of ten new law students moving in that year to maintain the ranks of the Inn and of the legal profession as a whole.[2] Superficially at least, the profession and its educational system functioned along time-tested, traditional lines, unhurried or undisturbed by external events. The central courts at Westminster deliberated in their leisurely manner over the interminable squabbles of those Englishmen fortunate enough to possess land; the upward movement from student to barrister to bencher, from apprentice to serjeant to judge continued; and the twice-yearly readings and moots at the Inns of Court were still providing both profit for students and prestige for lecturers.[3]

Yet the lawyers, perhaps just as much as the clerics, were to be profoundly affected by the events of the times, not only those wrought by the hand of the King and his compliant legislators, but those attributable to the will of God as well. For whatever effects the New Learning may have had upon scholarship in

[1] *L.I. Adm. Reg.* i, 47; throughout the century the number of university-trained lawyers rose; see below, p. 69.

[2] Among other prominent names were those of Robert Mounson, later judge of the Common Pleas (1572–79) and Richard Catlin, created Queen's Serjeant in 1556.

[3] For a list of readings in print for the sixteenth century, see *H.E.L.* v, 497–9; the importance of these lectures has been outlined by Putnam, pp. 177–81; Thorne, *Readings and Moots*, pp. ix–xviii, supplies a list of readers at the four Inns for the late fifteenth and early sixteenth centuries.

England, medicine and sanitation remained as medieval as they had been in the days of Edward III and Richard II. If the plague was hardly as severe as in the fourteenth century its growing subtlety and chronic nature tended to disrupt periodically the regime's carefully nurtured system of law and order. From Henry VII to Elizabeth pestilence and 'sweating sickness' frequently interfered with the workings of church and state and nowhere more severely than in legal London. Just as much as the conciliar courts with their civil lawyers, this was an external force which must have affected the machinery of the common law not only within the courts but even more acutely at the springs of learning, the congested Inns of Court in Holborn.[4]

In the summer following Bendlowes' admission to Lincoln's Inn, Richard Pollard, writing to Thomas Cromwell from the Middle Temple, declared that plague had closed the Inns and curtailed his reading; the sickness, he noted, was very sore.[5] Recurring bouts of pestilence upset the educational regime. The lists of readings during the fifteenth and early sixteenth centuries contain frequent entries to the effect that no reading was held because of plague.[6] The intensity of some of these outbreaks can be appreciated from the fact that in 1487, 1528, 1562 and 1578 it was necessary to close the central courts and continue the term outside Westminster at a later date.[7] The fifteen-thirties were particularly hard-hit. Time and again it is recorded that the city was ravaged by plague, 'especially at the Inns of Court'; that the judges were 'weary for fear' while the serjeants-at-law sought licence to depart; and that consequently, 'the Temple and Lincoln's Inn have broken commons, as well as Serjeants' Inn'.[8] These periodic outbreaks may have resulted in a temporary slackening in litigation, but the effect upon law-reporting was

4 Charles Creighton, *A History of Epidemics in Britain* (1965), i, 237–309.

5 *L. & P. Hen. VIII*, ix, no. 119.

6 Thorne, *Readings and Moots*, pp. xiii–xiv; Ives, 'Promotion in the Legal Profession', *L.Q.R.* lxxv (1959), 348–63.

7 *Materials for a History of the Reign of Henry VII* (R.S.) ii, 136; *L. & P. Hen. VIII*, iv, no. 4398; Dyer, 225b, 359b.

8 *L. & P. Hen. VIII*, v, nos. 1444, 1446, 1466, 1476.

more serious;[9] this may be inferred from the description of just such an event during the reign of Henry VIII:

If it happen that the plague of pestilence be any thing nigh their House they immediately break up their House, and every man goeth home into his Country, which is a great loss of learning: for if they had some House nigh London to resort unto, they might as well exercise their learning, as in the Temple, untill the plague were ceased.[10]

Similar disruptions affected the houses of Chancery as well.[11] The Inns constituted the principal centre for law-reporting of all types. It was the custom of practitioners and students alike to take rough notes of proceedings in court and then work them into coherent form during the evenings in their chambers.[12] It is difficult to resist the inference that recurrent epidemics of this sort must have been responsible to a degree for the erratic production of reports in the 'thirties and early 'forties.

If Bendlowes' early career was punctuated by what must have been construed as Divine punishment for unnamed sins, there were other difficulties which affected, if only indirectly, the practice of law-reporting. What prompted Maitland to stress the problems facing the common law in this period were the seemingly frequent and bitter complaints about its operation. It was traditional for laymen to vent their distaste for a profession of which they were ignorant and not a little afraid.[13] Somewhat more ominous, however, was the attitude of members of the Reformation Parliament, then in its fifth eventful year, who petitioned the king concerning 'delays in the law, wrangling over defective titles, heavy fees ... and inability to execute ...'. Justice, they reiterated, was expensive; 'nother sergeauntes nor

[9] Dr Blatcher's studies indicate that plague probably accounted for some decline in court business in the years 1535–6 and 1537–8; cf. *H.E.L.* iv, 255–6.

[10] Dugdale, *Origines Juridicales*, p. 197.

[11] In July 1551 the sweating sickness caused the death of over thirty students at the various Inns of Court and Chancery before they broke commons; D. S. Bland, *Early Records of Furnival's Inn*, p. 43.

[12] See below, Chap. V, pp. 167–8; *Lives of the Norths*, i, 31–2.

[13] G. R. Owst, *Literature and Pulpit in Medieval England* (1961), pp. 338–49, 495–6.

apprenticis woll for the preferment of theyr clyauntes cause goo barre at any time . . . without fee of iijs. iiijd.'[14] Throughout the later years of Henry VIII and the reign of Edward VI social reformers from Thomas Starkey to Martin Bucer were as vociferous about injustices arising from an archaic legal system as they were about abuses engendered by enclosures and usury.[15]

Too much should not be made of these signs of unrest. Despite its reliance upon a code dominated by feudal concepts and the fact that not a few of its number became prosperous on the proceeds of their practice, the legal profession in the sixteenth century had much to its credit. 'There was', in Holdsworth's opinion, 'an abundance of good men at the Bar; and good judicial appointments were made'.[16] Similar approving (if more prejudiced) comments were made by those viewing at closer range, notably Matthew Hale and Edward Coke.[17] Apart from the occasional political sacking the judges operated in a state of relative immunity from the harsher aspects of Tudor efficiency. And except when participating in the more notorious treason trials—which seem to have elicited the worst traits in every advocate—they appear in the reports to administer justice with scrupulous objectivity. Even modern critics of the common law, such as Sir Charles Ogilvie, acknowledge the considerable ability of common lawyers at this time.[18] Nevertheless, all too often both judges and reporters appear to have forgotten the needs of the litigant in their concern for resolving the more esoteric issues that could arise from essentially simple disputes. The authorities made a constant ritual of reminding the judges of their duty towards the Queen's subjects. When Roger Manwood was installed as Chief Baron of the

14 *L. & P. Hen. VIII*, vii, no. 1611 (3).

15 For a recent appraisal of this 'commonwealth' literature see Whitney Jones, *The Tudor Commonwealth 1529–1559* (1970).

16 *H.E.L.* v, 346.

17 Sir Matthew Hale, *History of the Common Law* (1739), p. 171; Co. Litt. Pref. xxix–xxx.

18 Sir Charles Ogilvie, *The King's Government and the Common Law, 1471–1641* (1958), pp. 1ff.

Exchequer in 1579 Lord Keeper Bacon exhorted him to treat every cause, from the Queen's downwards, with equal 'indifference'. The main attributes of a judge, he claimed, were discretion, uprightness, simplicity and diligence.[19] Four years later, when Anderson was elevated to the Chief Justiceship of the Common Pleas, the Lord Chancellor, Thomas Bromley, moved the judges to avoid 'intolerable expences en les sutors & pur prevention del danger que poit a vener per delay, ...'.[20] In Trinity term 1598 at the investiture of John Glanville as a puisne justice of the Common Pleas Lord Keeper Egerton, echoing his predecessors, told the assembled lawyers that a judge must know the thing whereof he is to judge, display the wisdom to arbitrate between suitors' claims and possess the integrity to withstand bribes and corruption.[21] With few exceptions members of the bench and bar seem to have met these standards while managing to gain a handsome living. In general, a practitioner's success usually grew in proportion to his ability, and those who did become wealthy had invariably earned their status.[21a]

Ironically, it was the flurry of legislation of Henry's reign aimed at reforming the law which gave rise to some of the most violent demonstrations of popular discontent. When Robert Aske petitioned for the redress of grievances on behalf of the Pilgrimage of Grace, he cited the Statute of Uses and its restrictions on the freedom of devising property.[22] The lawyers themselves, or at least those of senior rank, were partly to blame since the legislation relating to uses and enrolments had come about as compromise measures between the profession and the government.[23] Besides operating as a pressure group in society the legal profession actively looked after its own interests in Parliament. As the

[19] A full description of Manwood's installation, with Bacon's speech and the Chief Baron's reply, is in B.M. Add. MS 16169, ff. 67*v*–68*v*.

[20] Moore, 116. [21] B.M. Harg. MS 7, vol. ii, ff. 151*v*–52.

[21a] 2 Co. Rep. Pref. xi.

[22] M.H. & Ruth Dodds, *The Pilgrimage of Grace* (1915), i, 102–3, 364–5.

[23] T.F.T. Plucknett, *A Concise History of the Common Law* (1956), pp. 583–4; but cf. E.W. Ives, 'The Genesis of the Statute of Uses', *E.H.R.* lxxxii (1967), 686–7.

first non-resident members in the Commons to secure election from the boroughs,[24] lawyers played a dominant role in managing debates and determining the fate of many acts. Their power in the House was doubtless enhanced by their grasp of parliamentary procedure and attention to detail.[25] In addition, as judges they were virtually indispensable in the Lords and often had a decisive influence on the Council.[26]

For the most part, however, Henrician legal policy, particularly in its later stages, was probably the product of Thomas Cromwell and his associates. It compares closely, if unfavourably, with that of Edward I.[27] In Stubbs' opinion, it was only the urgency attached to ecclesiastical affairs and the resultant legislation which has led to virtual neglect of this legal code.[28] The Statutes of Uses and Enrolments were only the beginning. Some elements in this legislative programme were merely piecemeal attempts at reforming procedure: trial of murder in cities and towns, the non-suiting of plaintiffs, limitation of prescription and the Statute of Jeofails.[29] Others represented important constitutional changes in the court system: establishment of the Courts of Augmentations, First Fruits and Tenths, Wards and Liveries, and Surveyors.[30] And finally, there were those few acts which attempted to alter key sectors of the substantive law: treason,

[24] May McKisack, *The Parliamentary Representation of English Boroughs during the Middle Ages* (1932), pp. 117–18; Edward Porritt, *The Unreformed House of Commons* (1903), i, 512.

[25] E.R.Foster (ed.), *Proceedings in Parliament 1610* (1966), ii, 79, 89–92, 162–5. W.S.Holdsworth, *Essays in Law and History* (1946), p. 85; Neale, *House of Commons*, pp. 307–8.

[26] *H.E.L.* ii, 430–1.

[27] Elton, *Thd Tudor Revolution in Government* (1953), pp. 190–223; the then Chancellor, Thomas Audley, probably took an important part in preparing much of this legislation and supervising its passage through the House of Lords; S.E.Lehmberg, 'Early Tudor Parliamentary Procedure: Provisos in the Legislation of the Reformation Parliament', *E.H.R.* lxxxv (1970), 2.

[28] Stubbs, *Seventeen Lectures*, p. 293; K.W.M.Pickthorn, *Early Tudor Government, Henry VIII* (1934), p. 441.

[29] 1532, 23 Hen. VIII, chaps, 13, 15; 1540, 32 Hen. VIII, chaps. 2, 30.

[30] 1536, 27 Hen. VIII, chap. 27; 1540, 32 Hen. VIII, chaps. 45, 46; 1541, 33 Hen. VIII, chap. 39.

proclamations, wills and recoveries.[31] For sheer quantity the years 1539–40 were the most productive of the reign, while the programme as a whole proved as important to future generations as the religious code.

The effect of this new legislation upon the existing mode of law-reporting was immediate and decisive. Again, there is a marked parallel with the situation two-and-a-half centuries previously. Then, the great reforming statutes of Edward I gave rise to the vivid and comprehensive Yearbooks of Edward II which portray the work of the courts in harnessing the new law to the exigencies of fourteenth-century society.[32] In the same way the statutes of Henry VIII and their assimilation into the common law constitute an essential feature of private reporting from Bendlowes to Coke. Indeed, it was the need to elucidate the new legislation which contributed both to the compilation of new reports and to the development of modern canons of statutory interpretation.

In Easter term 1535, less than a year after taking up his studies, Bendlowes reported the first legal proceedings at which he was present.[33] This unremarkable start to forty years of reporting occurred by coincidence in the same year as marked the end of the printed Yearbooks. Both events would have passed unnoticed by contemporaries. Bendlowes' notes, though fairly extensive, were probably just the initial folios of the kind of note-book which every lawyer was expected to keep, while the publication of the Yearbooks invariably fell behind the terms reported and their demise was not the subject of comment by practitioners of the times.[34] It is abundantly clear, all the same, that the year 1535 lay within a period of flux, if not of crisis, for the common law. In addition to the effects of the new legal code, there were changes taking place through existing forms of action. Actions on the

[31] 1534, 25 Hen. VIII, chap. 22; 1544, 35 Hen. VIII, chap. 2; 1539, 31 Hen. VIII, chap. 8; 1540, 32 Hen. VIII, chaps. 1, 31.

[32] T. F. T. Plucknett, *Legislation of Edward I* (1949), pp. 13–17.

[33] *Bold v. Molyneux*, E. 26 & 27 Henry VIII; Bendl. 13.

[34] Plow. Pref. iii–iv; see above Chap. I, pp. 9–11, 24–5.

case, and specifically the offshoots assumpsit and trover, were in the process of gaining precedence over the older remedies of debt and detinue;[35] the central courts were at last beginning to recognize the rights of the copyholder in law;[36] and the jury, long notorious for its corruptibility, was rapidly assuming its posture of impartiality with witnesses supplying the evidence.[37] None of these developments or their effects can be assigned to one decade, let alone a single year, yet they do help to explain the changes which were taking place in the system of law-reporting during the latter part of Henry VIII's reign.

Although one of the less known of sixteenth-century reporters, William Bendlowes is a fair representative of his profession. He was, like most lawyers, a member of that much-discussed class, the gentry.[38] Born in 1516, he was the son of Christopher Bendlowes of Great Bardfield, Essex. His father was a prosperous yeoman who amassed sufficient wealth to purchase the manor of Brent Hall, Finchingfield.[39] William was sent to St John's College, Cambridge, but left without taking a degree, and proceeded directly to Lincoln's Inn. It was a sign of the times that many of Bendlowes' profession prefaced their careers with at least a few terms at the university.[40] Although this trend had begun at the end of the fifteenth century, it was still only a minority of students who had had a university education when Thomas More attended Lincoln's Inn. Yet in Elizabeth's reign, to judge from those who were members of parliament, a majority of lawyers had been to either Oxford or Cambridge; according to Coke the young student 'commonly cometh from one of the universities'.[41]

35 Plucknett, *Concise History*, pp. 374–5; C.H.S. Fifoot, *History and Sources of the Common Law* (1949), pp. 102–13, 330–40.

36 C. M. Gray, *Copyhold, Equity and the Common Law* (1963), pp. 56–64.

37 *H.E.L.* iii, 653–4.

38 Ives, 'Legal Profession', pp. 67–8, 79–86.

39 *D.N.B.* ii, 213; Hist. Parl.

40 Neale, *House of Commons*, pp. 304–5.

41 Chrimes, pp. 198–9; R.W. Chambers, *Thomas More* (1949), pp. 66–7; Neale, *House of Commons*, pp. 302–4; 3 Co. Rep. Pref. xixa.

From his admission in 1534 Bendlowes' career followed the well-trodden path of his more senior colleagues. One of these was William Rastell, who had entered the Inn in 1532.[42] The two men appear to have been personal friends and both were to display conservative religious leanings. Perhaps Rastell, with his knowledge of the printing trade, foresaw the need that would arise for new reports and encouraged his younger colleague to collect cases. It was also in the fifteen-thirties that Robert Brooke and James Dyer—future Chief Justices as well as reporters—joined the ranks of the Middle Temple.[43] The year 1534 also saw William Dalison admitted to Gray's Inn—one of the few things which he and Bendlowes had in common despite the fact that their work was later to be lumped together in the same volume.[44] Three years later the most famous of sixteenth-century reporters, Edmund Plowden, entered the profession.[45]

Five years after his admission Bendlowes was called to the bar;[46] and five years after that (1544), no doubt as the corollary of a successful start in practice, he married Eleanor, the daughter of Sir Edward Palmer and widow of John Berners.[47] It was also probably about this time that he inherited from his father the Bardfield and Brent Hall estates as well as other property.[48] The Black Books of Lincoln's Inn reveal his rise to prominence in the profession; as an utter-barrister he and his fellows were to 'have ther Clerkes in comens . . . so that they exercise ther larnyngs both within the howse and without', and in 1546 the Council of

[42] *L.I. Adm. Reg.* i, 46.

[43] The Middle Temple Admission Registers for the period between 1524 and 1551 have not survived so that the dates of entry of Brooke and Dyer can only be estimated with reference to their later careers.

[44] *G.I. Adm. Reg.*, p. 11.

[45] Plowden was a member of the Middle Temple; the date of his admission can be established from remarks in his Preface to the *Commentaries*.

[46] *Black Books of L.I.* i, 254.

[47] Bendlowes may by then have been a widower; see C.H. & T. Cooper, *Athenae Cantabrigienses* (1861), i, 495.

[48] J. G. Coverton, 'Some Local Memorials of and References to the Family of Bendlowes in Great Bardfield, Finchingfield and Neighborhood', unpublished essay (1934), Essex Record Office, T/G 98.

the Inn resolved that he and Rastell were to be called to the Bench at the next moot but one, 'and never loose auncyenty hereafter'. His appointment as reader for autumn 1548, however, was cancelled because of the plague which broke the learning vacation. After serving as Rastell's deputy in the Treasurership, Bendlowes assumed the office in 1550; he held it for four years, an unusually long tenure. It was during this period that Thavie's Inn was purchased, thus becoming the second Inn of Chancery affiliated with Lincoln's Inn.[49]

A brief parliamentary career began for Bendlowes in the autumn of 1553 when he sat for the borough of Helston. The following spring he represented West Looe and in November 1554 Dunheved. All three were Cornish boroughs, a circumstance which seems to befit his professional connections; these were concerned with the payment of homage dues to the Duchy. There was also a tradition by which Looe and Dunheved returned men affiliated with Lincoln's Inn.[50] Among others Bendlowes was associated in these parliaments with Robert Mounson, later a judge of the Common Pleas, with whom he represented Looe in April 1554, and with Clement Heigham, who was to serve briefly as Chief Baron of the Exchequer under Mary.[51]

Parallel with his temporary participation in national politics was Bendlowes' rising status in his home county of Essex. He was appointed a member of the subsidy commission of 1551 and became a Justice of the Peace in February 1554. Between 1562 and 1564 his name appears on commissions of the peace of various counties.[52] He seems to have been anxious to encourage small industry in his own area. Having purchased a house at Thaxted, he became, under Mary, the town's first recorder. Here he introduced fustian weavers and clothiers to help retrieve the fading economy.[53] About this time, however, a jarring note creeps into

[49] *Black Books of L.I.* i, 269, 275, 288, 295–9, 304–5, 311. [50] Hist. Parl.

[51] In October 1553 Bendlowes sat for Helston with Henry Nance, a resident of the area with property in the borough, and in November 1554 for Dunheved with John Kempthorn who was admitted to Lincoln's Inn in November 1552.

[52] Hist. Parl.

[53] Philip Morant, *History and Antiquities of the County of Essex* (1768), ii, 442.

the record of an otherwise reputable career. In 1555 John Carrowe, clerk of the peace for Essex, wrote to Sir William Petre complaining of Bendlowes' 'corrupt' conduct at quarter sessions which he supposedly displayed by preferring his own clients' causes to the detriment of other men's bills. In fact, Carrowe's displeasure appears to have stemmed from Bendlowes' demand that he render an account of monies received in virtue of his office. Nothing further seems to have emerged from the affair; in any event Carrowe retired from his post later in the year.[54]

As it turned out, the same year 1555 saw Bendlowes achieve his highest rank within the legal profession when he received his summons to become a serjeant-at-law.[55] In accordance with custom his Inn nominated him reader in Lammas vacation of that year. He was accorded 'four admittances and all other allowances that double readers have commonly had heretofore'.[56] It was no coincidence that he prospered under Mary. That he was a staunch adherent of Catholicism seems clear despite careful acquiescence after Elizabeth's accession. His election to the parliaments of 1553–4 was apparently acceptable to a regime anxious to procure representation of 'the catholic sort' of men. More significant was Bendlowes' appointment to the heresy commission for Essex which was issued in August 1556 and headed by the Earl of Oxford.[57] His inclusion was more than a formality since he appears to have taken his duties quite seriously and, along with Lord Darcy, pursued heretics in his county with considerable zeal.[58] In many of his duties during the 'fifties he was associated with a more prominent Catholic lawyer from Essex, Anthony Browne, who was Chief Justice of the Common Pleas until removed by Elizabeth in 1559. At the same time it is worth noting that, while Bendlowes served the cause of Rome, his brother-in-law, Sir Thomas Palmer, a fervent Protestant, was

[54] State Papers 11/5/3; F. G. Emmison, *Tudor Secretary* (1961), pp. 264–5.
[55] *C.P.R.* 1554–5, p. 59.
[56] *Black Books*, i, 312.
[57] J. E. Oxley, *The Reformation in Essex to the Death of Mary* (1965), p. 226.
[58] John Foxe, *Acts and Monuments* (1870), viii, 304–10; Oxley, p. 183.

executed for treason.[59] In gratitude for favours bestowed on him Bendlowes took advantage of mortmain concessions granted by the Crown to found a chantry in 1556 at Great Bardfield parish; here masses were sung not only for the souls of his own family but for Philip and Mary as well.[60]

After 1558, despite his manifest support of the Marian regime, Bendlowes escaped relatively unscathed. He probably lost the chance of a judgeship but his practice continued to prosper. From the evidence of his own reports and those of his contemporaries he was extremely active in the Court of Common Pleas for the next twenty years.[61] He continued to hold a place of honour in Lincoln's Inn and near the end of his career was elected a senior bencher.[62] The last professional reference to him comes in May 1582 at the investiture of Edmund Anderson as Chief Justice of the Common Pleas, when, as Recorder Fleetwood noted in a letter to Burghley, 'Father Benloos because he was auncient [i.e. senior serjeant] did put a short case'.[63] He had probably ceased active pleading in 1578, the year his reports terminate. He died on 9 November 1584, two days after making his will.[64] Besides leaving a number of bequests to charity, he remembered the institutions of his working life, Lincoln's, Thavie's and Serjeants' Inns.

The surviving evidence of this successful, if unspectacular, career tells something of the man but little of the lawyer or law-reporter. What manner of practice did he have? What sort of clients did he represent? How did he organize his activities in and out of term? And, most important, what motives lay behind the compilation of his reports? Much can be gleaned from the collection itself and those of his colleagues; otherwise reliance must be placed on the remarks of interested observers. One of these was John Stow, whose reference to Bendlowes was cited by Maitland

[59] Hist. Parl. [60] Morant, ii, 521; Oxley, p. 183.

[61] His name crops up as counsel regularly in the reports of Dyer, Dalison and numerous unprinted collections between 1553 and 1578.

[62] *D.N.B.* ii, 213; *Black Books*, i, 394. [63] Printed in Wallace, p. 138.

[64] Hist. Parl.; his will is registered in P.C.C. 10 Brudenell.

as evidence of a serious decline in business in the common law courts:[65]

In the Common Pleas no moe Sergeants but one, which was Sergeant Bouloise, who looked about him, there was elbow roome enough, which made the Lawyers complaine of their iniuries in that Tearme.[66]

Holdsworth has since cast doubt upon the impression of crisis thus given and indeed it now appears that in 1557 the Common Pleas enjoyed its busiest year in over a century.[66a] The explanation of what could only have been a temporary interruption in business may very well lie in the influenza epidemics which swept through England in the summers of 1557 and 1558.[67] Stow himself remarks on the effects which 'the quartaine agues' had on the price of corn and the mortality rate among the clergy and the old.[68] The original anecdote raises other questions with respect to the legal profession as a whole and the order of serjeants in particular. While there is no reason to question Stow's chronology, it would have been more appropriate had Bendlowes been confronted with the situation described in the following year:[69] it was in reference to Michaelmas term 1558 and Hilary 1559 that he and his heirs took pains to inform posterity that he was sole serjeant for seventy-three days.[69a] It was an unusual situation and one which

[65] Maitland, *English Law and the Renaissance*, pp. 22, 82.

[66] Stow, *Annals* (1631), p. 631. Despite the spelling the serjeant referred to could only be William Bendlowes.

[66a] This is based on the figures compiled by Dr Blatcher.

[67] Creighton, i, 401–5; John Strype, *Ecclesiastical Memorials* (1822), iii, pt. 2, 156–7.

[68] *Annals*, pp. 631, 634; for a modern assessment of the economic repercussions of these epidemics see F.J. Fisher, 'Influenza and Inflation in Tudor England', *Econ. Hist. Rev.* 2nd series, xviii (1965), 125–9.

[69] Cf. Peter Heylyn, *Ecclesia Restaurata* (1849), ii, 213, where the casual use of marginal annotations makes it appear as if the events Stow describes took place in 1558: the text itself is unambiguous.

[69a] Dugdale *Origines Juridicales*, p. 331; on his tomb at Great Bardfield, Essex, is an inscription which states that Bendlowes was sole serjeant from mid-November 1558 (the probable date of William Rastell's installation as a justice of the K.B.) to 26 January 1559 (the date on which the writ summoning Richard Weston as a serjeant was returnable); he also signed documents designating himself sole serjeant.

caused comment at the time.[70] The reasons for it were not related either to a purge by Marian authorities or to flagging business in the courts but rather to chance and the changing nature of lawsuits caused by the transition from oral to written pleadings.[71] Ten barristers had been called to take the coif in 1555 but a combination of death, exemption and promotion had by 1558 reduced this number to one.[72] In that year the government moved to fill the ranks once more by sending out twelve writs, but these abated on the death of Mary in Michaelmas term 1558. After a delay of three weeks the Elizabethan regime nominated ten new candidates seven of whom had been designated earlier.[73] Thus Bendlowes' unique status was really an accident and not a reflection on the state of the law. It should be borne in mind, however, that the relative decline in the number of practising serjeants may also be ascribed to the fact that many cases were now put on the record and steered through the court by attornies without benefit of serjeants to plead them.[74]

Yet bearing in mind that only serjeants were permitted to plead at the bar of the Common Pleas,[75] it seems to follow that Bendlowes was obliged to argue both sides of every action called to the court between 14 November 1558 and 26 January 1559. In practice no such anomalous situation is likely to have arisen. For one thing, the death of Queen Mary on 17 November caused a constriction of Michaelmas term with the abatement of unreturned writs and a general disruption in the judicial process.[76]

[70] Cf. Dyer's unprinted notes in the Inner Temple Library, Petyt MS 511, vol. 13, f. 38.

[71] S.F.C. Milsom, *Historical Foundations of the Common Law* (1969), p. 62.

[72] *C.P.R.* 1557–8, p. 457; Foss, v, 347, 415–16.

[73] *C.P.R.* 1558–60, p. 65.

[74] Serjeants would only be required for those cases in which the written pleadings ended in demurrer or where a special verdict taken at *nisis prius* was argued before the Common Pleas bench; Milsom, pp. 62–4.

[75] There were only rare exceptions to this rule; see, for instance, Plow. 425; Simpson, 'Circulation of the Yearbooks', p. 494.

[76] Except for a meeting of judges at Serjeants' Inn, no entries can be found reported for M. 1558 in Dyer, Dalison, Bendlowes, Plowden or the various MS collections examined to date; cf. Dyer, 165a. There is no plea roll for M. 5 & 6

More to the point, Bendlowes enjoyed his distinctive status, for the most part, during the Christmas vacation rather than in term time. During Michaelmas 1558 there were only eight possible days, and in Hilary 1559 five, during which he remained the only serjeant available for pleading.[77] In the circumstances, and given the casual procedure which attached to disputes of even the most urgent nature, it would have been a simple matter to postpone any hearings in the Common Pleas until the writs of the serjeants-elect had been returned on 26 January 1559.

In addition to monopolizing the work of arguing cases in the Common Pleas, the serjeants were also active in the King's Bench and, to a less extent, in the Court of Exchequer. Bendlowes, however, seems to have confined his own activities at Westminster to the Common Bench. The range of actions with which he was concerned, therefore, was governed by the jurisdiction of that court. Broadly speaking, this consisted of suits between private subjects begun by original writ out of Chancery.[78] This jurisdiction was exclusive in real actions, but these were rapidly losing favour in the eyes of litigants and there are few examples in Bendlowes' reports, although he did argue a number of possessory assizes, particularly novel disseisin.[79] More important were the traditional personal actions such as debt, detinue, account and covenant. These still constituted an essential part of the court's business in the sixteenth century, especially debt, which served as the principal remedy for the recovery of arrears of rent.[80] Bendlowes, it seems, was thoroughly steeped in Yearbook learning and specialized in the more traditional modes of litigation. Next to debt, the action with which Bendlowes seems to have been most concerned was trespass. Most of the entries in question dealt with the established remedy open to freeholders,

P. & M. in the King's Bench, while that for the Common Pleas is considerably abbreviated and merged with the roll for 1 Eliz.

[77] Michaelmas term 1558 ran from 7 October to 26 November, Hilary term from 20 January to 3 February 1559; Cheney, pp. 65–8, Table 5.

[78] Hastings, pp. 16–17; Plucknett, *Concise History*, pp. 355–6.

[79] See list of cases, p. 77; Hastings, p. 16.

[80] This coincided with the increasing use of leases for term of years.

trespass *quare clausum fregit*, rather than the more flexible *de ejectione firmae* which was being exploited by the King's Bench.[81]

Cases reported by Bendlowes at first hand classified according to subject-matter and in order of frequency.

Debt			21
Trespass	vi et armis	2	
	de bonis asportatis	2	
	quare clausum fregit	12	16
Quare impedit			12
Statutes, Henry VIII			11
Novel disseisin			9
Replevin			9
Dower			6
Covenant			5
Writ of entry			5
Leases			5
Detinue			4
Testaments			4
Waste			4
Action on the case			3
Formedon			3
Partition			3
Second Deliverance			3
Custom			3
Challenge to jurors			2
Scire Facias			2
Uses			2
Annuity			2
Statutes, Edward VI			2
Trials reported on circuit			2
Writ of right			1
Darrein presentment			1
Quare ejecit			1
Attaint			1
Disceit			1
Admiralty			1

[81] Plucknett, *Concise History*, pp. 373–4; F. W. Maitland, *The Forms of Action at Common Law* (1954), pp. 65–72.

Error	I
Statute of Winchester (13 Edward I)	I
Statute of Quia Emptores (18 Edward I)	I
Letters patent	I
Arbitration	I
Fines	I
Wardship	I

While the lines of demarcation were theoretically drawn between the areas of jurisdiction of the central courts, in reality competition in the sixteenth century was vigorous. The reports only hint at this internal struggle; indeed, they tend to emphasize the solidarity which undoubtedly existed between members of the profession. Of the three tribunals the Common Bench was probably the most important in terms of business and prestige when Bendlowes began practice; by the end of the century, however, the King's Bench had superseded its rival and taken the initiative.[82] It was around the writs of trespass and their offshoot, action on the case, that competition really revolved, since these were providing suitors with more efficient justice than older forms of action. Since neither tribunal had exclusive jurisdiction over trespass, the secret of success lay in getting the defendant into court as quickly as possible. In this the Common Pleas was notoriously inept and when the King's Bench evolved a technique for arresting defendants outside the confines of Middlesex by means of a fictitious complaint of trespass, it gained an advantage over its rival which was never relinquished.[83] At the best of times suits before the Common Bench tended to become mired in the tedious formalities of pleading seisin or title to land; the more stimulating subjects of crime and politics, on the other hand, helped enliven proceedings in the King's Bench. Roger North was later to lament a situation in which, because of the introduction of paper pleadings, the court was unaware of much of the business being carried

[82] Hastings, pp. 21–3 240–3; G. R. Y. Radcliffe & G. Cross, The *English Legal System* (1954), pp. 157, 172.

[83] M. Blatcher, 'Touching the Writ of Latitat: an Act "of no Great Moment"', *Elizabethan Government and Society* (1961), pp. 188–212; Milsom, pp. 54–6.

on; even the occasional real action which might require oral declaration at the bar was dispatched with some unintelligible mumblings by the serjeant.[84]

Since he never attained a place on the bench Bendlowes was denied access to many of the conferences where the more important issues of law were resolved; consequently, his reports lack the broader scope which characterizes the work of Dyer, Anderson, Popham and Coke. His cases tend to reflect the more staid, almost archaic atmosphere of an institution unable to cope with the rush of events which overtook it. Nevertheless, the Court of Common Pleas remained throughout the sixteenth century the principal forum of instruction for law students, and the work of its reporters continued as an integral part of the curriculum at the Inns of Court. Perhaps more than any contemporary collection of cases Bendlowes' Reports were designed as much for students as for practitioners.[85]

The decline of the Court of Common Pleas was accompanied by a certain loss of prestige for the order of serjeants. They remained, however, the elite of the legal profession, and in spite of the initial expenses involved Sir John Fortescue's words still held true when Bendlowes received his call in 1555: 'No advocate in the whole world enriches himself by reason of his office as much as the serjeant'.[86] Just how lucrative was the coif is uncertain, but one wearer of it under Henry VII, John Fineux, had an immense practice: after twenty-eight years as an apprentice and serjeant he held the stewardship of 129 manors and enjoyed the patronage of sixteen noblemen.[87] In 1500 a serjeant might expect £5 as a retainer and 40 marks plus expenses for acting as counsel during onc assize.[88] Serjeant John Spelman received 6s. 8d. 'for his counsell in putting in of the answer'.[89] By the end of the cen-

[84] *Lives of the Norths*, i, 30; he described proceedings in the King's Bench as consisting of 'more news than law'; ibid. p. 31.

[85] For a discussion of Bendlowes' original MS reports and their ostensible aim, see below, pp. 92–7; Hastings, p. 26; *Lives of the Norths*, i, 32.

[86] *De Laudibus*, p. 125. [87] Foss, v, 164.

[88] J. Manning, *Serviens ad Legem* (1840), p. 182.

[89] Editor's note in Elyot, *Boke named the Governour*, i, 150–1.

tury any reasonably competent pleader could expect to earn £40 in his first year of practice and as much as £600 per annum as a senior member of the bar.[90] Thomas Wilson, doubtless exaggerating, estimated in 1600 that judges and serjeants enjoyed an income of £20,000 to £30,000 a year; even when halved, such remuneration is impressive.[91] As for Bendlowes, from the lengthy list of his charitable donations, not to mention his landed estates, it is evident that he earned a good living from his practice. His clients ran the social gamut from the Queen to ordinary folk and included bishops, members of the nobility, merchants and even fellow lawyers.[92] But if his reports are any guide, Bendlowes catered primarily to the gentry with their interminable disputes over possession of manors, collection of rents and title to advowsons: men such as Richard Vaughan of Walthamstow, Essex, Sir Edmund Beaupre of Owtewell, Norfolk, Sir Geoffrey Cobb of Sandringham, Norfolk, Henry Vernon of Sudbury, Derbyshire, and John Crachfield of Herstmonceux, Sussex.[93] It was probably the standing of his clients as much as the character of the Court of Common Pleas which accounts for his traditionalist type of practice.

An ambitious and competent serjeant could expect two further appointments within his profession, those of King's Serjeant and judge. By Elizabeth's reign the first had become more or less honorary although it commanded an additional stipend; its holders were summoned by writs of assistance to attend the House of Lords, along with the judges, and give advice on technical legal points, and were called upon to advise the Council on questions

[90] *H.E.L.* v, 344, n. 1; cf. Plowden's receipt of annuities, below, Chap. VI, pp. 202–3.

[91] Thomas Wilson, *The State of England, Camd. Misc.* xvi (Camd. 3rd Series lii), 25.

[92] Bendlowes represented, for example, Gilbert Berkeley, Bishop of Bath and Wells (1575); William, Lord Sandys (1571); Evan Luce, a London mercer (1557); John Nyseham, a Shoreditch baker (1565); Roger Manwood, justice of the Court of Common Pleas (1573); Bendl. 265, 304, 62, 151, 217.

[93] Ibid. 100, 132, 141, 198 and 317.

of law.[94] The judiciary could only be recruited from the ranks of serjeants. This was one reason why the order continued to survive far beyond the sixteenth century. By the time Bendlowes received his call in 1555 the degree of serjeant had come to be looked upon primarily as a stepping-stone to the bench.[95] Already at least one and probably two advocates had been appointed serjeant and elevated to the bench simultaneously; fifty years later this practice was commonplace.[96] In normal circumstances, however, there was usually a gap of a few years before a member of the coif was promoted, during which he received valuable experience sitting as a justice of assize. Bendlowes first went on circuit in the Midlands with James Dyer following the death of William Stanford in 1558,[97] but he records at first hand only one trial at which he presided.[98]

As members of the same order serjeants and judges were in many ways equal in status. They lodged together at the same hostels and often served as justices of assize in concert. In court they tended to argue as colleagues on terms of equality, although there is no question that it was the bench which made the final decisions.[99] But during informal conferences outside Westminster Hall, at which serjeants were sometimes present, their opinions carried the same weight as those of the judges. This approximation of status between bench and senior bar also meant that the bond between client and barrister was less strict than nowadays. Thus it seemed to be quite in order for Roger Manwood to appear twice in *Winter's Case* (1572), first as serjeant and later as judge, notwithstanding any prejudice to his suitor's interests.[100] Some lawyers could be quite callous about this; when Justice Meade argued from the bench in the case of *Welcden v. Elkington* (1577),

[94] E.R. Adair & F.M. Grier Evans, 'Writs of Assistance, 1558–1700', *E.H.R.* xxxvi (1921), 366–7; Hastings, pp. 78–9.

[95] *H.E.L.* v, 340–2; Ives, 'Promotion in the Legal Profession', p. 357.

[96] Ives, 'Legal Profession', pp. 251–2; *H.E.L.* v, 341.

[97] I.T. Petyt MS 511, vol. 13, f. 38; Dyer, 163b.

[98] Bendl. 179.

[99] See Hemmant, i, p. xviii.

[100] Reported at length in B.M. Harg. MS 10, ff. 26–38.

he had changed his opinion since representing the defendant and went against his former client.[101] Richard Harper, on the other hand, continued to argue on behalf of a plaintiff whose counsel he had been even after his appointment as judge of the Common Bench.[102] Such conduct did not necessarily mean a denial of justice to the litigant since in many of these cases his interests were argued by two or more barristers.[103] The fact is that the line between the public and private sectors of the law was sometimes obscure and the reports reveal instances where Crown officers such as King's Serjeants, Attorney and Solicitor-General and even the Chancellor intervened to argue on behalf of private parties.[104] Bendlowes was never exposed to any such conflict of interest, but during twenty years' lodging at Serjeants' Inn, Fleet Street, he exerted considerable influence on his eminent colleagues.[105]

Sir Edward Coke declared that 'a substantial and compendious report of a case' should possess three attributes. First of all, it should help the reader to understand the law; secondly, ease any difficult points raised in the case; and thirdly, bring pleasure and profit to the studious.[106] Having surveyed something of Bendlowes' career and working environment, we may find it easier to appreciate at closer range his law reports and to determine their value to practitioners of the sixteenth and succeeding centuries. William Gregory, a judge of the later Stuart period, referring to a decision in Elizabeth's reign, stated that 'Dyer reports the case not so well as Anderson and Bendlowes'.[107] As a general rule, this is an opinion which most legal historians

[101] Dyer, 358b; cf. Plow. 519 and Bendl. 308.

[102] *Bullock v. Burdett*, Dyer, 281a; cf. *Vernon v. Vernon* (1572), Dyer, 317a, where Harper dissented in a case in which he was executor under the will in dispute.

[103] In *Welcden v. Elkington*, for example, Plowden reports the defendant as being represented by Serjs. Popham and Windham; Plow. 519; in his report of the case, Bendlowes states that he was also counsel; Bendl. 308.

[104] *Shelley's Case*, 1 Co. Rep. 105a; B.M. Harl. MS 1624, f. 55*v*.

[105] See below, Chap. V, pp. 192–3.

[106] 9 Co. Rep. Pref. xiib–xiva.

[107] Quoted by Wallace, pp. 126–7 from 1 Shower, 316.

would dispute on several grounds, not the least being that while Dyer's notes were first printed in 1585, neither Anderson's nor Bendlowes' were published in full until the second half of the seventeenth century.[108] The fact that the last-named was so long in being published in full is all the more difficult to understand in view of the comparatively large number of manuscript copies which survive.[109] The first appearance of any of Bendlowes' work in print goes back to 1609, when thirty-two of his reports, together with some cases attributed to William Dalison, were published as an appendix to Thomas Ashe's *Promptuary*.[110] This curious but useful volume was intended as a kind of concordance of Yearbook decisions which had some bearing on 'le exposition des statutes per equitie', and the entries from Bendlowes (and Dalison) serve as a gloss on later Henrician legislation.[111] The cases are taken at random out of one of the numerous Bendlowes collections then circulating in manuscript, but all are considerably abridged. The only thing they have in common is the reference to a particular act of parliament, generally from the period 1535–40. but in some cases going back to the fifteenth or fourteenth century.[112] Twenty-four years later the second edition of Keilwey's *Reports* came out, containing an appendix with precisely the same selection of cases from Bendlowes and Dalison; obviously these had been copied directly from Ashe, complete with printing errors.

The first serious attempt at putting into print a reasonably faithful version of Bendlowes' work came in 1661.[113] Unlike reports prepared during the Commonwealth, this volume reproduced the original law-French, though in a somewhat garbled condition. Many entries are considerably condensed and most are devoid of the pleadings which had been their chief attraction for students in the time of Elizabeth and James I. Ashe's edition had

108 Anderson was published in 1664, Bendlowes in 1661; Wallace, pp. 118, 142.

109 See list of MSS below, pp. 92–4.

110 *S.T.C.* no. 840; *Black Books of L.I.* ii, 149.

111 Cf. Plow. 465–8.

112 Including the Statute of Acton Burnel (1283), 11 Edw. I.

113 *S.T.C.* no. B. 1871.

given rise to the belief in a (non-existent) connection between Bendlowes and Dalison; in this version of 1661 the anonymous editor worsened the confusion by adding a considerable number of cases from the reigns of James I and Charles I. It was stated in the preface that only the entries from Henry VII to Elizabeth were the work of Bendlowes, but no clue was provided as to the authorship of the later cases.[114] The edition of 1661 is invariably cited in subsequent reports as 'New Benloe' notwithstanding the fact that it was published twenty-eight years before the definitive edition of 1689 which came to be known as 'Old Benloe'. The reason seems to be that 'Old Benloe' was also the name given to those manuscript copies of the reports which had been in circulation since the sixteenth century.[115] There are 166 'authentic' entries traceable to Bendlowes in the volume of 1661, although most of these are not his first-hand reports but short, summary cases which he probably extracted from some other source.[116] Collation with various manuscript versions suggests that the editor's original plan was to print only these abridged cases, and that in the course of his work he decided to add some of Bendlowes' original full-length reports. They were added at the end in a sequence completely at variance with that in 'Old Benloe'.

The last and most thorough publication of Bendlowes' *Reports* appeared more than a century after the author's death, in 1689. It was edited by Serjeant John Rowe. Presumably because of the association in Ashe, a collection of cases purportedly compiled by William Dalison was printed in the same volume but under separate pagination.[117] A majority of the entries which Bendlowes had initially amassed, 273 to be exact, were included in this edition.[118] The volume is distinguished by two features: firstly, the inclusion in many of the reported cases of written pleadings

[114] Pref. ii.

[115] Wallace, pp. 116–18, 135.

[116] The distinction between the various types of entries incorporated by Bendlowes is discussed more fully below, pp. 98–102.

[117] See below, Chap. IV, pp. 104, 113–14.

[118] The original manuscript contains 320 cases, and is discussed in greater detail below, pp. 94–8.

from the rolls, and secondly, a strict adherence to chronology. The latter was a clear departure from previous editions and the majority of manuscripts. Only one surviving manuscript collection is arranged in chronological sequence and this appears to have been prepared some time after 1625.[119] One cannot therefore accept Rowe's assertion that this edition represents 'the most authentic copy of his [Bendlowes'] whole work':[120] it is superior to previous printed versions but definitely inferior to some of the early manuscripts.

Although hardly surprising, it is unfortunate that Bendlowes' reputation as a law reporter should have come to rest on the four printed editions described, particularly that of 1689, for while this edition compares favourably with many such volumes published in the seventeenth century, it is filled with errors. The numbering of the entries is inaccurate; the black-letter type is out of date and abounds in unnecessary abbreviations taken directly from the manuscript model; the spelling of names of parties defies description; while the terms, years and roll numbers frequently bear no resemblance to the originals. Bendlowes' fate was not exceptional. Of the twenty-one sets of reports which contain entries from the sixteenth century, eighteen were not printed until after 1600.[121] Only two authors of that period lived to see their work published, Plowden and Coke. For the rest, except in the case of Dyer, the gap between compiling and printing was never less than fifty and could be as much as a hundred years. Even in their decline under Henry VII and VIII the Yearbooks received prompter and kinder treatment at the hands of the printers.

There was a veritable outburst of printing activity during the forty-year period from the Interregnum to the Revolution of 1688. More than fifty volumes of 'reports' were brought out,

[119] B.M. Add MS. 21068; see list of MSS below, p. 93.

[120] Pref. i; *H.E.L.* v, 368.

[121] *H.E.L.* v, 358–63; Veeder, 'The English Reports, 1292–1865', *H.L.R.* xv (1901), 3–4.

twenty-three during the 1650s alone.[122] Sir Harbottle Grimston, the editor of Croke's Reports, warned law students in 1657 about the increasing number of 'blind and misshapen reports' being put about 'through the sordid ignorance' of certain printers;[123] some were considered so suspect that the judges would refuse to accept them as authority in court.[124] The increase in unverifiable, contradictory precedents prompted Edward Bulstrode, a reporter himself, to observe that such volumes 'do rather cherish than extinguish law suites'.[125] The desire to achieve profitable circulation within the profession led some publishers to make inflated claims about their products without any real knowledge of the reporters concerned. Apart from a tendency to attribute authorship where this could not have been possible, some reports contain bogus endorsements purportedly by the author in question: such was the case in early editions of Godbolt, Popham and Owen.[126] Conversely, the work of reputable practitioners was sometimes printed without their knowledge or permission, and hence in a 'raw' state.[127] These tactics were easier to employ during the Commonwealth, after the disappearance of the Star Chamber which the Tudors had used to maintain a strict control over the licensing of printed books. Theft and pirating of manuscripts were even more blatant in Chief Justice Rolle's day than in Chief Justice Dyer's.[128]

One of the greatest sources of error by seventeenth-century printers was language. During the Commonwealth reports prepared for publication were often hastily translated from the original Latin or French by editors unfamiliar with either tongue or with the legal idiom. The authors' phraseology, abbreviations and particular style were all too often lost in the changeover.[129]

[122] Veeder, p. 3; Wallace, p. 16; *H.E.L.* v, 365–6.

[123] Croke Car. Pref. iv; Wallace, p. 15.

[124] Winfield, p. 184.

[125] 1 Bulstrode, 'Epistle Dedicatory', vi.

[126] Wallace, pp. 13–18; *H.E.L.* v, 367.

[127] See Plow. Pref. v; *H.E.L.* v, 365–6.

[128] *H.E.L.* v, 366; see also G.D.G.Hall, 'Bate's Case and "Lane's" Reports', *Bull. John Rylands Lib.* xxxv (1952–3), 405–27.

[129] Wallace, pp. 20–21; *H.E.L.* v, 368.

When law-French was reintroduced at the Restoration the situation became even more confused. As happened with Bendlowes, texts were blindly copied with little notion of grammar or orthography.[130] Thus other sixteenth-century collections such as those of Anderson, Moore and Savile, like the black-letter edition of the Yearbooks, lost much of their value through slovenly printing.

Until the Civil War law-French remained the medium of expression in almost all common law reports. This was a remarkable phenomenon which long outran the use of French as a spoken language. It was one factor in the success of England's indigenous legal system in resisting such encroachment as there was by the civil law of Europe. The irony of a foreign language assisting the survival of a native institution has not been lost on legal historians.[131] Like its distinctive costume and educational system, law-French was an integral part of the profession's exclusiveness.[132] 'Much part of the law', said Christopher St German in 1530, 'is in such speech that few men have knowledge of it', with the result that the gulf between secular and spiritual judges was unbridgeable.[133] It is not surprising that this language became supreme in the courts just at a time when it was ceasing to be spoken by the upper classes.[134] The resulting dichotomy is seen in an act of parliament of 1362 which ordered that henceforth pleading in the courts should be in English, while the statute itself was written in French;[135] the impact of the measure can be gauged from the comments of one chronicler who noted that it 'stode but a shorte whyle'.[136] But it is not simply professional obscurantism which accounts for the long survival of 'Anglo-Norman'. While having sunk to the level of jargon by the late fifteenth century, that language sustained its value as a precise, technical mode of expression. Fortescue conceded that it was

[130] See for example And. 345.

[131] Maitland, *Year Books 1 & 2 Edw. II*, pp. xxi–xxx, xxxiv–xxxvi.

[132] Cf. 3 Co. Rep. Pref. xxi–xxiii.

[133] *Doctor and Student*, Bk. ii (1721), Chap. 25, p. 221.

[134] Pike, *Year Books 20 Edw. III*, ii, lviii–lxviii; Chrimes, p. 194.

[135] Stat. 36 Edw. III, st. 1, chap. 15; *H.E.L.* ii, 477–9.

[136] *Fabyan's Chronicles* (1811), p. 476.

'commonly corrupted by a certain rudeness', yet pleaders found that they could express certain ideas more accurately in French than in English.[137]

Anglicization progressed rapidly during the sixteenth century; new words indicative of a greater variety in food, sport, domestic animals and objects of luxury came into vogue. The need for an increased vocabulary on the part of reporters was soon filled by barely-concealed English nouns, often with ludicrous results. Publicists and reformers exploited this linguistic anomaly when attacking the profession as a whole. Thomas Elyot condemned law-French as 'voyde of all eloquence' and suggested that the entire common law be put into Latin—a proposal which found favour among many disciples of the New Learning, including Thomas Starkey and Richard Morison.[138] Henry VIII took up the theme and commissioned three lawyers, Nicholas Bacon, Thomas Denton and Robert Cary, to prepare a report on the establishment of a students' hostel where training in 'the pure French and Latin tongues' would accompany the study of law.[139] Apologists for the profession were finding it difficult, but by no means impossible, to defend this 'hotchpot French stufft up with such variety of borrowed words'.[140] William Fulbecke reiterated that 'the words of the law, though they be rude in sound yet they are pregnant in sense',[141] and Coke, while readily admitting that by Littleton's time French was only meant to be read or written, insisted that many terms in law could not be expressed with necessary precision other than in French.[142]

The evidence indicates that by the sixteenth century law-French was no longer spoken, although formal 'pleadings' were

[137] *De Laudibus*, p. 115; *H.E.L.* ii, 480–1.

[138] Thomas Starkey, *A Dialogue between Cardinal Pole and Thomas Lupset*, E.E.T.S. Extra Series, xii, p. 193; Morison's proposals are found in B.M. Cotton MS Faustina C. 11, f. 5, and Royal MS A. 1.

[139] *Fortescutus Illustratus*, pp. 539–42.

[140] A. Fraunce, *The Lawiers Logic* (1588), Dedication, v.

[141] *A Parallele or Conference of the Civil Law . . . and the Common Law* (1601–2), p. 21.

[142] Co. Litt. Pref. xxxix, 9a.

still read by counsel in certain forms of real actions.[143] For the most part, however, English was employed when barristers argued in court.[144] On the other hand, the system of reporting cases remained the same as when Fortescue had described it:

> what is pleaded, disputed and decided in the royal courts is reported and put into book form, for future reference, always in the French speech. . . .[145]

This may help to explain why most law reports are disjointed and highly condensed; they were never verbatim transcripts but translated summaries, and hence the analogy with shorthand would not seem out of place. The ability to convert spoken English into accurate and coherent if not grammatical, law-French must have been a prerequisite for every reporter. Right to the end of the century, and beyond, case notes were taken in this manner.[146] No doubt the continued use of French in mooting at the Inns of Court helped to prolong its survival till the Restoration.

The Tudor barrister had actually to be familiar with three languages, French, English and Latin. While the last was primarily the medium of the clerks and their rolls, it also found its way into many reports in the form of maxims, extracts from the record or legal instruments, and phrases which the writer wished to emphasize.[147] Many legal issues were fought over 'faux latyn', usually in connection with badly drafted writs and indictments.[148] At least until the end of Henry VII's reign, if a conveyance was not put into Latin the warranty might not apply.[149] The Yearbooks contain instances where the use of Latin with its precise

[143] *Fortescutus Illustratus*, p. 545; *Lives of the Norths*, i, 30.

[144] Maitland, *Year Books, 1 & 2 Edw. II*, p. xxxv; but cf. Keilwey, 184, 185–6.

[145] *De Laudibus*, p. 115.

[146] As late as 1658 Francis North was taking notes in law-French: *Lives of the Norths*, i, 29; see also T.F.T. Plucknett, 'Ellesmere on Statutes', L.Q.R., lx (1944), p. 243.

[147] Dyer used Latin in his MS notes extensively; see below, p. 166.

[148] For example, Lib. of Congress Gell MS f. 69; B.M. Harg. MS 388, ff. 39, 74*v*; 4 Leon. 107; 5 Co. Rep. 121a.

[149] YB M. 10 Hen. VII, pl. 20, argument of Serj. Keble.

inflexions might have prevented disputes over the interpretation of words.[150] Of course, with Bendlowes the record forms a major part of his reports and there is as much Latin to be seen as French. A language with a fully documented and properly taught grammar, Latin did not deteriorate in the same way as law-French. It was to remain the medium of expression in the plea rolls until 1731.[151]

As the productions of separate individuals tailored to personal requirements, private reports exhibit wide variation in content and style. In many of the entries which he took at first hand, Bendlowes simply appended a brief commentary to a copy of the official record. Plowden and Coke also included the written pleadings in many of their reports but presented a full summary of the arguments of counsel and judges. Dyer and Dalison, and the majority of reporters in the latter part of the century, are usually content with noting essential issues or specific problems, with or without the final decision; save for the more important disputes entries are generally short and to the point. In Croke and Moore there is only the barest outline of the oral argument but fairly extensive coverage of rulings from the bench, while Anderson gives a full résumé of both the facts and the legal issues. Popham reported at length the arguments of bench and bar, but the actual number of cases is comparatively small. A few reporters tended to confine their observations to specific topics; for example, the first volume of Brownlow and Gouldesborough is mainly composed of practice cases, while Coke in his middle volumes includes blocks of entries on such subjects as 'appeals and indictments', 'actions for slander' and 'copyhold cases'.[152] On a broader scale, however, Coke made his *Reports* a vehicle for critical analysis of the law in dispute rather than a straightforward narrative. Without rules to guide them or the prospect of public access, early reporters did not confine their notes to strictly relevant material: such matters as the prevalence of plague, elevations to the bench, deaths of colleagues and the extraneous

[150] Ibid. pl. 16, Serj. Keble again. [151] Chrimes, p. 194; *H.E.L.* ii, 479.
[152] Wallace, p. 159; 4 Co. Rep. 39b–48a.

comments of bar and bench dot the pages of many printed collections. Only the most permissive of guide-lines could apply in these circumstances:

that is to reduce the sum and effect of all to such a method, as upon consideration had all the arguments the reporter himself thinketh to be fittest and clearest for the right understanding of the true reasons and causes of the judgement and resolution of the case in question.[153]

The reports reflect the changing attitudes of the profession and of the society it served. At the beginning of the century the imprint of the Yearbooks with their two hundred years of tradition was clear, but by the end an entirely new pattern of reporting was emerging.[154]

Holdsworth has pointed out certain parallels between the origin of the Yearbooks in the early fourteenth century and of private reports in the early sixteenth. There was no intention at the outset that such notes should benefit anyone but their author, yet eventually, through the medium of scriveners or printers, dissemination in both cases became more or less organized.[155] In one important respect, however, the two series differ in their inception. The authors of the Yearbooks remain unknown; at best we can say that they must have been fairly advanced students or members of the bar. The essence of private reports is that their authors were almost always prominent members of the legal profession, frequently judges.[156] They doubtless began by making notes in their commonplace books of cases they pleaded in court, witnessed or picked up from colleagues. They usually followed such notes with a memorandum of the parties and the term in which the suit was argued—especially late in the century when case citations became more precise.[157] These rough notes might eventually be fleshed out with excerpts from the record, additional comments by other advocates, the writer's personal interjections, or references to relevant statutes and previous court decisions.[158]

153 *Calvin's Case* (1608), 7 Co. Rep. 4a.

154 W. S. Holdsworth, *Sources and Literature of English Law* (1925), pp. 91–3.

155 *H.E.L.* v, 365; see below, Chap. IV, pp. 108–11.

156 See Appendix II, pp. 306–13.

157 Lewis, xlviii (1932), 230–4.

158 Veeder, p. 5.

Notebooks kept by judges were, generally speaking, superior to those of ordinary barristers; their compilers were better able to assess and summarize the essential elements of a trial and to give balance to opposing arguments of counsel.

Bendlowes was one of three serjeants-at-law in the sixteenth century whose reports survive in print.[159] His work, however, can be best appreciated by reference to the manuscript versions which barristers of Elizabeth's and James I's time would have read and copied. There are over twenty manuscripts clearly attributable to Bendlowes, of which seven are more or less complete. Approximately half were prepared in the early seventeenth century, but at least five of the full volumes were in use during the last fifteen years of Elizabeth's reign. One of these may well have been owned by Sir Edward Coke, who frequently cites cases out of Bendlowes in his *Reports* and *Institutes*.[160] All seven complete collections were prepared with considerable care and accuracy. This is all the more remarkable in view of the labour involved and the mixture of languages. Most, if not all, of these copies were transcribed by professional scriveners and they must surely represent only a fraction of those which circulated within the profession at that time.

SUMMARY LIST OF MANUSCRIPTS CONTAINING THE REPORTS OF WILLIAM BENDLOWES

A. *Complete collections*

1. *Bodl. Rawl. MS C.728:* 282 fols., late sixteenth century; flyleaf inscription designates the owner as William Bendlowes, Jr., but was probably compiled by the elder Bendlowes between 1573 and 1584; contains 321 entries.

2. *B.M. Add. MS 25189:* 159 fols., late sixteenth century; may have belonged to Edward Coke.

[159] The other two were John Carrell and Francis Moore; for details of reports by serjeants which were not printed see Appendix II, pp. 306–10.

[160] *Catalogue of the Library of Sir Edward Coke*, p. 26; see, for example, 1 Co. Rep. 15a, 24b, 96a; Co. Litt. 273b, 283a; 2 Inst. 228a, 281a; 4 Inst. 214a, 272a.

3. *Lib. of Congress MS 26:* 291 fols., late sixteenth century.

4. *B.M. Harl. MS 5142:* 186 fols., late sixteenth century.

5. *H.L.S. MS 16:* 488 fols., late sixteenth century; owned by John Savile, Baron of the Exchequer, 1598–1607. Ff. 5–224 comprise a full set of Bendlowes' Reports.

6. *B.M. Harl. MS 355:* 163 fols., late sixteenth or early seventeenth century.

7. *B.M. Add. MS 25001:* 250 fols., late sixteenth or early seventeenth century.

B. *Incomplete collections*

1. *L.I. Misc. MS 791:* 199 fols., early seventeenth century; includes only about half of the original entries; owned by Richard Levinge of Inner Temple (circa 1658), a Recorder of Chester.

2. *B.M. Add. MS 21068:* 333 fols., seventeenth century; follows same order as 1688 edition but contains only 215 out of the full 302 entries.

3. *B.M. Harg. MS 3:* 158 fols., early seventeenth century; contains 78 full-length cases, but none beyond 1568.

4. *B.M. Add. MS 25200:* 223 fols., seventeenth century; 26 entries between ff. 202–21*v* from 3 Hen. VIII to 4 Eliz.

5. *B.M. Harl. 5143:* 238 fols., late sixteenth to early seventeenth centuries; includes reports 5–12, 14–21 Eliz., 'ex reportes Bendlos'.

C. *Extracts and abridgments*

1. *B.M. Add. MS 25190:* 31 fols., late sixteenth century; contains 283 entries abridged from B.M. Add. MS 25189.

2. *C.U.L. MS Gg. 2. 5:* 553 fols., early seventeenth century; ff. 1–23*v* contain 233 numbered entries, T. 31 Hen. VIII—E. 20 Eliz.

3. *B.M. Harg. MS 33:* 11 fols., early seventeenth century; 126 abridged entries.

4. *Trinity College Dublin MS 704:* 21 fols., seventeenth century; selected cases between 1534 and 1562.

5. *B.M. Add. MS 36080:* 12 fols., late sixteenth century; 67 abridged entries arranged in rough chronological order.

6. *C.U.L. MS Dd. 13.24:* 98 fols., late sixteenth century; 60 entries consisting of Bendlowes' 'summary' cases.

7. *C.U.L. MS Ee. 6.12:* 85 fols., seventeenth century; ff. 1–16 contain extracts from Bendlowes, 1512–77.

8. *C.U.L. MS Dd. 10.37:* 170 fols., seventeenth century; ff. 154–63 consist of 67 entries, 10 Hen. VIII—17 Eliz.

9. *B.M. Lansd. MS 1072:* 228 fols., seventeenth century; a few entries from Bendlowes temp. Eliz. (ff. 56–65*v*).

10. *Longleat MS 240:* 190 fols., late sixteenth to early seventeenth century; ff. 187–9 consist of entries from Bendlowes copied by Edward Fenner, a justice of the King's Bench, 1590–1612.

11. *Bodl. Rawl. MS C.647:* 256 fols., seventeenth century; ff 163–5*v* include cases from 5 & 6 Eliz. Collected by Richard Powle of Lincoln's Inn temp. Eliz. and Jas. I.

12. *L.I. Misc. MS 361:* 200 fols., early seventeenth century; f. 12 contains 'certaine cases abridge hors del reportes de Benlose'.

For purposes of analysis and comparison the best, and indeed unique, source is what appears to be the reporter's own copy. This is a folio volume, containing 621 leaves, preserved in the Bodleian Library.[161] It consists of two distinct sections: folios 1 to 292 contain the reports of William Bendlowes, Sr., and folios 292*v* to 621 comprise a miscellaneous collection of cases, charters and commentaries mainly relating to family estates and compiled by William Bendlowes, Jr., the serjeant's son.[162] The subject of the present study, the first section, is prepared in the neat hand of copyists and is an entirely professional and businesslike piece of work. While the author does not reveal his identity, his son leaves little doubt in the matter: on the fly-leaf he has described the volume as 'An excellent learned booke made & compyled by Mr. Serjiant Bendlowes . . .'

One question immediately comes to mind: was this collection typical of the period in being essentially 'personal' and not intended for publication? At first glance this appears to be the case. As in most contemporary compilations of this kind, a fair amount of extraneous matter is found among the cases proper. At

[161] Rawlinson MS C. 728; this volume was brought to the attention of the writer by A.W.B. Simpson.

[162] Ff. 342–453 are blank.

folio 205, for instance, is an essay on the fall from grace of Somerset, Cromwell and Wolsey. At another point Bendlowes added a paragraph in Latin taken from an 'old book of the Exchequer', which sets out a system for dividing the calendar year into four equal quarters.[163] There is also a detailed description of the call of serjeants in 1577 which Rowe purposely omitted from his edition 'because the same is extant in Sir W. Dugdale'.[164] And at folios 282 to 289 is a list of judges who sat in the King's Bench and Common Pleas from the reign of Henry IV to that of Elizabeth. In addition to all this there is an assortment of charters, fines, sheriffs' returns and letters patent. The cases themselves seem to lack any definite sequence. Although they commence in the reign of Henry VIII[165] and follow a rough course through the next thirty-eight years, there is an abrupt departure upon reaching 16 Elizabeth (1573–4). At this point there is a series of 140 entries, each averaging only a few lines and taken at random from the years between 1512 and 1579.[166] Then the original sequence is resumed with full-length cases for the years 1574 to 1579.

The reports as found in this volume were evidently copied from a prepared text rather than being compiled from rough notes. The writing throughout is neat and the arrangement of entries consistent, being probably the product of two scribes. It is unlikely that either hand is Bendlowes'; lawyers were notorious for their illegible handwriting, and at the age of sixty-five or more his would not have been so steady. Certain additional entries and annotations of distinctly uneven appearance inserted at various points may have been written by the author.[167] Presumably, Bendlowes, having made preliminary notes in court and obtained relevant extracts from the plea rolls, prepared a draft from which the scriveners worked. For the first 233 folios one copyist was in charge; from folios 233*v* to 280 a different, but

[163] F. 233*v*; Dyer reports (345a) a case in which Bendlowes produced an abstract of this book.

[164] Ff. 265–9: Preface to Rowe's edition, ii; Dugdale, *Origines Juridicales*, pp. 119–27.

[165] There are a few precedents from Edw. III, Hen. VI and Hen. VII.

[166] Ff. 180–203*v*.

[167] For instance, ff. 215*v*–16, 269.

equally neat, hand takes over; and for the final twelve leaves the first scribe resumes. In all this there is one feature which stands out: the writing is varied according to the language, being slanted one way for the Latin pleadings and another for the French commentary and occasional English notes. This device was equivalent to the use of italic in printing, and indeed the printed reports follow its pattern. It appears that this 'fair copy' was made within a relatively short space of time and presumably for a particular purpose. Both in form and content it represents more than the day-to-day jottings of a busy lawyer.

As has already been noted, Bendlowes' reports terminate at 21 Elizabeth (1579). This may have been his last year of active practice, an inference borne out by the fact that he is not mentioned as a pleader in contemporary reports beyond this time.[168] Yet he did not die until 1584 and was fit enough in 1582 to 'put a short case' at Chief Justice Anderson's investiture. In effect, there was a period of four or five years in which he might have applied himself to the task of putting together the fruit of half-a-century's legal experience. There is, indeed, good reason to believe that Bendlowes began compiling his collection in 1573 or 1574. Inscribed on the title page, in addition to the remarks added by the Serjeant's son, is an informative statement which probably originated with Bendlowes himself. Among salient facts, he states that the book was composed in his fifty-seventh year which in turn is designated 16 Elizabeth. This being so it appears that the process was carried on for a period of between six and eleven years.[169]

It is possible that Bendlowes wished to take advantage of a rising demand for new cases. The situation had changed considerably in the years since he had first entered Lincoln's Inn. The second half of the sixteenth century witnessed an enormous increase in the printing of law books.[170] This was due in large

[168] Dyer, 361a; B.M. Harg. MS 8, f. 234; the last reference to Bendlowes occurs in M. 21 & 22 Eliz. in B.M. Lansd. MS 1084, f. 55*v*.

[169] He also notes that he had been a serjeant for nineteen years, which indicates that he began preparing this volume in 1574 rather than 1573.

[170] Putnam, p. 110; *H.E.L.* ii, 528–30; Beale, pp. 105–10.

measure to the enterprise of Richard Tottel, who began publishing in 1553 and dominated the trade for thirty-eight years.[171] In his last years at the bar Bendlowes must have been impressed by the fact that his colleague and fellow-Catholic Edmund Plowden had had his work put into print and that Robert Brooke's *Graunde Abridgement* came out posthumously in 1573.[172] He must also have been aware of the large number of cases collected by Chief Justice Dyer during the many years of their professional association at Westminster and on circuit. Whether Bendlowes had any intention of getting his cases published cannot be determined, but in view of the renewed interest in up-to-date material he at least ensured that an authoritative version was available for the use of the profession.

Whatever his motive, Bendlowes, like Dyer, never saw his collection in print. After his death, however, his son seems to have had this prospect in mind. In an inscription on the flyleaf of the Rawlinson manuscript, dated 1600, William Bendlowes the younger proclaimed the reports 'most worthye to be imprintedd for the utilitye & benefite of younge studentes of the lawes of this realme'. He sought the backing of the Chief Justices of both benches for his scheme.[173] While apparently unsuccessful in its immediate object, the attempt may have influenced Ashe's decision to include some of the entries in his *Promptuary*. It is also significant that Chief Justice Anderson extracted and abridged at least 130 of Bendlowes' cases for that section of his own reports covering the years 1535 to 1579,[174] and that a number of other lawyers borrowed quite freely from the collection either for their own benefit or for incorporation into another set of reports: several entries in the work of Moore and Leonard are attributable to Bendlowes.[175] This was the risk any industrious reporter had to

[171] Soule, 'Year Book Bibliography', p. 564; Bennett, ii, 156–66.

[172] J.D. Cowley, *A Bibliography of Abridgments* (1932), p. 26; Plowden was first printed in 1571; see below, Chap. VI, pp. 206–7.

[173] Inscription on flyleaf of Bodl. Rawl. C.728.

[174] 1 And. 1–57.

[175] Moore, 1–257; the Bendlowes entries are sprinkled at random through Moore's first 257 cases; 3 Leon. 1–14.

run, especially if he had shown himself a successful barrister. Despite their belated publication these reports must have been highly regarded in view of both the number of copies prepared and their close resemblance to the original volume.

There are two categories of cases to be found in Bendlowes' *Reports*: first, and most important, those which the author claims to have taken at first hand, and secondly, those—the greater number—for which no source is indicated. The ratio between the two is roughly two to three: to be exact, there are 125 entries in which Bendlowes either acted as counsel or was present at the trial. (This can be stated with reasonable certainty because he made a point of noting specifically those cases in which he was personally involved.) Taken as a whole, the reports of his 'own' cases represent a fair cross-section of the kind of practice enjoyed by this successful and long-lived serjeant-at-law. The earliest actions were set down during his student days. The very first, the leading case of *Bold v. Molineux* (1536), he concludes with the remark that he 'oyez et fuit present al dit argument et judgment'.[176] It appears that all the entries up to and including 3 Edward VI (1549) were the work of a student and rising barrister still learning his craft: until he became a serjeant Bendlowes entered the Common Pleas 'to listen and be present'. It was after promotion in 1555 that he began collecting the bulk of his reported cases. Almost without exception the hallmark of his involvement is the phrase, 'le author de cest liver fuit del counsel ove le dit plaintiff [or defendant]'. This idiosyncrasy was probably motivated more by a desire to establish 'copyright' than by mere egotism. While there is no reason to doubt the accuracy of Bendlowes' claim to participation, it is only fair to add that some of those disputes in which he claims to have pleaded are reported elsewhere, and sometimes without mention of his name.[177] This may be ascribed in part to the selectivity of the other reporters

[176] E. 26–27 Henry VIII, Bendl. 13 (Bodl. Rawl. C.728, f. 13).

[177] For example, *Welcden v. Elkington* (Bendl., 296; Dyer, 358b; Plow., 516), *Vernon v. Stanley* (Bendl. 198; Dyer, 315b; Dal., 107), *Cranmer's Case* (Bendl. 207; Dyer, 309a; B.M. Harg. MS 15, f. 27; Harg. 10, f. 38).

1. William Bendlowes, portrait by an unknown artist (1564). (By permission of St John's College, Cambridge.)

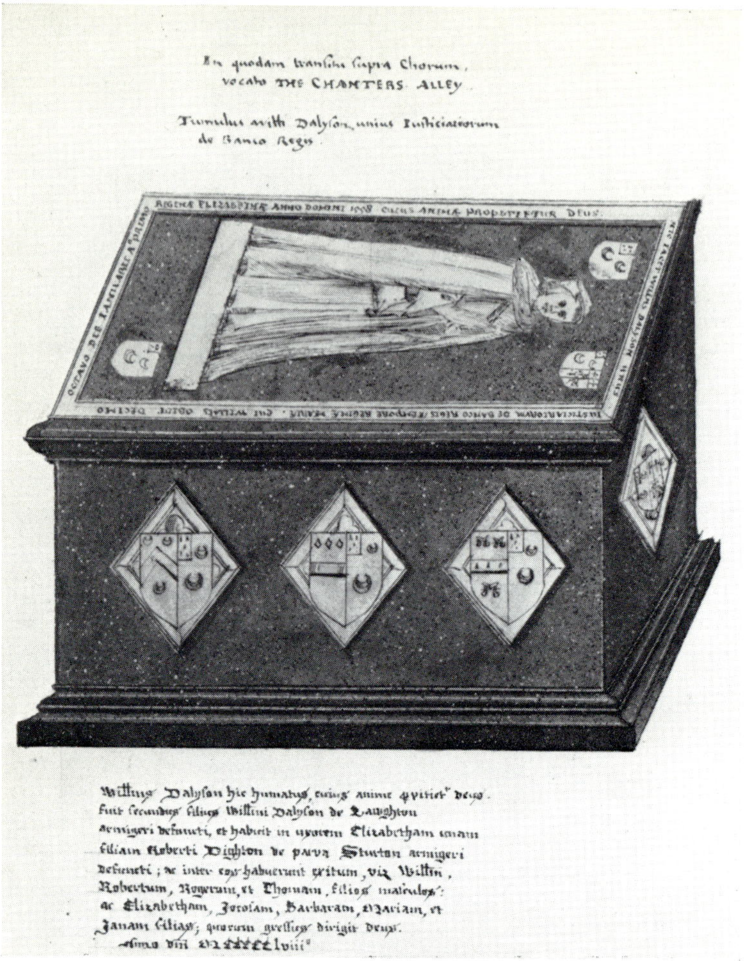

2. Sir William Dalison, drawn from the Dalison monument in Lincoln Cathedral by Sir William Dugdale and found in his volume 'Collection of Monuments in Various Countries'. (B.M. Loan MS 38, f. 102; by permission of the Trustees of the Winchelsea Settled Estates and by courtesy of the Trustees of the British Museum.)

concerned and in part to the casual use of the term 'counsel' which could apply to any advocate who happened to argue on behalf of a particular litigant.[178]

Notwithstanding the wide range of style and method exhibited in sixteenth-century reports, Bendlowes' compilation stands in a class apart. While Plowden and Coke also added written pleadings to their entries, they did so as part of a larger scheme, the presentation of a complete, if subjective, version of proceedings in court. Bendlowes' approach was less ambitious; in the words of Serjeant Rowe, 'the general way of his reporting was . . . to note upon the very record a short state of the point in question and the judgment given thereon'.[179] It should be added that many of his entries do include more extensive remarks by the author but approximately two-thirds accord with Rowe's description. It may be that if Bendlowes arranged his notes some years after the cases had been pleaded he was only able to supply the barest outline of proceedings and hence tended to rely heavily on the plea rolls. He must have taken to heart certain remarks made by Plowden on the deficiencies in orthodox Books of Entries: these merely reproduced precedents of pleading without any indication as to their effectiveness in court.[180] Just as the profession sought recent decisions, it likewise needed reliable pleadings which had been adequately tested under judicial scrutiny.[181] Plowden's reports, although exhaustive, are comparatively few in number; but with Bendlowes', pleaders were able not only to select from a much wider range of legal disputes covering a multitude of actual situations, but also to enjoy the advantage of having the names of the parties together with the correct terms and years of the reigns concerned. In addition, useful precedents were provided and a clear indication given of when these were most likely to succeed.

Forty-five of Bendlowes' first-hand reports do not contain pleadings from the official record; these are presumably cases of which he made full notes of his own. Yet even here the style is

178 See above, pp. 81–2. 179 Bendl. Pref. ii.

180 Plow. Pref. iv; cf. Rowe's comments, Bendl. Pref. ii.

181 Holdsworth, *Sources and Literature*, pp. 117–19.

much the same, with most of the reporter's attention concentrated on setting out the facts and legal issues—much as they would have been in the record. There is no attempt to reproduce arguments of either counsel or judges, although Bendlowes frequently concludes with a summary of 'lopinion des justices del Common Bank'. Even in cases where Bendlowes' arguments were given prominence by other reporters, he himself ignores them entirely. The only other feature of note in these particular reports is an emphasis on problems of interpretation. There are numerous extracts from wills, fines, patents and other legal instruments, although none, surprisingly enough, from statutes.[182] In effect, it is clear that in practically all his own work Bendlowes stands apart from his fellow-reporters.

While it is the 125 first-hand reports which represent the reporter's principal contribution to sixteenth-century legal literature, they form only part of the entire scheme. Reference has been made to a series of abridged decisions placed rather incongruously within the body of fuller reports. It is these which may give any reader the impression that no real formula was followed by Bendlowes when he compiled the volume. Not only is there no apparent reason for inserting them where they are, but the cases themselves do not seem to follow any pattern. Evidently some seventeenth-century copyists saw no significance either and reset them in chronological order. Yet when they are examined more closely in the original manuscript and with the marginal titles, a pattern of sorts emerges. Most of the cases are grouped under specific subjects which follow a roughly alphabetical order. Such titles as 'administrators', 'challenge', 'estrepment', 'surrender', and 'verdytt' are typical, but numerous others—about fifty—are found sprinkled throughout the series, which is, in fact, similar to the kind of commonplace book which every practising lawyer was expected to keep.[183] It can only be inferred

[182] For example, Bendl. 13, 25, 43, 75, 264, 390 (Bodl. MS Rawl. C.728, ff. 203*v*–9*v*).

[183] For example, Fleetwood's commonplace book, B.M. Harl. MSS 5153–4, and Coke's, C.U.L. MS Hh. 4, 4, 5.

that these short entries came from such a collection in Bendlowes' possession and that he merely added them to his larger scheme. His original intention was probably to provide an appendix to the full-length entries which cease at 16 Elizabeth—the year in which Bendlowes began putting his cases into book form. Presumably, he then proceeded to add further reports as he noted them up to 21 Elizabeth. Unlike most manuscript compilations of this sort, his was not arranged under folio headings so as to permit the addition of further notes which might come to the author's attention;[184] instead, it looks as if Bendlowes gathered together a number of random decisions noted over the years and sorted them into topics. Could he have been hoping to provide the best of both worlds, not only a set of reports but a minor abridgment as well? If so, the result is disappointing. Some of the titles are vague and misleading, while other entries have none at all. Whatever merits the scheme possessed were lost on subsequent editors who, as noted, changed the order when they came to print the *Reports*.

It is difficult to detect the source of these summary notes. The majority are taken from cases decided during Bendlowes' early career. When these entries are arranged in chronological order it can be seen that they run in a fairly regular sequence between 1532 and 1574.[185] One cluster of thirty cases occurs between 1533 and 1537, a feature which raises the possibility of a relationship with the last of the Yearbooks. Although none of Bendlowes' work can be linked with the printed Yearbooks, he does record one suit in 1536 which began in 'the book at large' in 1534.[186] On the basis of what has already been said on this subject, Bendlowes could well have been a potential Yearbook reporter; conversely, he might have copied cases from such a colleague at Lincoln's

[184] For example, B.M. Add. MS 35939; Royal MS 17 E. VII; Essex County R.O. D/DP/L35.

[185] The earliest of these summary cases dates from 1514.

[186] *Levet v. Lewkener*, H. 28 Hen. VIII, Bendl. 18; cf. *Shelley's Case*, 1 Co. Rep. 96a; '28 H. 8 reported by Serjeant Bendloes which case began 26 H. 8 in the Book at Large . . .'; Yelverton, *Reports*, 33, cites the case from Fitzherbert as 26 Hen. VIII pl. 7. See Appendix III, p. 314.

Inn. It is even possible that he selected entries from the plea rolls and presented them in condensed form. In any event, like those in the rest of the reports, most originated in the Common Pleas. In one or two instances he has duplicated his work, the same case being reproduced both at length and in a shortened form.[187]

Taken together, the first-hand and summary cases number 264. There still remain forty-six entries (plus a number of miscellaneous items such as fines, patents and charters). These also have no acknowledged author but occur intermittently throughout the manuscript. Some are nothing more than pleadings taken from much earlier decisions; one, for instance, goes back to Edward III.[188] Another case dates back to 18 Henry IV and ends with the following, somewhat questionable, comment:

> le author de ce lyver conust bien que les dits services sont faits a ce jour.[189]

A similar statement occurs in a report from early Henry VIII.[190] In these and other entries Bendlowes seems to have had a special interest either in the parties or the procedure. One or two of the disputes relate to his home county of Essex,[191] others to contemporary trials of note which also attracted the attention of his fellow-reporters.[192]

While, taken as whole, his reports were quite distinct from those of his colleagues, it is not surprising to find a fair amount of duplication. This is most evident in relation to the cases of Dyer, whose career ran parallel with Bendlowes', though on a higher plane. There are over a hundred examples where they report the same suit, yet in the vast majority there is no evidence of copying or even collaboration. The same is true of the smaller number of

[187] See *Bilota v. Poyntel*, T. 4 & 5 P. & M., Bendl. 58, 64; *Vernon v. Stanley*, M. 13 & 14 Eliz., Bendl. 198, 204.

[188] Bendl. 1 (Bodl. Rawl. C.728, f. 258*v*).

[189] Ibid. 3 (Bodl. Rawl. C.728, f. 17). The suit concerned parties in Essex and presumably Bendlowes had access to additional evidence on the matter.

[190] Ibid. 9 (Bodl. Rawl. C.728, f. 18).

[191] Ibid. 3, 89.

[192] For instance, *Vernon v. Vernon*, T. 14 Eliz., Bendl. 210; *Eyston v. Studd*, E. 16 Eliz., Bendl. 238. See Appendix III, pp. 324, 326.

reports duplicated in Plowden, Dalison and a wide assortment of unprinted collections.[193]

For the period between the end of the Yearbooks and Bendlowes' death in 1584 there are comparatively few recognized law-reporters and even fewer whose work went into print.[194] This makes their collections all the more valuable for those wishing to study the law and the legal profession in the post-Yearbook era. In view of the considerable individuality exhibited by these private reports it can be of value to have more than one version of an important or influential decision. Sometimes there are three, four and even five distinct accounts of the same case.[195] This element of independence could be just as vital to the propagation of current case-law as the sort of cooperation exemplified in the reports of Carrell and Spelman. Whatever their purpose or the style they employed, Bendlowes and his contemporaries succeeded in preserving for their successors and posterity a valuable corpus of doctrine and dicta reflecting one of the most eventful half-centuries in the history of English law.

193 For details see Appendix III, pp. 314–27.

194 *H.E.L.* v, 358–63.

195 Wallace, pp. 41–2.

CHAPTER IV

William Dalison and Richard Harper

MUCH of the history of the printing of Bendlowes' *Reports*, as discussed in the previous chapter, was coupled with the collection attributed to William Dalison. Entries under the names of both authors appeared as an appendix first to Thomas Ashe's *Promptuary* (1609) and a quarter-of-a-century later to the second edition of Keilwey (1633).[1] Finally, the definitive edition of 1689, generally designated as 'Benloe and Dalison', was produced by John Rowe.[2] This, however, is where the connection ceases. The original association probably arose from the composition of the manuscripts in Ashe's possession and from then on it was propelled by its own momentum. In content, style and method of reporting, as well as the careers of the reporters themselves, the two sections, as found in the Rowe edition, have almost nothing in common. Furthermore, if Bendlowes' collection raises problems with regard to the printing trade, Dalison's poses equally taxing questions on the circulation of legal manuscripts and their attribution. In this chapter an attempt will be made to reconstruct the collection credited to William Dalison and to review the wider topic of the significance of manuscript reports in the post-Yearbook period.

If the production of and reliance on printed law books expanded during the sixteenth century, particularly under Elizabeth, what can be said of manuscript material during the same span? Attention has already been drawn to the fact that in its early years printing made relatively little impact and that the number and accessibility of legal manuscripts remained of far greater significance.[3] Even the increased output of books in the second half of

[1] *S.T.C.* nos. 840, 14902. [2] Ibid. no. B.1870.

[3] This has recently been corroborated by Dr E.W. Ives; see 'A Lawyer's Library in 1500', *L.Q.R.* lxxxv (1969), 106, 108; Putnam, p. 175.

the century was not all that it may appear to be. Legal printers, like the profession for which they catered, were conservative and wary of innovation. By far the greatest proportion of their output consisted of reprints of well-established works such as the Yearbooks, Statutes-at-Large or Littleton's *Tenures*, or of the publication of material which had long circulated in manuscript. Since commercial rather than professional considerations motivated such men as Redmond and Tottel, few sixteenth-century reports were printed before the period of the Commonwealth. Consequently Elizabethan lawyers had virtually no contemporary cases in print until 1571, and it is not surprising that they turned to the practice of compiling their own reports. Without even the semi-organized system of note-taking which existed during the Yearbook era, every practitioner was obliged to supplement the Abridgments with his own or someone else's collection. This must go far towards explaining the fact that, notwithstanding the subsequent flurry of printing, there remains a tremendous residue of manuscript reports from the years 1558 to 1603.

The student of law-reporting in this period can make no serious appraisal of his subject without bestowing attention upon this neglected mass of material. Wallace, in his survey of law reporters, published as an appendix 'a very scarce pamphlet' compiled by one Richard Pheney in 1834.[4] This appears to have been the only attempt hitherto made to tabulate early manuscript collections.[5] For the period from Henry VII to Elizabeth Pheney lists eighty-eight different sets of unprinted reports. The present writer has so far located more than 300 separate collections. Some of these contain only a few entries, others are found among readings, moots, abridgments, pleadings, statutes or treatises; but there are those which cover 400 to 500 folios and may contain as many as 1,500 cases. As in the printed compilations, the courts concerned reveal what sort of practice the author enjoyed, and when, and are not a sign of careful planning. Towards the end of

[4] Wallace, pp. 595, 602–12.

[5] Except for the 'Preliminary Edition' of a *Register of Year Book Manuscripts* (S.S.) prepared by Dr Jennifer Nicholson.

the century there appears to have been a trend towards specialization, with a higher percentage of reporters working exclusively in the King's Bench. Throughout, all the reporters attempt in varied ways, either as compilers or copyists, to collect and convey practical information to the advocate.

So unwieldy a mass of material, written in many different hands and employing law-French in various degrees of corruption, poses obvious difficulties. It has been found necessary to impose somewhat arbitrary priorities, choosing particular collections to serve as examples of the whole. Only so could the reports be viewed in perspective and any conclusions drawn. Of the many ways in which these manuscripts might be classified the following division into two principal categories is the simplest and most useful:

(1) *Manuscript versions of printed reports.* Almost all published reports of cases from the sixteenth century have their counterparts which survive in manuscript, either in whole or in part. Bendlowes, Keilwey, Dalison and Moore are typical of volumes which circulated for many years before going into print. But in the case of Plowden and Coke, two reporters whose notes were published in their own lifetime, the only hand-written copies which have so far come to light were prepared subsequent to publication and consist mainly of selected entries or abridgments.[6] On the other hand, a number of collections can be found which contain unprinted material attributable to authors who have had other cases published. This is, perhaps, to be expected where long delays occurred between compilation and publication; most of the printed reports of the sixteenth century are in this sense 'incomplete'.[7] A variant of this is found in the work of James Dyer; here an enterprising copyist with access to the Chief Justice's original manuscript purposely selected those entries

[6] *H.E.L.* v, 369; see also the articles by Simpson on Spelman and 'Keilwey', and Plucknett's analysis of Coke's Reports.

[7] *H.E.L.* v, 365–8.

which had not been put into print and transcribed them into a separate volume.[8]

For the most part, such unprinted material lies scattered in isolated pockets, the product of error or neglect on the part of scribes and editors. All too often manuscript collections are put together from the efforts of several reporters whose work may or may not have been published. Reports of this kind are the most difficult to disentangle, particularly where the copyist has seen fit to amend the entries to suit his own requirements. Since collectors were often anxious to provide themselves with a set of cases extending in chronological sequence over several years, they had no hesitation in dismembering existing sets without regard to their original authorship.[9]

(2) *Unprinted reports.* These account for the larger proportion of surviving manuscripts, though by no means the most widely used. They range from the barely legible jottings of barristers taken in court during the hearing of a suit to polished, carefully prepared copies of widely circulated reports written by professional scribes. They may be the work of the advocate in whose possession they resided or they may have been taken from the notes of a colleague. Individual entries follow no prescribed form but vary from concise statements of law to lengthy analyses more in the nature of minor treatises. The authors of some of these collections have been identified but the majority remain unattributed, especially those compiled at the end of the century when their number increases.[10] Like private reports as a whole they have one thing in common, the attempt on the part of the compilers to attain two conflicting objectives. Every pleader, provided he had access to the standard printed literature, sought a reliable guide to the case law of his time coupled with a set of reports of limited access. For the industrious and enterprising reporter the problem lay not in collecting relevant cases but in restricting their

[8] This volume is found in the I.T. Library, Petyt MS 511, vol. 13; a copy exists at Herts. R.O. Gorhambury MS XII. A.6.A.; see below, Chap. V, pp. 165–6.

[9] Hall, 'Bate's Case', p. 412.

[10] See Appendix I, pp. 290–305.

circulation. All too often the resultant compilation was too narrow in chronology or subject-matter for any but the most limited objectives; otherwise every opposing barrister would soon ferret out the source in question. The evidence of surviving manuscripts points to this: the most competently reported cases or those embracing a fairly general range of subjects are frequently duplicated, whereas those collections extending over only a few terms or years, or limited to specific causes, were less likely to be copied unless the reporter were an advocate of high rank or reputation.

As a source for the development of the common law under the Tudors manuscript collections should help historians to correct or at least to supplement the sometimes misleading evidence of printed reports. Surprisingly little has yet been produced along these lines, although additional light has been shed by unpublished decisions on such topics as copyhold tenure, impositions and perpetuities.[11] Preliminary investigations indicate that valuable material remains to be exploited on such subjects as proclamations, jury trials, and the development of trover and of action on the case for words.[12] Undoubtedly the main reason for the neglect of this material is its very bulk and the intrinsic difficulty involved in searching for, let alone finding, relevant cases. Although a majority of manuscript reports contain tables of one sort or another, these are seldom exhaustive and generally unreliable.

The number of volumes which survive emphasizes the fact that the practice of collecting cases not only continued after the demise of the Yearbooks but strengthened as the century progressed. There is, however, a gap of some thirty years after 1535 during which the number of existing manuscripts dips fairly low. Granted that the rate of survival remained fairly constant, it is to be inferred that the factors which militated against the production of Yearbooks continued to operate for another generation. This

[11] Gray, p. 63; G.D.G. Hall, 'Impositions and the Courts', *L.Q.R.* lxix (1953), 207–8; A.W.B. Simpson, *Introduction to the History of Land Law* (1961), pp. 201–2.

[12] Useful collections on the above topics include B.M. Harl. MS 5141 (Dalison), Lansd. 1084, Harg. 8 and H.L.S. MS 16.

appears to be reflected in the volume of litigation in the common law tribunals which, having declined in the later fifteenth century, remained stagnant during the first half of the sixteenth. Coupled with the disruptive effects of the plague, this may have discouraged advocates from carrying on the work of the Yearbook reporters and compiling regular reports.[13] For the last ten years of Henry VIII the collections of Dyer and Bendlowes, together with the volume owned by Anthony Gell and Brooke's Abridgment, constitute virtually the entire output.[14]

The pace began to quicken during the reigns of Edward VI and Mary and the first decade of Elizabeth's. By this time the last of the Yearbooks had been printed and the lack of any published decisions beyond 1535 must have proved a hindrance to pleaders. Consequently more of them, together with the judges, began supplementing their commonplace books with up-to-date cases. But the most significant increase was to come in the last quarter of the century: over two-thirds of all extant manuscripts were either prepared at that time or served as models for seventeenth-century copyists. In contrast to previous compilations these later reports usually cover only a few years, although the number of entries per term and year is quite often greater; this fact, coupled with the greater diversity of subject-matter and less frequent repetition of cases, supports the conclusion that a greater proportion of lawyers were preparing their own reports than had done so earlier. By the same token these practitioners were obliged to make the best of the skimpy material for the period 1535 to 1570. It is clear that, notwithstanding the publication of Plowden, Brooke and Dyer, the demand for 'new' mid-century reports remained strong well into the seventeenth century: hence the comparatively large number of manuscript copies of Bendlowes' Reports and those attributed to William Dalison and his contemporaries.

[13] Information on the rise and fall of business in the courts was kindly provided by Dr Blatcher.

[14] These books were supplemented, of course, by a large number of scattered decisions from various sources, some attributable, some not; see Appendices I and II, pp. 257–313.

To judge from their orthography many late-sixteenth century collections of contemporary cases were written by the lawyers themselves either as students or practitioners. It has been suggested that, in addition to the accepted digests of the law, pupils at the Inns were encouraged to study and copy the commonplace books of the barristers by whom they were sponsored. This was in keeping with the traditional belief that a wise student learned more by applying himself to good notes of an experienced reporter than by making shoddy ones of his own.[15] 'The drudgery of transcription', however, could not continue indefinitely and young practitioners were also exhorted to prepare their own reports. According to William Fulbecke, 'There hath never bin any learned in the Law, . . . who hath not made a collection of his owne'.[16] Such a practice must have developed in Elizabeth's reign when the number of manuscripts in circulation had increased and by the turn of the century it was fairly common for students and junior barristers to compile their own notes in court in imitation of their seniors. These notes tended to follow the orthodox method employed by Dyer rather than the more scholarly approach of Plowden, that is to say, they were concise, factual notes covering a connected run of years and terms, and susceptible of easy reference.

The fact remains that a considerable number of these unpublished collections are the work of professional copyists. This is especially true of those covering the lean years between 1535 and 1570. It is a reasonable supposition that serjeants and senior apprentices would wish to amplify material provided by the printers for this period with less well known but useful cases. For a volume as extensive as Bendlowes' the solution was to retain the services of a scrivener, but the student or young practitioner might have to content himself with abbreviated, personal transcriptions of selected portions. Coke exemplifies both processes. He personally

[15] *Cal. I.T. Recs.* i, p. xxxvi; Putnam, p. 162.

[16] Fulbecke, *Parallele*, p. 44; when Sir Simonds D'Ewes ended his legal studies in 1626 he lamented his leaving the Middle Temple and his 'reporting of law-cases at the Court of Common Pleas'; *Autobiography*, i, 307.

abstracted certain entries from Bendlowes' casebook in 1578; then at the turn of the century he purchased, or had copied, a full set of the reports.[17]

Some consideration must be given to the role of professional copyists during this period. We have already noticed the suggestion that the gap between preparation and printing of the later Yearbooks was due to some sort of scribal monopoly. If there are grounds for believing that the activities of the printers were hampered because of the hostility of professional scribes,[18] no evidence of this kind is forthcoming from the surviving records of the Scriveners Company of London, whose influence would surely have been dominant. On the other hand, it is worth noting that the number of scriveners in and around London rose rapidly just at a time when printing had become well established. Between 1501 and 1551 eighty-four new members were admitted, of whom twenty-five joined between 1541 and 1550. During the next fifty years (1551–1600) over 300 new signatories appear on the Company's records, a three-and-a-half-fold increase.[19] While a primary cause of the increase was the undertaking of additional kinds of work such as the negotiation of loans, the scriveners obviously benefited from the expansion of general legal business. Instruments such as deeds, charters, marriage settlements and the like increased in proportion to the population and its activities. At the same time more and more attorneys were drafting legal instruments themselves. The scriveners compensated for this in part by undertaking work on a wider scale although still retaining a close connection with the legal profession.[20] Among those trained as 'writers of the court letter' were clerks and notaries as well as public scriveners.[21] All were familiar with the languages of the law; it is significant that the oath which was taken by newly-

[17] The earlier set, in Coke's hand, is in B.M. Harl. MS 6687, ff. 49–56*v*; the complete set forms Add. MS 25189; see above, Chap. III, pp. 91–2.

[18] *H.E.L.* ii. 542–3.

[19] Hilary Jenkinson, 'The Teaching and Practice of Handwriting in England', *History*, xi (1926–27), 130–38.

[20] Michael Birks, *Gentlemen of the Law* (1960), pp. 78–84.

[21] Hilary Jenkinson, *Later Court Hand* (1927), p. 30.

enfranchised members was in 'old law French'.[22] While there is a lack of evidence it is more than likely that the London scriveners did most of the copying of manuscript reports in the sixteenth century: a comparison of the styles of handwriting found in the 'Common Paper' and in many of the surviving collections lends credence to this.[23] Presumably, when an advocate desired a copy of available cases he ordered it from a convenient shop where the scrivener might well employ several apprentices under him. Some of these shops were located close to the Inns of Court and it seems that a brisk business in new and used manuscript books continued into the seventeenth century.[24] Just as there seems to have been continuity in the publishing trade, so too professional writers continued to flourish throughout the century.[25] Each group contributed to the evolution of law reporting.

Irrespectively of which manuscript reports have survived, it seems that practically every barrister who pleaded before the central courts supplemented printed reports with written notes of some sort.[26] These may not have been of his own making and their contents are not always easy to classify. Even to decide whether a particular collection of notes merits the description of 'reports' is not a simple matter. While the respective functions and limitations of reports and plea rolls were well understood there was little discrimination in the matter cited in court. Hence, contemporary criteria as to what constituted valid law-reports are not always reliable. One modern authority has stated that 'reporting begins when cases are collected of set purpose for professional use and study'.[27] Such a stage had long been reached by common lawyers, yet for the latter part of the sixteenth century there arises the question how much circulation there was of

[22] *The Case of the Free Scriveners of London* (1749), pp. 30–1.

[23] The 'Common Paper' is described by Jenkinson, *Later Court Hand*, p. 4; the MS itself is deposited in the City of London Guildhall Library.

[24] *Cal. of M.T. Recs.* i, 8; B.M. Harl. MS 4585, f. 453*v* and Harg. 50, f. 1*v* contain warranties or conditions of sale of the collections in question.

[25] George Unwin, *The Gilds and Companies of London* (1938), pp. 302, 386.

[26] *H.E.L.* v, 365.

[27] Sir Frederick Pollock, *First Book of Jurisprudence* (1929), p. 294; cf. Coke's definition, Co. Litt. 293a.

the numerous manuscripts being produced. Even in their decline the Yearbooks circulated freely; private reports such as Dyer's and Plowden's may originally have been for personal use but once printed they achieved widespread circulation. The collections prepared by Bendlowes, 'Dalison', and later reporters were copied many times and widely used. Could a manuscript casebook which remained in sole possession of its author be regarded as a reliable set of reports? If such a compilation were never exposed to contemporary professional criticism, is the legal historian entitled to rely on its dicta? The question is probably academic since it is virtually impossible to prove that even the most insignificant compilation did not circulate or influence in some way later jurists: even a single decision from an anonymous set of notes could have lasting effects.[28] Throughout the seventeenth century cases continued to be cited, copied and printed from private collections extending back to the reign of Henry VII. The fact remains, however, that something in excess of one-quarter of the unprinted reports from the reign of Elizabeth appear to have had little if any circulation: they were truly 'private' reports.

Discussion is confined here to the relatively few but important manuscript collections from the immediate post-Yearbook period. It was one of these 'wandering and masterless Reports' decried by Coke which came to be known as 'Dalison's Reports'.[29] A close examination of this volume will illustrate a number of problems relating to the preparation and circulation of manuscripts in general.

The 'divers special cases . . . colligees par Gulielme Dalison un des justices del Bank le Roy', published by John Rowe, contain entries extending from 38 Henry VIII to 16 Elizabeth (1546–74). There are 402 in all, but a number of gaps exist in the sequence of terms and years, the most notable being the absence of decisions between 1565 and 1571. What has long been realized about this set of reports is that the majority of these cases were decided after

[28] Simpson, *Land Law*, p. 201. [29] 1 Co. Rep. Pref. iv.

Dalison's death early in 1559.[30] Rowe himself acknowledges this and refers to some earlier occasions when this fact arose as an issue in court. Gouldesborough records in 1601 that Coke, then Attorney-General, cited a case purportedly out of Dalison's notebook from 1567; Serjeant Godfrey denied its validity, pointing out that Dalison had died 'long before Anno 9 Eliz.'.[31] Coke obviously had access to a manuscript copy of the collection as early as 1590, nineteen years before Ashe's publication, yet in his First Institute he cites three entries from 'Dalison', apparently taken from Ashe—but again all later than 1559.[32] In 1631 the attribution of these decisions was again challenged, this time by Chief Justice Hobert, himself a law reporter, who demanded of Serjeant Hendon 'by what warrant those reports of Dalisons came into print'.[33] A fair question, and one which reflects the confusion existing at the time over the origin and authorship of that 'ocean of reportes' which was engulfing the profession.[34]

The search for William Dalison and his work really begins with William Lambarde. In his *Perambulation of Kent*, published in 1576, Lambarde cites a case from 3 & 4 Philip & Mary (1556–7) '(as Justice Dalison reporteth)'.[35] This is the earliest printed reference to the reporter's work. It turns out that Lambarde married the widow of Dalison's eldest son and through her must have come into possession of the original notes. In any event, Lambarde prepared his own set, which is now part of the Harleian collection in the British Museum.[36] Miss Putnam referred to the manuscript and gave the impression that it was Dalison's own copy.[37] At various points in the text, however, Lambarde makes it clear that he prepared this particular copy, and at the end there is this unambiguous colophon:

[30] His will (P.C.C. 9 Chaynay), dated 8 January 1559, was proved in the following April.

[31] Gould. 153; cited in the margin of Rowe's Preface; cf. Wallace, p. 116.

[32] Co. Litt. 53b, 111b; cf. 3 Inst. 59, 61, 72.

[33] Croke Car. Pref. iv.

[34] Fulbecke, *A Parallele*, p. 5.

[35] *Perambulation of Kent* (*S.T.C.* no. 15175), p. 398.

[36] B.M. Harl. MS 5141.

[37] Putnam, p. 111.

3. Richard Harper, taken from the effigy in Swarkestone parish church, Derbyshire, (By permission of Dr J. H. Baker.)

4. Sir James Dyer, portrait by an unknown artist. (National Portrait Gallery, London.)

Hucusque ex libro manu Willelmi Dallison conscripto Willelmus Lambert exaravit 1569.[38]

The entries are written in a neat hand and were obviously taken down with considerable care. There are, in all, 241 decisions noted, still only half the total of those printed under Dalison's name in 1689. Their chronological sequence and limits are at considerable variance with Rowe's edition; the entire manuscript covers a span of only six years (1552–8).

This set of reports corresponds quite neatly with Dalison's somewhat abbreviated career. He was the son of William Dalison of Laughton, Lincolnshire, a prominent member of the county gentry who served as sheriff in 1545–6.[39] The date of the younger Dalison's birth is not known, but having received 'some education' at Cambridge [40] he entered Gray's Inn in 1534. The age at which law students seemed to be gaining admission at this time was usually about nineteen or twenty, so that Dalison was probably born around 1515.[41] He must have shown great promise since he was called to the bar after only three years' study, in 1537. In 1542 he became 'an ancient' of his Inn and he delivered his first reading in the Autumn vacation of 1548.[42] During the course of the late 'forties he seems to have taken on the expected round of tasks appropriate to his rank and seniority: these included various commissions of post mortem, sewers and the peace.[43] He assisted in carrying out some of the less popular policies of Edward VI's Protectors. In 1550 he and others set about collecting in Lincolnshire the third payment of a relief granted by the first Parliament of the reign.[44] He was a member of the commission which was

[38] B.M. Harl. MS 5141, f. 45.

[39] *D.N.B.* v, 391; *C.P.R.* 1553–4, p. 436; *L. & P. Hen. VIII*, ii, no. 472.

[40] Cooper, *Athenae*, i, 191.

[41] Bendlowes, Dyer, Plowden, Coke, Egerton and Anderson were all twenty or close to it.

[42] G.I. *Pension Book*, i, 499; Foss, v, 478.

[43] *C.P.R.* 1547–8, p. 78; 1549–51, pp. 67, 216; *L. & P. Hen. VIII*, xxi, no. 504 (4).

[44] *C.P.R.* 1553, p. 355.

appointed in 1551 to make an inventory of church assets in Lincoln,[45] but as a former resident of the city he was not excessively diligent in this task: the mayor and aldermen were anxious to retain valuables from disused churches and offered him forty shillings to sign the certificate of inventory without undue investigation; he apparently acceded to this questionable request and nothing more was heard of the matter.[46] It should be added that by this time Mary had become Queen and no doubt the zeal of the commission had slackened.

Dalison received his call as serjeant-at-law in 1552.[47] He was in distinguished company, with Robert Brooke, William Stanford and James Dyer among the other appointees; all were to become judges soon afterwards and were to contribute richly to the legal literature of the period. It was Dalison's own Inn which played host to the new serjeants at their traditional feast, a description of which has been left by Henry Machyn the diarist.[48] The records of Gray's Inn contain an entry that in accordance with custom the Pension awarded Dalison and Stanford the sum of five pounds each and a pair of gloves.[49] Dalison presented his second lecture that autumn with a learned analysis of statute 32 Henry VIII, chapter 33, 'that wrongful disseisin is no descent in law'.[50] It is this reading which, Dyer reports, was approved by the judges after 'a diligent review' at Serjeants' Inn in 1562.[51] Presumably Dalison followed the usual course by moving out of Gray's Inn and into one of the two hostels reserved for judges and serjeants—it was probably the one in Chancery Lane[52]—but like Bendlowes he continued to maintain chambers at his old Inn. It seems, indeed, that many of these rooms were held on long leases: Dalison's son William began studying law in 1552 and probably occupied his father's old quarters, and in 1594 Maximilian, the

[45] Ibid. 1550–3, p. 396.

[46] *H.M.C. Fourteenth Rep. App. VIII*, 46.

[47] *C.P.R.* 1550–3, p. 355; he was made King's Serjeant in 1555; Foss, v, 478.

[48] *Camden Old Series* xlii, 26, 327.

[49] *Pension Book*, i, 496.

[50] Foss, v, 479.

[51] Dyer, 219a.

[52] B.M. Harl. MS 5141, ff. 26–8; Plow. 75.

reporter's grandson, took possession of both the chambers and law-books of his grandfather.[53]

As pleader Dalison is named only occasionally in the reports of his colleagues and then not before he had received his call as serjeant. Like a number of other advocates of his day he seems to have concentrated before 1552 on administrative duties rather than litigation.[54] The earliest reference to his arguments occurs in Plowden's report of a conference at Serjeants' Inn, Chancery Lane, where he is designated a serjeant-elect.[55] Dalison also represented the defendant in the leading case of *Buckley v. Rice Thomas* (1555), and acted as counsel in a Court of Wards dispute, as reported earlier in the year.[56] The only other glimpse of him as a pleader comes from three entries in the Gell manuscript; in none of these were his arguments especially noteworthy or persuasive.[57] It should be added that his duties on various commissions of peace and assize occupied part of Dalison's time: he and Edward Saunders, later Chief Justice of the King's Bench, were often paired on circuit, generally in the North and in Lincolnshire.[58]

In common with many lawyers of his time, Dalison had a brief spell in the House of Commons, but his parliamentary career was even more perfunctory and seemingly less distinguished than Bendlowes'. He sat only once, in the first Marian parliament of (October) 1553, as one of the knights of the shire for the county of Lincoln.[59] The only fact known about his

[53] *G.I. Adm. Reg.* pp. 22, 85; see also Dalison's will P.C.C. 9 Chaynay, and an inventory of assets belonging to his son, Kent County Record Office, Dalison MSS, E. 1, 1/2.

[54] Cf. the career of Nicholas Hare, above, Chap. II, pp. 47–8.

[55] *Wimbish v. Willoughby* (1552), Plow. 72 at p. 75.

[56] Ibid. 112, 121.

[57] Lib. of Congress Gell MS, ff. 126, 135; Dyer alludes briefly to him in his unpublished notes; I.T. Petyt MS 511, vol. 13, f. 35*v*.

[58] *C.P.R.* 1553–4, pp. 18, 21, 22, 25, 26, 31, 33–4; 1554–5, pp. 105–6, 109; 1555–7, pp. 144, 454, 521.

[59] In the *Official Returns* Dalison's name is missing and only the description 'serviens ad legem' remains. In Browne Willis, *Notitia Parliamentaria* (1750), iii, 28, Dalison is listed as one of the members for Lincs. in October 1553; this sometimes unreliable source is corroborated by Bodl. MS e Mus. 17 which lists

membership is the negative one that he was not among those who 'stood for the true religion', that is, for Reform.[60] His membership went unrecorded in the *Commons Journal* and he never sat again.

During the remainder of Mary's reign Dalison rose to the summit of his profession. In February 1554 he was nominated a Justice of the Duchy of Lancaster in company with his circuit-partner Edward Saunders.[61] As often happened, this heralded an appointment to the bench of one of the central courts. After William Portman was made Chief Justice at the death of Thomas Bromley, Dalison filled the vacancy as a puisne judge of the King's Bench; shortly afterwards he was knighted.[62] Again, there is little to be gleaned from the reports as to his pronouncements from the bench, although he presided at some notable Exchequer Chamber cases.[63] Dyer mentions his participation in some adjudications but without reproducing any of his arguments.[64] This is hardly a fair criterion, however, since very few King's Bench cases have been recorded during his tenure except by Dalison himself; moreover, even here he restricted quotation from his own arguments to three or four principal causes, and this not out of modesty but because of his style of reporting.[65] From this meagre evidence, nevertheless, he appears to have been a competent jurist, if nothing more.

From the available evidence—his election as a trustworthy member to Mary's first parliament, his close association with Saunders and his background in Lincolnshire—it appears that Dalison's religious posture was distinctly conservative, yet he seems to have prospered under Edward VI as well as under Mary. His patent as judge was also renewed under Elizabeth, but he did

Dalison as the 'serviens ad legem' in question. This manuscript was brought to the writer's attention by Prof. S.T. Bindoff.

[60] Bodl. MS e Mus. 17.

[61] Robert Somerville, *History of the Duchy of Lancaster* (1953), i, 473.

[62] *C.P.R.* 1555–7, p. 144; *D.N.B.* xiii, 391; Foss. v, 478–9.

[63] For instance, *Basset's Case* (1557), Dyer, 136a; B.M. Harl. MS 5141, f. 38.

[64] Dyer, 123a, 128a, 128b, 131a.

[65] B.M. Harl. MS 5141, ff. 28, 35*v*, 40*v*; cf. Dyer, 123a.

not live long enough to be involved in the 'purge' which took place during the Christmas vacation of 1558–9; he died shortly after making his will in January 1559.[66]

According to that will the bulk of Dalison's printed law books were to go to his son, although the manuscript from which his 'Reports' later emerged seems to have passed into Lambarde's hands, at least temporarily.[67] As found in the Harleian Manuscripts the collection stands in sharp contrast to the work of his contemporaries. It lacks, first of all, the chronological sweep which characterizes Dyer and Bendlowes; secondly, there is none of the painstaking analysis of issues or lengthy arguments so typical of Plowden. Perhaps more surprising, nowhere is the stamp of the Yearbooks—the last of which were just being printed—to be found. When viewed within Rowe's printed version the peculiar nature of Dalison's compilation is lost, especially since only seventy-eight of his own entries are included; but when seen in its entirety and in isolation his work shows features which exemplify the individualistic character of early private reporting. The manuscript, which consists of forty-five leaves bound together with a number of later tracts, covers only twelve terms, that is, half the possible number for the six years included. This is in itself not unusual, any more than is the fact that the number of entries per term varies from one to fifty-two; both are probably related to the diverse commitments of the author at the time, although all the reports were drafted during his tenure as serjeant and judge.

When we turn to the nature of the entries themselves, we find a lack of 'cases' in the accepted sense. Less than twenty make mention of the parties by name. Even at this rough-and-ready stage of law reporting, such a negative feature is striking. Again, the presence of counsel or the gist of their arguments is rarely mentioned, and the decisions of judges sitting in open court are subordinate to the more numerous extra-judicial proceedings: almost half the 'cases' emanate from the two Serjeants' Inns,

[66] P.C.C. 9 Chaynay.

[67] There is no reference to manuscripts of any kind.

Fleet Street and Chancery Lane.[68] The first ninety-three entries cover three terms in the space of a year: Michaelmas 6 Edward VI, Hilary 6 & 7 Edward VI and Michaelmas 1 Mary (1552–3). Sixty-three were adjudicated or debated among the judges at Serjeants' Inn, Fleet Street, the residue were for the most part reported from the King's Bench and Common Pleas where, presumably, Dalison was then pleading.

Another feature of this first year's reporting is the special prominence accorded two particular judges, James Hales of the Common Pleas and William Portman of the King's Bench. It is more than likely that they both resided at the Fleet Street Inn, that they participated in a great deal of extra-judicial argument, and above all that they were highly regarded in official circles.[69] Plowden, in a report from the preceding year, notes that Chancellor Rich sent for Portman and Hales 'to have their advice what the common law was' in a chancery suit.[70] Apart from the fact that both had been created serjeants in 1540, they had little else in common besides astute legal minds: but between them, to judge from Dalison, they exercised considerable influence on the formation of common law principles during the early 1550s.[71]

In Hilary term 1553 the reports concentrate more on suits in the King's Bench.[72] Here again Portman's name occurs frequently, but this time in conjunction with that of the Chief Justice of his own court, Thomas Bromley. Dalison himself makes his first appearance this term in 'un graund question' relating to patents which was discussed at Serjeants' Inn.[73] Not unnaturally, the emphasis in most of the King's Bench matter is on criminal law. There is little involved argument between bench and bar; rather, the author seems intent on conveying accurately decisions on the

[68] For a discussion of extra-judicial proceedings see below, Chap. V, pp. 177–97; cf. Putnam, p. 198.

[69] They were linked together as early as 1544; Lib. of Congress Gell MS. f, 74.

[70] *Ross v. Pope*, E. 5 Edw. VI, Plow. 72.

[71] The opinions and pronouncements of Hales and Portman are cited on at least forty occasions.

[72] B.M. Harl. MS 5141, ff. 17–23. [73] Ibid. f. 19.

legal issues. In common with reporters of his own day and with Coke later, Dalison strove to establish a consensus of the court or conference concerned in order to express the 'clere ley'.[74]

A further significant group of cases is found in Michaelmas 1 & 2 Philip & Mary (1554). About half of the thirty-six entries for this term originated in Serjeants' Inn, Chancery Lane. Of particular interest are the final ten 'cases' which were decided by 'toute les Justices assembles', probably at one and the same sitting. All relate to capital crimes and, fittingly for the year 1554, treason, as related to the imagining and encompassing of the monarch's death, receives particular attention.[75] New names appear, including Serjeants Gawdy and Rokeby and Justices Robert Brooke and William Stanford, the latter having recently been appointed to the Bench.[76]

It was not until Easter term 1556 that Dalison reported the first of his few full-length court decisions. It was his debut as a judge, which came at a time when the Court had a complement of only three justices on the bench.[77] The rest of the manuscript reflects a wider range of material, as befitted the experience of a senior magistrate—about one-half emanate from the King's Bench, the remainder from the two Serjeants' Inns. Another departure was the report of 'le Serieants Case' in 1556. It took the form of a regular piece of litigation in the Common Pleas in which the newly-appointed serjeants all contributed arguments.[78] The chronology towards the end of the collection becomes confused but it appears that Dalison's final reports relate to Trinity term 1558. One of the last notable trials in which he sat was *Lord North's Case*, a leading decision on the responsibility of public servants for obligations executed on behalf of the crown.[79]

[74] 3 Co. Rep. Pref. xvib; see below, Chap. V, pp. 189–90.

[75] Harl. 5141, ff. 27–8.

[76] Foss, v, 359, 390; Gawdy and Rokeby probably resided at Serjeants' Inn, Chancery Lane.

[77] *Granado v. Dyer*, E. 2 & 3 P. & M., Harl. 5141, f. 28; cf. Dyer, 123a.

[78] *Hill v. Grange*, H. 2 & 3 P. & M.; reported also by Dyer, Plowden and Brooke; see Appendix III, p. 317.

[79] Harl. 5141, f. 41*v*; cf. Dyer, 161a.

A comparison of the printed 'Dalison' with Harleian MS 5141 answers some questions but raises others. Seventy-eight entries have been extracted from the original collection extending from 7 Edward VI to 4 & 5 Philip & Mary. These exist as a consecutive series within the body of the printed edition and evidently were inserted to fill a gap between Michaelmas 4 Edward VI and 2 Elizabeth.[80] With a delay of more than a century between compilation and publication discrepancies were bound to occur. Although the sequence is vaguely reminiscent of that of the original, individual terms and cases have become hopelessly entangled. Some entries have been run together in two's and three's while others, conversely, have been unaccountably split up. Many have been abridged or amended almost beyond recognition. Names have not so much been misspelt as changed—'Browne' instead of 'Bromley' being a common error. In short, the ravages of constant recopying and seventeenth-century printing are all too apparent.

That Dalison was the author of at least a portion of 'Dalison's' Reports seems fairly certain. But two obvious questions then arise. First, who reported and compiled the large residue of cases comprised in Rowe's edition? Secondly, how did these two (or more) collections come to be entangled? Neither question, it appears, can be answered with certainty but some fairly reasonable conclusions may be drawn. And in seeking solutions many of the problems relating to manuscript reports in general are touched upon.

There are, in fact, a formidable number of manuscript reports extant which contain in varying proportions cases printed under Dalison's name but actually decided after his death. Thirty such manuscripts have so far been located.[81] The name most commonly associated with these collections is that of Richard Harper, a judge of the Court of Common Pleas during Elizabeth's reign. Although they were contemporaries, Harper's name has never been linked with Dalison's, either as advocate or reporter. But the title of 'Justice Harper's Reports' has been applied to several

[80] Dal. 8–26. [81] See list, pp. 123–6.

volumes; a number are found among the Hargrave Manuscripts. One such folio book, Hargrave MS 6, was copied in the late sixteenth century and contains entries ranging from 38 Henry VIII to Michaelmas 26 & 27 Elizabeth (1546–84). At the top of the first page of cases, in the same hand as that of the text, is written the simple heading 'Harpers Reports'—not in itself convincing evidence of authorship. But it is worth noting that this particular volume was owned by William Nichols, who entered the Middle Temple in 1582, a mere five years after Harper's death.[82] Another manuscript from the Hargrave Collection—number 8—is almost identical in content; the catalogue lists it as 'another copy' of reports by Judge Harper, but Hargrave may simply have assumed Harper's authorship from his earlier acquisition.[82a] From internal evidence it appears that this volume was transcribed between 1585, when Dyer's Reports were put into print, and the end of the century.

SUMMARY LIST OF MANUSCRIPTS CONTAINING THE REPORTS OF RICHARD HARPER

A. *Autonomous collections*

1. *B.M. Harg. 6:* 79 fols., late sixteenth century; 'reports by Judge Harpur of cases 38 H. 8—M. 26 & 27 Eliz.'; probably owned initially by William Nichols of the Middle Temple (adm. 1582).

2. *B.M. Harg. MS 8:* 277 fols., early seventeenth century; described by Edward Umfreville as 'another copy of the reports of Judge Harpur, 38 H. 8—26 & 27 Eliz.'

3. *C.U.L. MS Ll. 3.14:* 283 fols., early seventeenth century; follows closely Harg. 8 and may possibly be the work of the same scrivener.

4. *B.M. Harg. MS 4:* 342 fols., early seventeenth century; ff. 94–289 contain a collection of cases ascribed to Harper, 38 Hen. VIII—9 Eliz.; several cases reported for 4 & 5 P. & M.

5. *Bodl. Rawl. MS C.112:* 271 fols., late sixteenth century; a collection

[82] *M.T. Adm. Reg.* i, 49.

[82a] B.M. Harg. MSS 6 and 8 were previously in the possession of Edward Umfreville who noted the connection of both volumes with Harper.

erroneously ascribed to Dalison, 38 Hen. VIII—9 Eliz. (together with additional material of unknown origin).

6. *Longleat MS 221:* 102 fols., late sixteenth or early seventeenth century; cases attributable to Harper, 38 Hen. VIII—9 Eliz.

7. *B.M. Harl. MS 1624:* 328 fols., seventeenth century; ff. 55*v*–83 contain cases corresponding to B.M. Harg. MS 4 ff. 110–54 for M. 4 Edw. VI—M. 3 Eliz. and H. 5 Eliz.

8. *L.I. Mayn. MS 86:* 111 fols., seventeenth century; ff. 55*v*–83 contain a series of entries which correspond to the Harper collection in B.M. Harl. MS 1624.

9. *B.M. Harg MS 10:* 72 fols., late sixteenth century; reports ascribed to Harper, H. 2—M. 15 & 16 Eliz.

10. *B.M. Harg. MS 374:* 169 fols., early seventeenth century; reports ascribed to Harper by Edward Umfreville, 2–16 Eliz.; similar in content to B.M. Harg. MS 6 for the period covered.

11. *B.M. Lansd. MS 1060:* 182 fols., late sixteenth or early seventeenth century; another incomplete collection ascribed to Harper by Edward Umfreville; ff. 6–22 contain a series for M. 1 & 2—7 Eliz.

12. *H.L.S. MS 2079:* 170 fols., early seventeenth century; ff. 3–24*v* contain entries attributable to Harper, M. 1 & 2—7 Eliz.

13. *L.I. Hill MS 123:* 98 fols., seventeenth century; ff. 1–66 contain 549 numbered reports, 38 Hen. VIII—T. 6 Eliz. traceable in part to Dalison but consisting mainly of cases associated with Harper.

14. *B.M. Add. MS 24845:* 519 fols., seventeenth century; ff. 1–117*v* contain cases 38 Hen. VIII—M. 15 & 16 Eliz. which combine collections compiled by Dalison and Harper. The printed edition of 1689 is closely modelled on this collection which may have been prepared in the same period for Henry Bradshawe of Gray's Inn (adm. 1686).

B. *Abridged or selected extracts*

1. *L.I. Misc. MS 487:* 365 fols., late sixteenth century; ff. 170–354*v* contain, among others, reports for the years 1560–75.

1a. *B.M. Harg. MS 9:* 280 fols., late sixteenth or early seventeenth century; selected entries, 1–20 Eliz., found between f. 1 and f. 277.

2. *B.M. Harg. MS 15:* 206 fols., sixteenth and seventeenth centuries; reports attributable to Harper, M. 7 & 8—M. 14 & 15 Eliz. (ff. 10–49); volume owned by Christopher Yelverton.

3. *C.U.L. MS Dd. 5.50:* 70 fols., early seventeenth century; ff. 59–62 contain an abridged selection of cases for M. 1, E. 3, M. 4, E. 5 Edw. VI and M. 3 & 4 Eliz.

4. *Longleat MS 240:* 190 fols., seventeenth century; ff. 1–14 and 41*v*–188*v* contain cases, 1–20 Eliz., related to Harper's work.

5. *B.M. Harg. MS 37:* 184 fols., early seventeenth century; selections from Harper amongst ff. 119*v*–48; M. 2 & 3—H. 7 Eliz.; owned by Henry Calthorpe, reporter and Recorder of London (1635–6).

6. *B.M. Lansd. MS 1086:* 144 fols., early seventeenth century; ff. 97–127*v* include selections from Harper's reports, M. 2 & 3—M. 6 & 7 Eliz.

7. *B.M. Lansd. MS 1121:* 120 fols., early seventeenth century; ff. 67–79 consist of random reports, M. 38 Hen. VIII—H. 5 Eliz.

8. *L.I. Misc. MS 361:* 200 fols., early seventeenth century; ff. 198–205 consist of a selection entitled 'Harpers Reports', H. 2—H. 9 Eliz.

9. *B.M. Add. MS 25198:* 308 fols., seventeenth century; ff. 283*v*–97 include abridged extracts of Harper cases, M. 38—H. 9 Eliz.

10. *L.I. Misc. MS 791:* 199 fols., early seventeenth century; ff. 1–14 contain a selection of cases described as 'Justice Harpers Reports', M. 38 Hen. VIII—H. 26 Eliz.

11. *B.M. Lansd. MS 1133:* 161 fols., seventeenth century; ff. 128–37 comprise selected leading cases associated with Harper collections.

12. *I.T. Petyt MS 516, vol. 6:* 143 fols., seventeenth century, selected reports, 13–20 Eliz. (ff. 1–51).

13. *B.M. Harg. MS 373:* 229 fols., late sixteenth century; 'Jordan's Collectanea'; leading cases from Harper are found between f. 23 and f. 141.

14. *MS belonging to Sir John Neale:* 178 fols., seventeenth century; ff. 26–35 contain a series of abridged entries designated 'Justice Harpers Reports', 9–12 Eliz.; the volume was owned and compiled by Timothy Turner of Gray's Inn.

15. *I.T. Barr. MS 17:* 249 fols., early seventeenth century, small quarto volume; ff. 14*v*–17 comprise reports from E. 6—M. 16 & 17 Eliz. taken 'ex libro Harper'.

16. *B.M. Add. MS 25188:* 100 fols., late sixteenth century; small quarto volume of selected cases associated with Harper, 38 Hen. VIII—13 Eliz.

17. *B.M. Harl. MS 6707:* 118 fols. late sixteenth or early seventeenth century; selected leading decisions, including *Bullock v. Burdett* (1565) and *Mutton's Case* (1568) (ff. 50–3*v*, 96–110*v*).

18. *B.M. Harl. MS 1696:* 22 fols., seventeenth century; a few entries among reports for 5–31 Eliz. attributable to Harper.

19. *B.M. Lansd. MS 1095:* 140 fols., early seventeenth century; ff. 101–26 include selections, M. 6 & 7—T. Eliz., some of which can be connected with the work of Harper.

20. *C.U.L. MS Gg. 2.5:* 553 fols., early seventeenth century; a composite collection of reports including Harper cases for M. 4 & 5 P. & M.—6 Eliz. (ff. 24–76).

21. *Lib. of Congress Gell MS:* 145 fols., second half of sixteenth century; ff. 97–101*v* include cases related to designated Harper collections, M. 38 Hen. VIII, M. 1, T. 2 Edw. VI; volume owned by Anthony Gell of the Inner Temple (adm. 1547).

22. *C.U.L. MS Gg. 3.3:* 44 fols., early seventeenth century; a volume containing six lengthy reports, two of which, *Vernon v. Vernon* (1573) and *Sheldon v. Gilbert* (1574), are found in Harper collections; at f. 16 is a note to the effect that the cases were taken 'ex reports Will. Watson de Interiori Templo'.

23. *B.M. Lansd. MS 1072:* 228 fols., early seventeenth century; includes two cases associated with Harper: *Mutton v. Mutton* (1571), ff. 66–75*v*, and *Winter's Case* (1572), ff. 76–92.

24. *Herts. R.O. Gorhambury MS XII, A.6.A:* 185 fols., late sixteenth century; ff. 74–79*v* comprise reports 'ex libro Harper' probably extracted by George Croke.

Another set of reports which has been attributed to Richard Harper is Hargrave MS 10. This is made up of a selection of cases found in the aforementioned collections but for the most part reported at greater length; they cover the years 1560 to 1573. Again, the only explicit connection with Harper is a note to this effect inserted by Edward Umfreville who apparently took possession of the volume while a student in 1724.[83] Two references

[83] On the flyleaf, among various other notations, Umfreville, who was a legal antiquarian of some authority, draws attention to the fact that many of these cases were printed in Rowe's edition of 'Dalison'.

within the reports themselves may be construed as suggestive of Harper's authorship. In one there is a reference to him as arguing a case while 'adonque seriant';[84] elsewhere it is recorded that when Anthony Browne died in 1567, 'Harper Sgt. fuit fait Justice de mesme le lieu'.[85] Moreover, it is to be noted that Harper's name and opinions figure prominently in almost every entry. Yet another volume which passed into the possession of Francis Hargrave is described by him as 'Mr. Justice Harper's Reports'; he adds that it was 'so cited per E.U.', that is, Edward Umfreville, who owned many of these manuscripts previously.[86]

Harper's name also appears elsewhere. A volume, probably compiled by George Croke, a reporter himself, contains 'cases ex libro Harper' to which Croke as an Inner Templar may have had access.[87] Another repository of valuable legal manuscripts is Lincoln's Inn; among them are two further sets of decisions ascribed to Harper. One set, which once belonged to Richard Levinge, contains cases which run between the years 1546 and 1584; an indication of their authorship is a note at the top of the first folio in the same hand as the text.[88] The second Lincoln's Inn volume forms part of the Rodd Collection and contains, in addition to seven folios attributed to Harper, entries from the work of Bendlowes, Owen and Coke.[89] Finally, there is yet another collection which names Harper as its author, this one having belonged to Timothy Turner of Gray's Inn who commenced his studies early in the seventeenth century.[90] In none of these manuscripts does the reporter refer to himself in the first

[84] B.M. Harg. MS 10, f. 10.

[85] Ibid. f. 19.

[86] B.M. Harg. MS 374; Hargrave refers to his 'two other copies in folio', Harg. 6 and 8, noting that 'all three vary according to the judgment of the several excerpts'; Harg. 374, f. 55.

[87] Herts. R.O. Gorhambury MS XII. A.6.A. ff. 74–9*v*; see also B.M. Lansd. MS 1060, ff. 6–22, 50–8; Lansd. 1072, ff. 56–92.

[88] L.I. Misc. MS 791, ff. 1–14; Levinge was admitted to the Inner Temple in 1647; *I.T. Adm. Reg.* p. 328.

[89] L.I. Misc. MS 361, ff. 198–205.

[90] The manuscript is now owned by Sir John Neale who kindly lent it to the writer for perusal; 'Harper' cases are found at ff. 26–47.

person or give any clear indication of his identity: all references to Harper are in the third person. This in itself, however, is not an objection, as many reporters, most notably Dyer, cite their own opinions in this impersonal manner.[91]

The earliest citation of a case ascribed to Harper—one of the few to be found—occurs in an entry for Trinity 37 Elizabeth (1595) out of an anonymous manuscript collection:[92] the precedent was cited by Serjeant Drew, who, like Harper, was a member of the Inner Temple.[93] There are, in addition, a number of marginal references to Harper's reports to be found in certain printed volumes. In his edition of Dyer (1688), Chief Justice Treby has four such, all of which can be identified in one or more surviving Harper manuscripts.[94] The case of *Ayer v. Orme* argued in Easter term 1563, for instance, seems to link up with the Richard Harper who was practising during the fifteen-sixties and 'seventies: it turns up in at least nine manuscripts with which his name is connected, as well as in the published volumes of Bendlowes and 'Dalison'.[95] Dyer's report of the decision of *Dauncy v. Southwell* (1560) also has its counterpart in several Harper manuscripts,[96] but in this case there is corroborative evidence from another source. In Trinity 41 Elizabeth (1599) Lawrence Tanfield, an Inner Templar and reporter in his own right, is recorded as saying that:

Southwell et Dancy's Case . . . est brefement report per Dyer 184: mes il ad view un large report de cet case lou il fuit notablement largue et adjudge comme devant.[97]

[91] There is in Harg. 10 at f. 39, following the report of *Cranmer's Case*, a note: 'Vide contra en mon reporte f. 7 et 55b'; this does not seem to refer to the same volume and may relate to a separate collection.

[92] B.M. Harg. MS 356, f. 67; the reference was to *Barber's Case*, 18 Eliz.

[93] The same case was also reported by Justice Francis Rhodes; Croke Eliz., 399 and Harg. MS 7, vol. 1, f. 17*v*.

[94] Dyer, 184a, 222a, 264b, 272a; cf. Harg. 4, ff. 159, 186*v*; Harg. 8, ff. 132, 147*v*.

[95] See Appendix III, p. 320.

[96] Reported most fully in Harg. 4, ff. 159–61*v*, and Harg. 10, ff. 2–4.

[97] *Ewens v. Labram*, B.M. Harg. MS 7, vol. i, f. 193*v*; a later annotator has written the name of Harper in the margin.

Although Harper is not referred to by name, 'his' version of the case runs to six pages and includes arguments by both counsel and judges. It is more than likely that Treby had access to one of the sets of notes attributed to Harper and presumably still in circulation. His work was cited by other seventeenth-century reporters as well. Palmer refers to one of several entries found in the Harper manuscripts relating to copyholders,[98] while Keble alludes to two cases purportedly decided in 1566 and 1576 respectively.[99]

This series of citations constitutes *prima facie* evidence that a Justice Harper was collecting or reporting cases during the middle years of Elizabeth's reign and probably earlier. And notwithstanding the casual system of attribution then prevalent, there must surely have been some basis for the attachment of his name to so many manuscripts. On these grounds the jurist concerned and his career merit examination.

Richard Harper has been denied even the scant attention accorded to Dalison in the *Dictionary of National Biography*. His date of birth is unknown and his parentage uncertain, although he was probably the son of Henry Harper of Rushall, Staffordshire.[100] He did not attend either of the universities but went directly into the study of law. His name appears on the register of Barnard's Inn, one of the houses of Chancery affiliated with the Inner Temple,[101] and it was to the latter institution that he proceeded in November 1537 under the sponsorship of John Porte, a justice of the King's Bench.[102] In the course of the next twenty years he executed the duties and assumed the offices expected of one who intended to make the law his career: he collected dues, organized dinners, audited accounts and attended upon readers. He became in due course (1552) a bencher and in 1554 was nominated Autumn Reader.[103]

98 Palmer's *Reports*, 416; but see Wallace, p. 254.

99 1 Keble, 341; 2 Keble, 328; see Wallace, p. 315.

100 It is not certain whether Henry was his father or grand-father; Thomas Wotton, *The Baronetage of England* (1771), i, 256; will of Margaret Harper of Rushall, Staffs., P.C.C. 21 Holdar.

101 Pugh, p. 207; Foss, v. 496–7.

102 *Cal. I.T. Recs.* i, 117.

103 Ibid. i, 120, 168, 172–4, 177, 182, 199.

Beyond the confines of the Temple and Westminster Harper began building himself a practice. Like Dalison he concentrated on his home area. He represented the executors of John Porter of Derbyshire when the Council was investigating arrears of rent within the survey of Augmentations.[104] Another of his clients was Sir Henry Vernon of Haddon Hall, a substantial landowner with connections in both Derbyshire and Staffordshire. Harper was appointed an executor of his estate and was to assist in adjudicating two of the numerous law-suits which arose among Vernon's heirs after his death in 1569.[105] As a junior barrister he probably gained experience in pleading by arguing cases before the justices of assize of the west Midland circuit. He also sat on the usual array of inquisitions post mortem, and during his years as an apprentice-at-law he was frequently included on commissions of gaol delivery for Oxford.[106]

One of the more intriguing facets of Harper's career was his association with the affairs of the Palatinate of Chester, where he seems to have resided for a time.[107] He may also have had personal connections there; John Porte, his early sponsor, was a native of the city.[108] He himself was made a freeman in 1555 and an alderman three years later.[109] It was fitting, therefore, that he should have been on a commission in 1568–9 which investigated the rights and privileges of the county palatine against 'forrayne officers' of the realm.[110] These liberties, particularly the maintenance of

[104] *L. & P. Hen. VIII*, xxi, no. 1280.

[105] C.J. Black, 'The Administration and Parliamentary Representation of Nottinghamshire and Derbyshire', unpublished Ph.D. thesis (London, 1965), p. 461; see list of leading cases, Appendix III, pp. 324, 325.

[106] *C.P.R.* 1557–8, pp. 365, 452–3; he may also have been the Richard Harper who offered to protect the interests of Sir Thomas Barrington of Hatfield Regis, Essex, sometime in the 'forties or 'fifties; *H.M.C. Seventh Rep. App.*, p. 538.

[107] On the Pardon Roll, 1 Eliz. (15 Jan. 1559), he is described as 'Richard Harpur *alias* Harpar late of the Inner Temple, London, *alias* late of Sayncte Jones, co. Chester, *alias* of Chester, alderman'; *C.P.R.* 1558–60, p. 191.

[108] *Cal. I.T. Recs.* i, 117; Foss, v, 228; Black, p. 415.

[109] *The Rolls of the Freemen of the City of Chester*, *Rec. Soc.* li, pt. I, pp. xi, 30.

[110] *C.P.R.* 1566–9, 441; *C.S.P. Dom.* Add. 1566–9, 73–4. cf. B.M. Harl. MS 2077, ff. 65–5*v*, for Dyer's opinion on the privileges of the County Palatine; see

autonomous courts, were, it seems, frequently challenged by disgruntled litigants. It was not until 1574 that Harper, now a judge, and two other aldermen, Robert Snagge and Randle Leech, after appearing before the Court of Chancery, were able to re-establish the city's status. The old charter was accordingly surrendered and a new one issued which confirmed those privileges conferred initially in 1506.[111]

Whatever his clients or associations, Harper was first and foremost a barrister and presumably earned his call to become serjeant in 1558 by pleading before the courts at Westminster. His writ was one of twelve issued by Mary in October 1558. Elizabeth succeeded before their return and when she reissued them three names were dropped, notably that of Edmund Plowden. Apparently Harper was acceptable to both regimes.[112] He was soon commissioned as a justice of assize. From 1559 until his promotion to the bench in 1567 he toured the counties of the south and west in company with Richard Weston who had been created serjeant and raised to the bench in 1559.[113] As was customary Harper was also appointed to commissions of the peace in the counties he visited on circuit.[114]

His elevation to the Common Bench came in succession to Anthony Browne who died in 1567; he also assumed Browne's circuit in the North in company with Serjeant Christopher Wray.[115] In addition to discharging the normal duties of his office, he was from time to time empowered to hear appeals in error from the city courts of London.[116] A further recognition of his ability came in 1571 when he was named Chief Justice of

also *H.M.C. De L'Isle*, i, 344–5; Penry Williams, *The Council in the Marches of Wales under Elizabeth I* (1958), pp. 198–9.

111 M. Weinbaum, *Borough Charters* (1943), pp. xxxiv–xxxv, 10–11; *Chester Poll Books and Election Pamphlets 1747–1827*, ii, Appendix, p. 8.

112 *C.P.R.* 1557–8, p. 457; 1558–60, p. 65.

113 Ibid. 1558–60, pp. 18, 59, 104; 1560–3, 1563–6, *passim*; Foss, v, 543–4.

114 *C.P.R.* 1560–3, pp. 435–6; 1563–6, pp. 20, 27–8, 105.

115 The patent of Harper's appointment has not survived but Plowden notes his succession to Browne; Plow. 356.

116 *C.P.R.* 1566–9, pp. 130, 347–8; 1569–72, pp. 431, 434; discussed below, Chap. V, p. 175.

the Duchy of Lancaster.[117] Like other members of the bar who had 'made good', Harper moved to establish his place in the ranks of the landed gentry: in 1566 he acquired the manor of Repington in Derbyshire.[118] His tenure as justice lasted ten years: the last professional reference to him occurs in Trinity term 1576. In the following autumn the courts were adjourned because of plague. It may be that Harper fell victim to the pestilence, for he died in January 1577, when probably in his early sixties.[119]

At both bar and bench Harper was clearly learned and fluent; his arguments figure prominently in the reports of Plowden, Dyer and Bendlowes, as well as in numerous manuscript collections including those attributed to himself.[120] He knew his law and had the ability to cite previous decisions which were both relevant and accurate, a quality which would make him an ideal reporter. His argument on the subject of uses in *Brent's Case* was not only a model of clarity but comes nearer to historical truth than any other contemporary speculations on the subject.[121] At the same time there is a hint of stubbornness in his work on the bench; on a number of occasions Dyer and Plowden record his spirited dissents when outvoted by his colleagues.[122]

If Richard Harper was the author of the reports with which he is credited there is no indication of the fact in his will. He makes no reference to manuscripts although he did bequeath his law books at Serjeants' Inn to his son Richard.[123] This in itself is not unusual since reference to manuscript reports in the wills of lawyers is very rare.[124] Whatever cases he may have collected were soon dispersed far and wide and it poses a difficult task to disentangle his original work from later accretions. It is the great

[117] Somerville, i, 471. [118] *C.P.R.* 1563–6, p. 417.

[119] Dyer, 351b, 353b; Plow. 498; *A.P.C.* 1575–7, p. 230; according to the inscription on his tomb at Swarkeston, Derbyshire, Harper died on 19 January.

[120] Especially Plow. 414 and Bendl. 212, the latter a rare instance of Bendlowes' naming a pleader other than himself.

[121] Reported in 2 Leon. 16–17; *H.E.L.* iv, 450, n. 1.

[122] Dyer, 279a, 317a, 317b; Plow. 411–14; Harper, like many judges, was involved in law-suits of his own; see I.T. Petyt MS 511, vol. 13, f. 43*v*.

[123] P.C.C. 9 Doughty.

[124] For the example of Dyer see below, Chap. V, pp. 158–9.

discrepancies among the thirty or more manuscript reports attributable to Harper which mark them off from those of William Bendlowes. Whereas these latter retain a fairly close similarity with one another even where abridged, the 'Harper' manuscripts are often carelessly copied, diluted with foreign cases or submerged in an entirely different collection. Their chronology and the order of their entries within a given term vary widely from one volume to the next. It is virtually impossible to arrange these disparate compilations into meaningful groups; the only realistic approach is to determine which cases appear regularly among them and then, and on the basis of these, to try to assess both Harper's claim and his merits as a reporter.

To begin with, it is necessary to establish the chronological limits of the reports and to relate these to Harper's professional career. There are fourteen volumes to be found devoted exclusively to cases which he is supposed to have reported.[125] Several of these, including Hargrave MSS 6 and 8, run from Michaelmas 38 Henry VIII to Trinity 27 Elizabeth (1546–1585), a fact which prompts the immediate objection that many of the entries concerned are from cases decided after Harper's death in 1577. This need not invalidate his authorship of the remainder any more than it does the work of Dalison. The late Miss I.D. Thornley, in preparing a commentary on one such compilation in Lincoln's Inn Library, concluded that 'they could not be the reports of Harper who became a judge in 1567 and died in 1577':[126] her verdict was based, apparently, on the erroneous assumption that 'Justice Harper's Reports' could only mean decisions taken while he was on the bench. Apart from the final ten years, the period in question accords well with Harper's professional career; moreover, it appears that Miss Thornley failed to notice that the copyist of this particular manuscript wrote after the final entry for 1576, 'finis reports Justice Harper & vita'.[127] In

[125] See list above, pp. 123–4.

[126] L.I. Misc. MS 791, ff. 1–14; Miss Thornley's remarks are found in a typescript report annexed to the manuscript.

[127] Ibid. f. 12*v*.

fact, some of the autonomous collections do terminate at Michaelmas 18 & 19 Elizabeth (1576)—the last term in which he could have officiated.

Having reduced the possible scope of Harper's work to the thirty-year period when he was at the bar and on the bench, we must clear away certain anomalies. A number of versions include sizeable sections labelled as cases from the King's Bench (although some of the decisions in fact emanate from the Common Pleas or were argued extra-judicially).[128] Nevertheless, for the years 1572 and 1573 there are reports originating in the King's Bench when Harper was already a judge in the Common Pleas: whether these were borrowed by him from a colleague's case-book or added later by another practitioner or enterprising scrivener cannot be determined.[129] By contrast, other collections do not extend beyond 1567, while a few contain a gap of three years between Easter 10 and Michaelmas 13 & 14 Elizabeth (1568–71).[130] The extracts printed by Thomas Ashe (1609) only run to 1564, while Rowe's edition of 1689 goes no further than 1574. The majority of manuscripts, however, contain an important series of reports for the years 1571 to 1576 which emanate for the most part from the Court of Common Pleas and are consistent in terms of style and method with those of the earlier terms.

In theory it is possible, and in view of the evidence it is likely, that most of the material collected between 1547 and 1576 can be ascribed to Harper. Yet in this regard one further cluster of cases merits attention. On average the number of entries per term in most versions is about fifteen. Yet five collections yield the exceptionally high figure of 106 cases for a single term, Michaelmas 4 & 5 Philip & Mary (1557); the total for the entire regnal year

[128] Particularly B.M. Harg. MSS 6 & 8, C.U.L. MS Ll.3.14 and L.I. Misc. MS 791.

[129] Two MS volumes, B.M. Harg. 8 and C.U.L. Ll.3.14, are almost identical and appear so similar in handwriting as probably to have been prepared by the same scrivener.

[130] See list above, pp. 123–6.

(1557–8) is 205.[131] This contrasts sharply with the two entries for the same period found in the majority of full-fledged compilations associated with Harper.[132] The comparable section in Dyer contains thirty-eight reports, while Bendlowes and Dalison each have twenty-four.[133] Does this large bloc represent the output of another reporter or even that of several? The dates suggest the possibility of Dalison, but there is no connection whatever between the entries in Lambarde's transcription and those under examination. Why should Harper, or any other practitioner for that matter, have been prompted to record litigation on such a scale in a particular year? In the absence of further evidence no authoritative answer can be given.

This last year of Mary's tragic reign produced upheavals in the legal profession. Six changes occurred among the personnel on the bench, including the appointment of a new Chief Justice of the Common Pleas and a Chief Baron of the Exchequer. Only in the year previously Edward Saunders had assumed the same position in the King's Bench.[134] The number of serjeants had plummeted as a result of death or promotion from a total of sixteen in 1556 to one in 1558. Yet the latter year also seems to have been an extremely busy one for the barristers in both the King's Bench and Common Pleas. Despite the adverse affects wrought by recurrent bouts of plague and influenza the amount of litigation had risen since 1529 and was to reach an all-time high in the year 1558.[135] During the period encompassed by Michaelmas and Trinity 4 & 5 Philip & Mary (1557–8) Harper does not himself appear as a pleader. This is only to be expected since the reports concerned emanate exclusively from the Court of Common Pleas and his call to the coif did not come until late in October,

[131] B.M. Harg. MS 4; Harl. MS 1624; Bodl. Rawl. MS C.112; C.U.L. MS Gg. 2.5; L.I. Mayn. MS 86.

[132] For instance, B.M. Harg. MS 8, f. 14.

[133] Dyer, 150b–64b; Bendl. 57–74; B.M. Harl. MS 5141, ff. 39*v*–45.

[134] *C.P.R.* 1555–7, p. 363; 1557–8, pp. 60, 459; Foss, v, 338–47.

[135] According to figures compiled by Dr Blatcher the amount of business in the three common law courts more than doubled between 1529 and 1558, despite the intrusion of five periods of plague and the influenza outbreaks of 1557 and 1558; see above, pp. 73–6.

a month before Mary's death. Therefore it may well be that in anticipation of his promotion he spent much of his time in this court taking notes and familiarizing himself with the techniques of pleading.[136] The resulting reports closely resemble in style those attributed to Harper for the years 1546–52 and 1559–76.

On the assumption that Harper was the reporter in question, it becomes clear, when his work is segregated from that of Dalison, just how different were their methods. While both intersperse short notes of judgments with fuller reports of leading decisions, Harper does so on a far larger scale and restricts himself almost exclusively to rulings in open court. Apart from occasional Exchequer Chamber cases there are few references to Serjeants' Inn, which occupied so much of Dalison's attention.[137] Because of their thirty-year span the variety of both pleadings and pleaders is much wider in Harper than in Dalison. As a guide to the development of the law he also has more to offer the historian. Despite the brevity of many of his entries, Harper's attention to sophisticated argument is reminiscent on occasion both of the Yearbooks and of Plowden. In terms of subject-matter he follows the well-trodden path of land law, and unlike his 'partner' rarely strays into the field of criminal law. To judge from the number of times his opinions are quoted, the jurist who most influenced Harper was James Dyer.[138] This is evident even before Harper went to the bench; but how much it affected his mode of reporting is difficult to say although their style is similar.

Harper's tenure as judge came at a time when a number of notable suits were adjudicated. He was in distinguished company. Besides Dyer, the Chief Justice, he shared duties with Robert Mounson of Lincoln's Inn and Roger Manwood, later Chief Baron of the Exchequer, both of whom may have done some

[136] From information brought to the writer's attention by Prof. S.T. Bindoff, it may have been customary for aspiring serjeants to cease active practice for a time in order to prepare themselves; this was certainly the aim of Humphrey Mosley of the Middle Temple in 1554, although in fact he was never called; Thynne Papers, ii, 194–94*v* (Longleat).

[137] See below, Chap. V, pp. 180–1; B.M. Lansd. MS 1077, f. 26*v*.

[138] This is particularly noticeable between 1546 and 1566.

reporting of their own.[139] It was in their company that the leading decision, *Winter's Case* (1572), was formulated.[140] This is one of the longest single reports yet found in manuscript for the sixteenth century and is comparable with the printed giants prepared by Coke. It was argued in 1572–3, when Harper's authorship is less certain than ever, although in the most elaborate version his name has been appended to the margin.[141] The case demonstrates most strikingly the variation in approach between individual reporters. Dyer covers the salient features of the dispute—reversion of a leasehold under statute 32 Henry VIII, chapter 34—in two pages, Harper takes forty-two. The difference is that Dyer gives scant attention to the arguments of colleagues at bar or bench whereas Harper reproduces at great length the speeches of nine barristers and judges, including two by Manwood.[142] Because of the complexity of the case Dyer's talent for distilling the issues may have been more appreciated than Harper's energy. Similar comparisons could be made with such decisions as *Bracebridge's Case* (1573), *Vernon v. Vernon* (1572) and *Brent's Case* (1575),[143] all debated while Harper sat on the bench. Yet it should be remembered that this was precisely the style adopted by Coke for almost all his reports; in view of his known passion for legal manuscripts it would be surprising if he had not possessed a copy of this volume.[144] At the same time 'Harper' was manifestly capable of digesting a wide range of subjects and producing valuable summaries of the law involved. From the number of copies that survive it is clear that his work was widely used, if not justly recognized.

To repeat: did Richard Harper, judge of the Court of Common Pleas from 1567 to 1576, prepare the reports to which his name is attached? The evidence, although circumstantial, does suggest that he was directly involved in compiling most of the cases attributed to him between 1546 and 1576. Notwithstanding the

139 See below, pp. 143–5. 140 E. 14 & M. 14 & 15 Eliz., Dyer, 308b.

141 B.M. Lansd. MS 1072, f. 69. 142 Ibid. ff. 69, 80.

143 Dyer, 252a, 339b; I.T. Petyt MS 511, vol. 13, f. 58; B.M. Harg. MS 10, ff. 40*v*, 47; Harg. 8, f. 215; 1 Co. Rep. Pref.; see Appendix III, pp. 324–5, 327.

144 If he did, he was apparently unaware of its origin.

errors and accretions wrought by three generations of scriveners and practitioners, there is still to be found a solid core of material which could only have been produced in the first instance by a jurist in Harper's position. In default of a stronger candidate his claim merits recognition.

A further question remains to be answered: how did Dalison and Harper, authors of distinctly different types of reports, come to be joined? The process was evidently a *fait accompli* by the outset of James I's reign when Thomas Ashe prepared his *Promptuary* with its appendix containing cases from Bendlowes and 'Dalison': presumably he extracted these from a manuscript then in circulation which combined entries by both reporters. It must also have been such a composite collection that Rowe employed eighty years later when he put out his definitive edition. Two such manuscripts still exist, one in the library of Lincoln's Inn, the other at the British Museum.[145] Both were copied within the first half of the seventeenth century, the former actually bearing the date September 1633. Clearly they emanated from a common source although, as might be expected, they exhibit marked differences. The Lincoln's Inn version consists of ninety-eight folios, copied in a single, easily legible hand, of which thirty-six contain Dalison–Harper cases; in all, it contains 549 numbered entries extending from Michaelmas 38 Henry VIII to Trinity 6 Elizabeth (1547–64). As Rowe's printed volume runs to 16 Elizabeth, this version could not have served as the text of that work. But it may well have been a copy of the manuscript used by Ashe.[146] It is to be noted in passing that the volume includes no reference to Harper, but that at the top of the first folio one finds the inscription 'secundum Justice Dalison'.

The British Museum copy provides considerably more food for thought while at the same time clearing up some of the confused background to both sets of reports. It is a much larger collection, containing 519 folios and entries running from 1547 to 1599. Written in a clear, seventeenth-century hand, it is, like the other

[145] L.I. Hill MS, 123; B.M. Add. MS 24845.
[146] Ashe also terminates his extracts at 1564.

relevant collections, in law-French.[147] Taken as a whole the volume represents an intriguing cross-section of half-a-century's law-reporting. In addition to the Harper and Dalison material there are identifiable samples from the work of Dyer, Plowden and Coke, among others.[148] None of these is named in the text and their respective entries run into one another without discernible break while following roughly chronological lines. From marginal notations it appears that the owner recognized those collections then in print but not always their original source. The manuscript is a classic example of the sort so commonly in circulation throughout the seventeenth century.

The section of particular relevance to this study covers the first 114 leaves, from Michaelmas 38 Henry VIII to Michaelmas 15 & 16 Elizabeth. From a collation of the entries here with those in the printed edition of 1689 it becomes obvious that Rowe's version of 'Dalison's' *Reports* was taken from just such a manuscript. There are enough discrepancies in the text to accord with the lapse of time between the original fusion of the two collections and their eventual publication. In fact, the date of the initial Dalison–Harper version can be established with some degree of certainty as 1583–4. On folio 24*v*, at the conclusion of the cases for 1 Mary, the scrivener has added the date, 'Le vint iour del moyis de December 1583'. Two months later he had evidently reached the end of 6 Elizabeth in his work:

> Le fyn de le sixieme ann de la Royne Elizabeth le 21 ior del Februarie anno 20 (sic) le dit Royne 1583 [1584].[149]

Whoever prepared the original, or at least an early copy, of this joint effort probably appended these dates, and the seventeenth-century copyist followed suit. In other words, at a comparatively early date 'Dalison's Reports' had come into existence.

[147] The name of Henry Bradshaw appears at the bottom of f. 1; he may have been the member of Gray's Inn admitted in 1686; *G.I. Adm. Reg.* p. 337.

[148] Ff. 114*v*–17*v*, 122*v*–5, 165*v*.

[149] B.M. Add. MS 24845, f. 82*v*; at some stage a scribe must have copied 20 instead of 26 Eliz.

If such a dual collection was already circulating within the profession during the fifteen-eighties why did all the credit for it come to attach to Dalison alone? Richard Harper had died only a few years previously, yet there is no hint of his collaboration, let alone any recognition that he or anyone else collected the majority of the cases; Dalison, on the other hand, had been dead for twenty-five years. Such a lapse in the collective memory of the profession may appear irrational but is not difficult to understand. It may be presumed that Harper never prepared his notes for anyone's use but his own. Unlike Bendlowes he had probably neither the time nor the inclination to produce a fair copy, nor did he take the trouble to designate himself a reporter. It is possible that after his death his rough notes were loaned out, perhaps by his son, and hastily transcribed and circulated. While certain copyists might credit Harper with the authorship, others doubtless did not, and evidently it was the work of one of these which was combined by some resourceful lawyer or scribe with extracts of Dalison's work. That the name of the lesser contributor should have survived may be due to Lambarde's initiative in citing Dalison in the *Perambulation of Kent* and *Eirenarcha*, and in having in his possession an accurate copy of the original collection.[150] Whatever the reason, Dalison's name appears twice in the text of Additional MS 24845 within the formula 'Finis secundum Dalison Justice del Banke le Roy'.[151] It is also to be noted that William Dalison, Jr., died in 1581:[152] he had been bequeathed his father's 'bookes of the lawes', but whether this included manuscript cases cannot be determined since none is mentioned in an inventory of the judge's books dated 1584.[153] Could an unauthorized version have begun to circulate after the younger Dalison's death? The shortness of the interval between his death and the production of the joint

150 *Perambulation*, p. 398; *Eirenarcha* (1581), p. 466; Putnam, p. 111 n. 1.

151 These annotations, ff. 22, 35*v*, in fact follow the entries originally collected by Dalison; presumably the original copyist of the combined reports knew that Dalison only reported some of the cases but was unaware of the identity of the other reporter.

152 See P.C.C. 40 Darcy.

153 Kent County Record Office, Dalison MSS, Inventory, E.1. 1/2.

collection makes this a tempting hypothesis, but nothing more. Unfortunately, neither Dalison nor Harper possessed the eminence of Dyer or the prudence of Bendlowes; otherwise both might have received the credit which was their due.

There are only five sets of printed law reports which deal at first hand with litigation in the period between 1535 and 1580, those of Plowden, Dyer, Brooke, Bendlowes and 'Dalison'; and of these the two last-named were available to Tudor lawyers only in manuscript. It would be logical to assume that this meagre ration was supplemented by a wide array of case-collections and notebooks; yet on the strength of the material that has come down to us we must conclude that those lawyers who took it upon themselves to report current decisions were few in number, particularly in the years preceding Elizabeth's accession. Apart from the cases ascribed to Pollard and Spelman and those put together by Anthony Gell, which cover the period immediately following the Yearbooks, little remains.[154] Plucknett's claim that reporting as a professional activity was at a low ebb and barely survived until its renaissance under Elizabeth seems to be borne out.[155] The picture, however, is not so bleak as first appears; there is evidence, albeit fragmentary, that considerably more practitioners were collecting cases during the mid-century period than is generally supposed. But because many of these notebooks did not circulate or were not widely reproduced, their survival rate has been low; several of the authors concerned, it seems, did not live long enough to benefit from the renewal of interest in recent decisions which was to arise in the 'seventies. Certainly there was no lack either of able barristers or of business for them.

Typical of those whose work has not survived but who evidently was recognized as a law-reporter in his own day is John Whiddon (d. 1576). The only indication that he collected his own cases comes from an unprinted note of Dyer's, which states that Whiddon

[154] See above, Chap. II, pp. 50–8.
[155] Plucknett, 'Early English Legal Literature', pp. 111–13.

mira un report per luy mesme que auters ne remembre del opinion des iustices M. 3 & 4 Phil. et Mar . . .[156]

Around 1570, when this remark was made, Whiddon was a senior judge, having sat in the King's Bench since 1553.[157] The loss of what may have been an extensive set of notes is especially regrettable since that court has been inadequately reported during this middle period.

During much of the time that Whiddon sat as a judge, the King's Bench was presided over by Robert Catlin (d. 1574):[158] he had been appointed to replace Edward Saunders whom Elizabeth removed in 1558. Catlin also kept a note-book which must have had limited circulation in his lifetime, although no trace of it remains. Again, it is the meticulous pen of Dyer which records the fact. In the case of *Vernon v. Madder* (1571) the correct text of the statute Westminster II, chapter 3, is confirmed by reference to the 'librum scriptum' of Lord Catlin:[159] while this suggests a mere collection of statutes, in an earlier entry from Dyer's manuscript there is a citation of a case 'in libro Catlin'.[160] Such a mixture of assorted material is characteristic of much unprinted legal writing of the sixteenth century; many advocates preferred to maintain a single volume which could serve as a source of reports, pleadings and statutes, as well as giving definitions of terms, legal maxims and precedents of writs.[161]

An indiscriminate collection of this type has been found originating with John Birche (1515–81), who became third baron of the Exchequer in 1562.[162] Within the judicial hierarchy puisne barons of the Exchequer occupied a somewhat inferior position. Although trained lawyers, they were not necessarily serjeants and it was only in 1579 that they were granted formal equality of status with judges of the other two central tribunals.[163] Birche

[156] I.T. Petyt MS 511, vol. 13, f. 59.

[157] He remained on the bench until his death in 1575; Foss, v, 545–6.

[158] Robert should not be confused with his older kinsman Richard Catlin who had been created serjeant in 1552.

[159] Dyer, 298a. [160] B.M. Harg. MS 26, f. 167.

[161] *H.E.L.* v, 370–2. [162] Foss, v, 461–2.

[163] Plucknett, *Concise History*, pp. 170–1.

himself was probably the first puisne baron to have been a serjeant.[164] Since even less material is available for the Exchequer of Pleas at this period than for the King's Bench, Birche's notes are all the more valuable. They consist of ninety-five folio leaves and form part of a more general legal manuscript.[165] Only in the loosest sense could this collection be described as reports. Writing on random scraps of paper, including old letters addressed to himself, Birche jotted down references to Yearbooks, printed Abridgments, Plowden's *Commentaries* and various treatises. Arranged vaguely under subject headings, the material must have facilitated the author's frequent searches for relevant points of law when dispensing justice. Included among these jottings are citations of cases from 11 to 15 Elizabeth (1568–73): these citations evidently refer to another set of notes, which Birche described as 'mon bref reports' and which he kept in his 'petit livers',[166] but which are not found in the present volume and do not seem to have survived elsewhere.

The Chief Baron of the Exchequer was traditionally regarded as on a higher plane than his associates, rather than first among equals: even before 1579 he was chosen from the ranks of the serjeants or judges. Among the latter was Roger Manwood, who seems to have kept a set of reports during his tenure in the Common Pleas as well as when Chief Baron.[167] Neither the character nor the content of these cases is known since they could hardly be said to have circulated in the accepted sense. During the course of a suit in 1623 Serjeant Harvey vouched 'as authority a note which he said he had seen in Justice Manwood's study'.[168] Apart from illustrating the casual manner of citation which still persisted, this demonstrates how easily a man's notes could become public property. Manwood himself makes only one

[164] Foss doubts this, claiming that there were two John Birches; Foss, v, 461–2; the Admission Register, however, shows only the one John Birche admitted to Gray's Inn in 1537; *G.I. Adm. Reg.* p. 13.

[165] B.M. Harl. MS 785, ff. 104–98. [166] Ibid. f. 119.

[167] He was a justice of the Common Pleas 1572–9 and Chief Baron of the Exchequer 1579–93; Foss, v, 516–23; see also 3 Co. Rep. 26a.

[168] Winch's *Reports*, 153; noted by Wallace, p. 117.

vague reference to 'my booke', which may or may not have been a set of personal reports.[169]

Neither John Birche nor Roger Manwood could properly be described as 'law-reporters', despite the fact that they may have collected cases in one form or another. The same kind of ambiguity applies to a number of other practitioners at this time. It results from the close lines of communication which existed between senior members of the profession and which constituted a vital element in the judicial process. Plowden, the most diligent of note-takers, often relied 'sur credyble report de ceux que fueront present' when unable to attend a particular trial.[170] One of those named in this capacity was Edward Saunders, who began his career about the same time as John Whiddon. After taking the degree of serjeant in 1540 and enjoying his brief term as Chief Justice of the King's Bench, he settled comfortably for twenty years under Elizabeth as Chief Baron.[171] As fellow Catholics and members of the same Inn, Saunders and Plowden were close associates and personal friends,[172] and the *Commentaries* show Plowden making full use of the Chief Baron's position and expertise. Thus, in *Sir Thomas Wroth's Case* (1573), an Exchequer plea, Plowden submitted his report to Saunders, who 'corrected and reformed it with his own hand', and added a relevant decision from the Exchequer Chamber in support.[173] Interestingly enough, Dyer recorded the same case in his notebook, albeit somewhat perfunctorily, and in a different context: judgment, he added, was given for the plaintiff, 'by report of Saunders'. Dyer, too, made frequent use of his colleague's 'reports' and opinions, partly because they both had chambers in Serjeants' Inn, Fleet Street.[174]

[169] *A brief declaration . . . concerning private dwelling houses* (1636), p. 20; Popham records a case which he 'heard . . . reported by Manwood late Chief Baron of the Exchequer'; Poph. 48.

[170] For example, Plow. 342, 514.

[171] *M.T. Adm. Reg.* i, 12; Foss v, 537–9; certain corrections to Foss and the *D.N.B.* (xvii, 811) are made in the History of Parliament Trust biography of Saunders.

[172] See Saunders' will: P.C.C. 41 Carew (1576).

[173] Plow. 452 at p. 459.

[174] Dyer, 239a, 269a, 292b, 326a.

Another colleague of Dyer's who sat with him on the Common Bench for five years was Robert Mounson. His claim to consideration as a reporter rests on one entry found within a collection of leading decisions from Elizabeth's time.[175] The case in question is *Vernon v. Vernon*, which was argued over Michaelmas, Hilary and Easter terms, 1572–3. It has the distinction of having been reported in five different versions, four by participants and one by a student,[176] and thus affords a valuable study in various techniques as well as in the shift of emphasis from one version to another. Mounson's report is comparatively brief, about fifteen lines. Having stated the issue, which concerned a widow's right to life estate within the intent of statute 27 Henry VIII chapter 10, he went on to outline the argument on the defendant's demurrer in law.[177] Oddly enough he ignores the opinions of the judges—including himself—while concentrating on those of counsel, namely Serjeants Lovelace, Meade, Bendlowes, Gawdy and Jeffrey. If this isolated report is part of a larger collection no trace of such is evident: the bulk of the decisions in the manuscript concerned cannot be ascribed to any other lawyer.[178]

Evidence of a flimsier kind suggests that a number of other distinguished practitioners prepared 'reports' of one sort or another. Henry Calthorpe, a Recorder of London during the reign of James I, sought authority from the case of *Horn v. Fortesque* (1565) which, he asserted, was noted in Sir Anthony Browne's Reports, 7 Elizabeth.[179] If such a collection ever existed it has either been lost or absorbed in other volumes: but in view of the lapse of time between Browne's death in 1567 and Calthorpe's citation in 1627 the attribution itself must be treated cautiously. It is surprising that Plowden, a colleague and great admirer of

[175] B.M. Add. MS 35953, f. 29.

[176] Dyer, 317a; Bendl. 210; B.M. Harg. MS 10 (Harper), f. 47; Add. MS 35953 (Mounson), f. 29; 4 Co. Rep. 1a; see Appendix III, p. 324.

[177] The demurrer was taken upon plaintiff's replication and the ensuing argument involved various technical points of pleading.

[178] The volume consists primarily of cases from James I and is written in various hands of the early seventeenth century; cf. Plow. 522.

[179] Palmer's *Reports*, 459; noted by Wallace, p. 107 n. 1.

Browne's, did not make at least a passing reference to his work.[180] Indeed, belief in its existence may have arisen from a misunderstanding. As was observed with regard to the activities of Saunders, 'report' could denote merely the passing of useful information by word of mouth rather than the transmission of material from a written collection. Thus Dyer, on one occasion, in referring to 'the report of Baron Fortescue', was undoubtedly alluding to certain information conveyed to him verbally about an Exchequer decision.[181] Such informal relaying of information would naturally take place when members of the bench and bar met in or around the precincts of Westminster or conferred at the Inns. Dalison recalls such an occasion at Serjeants' Inn, Chancery Lane, where the same Anthony Browne 'reported' on the legal relationship between servant and master:[182] perhaps it was just such an episode as this which gave rise to the notion of his 'reports'.

The distinction between what is and what is not a report can be even more subtle than the examples above indicate. Consider, for instance, the status of Ranulph Cholmeley (c. 1515–63).[183] Called to the bar in 1543, he sat as one of the members for the City of London in eight successive parliaments; he received his call to the coif in 1558 and was appointed a justice of assize for the Southern circuit in 1559.[184] Cholmeley's principal contribution to the study of legal history is a unique set of Yearbooks which he bequeathed to Lincoln's Inn. He also left a number of manuscripts, but nothing survives in the way of personal reports.[185] Yet there is evidence that he compiled some sort of record of his work in the courts. Again, it is Dyer who supplies the clue: in his account of *Cranmer's Case* (1572) he cites a case

[180] Plow. 356, 376.

[181] Dyer, 54a; Lewis Fortescue sat as fourth baron of the Exchequer circa 1542–6.

[182] B.M. Harl. MS 5141, f. 41*v* (1558).

[183] Not to be confused with his kinsman and benefactor, Roger Cholmeley, Chief Justice of the King's Bench 1552–3.

[184] His career is traced in a biography for the History of Parliament Trust.

[185] A. W. Reed, *Early Tudor Drama* (1926), pp. 92–3; *Black Books of L.I.* i, 341.

from 1 Elizabeth adding that Cholmeley, late serjeant and Recorder of London, 'ad relinquish en son report' that the opinions of Catlin and Browne supported the issue at hand.[186] Presumably Cholmeley had prepared some notes on at least one case in 1559, but whether these were part of a series cannot be established: he may belong to the substantial number of Tudor lawyers whose literary remains have been lost.

When Cholmeley was appointed Recorder of London in 1554 he succeeded Robert Brooke, who became Chief Justice of the Common Pleas in the same year.[187] Brooke is best remembered for his *Graunde Abridgement* for which he compiled material until his death in 1558.[188] The work was published in 1573 by Richard Tottel, who enhanced its value by providing cross-references to it in his subsequent publications.[189] The new Abridgment was immediately accepted as the logical successor to Fitzherbert and apparently led to the latter's neglect.[190] Although the two volumes are similar in subject-matter and organization, Brooke endeavoured to prune away that material from Fitzherbert which had become out-dated; he summarized some of the longer cases or divided them into more manageable units. The result is a larger volume with more entries than Fitzherbert's Abridgment.[191] This increase is due in part to the inclusion of a useful series of cases from the last decade of Henry VIII and the reigns of Edward VI and Mary. In addition, Brooke widened his scope by abstracting a selection of readings together with material from *Doctor and Student*, the Books of Entries and the Old and New Natura Brevium. In effect, Brooke began where Fitzherbert left off by providing an epitome of the common law as it stood at mid-century.

[186] Dyer, 310a. [187] Foss, v, 359.

[188] His will is registered in P.C.C. 54 Noodes.

[189] There has been some question as to the date of Brooke; it has been suggested that the first edition came out in 1568 although no copies survive and no record of such a printing can be found; Cowley, pp. xlix–1; Putnam, p. 210; there is a reference to Brooke in a case from H. 1570 (Dyer, 287a), but this could have been inserted by the editors.

[190] See Fleetwood, *Annalium*, p. i. [191] Details are in Winfield, pp. 233–4.

Brooke merits recognition not merely as an abridger of cases but as a reporter in his own right. This must have occurred to Tottel who commissioned an Irish lawyer of Lincoln's Inn, Richard Bellewe, to publish the more recent entries from the Abridgment as a separate volume in 1578.[192] Evidently some practitioners had already tried to adapt Brooke in this manner for their own use by arranging certain cases in chronological order.[193] Elizabethan judges came to equate Brooke's material with that of the later Yearbooks. His reports, especially those containing judicial opinions from the fifteen-forties and 'fifties, were regarded with cautious respect. Dyer records instances where Brooke's dicta carried considerable weight, but he also notes cases where 'divers opinions' were against him.[194] Coke invariably cites decisions from the Abridgment rather than Bellewe's 'New Cases', yet on occasion he specifically characterizes Brooke's work as reports. Coke's wariness of abridgments in general, however, seems to have made him reluctant in accepting Brooke's dicta, and he cites numerous examples where such were held 'to be no law'.[195]

In terms of numbers, Brooke's later entries are insignificant when compared with the Abridgment as a whole. There are approximately 425 entries relating to the post-Yearbook period out of a total of 20,717, and a number of these are repeated several times under various headings.[196] Yet to a greater extent than Fitzherbert, Brooke probably reported many of his cases at first hand; they clearly have certain traits which are consistent

[192] Ibid. p. 234.

[193] B.M. Harg. MS 2 is composed of cases out of Brooke from Henry VIII, Edw. VI and Mary arranged chronologically; Harg. 5, ff. 107–10*v* contains a few entries from Brooke; the compiler of Bodl. Rawl. MS C.644 has attempted to break down various headings in both Brooke and Fitzherbert into subheadings, perhaps in accordance with the advice proferred by William Stanford; *H.E.L.* v, 376.

[194] Dyer, 309a, 311b, 317b, 319a, 322b; B.M. Lansd. MS 1084, ff. 58*v*–9.

[195] 1 Co. Rep. 103a; 3 Co. Rep. 39b; 5 Co. Rep. 13b, 59b; cf. Croke Eliz. 147.

[196] Winfield, pp. 233–4; Bellewe extracted 533 entries, but these include 34 taken from readings including that of Thomas Frowick.

with his later career. Among the many new titles he added to his Abridgment was that of 'London' which seems to reflect his background as member of parliament, common serjeant and, later, Recorder of the City.[197] Fitzherbert was not elevated to the bench until some seven years after the appearance of his great volume and it is evident that he extracted most of his material from reports already in circulation. Brooke, on the other hand, has inserted into his collection cases that were decided while he was presiding in the Common Pleas. A number of leading decisions reported independently by his contemporaries are noted at some length complete with the names of parties involved. Such disputes as *Throckmorton v. Tracy* (1555) and *Hyde v. Umpton* (1556) were resolved in the Common Pleas with his active assistance, a fact corroborated by Dyer, Plowden and Bendlowes as well as Brooke himself.[198] He also reports the *Serjeants' Case* of 1556 and certain extra-judicial conferences at Serjeants' Inns which quite clearly were the product of personal observation.[199] In the latter respect he was part of the movement away from the narrower approach of the Yearbooks towards the more flexible style of reporting being practised by the judges. This method, exemplified in Dalison's small collection, was to be fully exploited by Dyer in the reign of Elizabeth.

[197] The title contains 31 entries.

[198] Brooke, tit. 'Attornment', no. 61, 'Testament', no. 26; cf. Plow. 145; Dyer, 130a, 150b; Bendl. 49.

[199] Brooke, tit. 'Entre congeable', no. 139, 'Lease', no. 65, 'Mayntenance', no. 38, 'Challenge', no. 216, 'Corone', no. 220, 'Trials', no. 151.

CHAPTER V

James Dyer

AN attempt has been made to show that the reports of Bendlowes and Dalison, regardless of intrinsic merit, lost much of their value through posthumous and inaccurate publication. By way of contrast the more famous compilations of Dyer and Plowden represent the greatest achievement in sixteenth-century reporting. Much of the credit for this undoubtedly lay in prompt, accurate editing; at the same time few practitioners were so highly regarded by contemporaries. Dyer, in particular, had both luck and skill on his side. As an able and respected judge his dicta were eagerly recorded; having been appointed to the Bench relatively early in life he remained an influential jurist for thirty-five years, amassing in the process an unrivalled stock of legal knowledge. To some extent Dyer the judge guaranteed a market for anything he wrote; he 'made' his reports rather than the reverse. On the other hand, with a staggering array of official duties to occupy his time, it is a tribute to the man that he found the opportunity to collect as much material as he did. To a greater degree than either Harper's or Dalison's—not to mention Bendlowes'—Dyer's *Reports* are an admirable reflection of his office and ability.

James Dyer was the product of West Country gentry, a favoured breeding ground for successful advocates.[1] Born in 1512 at Roundhill, Somerset, he was the second son of Richard Dyer of Wincanton. He apparently spent some time at Oxford, probably at Broadgate Hall,[2] but like Bendlowes and many other lawyers of the period he never took a degree.[3] According to George Whetstone, Dyer's poet-biographer, writing two months

[1] Ives, 'Legal Profession', pp. 116–22.
[2] *D.N.B.* vi, 286; Vaillant, 'Life of Sir James Dyer', p. ii.
[3] D.*N.B.* vi, 287.

after his death, he had embarked on the study of law at Strand Inn.[4] Presumably he spent one or two years 'learning the elements' of the law before moving into the parent Inn sometime between 1530 and 1533—a date which can only be conjectured since the records of admission for this period were destroyed. It is known that he began pleading before the King's Bench in the spring of 1536 and had been recommended to Thomas Cromwell as a counsellor about this time.[5] Even this piecemeal evidence suggests considerable talent and an auspicious start for a junior practitioner not yet thirty years old.

From the testimony of his own writings, both printed and unprinted, as well as from the evidence of others' reports, there can be little doubt that by the latter part of Henry VIII's reign Dyer had 'arrived'; throughout the 'forties he was a frequent pleader in the courts at Westminster and by 1544 was already being designated 'apprentice-at-law'.[6] It is no surprise therefore that his call to the degree of serjeant came during Edward VI's reign when he was only forty years of age. As an advocate of undoubted ability and unobtrusive Protestant leanings he was a logical choice for the call of 1552.[7] Religion, however, seems to have played little part in the selection of the nine serjeants-elect; in addition to Dalison, Keilwey and Carrell, such Catholic lawyers as Robert Brooke and William Stanford were included. In what may have been a relatively recent practice, the newly-created serjeants pleaded 'their case' in Easter term 7 Edward VI (1553).[8] In his report of the proceedings Dyer, not unnaturally, gave major attention to his own arguments which analysed the

[4] Foss claims that it was New Inn, but since both hostels were Inns of Chancery under the aegis of the Middle Temple the point is of little importance. Whetstone, 'A remembraunce of . . . Sir James Dyer', *Frondes Caducae* (1816), p. 2; cf. *Cal. I.T. Recs.* i, 178; Foss, v, 480.

[5] Dyer, 34a; biography of Dyer prepared by the History of Parliament Trust.

[6] Dyer, 34a–8a; Lib. of Congress, Gell MS, f. 84.

[7] *C.P.R.* 1550–3, p. 355; he had also been considered for mastership of the Rolls; *D.N.B.* vi, 286.

[8] No cases are so designated in the Yearbooks of Henry VII and VIII.

subject of tithing as incorporated into the common law by the statute 32 Henry VIII, chapter 7.[9]

One custom of proven antiquity was that of each new serjeant's presenting a reading at his Inn. Dyer was appointed Autumn Reader for 1552[10] and delivered a series of lectures on the two Statutes of Wills, 1540 and 1542.[11] The purpose of readings at this time—like the law itself—was changing. While they remained an essential part of every student's course of instruction there was a growing tendency for readers to use the opportunity for impressing colleagues with their own erudition.[12] Again, the tradition of taking 'ancient' statutes as a text was declining. With the mass of legislation recently pushed through Parliament still in need of digestion, it is difficult to determine whether Dyer was trying to enhance his reputation or enlighten young barristers of his Inn on two key elements in the Henrician legal code. Although by no means the first to do so, Dyer was still something of an innovator in expounding recent acts.[13] The readings were eventually published—in a condensed form—probably on account of Dyer's great reputation with seventeenth-century practitioners.[14]

Promotion came quickly. In November 1552, having just completed his reading and been installed as serjeant, Dyer was given the further honour of being named King's Serjeant—the last rung on the professional ladder below a judgeship.[15] In February 1553 he was drafted directly into the ranks of Tudor administration when named second justice of the Duchy of Lancaster, and on 12 June, shortly before Edward's death, he became Chief Justice of the Duchy.[16] This may help to account for the small number of entries found in his reports for Easter and Trinity terms 1553: but a more likely explanation is to be found in his brief yet eminent

[9] *Dean and Chapter of Bristol v. Clerke,* Dyer, 83a–7b.

[10] *Cal. M.T. Recs.* i, 86.

[11] 32 Hen. VIII, chap. 1, 34 & 35 Hen. VIII, chap. 5.

[12] Thorne, *Readings and Moots*, p. xvii.

[13] B.M. Harg, MS 87 'Collection of readings on various statutes'; Thorne, *Readings and Moots*, p. xvii n. 1.

[14] *Three Learned Readings* (1648), pp. 1–67.

[15] *C.P.R.* 1550–3, p. 269.

[16] Somerville, i, 470, 473.

parliamentary career. Dyer had first been elected to the Commons as a burgess for Wells in 1542, probably under the patronage of John Mawdley who sat for the borough at least twice, the last occasion being in 1539.[17] Five years later (1547) Dyer turned from his own county to Cambridgeshire where he was returned as a knight of the shire in Edward VI's first parliament.[18] He was re-elected in March 1553 and chosen Speaker, a position frequently occupied by promising advocates.[19] The choice of Speaker was always a matter of importance but especially so in this parliament: as early as January Northumberland had been addressing himself to the matter in order that the person nominated 'might have secret warning thereof, as always it hath been used, because he may the better prepare himself towards his proposition'.[20] Dyer's selection for the office probably rested on three attributes: his reputation as a lawyer, his adherence to Protestantism, and—perhaps most significant—his lack of any political connection with the Somerset regime. The parliament may have been designated as an instrument of Northumberland's succession plan, although in the end it did nothing about this—or little else, for that matter. Dyer's own role has been left unrecorded: whether parliament's failure to produce any political decision was due to him is not known, but he was knighted sometime before 20 June 1553, presumably in recognition of his services as Speaker.[21]

With the accession of Mary any further plans for a political career must have been abandoned. While apparently retaining a

[17] Dyer's election to the parliament of 1542 has been brought to light by the History of Parliament Trust.

[18] It appears that Dyer settled in Cambridgeshire shortly after his marriage to Margaret Aborough, the widow of Thomas Elyot, and acquired possession of the latter's estates; Hist. Parl.

N.B.

[19] *Official Returns*, i, 375, 378; Dyer was one of 15 candidates known to have been recommended by the Privy Council; Strype, *Ecclesiastical Memorials*, II, ii, 65–6; A.F. Pollard, *Political History of England 1547–1603*, vi, 74–6.

[20] P.F. Tytler, *The Reigns of Edward VI and Mary* (1839), ii, 163; J.S. Roskell, *The Commons and their Speakers in English Parliaments 1376–1523* (1965), pp. 59–75.

[21] *Commons Journal*, i, 24, 26; Hist. Parl.

keen interest in the workings of government,[22] Dyer dedicated himself to the law. It was in this reign that he achieved real prominence in the profession. His patent as Queen's Serjeant was renewed and he continued to act as legal counsel to the Crown. This seems all the more fortunate in view of the fact that he had signed the letters patent and witnessed Edward VI's will by which it was intended to exclude Princess Mary's succession.[23] At this juncture he began making what was to be a yearly ritual until the end of his life, his circuit in the Midlands as a justice of assize.[24] But it was in London that he made his position clear as a supporter of vested authority through the minor part he played in the Throckmorton trial in the wake of Wyatt's uprising.[25]

Under Mary, Dyer was also appointed Recorder of Cambridge, at a time when this office was gaining considerable prestige.[26] In Trinity term 1557 the London Court of Hustings retained him to seek an opinion of the justices of the Common Bench concerning possession of a church cellar which was in dispute between the parson and the Mercers' Company;[27] this must have been fairly near to the date of his own elevation to the bench of the same court, namely, 8 May. A year later he was made a judge of the Queen's Bench 'during pleasure'; this was a temporary appointment to cover the illness of Francis Morgan while Dyer continued to hold his patent in the Common Pleas. With Morgan's death in the following August (1558) and William Rastell's elevation in his place, Dyer reverted to his former seat.[28] Judicial appointments under Mary (as opposed to the treatment meted out to certain incumbents) appear to do the regime credit. This

[22] Lloyd refers to a work ascribed to Dyer containing forty-six rules 'for the preservation of the Commonwealth'; *State Worthies*, p. 596.

[23] Foss, v, 481; cf. his notes on Montague and Cholmeley, ibid. 295, 311.

[24] I.T. Petyt MS 511, vol. 13, ff. 34–47.

[25] *State Trials*, i, 870 at p. 883; Vaillant, 'Life of Dyer', p. iii; opposition to the Marian regime as centred on Wyatt's rebellion (1554) and the Dudley conspiracy (1556) is examined by D.M. Loades, *Two Tudor Conspiracies* (1965).

[26] Vaillant, 'Life of Dyer', pp. iii–iv; the rise of this office is traced in Ives, 'Legal Profession', pp. 347–68.

[27] Plow. *Panel v. Moor*, 93; *C.P.R.* 1557–8, p. 453.

[28] Foss, v, 482; *C.P.R.* 1555–7, p. 363; 1557–8, pp. 244, 457.

is a tribute less to the Chancellors Gardiner and Heath than to the foresight of the new Chief Justices. Once the suspect Mountague and Cholmeley had been removed from their posts, promotion was invariably based on merit, notwithstanding a preference for such conservatives as Rastell, Brooke, Stanford, Saunders and Anthony Browne.[29]

Having achieved preferment with relative ease and speed Dyer set about consolidating his economic and social standing. In addition to the land he held in right of his wife, he purchased an estate in Great Stoughton in Huntingdonshire in the summer of 1558. A few years later he bought land in London for a town house. Unlike many of his colleagues he did not reside in one of the Serjeants' hostels during term time although he had chambers there.[30] If he prospered from his treatment under Mary, Dyer reached the apex of his career with the fall from grace of some of his colleagues under Elizabeth. No immediate changes were made when Elizabeth succeeded, probably because Mary died in the middle of Michaelmas term. During vacation before Hilary term, however, both Chief Justices—Edward Saunders and Anthony Browne—were removed. Saunders vacated the King's Bench for the less prestigious if more profitable position of Chief Baron, Browne was made a puisne judge of the Common Pleas, and Dyer moved up to take his place as Chief Justice.[31] He was to serve in this capacity for twenty-three years and the majority of his reported cases relate to this fruitful period.

Thanks to his own diligence in recording events in his life and to the testimony of contemporaries, including some who felt the full force of his judicial power, it is possible to sketch a portrait of Dyer the man and jurist. His personal honesty and scrupulousness are attested by Whetstone, who eulogizes Dyer's fair, if uncompromising, attitude towards litigants of every rank,[32]

[29] Burnet, ii, 398–9; Foss, v, 295, 311, 371; as to the fate of the unfortunate James Hales, see below, Chap. VI, pp. 224–6.

[30] *C.P.R.* 1557–8, p. 9; 1560–3, p. 403; Dyer, 313b; Hist. Parl.

[31] *C.P.R.* 1558–60, pp. 58, 59, 65; Foss, v, 482.

[32] *Remembraunce*, stanzas 10, 12; cf. *A.P.C.* 1578–80, p. 63.

while Coke refers to his 'great piety and sincerity, who from his heart abhorred all corruption and deceit'.[33] On becoming Chief Justice Dyer sought to root out corruption among officials in his court. A speech attributed to him on the 'manner of reforming the abuses of Common-Pleas' was printed in 1674: having more clerks than the other two common law tribunals meant, in Dyer's opinion, 'many times most faults, errors and misdoings'.[34] As might be expected, good intentions were not enough; in 1575 he noted in his case book 'that a quest of officers and atturnies and clarkes of the comen place was charged' for misdemeanors committed since the last pardon.[35] Yet if supervision of his officials was difficult there was a greater challenge in maintaining his right to appoint them. The Crown constantly tried to preempt the Chief Justice's prerogative of choosing certain key officers to the Common Bench. Since this was an important source of patronage and income, Dyer's concern was obviously self-interested. At the same time his legal mind was always at work and his reports contain a number of references to the subject. These include the case of *Skrogges v. Coleshill* (1559) involving his predecessor Anthony Browne,[36] and precedents from Henry VI and Henry VIII which confirmed that the office of chirographer was in the gift of the king.[37] He was himself involved in controversy with the Privy Council over the installation of various men, including John Hales, to the clerkship of the Hanaper, and Hales in turn clashed with Dyer on appointments to positions under the Keeper of the Seal of the Common Pleas.[38] There was also adverse comment when Dyer raised the fees of those offices in his gift.[39]

A judge should dispense justice, not patronage. During his long tenure Dyer seems to have made enemies, especially among

[33] 9 Co. Rep. 14b. [34] *Praxis Utriusque Banci* (1674), pp. 40, 43.

[35] I.T. Petyt MS 511, vol. 13, f. 65.

[36] Dyer, 175a; Hastings, p. 101; a version in English is found in B.M. Harg. MS 9, f. 16.

[37] Dyer, 176a; see Appendix III, p. 319.

[38] *A.P.C.* 1558–70, pp. 192, 196; *Kemp v. Hales* (1560), Dyer, 179b; Petyt MS 511, vol. 13, f. 66*v*.

[39] B.M. Lansd. MS 23, f. 162.

the gentry in the counties where his circuit took him. In June 1576 William Porter wrote to Cecil charging the Chief Justice with false judgment: significantly there was no imputation of dishonesty but simply the bearing of 'an olde grudge'—a not unfamiliar cry from losing parties in a lawsuit.[40] There is a well-documented encounter with some gentlemen of Warwickshire in the years 1574–9 which vividly portrays the friction which could result when the power of the central government was imposed upon justices of the peace and sheriffs.[41]

Dyer was probably not the easiest person to challenge in terms of either status or intellect. Reading between the lines of his *Reports* one finds hints that he did not suffer fools gladly. Even before becoming a judge he freqently 'quaered' the opinions of his seniors with greater readiness than most lawyers of his age. On a question of execution upon property he doubted the opinion of Justices Hales and Bromley 'because it was against the opinion of many in the Temple'.[42] When Sir John Baldwin made a lone dissent in a case of debt reported in Michaelmas term 1538, Dyer pointedly commented that neither he nor anyone else was able to understand his refutation.[43] Chief Justice Brooke, author of the Abridgment, was shown by Dyer to have adjudicated one important suit in a questionable fashion: Brooke, it seems, had prepared an argument on both sides, 'and if any one of his companions had been against the lease he would have argued for it . . .'[44]—an attitude hardly in keeping with the growing trend towards judicial consistency. Dyer was never one to hide his own light under a bushel and on occasion reveals some subtle piece of interpretation which the judges may have missed.[45]

As Chief Justice, Dyer did not hesitate to criticise humbler members of the profession when he saw fit. He was acknowledged as an authority on correct forms of pleading and the proper

[40] Ibid. f. 196.

[41] Petyt MS 511, vol. 13, ff. *66v–9v*; printed in part by Vaillant, pp. vii–xii; *A.P.C.* 1571–5, pp. 243, 277, 320.

[42] Dyer, 67b. [43] Ibid. 43a. [44] Ibid. 126b.

[45] For example, *Marshall v. Eure*, T. 29 Hen. VIII, ibid. 37b at p. 38a.

entry of judgments:[46] thus in recording a case of trespass in 1566 he remarks that judgment had to be stayed because the original writ had not been returned into the King's Bench—'And this by the negligence of Kyme the attorney'.[47] He could on occasion show glimpses of dry wit. In 1570 when one Blancharde, a solicitor, was committed to the Fleet for slandering Leicester and Cecil, Dyer opined that he spoke 'more for monie than malice'.[48]

Dyer's professional ability nevertheless commanded respect from his colleagues at bar and bench. He was a personal friend of Chancellor Thomas Bromley and in matters of law enforcement had the clear support of the Queen and Privy Council. His high rank, combined with his long experience in the courts, gave his pronouncements great weight. In the *Reports* he allots ample space to his own arguments, but case books covering the same period confirm that he frequently played a dominant role in fashioning decisions. This was especially true in those 'leading' cases through which the common law was being remoulded in the mid-sixteenth century.[49] It is worth noting in this respect that the conventions observed in courtroom argument had a certain influence. As in mooting at the Inns, advocates and judges in formal litigation argued according to seniority, the Chief Justice invariably putting his views last, thus precluding any reply from counsel.[50] Time did not weaken Dyer's reputation, rather the reverse, for later generations of lawyers regarded his dicta more as settled law than opinion. Coke for one constantly cited his arguments, while almost all the printed and manuscript reports of the first half of the seventeenth century refer to his judgments.

Dyer died in 1582 at the age of seventy. Only three years elapsed before a selection of his notes was printed by Tottel

[46] 9 Co. Rep. 14b. [47] Dyer, 256b.

[48] Petyt MS 511, vol. 13, f. 52*v*.

[49] See particularly *Stowell v. Zouch*, H. 11 Eliz, Plow. 358, 374; *Winter's Case*, H. 15 Eliz. Harg. MS 10. ff. 26–38; *Brent's Case*, H. 17 Eliz. Harg. MS 8, ff. 215–228; see Appendix III, pp. 323, 327.

[50] For an exception to this see Plow. 358, 374.

under the title of 'ascuns novel cases'.[51] Having no children of his own, Dyer bequeathed his law books, including those 'reports of myne owne hand wrytinge', to his nephew Richard Farwell: evidently he was more than usually aware of their value to his colleagues since only rarely did lawyers of that period specifically mention their own case books.[52] The choice of beneficiaries was a sound one. Farwell and another nephew, James Dyer, also a lawyer, found themselves in possession of a manuscript containing a mass of case reports, observations on friends, obituaries, notes of trials on circuit and various other matters related directly or indirectly to the common law. The prospective editors came under the same kind of pressure as was described by Plowden before 1571.[53] Members of the legal fraternity familiar with the late Chief Justice's forensic skill, and presumably aware of the notes he had compiled, pressed the executors for 'the view thereof'. Edmund Anderson, Dyer's successor as Chief Justice, had access to his notes prior to publication, but they do not seem to have circulated within the profession.[54]

The nephews, in consultation with 'other more exquisitely skilled, and of farre better judgment', selected what were considered cases of greatest profit to both students and advocates.[55] The finished product was clearly a commercial success and Farwell and Dyer supervised two further editions, one brought out by Tottel in 1592, the other by Thomas Wight in 1601.[56] All three editions were in the fairly readable law-French used initially by the author. A new version prepared in 1688 by Chief Justice Treby was also in French: it contains a large number of marginal references, presumably of value to the lawyers of his day, but less so to legal historians of the present. The last, and best, edition

[51] Beale, no. R.-481, p. 108.

[52] His testament is registered in P.C.C. 28 Tirwhite.

[53] See below, Chap. VI, pp. 206–7.

[54] Anderson compiled a notebook of cases reported by Dyer from the years 1559–65; the writer is indebted to Prof. S. E. Thorne who owns the MS in question; see Appendix I, p. 276; cf. 1 And. 106.

[55] Preface 'to the Students of the Common Laws', p. ii.

[56] Beale, nos. R.-481–2; *S.T.C.* nos. 7388–90.

of Dyer's work was a three-volume version edited by John Vaillant of the Inner Temple and printed in 1794. Although his work is clogged with the accumulated citations of two centuries, Vaillant made a creditable English translation and included excerpts from manuscript cases hitherto unpublished.[57] In short, the *Reports* were rescued from the scriveners of the sixteenth century and unlicensed printers of the seventeenth. If Dyer's collection received fair treatment at the hand of the publishers, this was thoroughly deserved.

The success of Dyer's *Reports* was immediate and far-reaching. As a judge he had been highly respected, but for barristers of the succeeding hundred years and more his reports were indispensable. Until the seventeenth century the only private reports cited with regularity by pleaders were those of Plowden and Dyer, together with the 'New Cases' of Brooke.[58] A fairly comprehensive examination of existing manuscript notebooks, as well as printed reports, from the late sixteenth and early seventeenth centuries indicates that Dyer's work was second only to the Yearbooks as a source of authority. The editor of Croke's Reports, Sir Harbottle Grimston, looked upon Dyer as the real successor to the Yearbook reporters: 'If we have . . . failed in the number of persons reporting it hath been amply recompensed in the Grandure and Authority of one single Author, Sir James Dyer.'[59] Others qualified to give an opinion, however, were not as wholeheartedly taken with Dyer's methods. While acknowledging the debt which lawyers owed him, Francis Bacon regarded his work as 'but a kind of note book'.[60] Thomas Egerton doubted the value of any reports which the author wrote as he heard and which he filled out with numerous opinions and doubts;[61] and even Coke was disposed to point out omissions and

[57]. These were taken from I.T. Petyt MS 511, vol. 13, ff. 49–70*v*; in a report from 1586 Coke cites a case from Dyer 'now newly printed'; 9 Co. Rep. 12b.

[58] Brooke's *New Cases* were reprinted twice after their appearance in 1578; a second edition came out in 1587, a third in 1597; Beale, p. 287.

[59] Croke, Car. Pref. ii.

[60] Spedding, v. 86.

[61] Cited in *H.E.L.* v, 364–5 from John Hawarde, *Les Reportes del Cases in Camera Stallata* (1894), p. 127.

contradictions, although he considered the *Reports* as a whole contained 'summary and fruitful observations'.[62]

The burden of most contemporary criticism followed Bacon's dictum that 'great judges are unfit persons to be reporters, for they have either too little leisure or too much authority'.[63] Despite the fact that Bacon held a brief for the purported reestablishment of professional reporting, it is nevertheless true that Dyer was vulnerable on the first count, if not the second. His editors had anticipated just such a charge. They acknowledged that readers would not find the cases as 'fully argued and largely disputed as in other bookes and reports of law', admitting that, industrious as Dyer had been, the office of Chief Justice was so onerous that 'he wanted time and leisure' to rewrite cases with more extensive arguments. All the same, they believed that for the 'paineful and diligent student' there was much of value to be had from his work.[64]

It is possible that, like Bendlowes, Dyer had contemplated publishing his collection just as Plowden had done in 1571. The editors suggest in their preface that he intended revising his work.[65] There are, indeed, signs that he had begun by bringing some of the older cases up to date with the introduction of more recent precedents.[66] This runs contrary to Coke's assertion that Dyer never intended his work to be placed on public view, and it has long been held that none of the sixteenth-century reports after 1535 was designed for publication.[67] Yet in the light of the evidence this view needs to be qualified. Admittedly Dyer, when he began compiling notes in the fifteen-thirties, could not have foreseen the demand for fresh reports which arose in Elizabeth's time, but there is no reason why he should not have decided to meet this demand once it manifested itself, especially after seeing how quickly Plowden's *Commentaries* were accepted. As a close

[62] 2 Co. Rep. 79a; 3 Co. Rep. Pref. v. [63] Spedding, v, 86.

[64] Dyer, Pref. ii–iii. [65] Ibid.

[66] For example, Dyer, 59b, 72b, 92b, 96a; cf. 2 Leon. 19, where Dyer cited a case 'reported by himself'.

[67] *H.E.L.* v, 364–6; Wallace, pp. 9–11.

associate of both Bendlowes and Plowden, and no doubt aware of what happened to collections which went into unauthorized circulation, Dyer must have appreciated the wisdom of going into print as a means of protecting a valuable asset. Given his close proximity to the last of the Yearbooks, the role of successor might well have appealed to him.[68]

Dyer's printed reports contain approximately 1,120 entries. Although most are fairly short—less than a quarto page—a substantial number run to five or six pages. The latter are usually 'principal' cases over which Dyer presided or which he discussed with colleagues in the Exchequer Chamber. In their order as printed, the reports cover a period of sixty-eight years, from Easter 4 Henry VIII to Michaelmas 23 & 24 Elizabeth (1513–81). There are, indeed, entries extending back to the reign of Henry VII, but these were incorporated into the body of later cases—presumably as Dyer either read them or heard them cited in court:[69] some were abstracted from Keilwey's *Reports*, like the *Duke of Buckingham's Case* (1514) which is catalogued under the year 1570.[70] Two entries for 1527 were originally reported in the Yearbook for 19 Henry VIII. Dyer probably possessed his own manuscript of this since his version is fuller and more fluent than that of the printed editions. There are also six cases entered under Easter 4 and Michaelmas 6 Henry VIII which have not been traced: they could not, it appears, have been taken from the Yearbooks but were perhaps copied from Serjeant John Carrell's notebook, although none of them turns up in collections associated with Carrell.[71]

The stage at which Dyer began his own reporting is more problematical. The earliest possible date is Trinity term 1532, in which he notes another Exchequer Chamber case,[72] that is, about the time he took up studies at the Middle Temple; but the uncertain date of Dyer's admission, taken with the uncharacteristic

[68] Plowden was apparently thinking along the same lines; see the Preface to his *Commentaries*, p. iv.

[69] Dyer, 197b–8a, 285a–6b.

[70] Ibid. 285b, pl. 39; cf. Keil. 170.

[71] Simpson, 'Keilwey', pp. 89–105.

[72] *Rushden's Case*, Dyer, 4b.

wording of the entry, casts doubt upon its origin.[73] Next are half-a-dozen cases for the years 1533 and 1534 which could have been the jottings of a law student but may just as easily have come from an unprinted Yearbook which they strongly resemble.[74] It is only with Easter 1536, the year of Dyer's admission to the bar, that cases commence in a regular series. Here in all probability are first-hand reports. The entries take on a more personal flavour. While he does not himself argue—most of the actions were heard in the Common Pleas—Dyer 'quaeries' with authority the points put in argument by the serjeants and judges. The regnal year 28–29 Henry VIII was, in fact, one of the reporter's most productive, with a total of seventy-three cases.[75]

Some writers have assigned the beginning of Dyer's active reporting career to a later date. Thus Wallace contends that his own reports begin about 6 Edward VI (1552), a view which appears to be based on the belief that Dyer could only have compiled cases from the Common Pleas after his call to the coif.[76] Vaillant takes the more logical position that Dyer began collecting material as soon as he was called to the bar in 1536. Most convincing of all is the fact that Dyer refers to his own participation in certain suits as early as 1538:[77] since the latter were pleaded in the King's Bench the question of his call is irrelevant. This is also the period when the collection includes disputes taken from a variety of tribunals—Chancery, Exchequer, Augmentations, Wards and Liveries and even moots in the Temple[78]—the natural result of an apprentice's learning his craft. It is fairly certain that Dyer the reporter began his career in 1536, if not earlier.

From the reign of Edward VI to the end of 1580 the number of entries in each year remains more or less constant at between thirty-five and forty-five. Only in the spring of 1581 does the pace falter. There are seven cases for Easter term, four of which were

[73] The entry begins, 'the case . . . *was reported* as follows . . .'; ibid. 4b.
[74] There are printed Yearbooks for 26 but not for 25 Hen. VIII.
[75] Dyer, 6a–34b. [76] Wallace, p. 131.
[77] Dyer, 34a; Vaillant, 'Life of Dyer', p. ii n. b.
[78] Dyer, 24a, 30a, 30b, 31a, 45b.

special adjudications decided in conference with other judges and legal officers; Trinity contains four short decisions; and from Michaelmas, three or four months before Dyer's death, comes one final case.[79] Any observations on the number of entries in the published volume are bound to be suspect since the original manuscript or a complete copy of it no longer exists. There are, however, a number of volumes which contain fairly substantial extracts and supply a useful basis of comparison; these succeed, in part, in placing the printed version in proper perspective. Since the copyists tended to record those decisions not already published, they help to present a more reliable picture of Dyer's technique as well as to demonstrate the wide array of topics covered.

After being used for the first three editions, the original collection, like so much other material of this sort, fell into the hands of Edward Coke. This may have occurred about 1613–14 since Coke first refers to the manuscript as in his possession in the preface to Part X of his *Reports*.[80] No further references to it are found in subsequent volumes except once in the posthumous twelfth part,[81] but in the reports of a colleague of his Coke is quoted in 1615 as describing one of Dyer's books as 'a manuscript written with his own hand which I have, in which there are many cases not in the printed book'.[82] Throughout the *Institutes* Coke makes full use of this collection and emphasizes the fact that the cases cited were in Dyer's *propria manu*.[83] Other seventeenth-century lawyers had access to these notebooks or obtained copies of cases. Chief Justice Anderson introduces 'un note escry per Sir James Dyer' into his report of the Somerville treason trial;[84] there are seven folios in Hargrave MS 26 which appear to be a second- or third-hand copy of the original; and further short excerpts have been traced in three other volumes in the Hargrave

[79] Ibid. 376b–7b. [80] Printed in 1614; *S.T.C.* no. 5518.

[81] 12 Co. Rep. 43. [82] 3 Bulstrode, 49.

[83] For instance, Co. Litt. 13b, 58b, 148b; 2 Inst. 61, 657; 3 Inst. 24, 61, 126–7; 4 Inst. 160; Coke describes the collection in his catalogue as 'Foure bookes of the collection of cases by the lord Dier in folio whereof two are written with his owne proper hand'; *Catalogue*, p. 23.

[84] 1 And., 106.

Collection, two of which are based on copies made by Chief Justice Hyde from the original reports.[85]

The largest and most important surviving collection resides among the Petyt Manuscripts in the Inner Temple Library.[86] It was 'discovered' by Vaillant who refers to it in his Advertisement and inserts selections as lengthy footnotes in the edition of 1794. The cases in question cover only thirty-six folios but number approximately 360, thus consisting mainly of short, factual statements of law. The collection is divided into two sections: the first contains notes taken by Dyer during his twice-yearly circuit through the Midlands, and the second a selection referred to by the copyist as 'certeine cases of the Lord Diers collection which ... hee thought not fitt to make them vulgarr'.[87]

The 224 entries representing Dyer's thirty years as a justice of assize were largely ignored by the original editors.[88] This is not surprising since it was their purpose to present, as Plowden had done, significant issues of law as argued at Westminster Hall. For the student of legal history this is unfortunate since circuit cases rarely received attention from reporters. While the system itself has been adequately expounded by writers such as Holdsworth and Turner many details of procedure and subject-matter are lacking. Moreover, the importance of the assizes as a training ground for young barristers has yet to be explored.[89] Dyer's authorship of these particular reports is only tentatively acknowledged by the scribe who prepared the Petyt manuscript, but chronology and geography leave little doubt. The series begins in autumn 1553, shortly after Dyer's call as a serjeant which made him eligible for commissions of assize, and terminates in autumn

[85] B.M. Harg. MS 27, ff. 92–2*v*; 132, ff. 66*v*–7; 403, ff. 147*v*–53*v*.

[86] Petyt MS 511, vol. 13.

[87] There is another collection very similar to the Petyt MS; it is among the papers once the property of Harbottle Grimston; Herts. R.O. Gorhambury MS XII, A.6, ff. 1–26.

[88] The only exception is a series of entries entitled 'Cases in the Course of our Circuit last Lent', printed under 1 Mary; Dyer, 99a–100a.

[89] John Savile, a baron of the Exchequer (1598–1607), began pleading before Justices Wray and Harper on the Northern Circuit; 'Autobiography of Baron Savile', *Yorks. Arch. Jour.* xv (1900), 423.

1581. The counties through which he toured throughout this period remained those in the Midland circuit, and these are the ones specifically covered in the manuscript:[90] he was, in fact, the only person whose career satisfied these conditions.[91]

The remaining 136 entries are, for the most part, taken from cases argued in the Court of Common Pleas. They begin in the first year of Elizabeth and hence are exclusively the product of Dyer's tenure as Chief Justice. Most were neglected by Farwell and the younger Dyer when they edited the notes for publication. Some deal with problems referred to the court from criminal prosecutions in the counties; others were simply too brief for inclusion, even where concerned with notable trials.[92] A few relate to colleagues, their promotions, demotions and death. These represent a kind of running commentary on the great and small matters of interest which commanded the attention of an astute and conscientious magistrate. The language in both series is a seemingly confused mixture of French, English and Latin. In fact, each of these is employed for specific items. Law-French occupies its traditional role as the vehicle for the reporting of legal argument; Latin serves as the medium for formal statements not directly relating to litigation, such as passing references to fellow-judges and barristers and problems concerned with court officials; English quite appropriately serves as the vulgar means of expression in matters outside the confines of Westminster. The surprisingly frequent use of English by Dyer reinforces the impression that it was in the process of supplanting French as the principal language of common lawyers.

It has been suggested that Dyer also compiled an abridgment of some sort, which, it was believed, existed in manuscript. The notion may have originated with one Thomas Cole, an official of the Court of Wards, who prepared lists of deceased persons of

[90] *C.P.R.* 1563–6, p. 37; 1569–72, p. 215.

[91] He was accompanied for many years by Christopher Barham who only became serjeant in 1567.

[92] One such case is *Stowell v. Zouch*, H. 11 Eliz. (Petyt 511, vol. 13, f. 50), which Plowden reports at length; Plow. 353–76.

note with information about their property. Cole refers to Dyer's death in connection with his estate in London and adds that he made 'the abridgment of the lawe'.[93] Vaillant denies the existence of such a work,[94] and it is probable that Cole was either referring to a printed abridgment published by Wight in 1602[95] or misconstruing the bequest in Dyer's will of all his 'bookes of the lawe as well abridgements and reports of myne owne hand wrytinge': the abridgments in question were those printed by Fitzherbert and Brooke.[96]

There are grounds for accepting the claim that Dyer was a logical successor to the Yearbooks;[97] yet it might be more accurate to say that he bridged the gap between their disappearance in 1535 and the resumption of regular reporting after 1580. He was not, of course, the first 'private' collector of contemporary cases, nor the first to have his notes published. Yet in many respects his work is reminiscent of the Yearbooks, especially in the earlier sections: the emphasis on the Court of Common Pleas and the attempt to cover as many terms and years as possible are two obvious examples. At the same time it is not surprising that over the course of thirty-five years Dyer's methods of reporting changed: his maturing as an advocate and jurist was bound to show itself in his writing.

From the very first he appears to have been a thorough and conscientious student. Campbell relates how as a young barrister Dyer attended the courts every morning from seven to eleven with his notebook at the ready, copying in shorthand any arguments or decisions of value: upon returning to his chamber at the Middle Temple in the evening he would rework his jottings into coherent reports.[98] While Campbell fails (or is unable) to name the 'prose authority' on which he bases this little sketch, it is quite plausible inasmuch as it conforms to the regime of serious

93 B.M. Harl. MS 760, ff. 250*v*, 450; cf. Lloyd, p. 596.
94 'Life of Dyer', pp. xiv–xv; cf. Vaillant's remarks in Dyer, 238b.
95 *S.T.C.* nos. 7385, 7386.
96 P.C.C. 28 Tirwhite.
97 Pike, p. lxxviii.
98 J. Campbell, *Lives of the Chief Justices* (1849), i, 180.

law students of the time.[99] In an age when the canons of citation were as yet unformulated a training in sound note-taking could prove invaluable. On one occasion, just after being raised to the bench, Dyer was taxed by Serjeant Bendlowes with a case they had once pleaded together at the bar. In his judgment—as noted by another reporter—Dyer denied Bendlowes' interpretation of the outcome of that case: 'ieo bien remember lopinion del corte . . . car ieo comit un note de ceo al escripture'.[100]

Although it abounds in brief, summary reports which tend to stress perhaps one or two points, the section before 1547 is notably discursive in style, giving full play to the sometimes rambling arguments of the judges. While conversant with his craft and ready to find fault, Dyer was apparently not yet discriminating enough to display fully that brutal conciseness which marks his work under Elizabeth. When he began his studies the Common Bench was supreme among common law tribunals and the principal training-ground for aspiring barristers. It was in turn dominated by Anthony Fitzherbert, one of the greatest legal scholars of the day, who until his death in 1538 must have exerted a strong influence on Dyer.[101] The *Reports* from Easter 28 to Trinity 29 Henry VIII contain seventy-eight entries of which about half give prominence to Fitzherbert's arguments, and this despite the fact that Dyer himself was pleading many of his actions in the King's Bench.[102]

With his second burst of reporting, beginning in Michaelmas term 1552, Dyer as a newly-created serjeant concentrated on suits in the Common Pleas. During the remainder of Edward VI's reign and most of Mary's, his notes are concerned primarily with the intricacies of land law and recent Henrician legislation.[103] The style becomes more matter-of-fact. The arguments of colleagues are more relevant to the cause of action; rather than

[99] Fortescue, *De Laudibus*, pp. 21, 23, 117–21; Waterhous, *Fortescutus Illustratus*, pp. 539–46.

[100] Bodl. Rawl. MS C.112, f. 414.

[101] Putnam, pp. 32–3.

[102] Dyer, 6a–37a.

[103] In addition, there are a number of Exchequer Chamber decisions and problems referred from the circuits; ibid. 92a, 93a, 98a, 98b.

quote at length Dyer tends to summarize the heart of their contentions, always keeping the legal issues in view. Presumably, as an active pleader at the Common Bench he had less time at his disposal for taking notes, so that while he sought to cover the maximum range of problems, 'strictness and brevity' became the rule, lengthy reports the exception.

Finally, and most characteristic of Dyer's method, are the entries for the years 1557 to 1582 when as a judge he was helping to interpret the law as well as to record it. Henceforth, he often refers to himself in the third person as one of four justices on the bench, a bench which over the years included Richard Harper, Christopher Wray and Roger Manwood, all sound jurists and law reporters in their own right.[104] It was an era to which Coke looked back as 'furnished with men of excellent judgment, gravity and wisdom'.[105] As Chief Justice, Dyer recorded a total of 688 cases, precisely sixty per cent of the printed total: in addition there are the 136 entries collected in the Petyt manuscript. An essential feature of this combined group is variety. While the majority of causes emanated from the Common Pleas a sizeable proportion relates to other tribunals, as well as to various dialogues between judges and officials.[106] Unlike those of earlier sections, very few entries contain 'sudden sayings of the judges' or points raised and debated without decision.[107]

On average the length of individual reports is shorter in this period; there is a minimum of verbatim argument but a maximum of penetration into both procedural and substantive issues. Dyer's style has progressed to the point where, except for the really significant trials, individual arguments are subordinated to an assessment of the consensus on each side. Unlike Coke or Plowden, Dyer rarely introduces personal asides, though he does favour his own opinions. Much greater emphasis is given to the effect of statutes and new forms of action as well as to problems

[104] See above, Chap. IV, pp. 136–143 and Appendix II, pp. 306–09.
[105] Co. Litt. Pref. xxix.
[106] The subject of the decision-making process is discussed below, pp. 177–97.
[107] Roger North, *A Discourse on the Study of the Laws* (1824), p. 157.

resulting from the establishment of new courts,[108] but considerable space is still devoted to the traditional writs, debt, quare impedit, trespass, account, dower and wardship. On the other hand, few entries deal with the possessory assizes or the personal actions of detinue and replevin for which quicker remedies were being found.[109] A significant number of suits is concerned with offices—either the right to retain or dispose of them—and with the royal prerogative.[110]

Even at their most business-like the reports retain their essentially personal and informal character. It is possible to trace promotions in the author's career from entries in the book. Sometimes there is a simple statement of fact, such as Dyer's call to become serjeant, along with six of his confreres;[111] but when appointed judge of the Common Pleas in 1557 he appended to a memorandum of the occasion a copy of the letters patent.[112] His rise to prominence also involved certain problems; in Easter term 1558 he records that doubts were raised over his temporary transfer to the King's Bench,[113] and further difficulties are reported when he replaced Anthony Browne as Chief Justice.[114] Items of a similar nature were omitted from the published volume: these generally relate to the death of less vigorous colleagues and their replacement from the ranks below.[115] Occasionally, Dyer notes extraneous events such as Queen Elizabeth's ride into the city to bestow its new title on the Royal Exchange.[116] On the whole, however, he can be said to have strayed little from the narrow professional path of common law issues: his aim was to build up a stock of precedents for his daily work and perhaps ultimately as a guide to successors.

While many of his entries are brief, Dyer displays his skill as a

[108] Dyer, 50a, 178b, 240b, 242b.

[109] This subject is best discussed by Maitland, *The Forms of Action at Common Law*, pp. 61–72.

[110] Dyer, 167a, 195a, 213b, 225a, 285b, 328a, 335a.

[111] Ibid. 72a. [112] Ibid. 144a.

[113] Ibid. 158b; cf. Brooke, tit. 'Commissions', no. 25.

[114] Dyer, 173b. [115] I.T. Petyt MS 511, vol. 13, ff. 59*v*–60*v*.

[116] Ibid. f. 53.

reporter and legal scholar in the range of citations and sources. Many of these reflect what the profession as a whole studied and utilized. There were, first and foremost, the Yearbooks, which formed the staple of decided cases; the Abridgments, Statham, Fitzherbert and, later, Brooke;[117] and the two Books of Assizes, Pynson's and Rastell's, both of which were cited frequently.[118] Recourse to the standard medieval texts—Glanvil, Bracton, Fleta, Britton and Littleton—was supplemented by reference to more recent printed works, notably *Doctor and Student* and Stanford's *Plees of the Crown* and treatise on the prerogative.[119] Occasional references are also made to Fitzherbert's *Diversite des Courtes* and treatise on justices of the peace.[120] There was of course the old Register of Writs, but this was rapidly being supplanted by a work wrongly ascribed to Fitzherbert, the *Nouvel Natura Brevium*, which in turn was an improved version on the Old Natura Brevium.[121] Similarly, the profession was apparently supplementing the plea rolls with various Books of Entries of which Dyer cites three.[122] Unlike Bendlowes he rarely includes verbatim portions of the record in his reports, although he does sometimes base an entry on them.[123]

Supporting this orthodox selection of printed literature is an impressive array of manuscript material reported or cited by Dyer. Apart from his own notes, it seems likely that he had access

[117] Citations of Fitzherbert increase noticeably after publication of the second edition in 1565.

[118] *The Abridgment of the Book of Assizes* (1510) is an authentic abridgment, Rastell's *Book of Assizes* (1516) merely summarizes cases from the reign of Edw. III; Holdsworth, *Sources*, pp. 104–9.

[119] *Doctor and Student* consists of two dialogues written by Christopher St German and printed respectively in 1523 and 1530; Stanford's *Plees of the Crown* was published posthumously in 1560, the *Exposicion of the Kinge's Prerogative* in 1567; Beale, p. 304.

[120] Published in 1526 and 1538 respectively; Dyer 376a and Petyt 511, vol. 13, f. 35; Beale, pp. 290, 297.

[121] Fitzherbert's *Natura Brevium* was first printed in 1534.

[122] The earliest collection was put out by Pynson in 1510; its successor, the Old Book of Entries (1546), was published by Smythe; and the best collection, that of Rastell, came out in 1566; Dyer, 192b, 266b, 338b.

[123] For instance, ibid. 67a, 197a.

to certain manuscript Yearbooks as well as to the notes of Serjeant Carrell.[124] In 1572 he has recourse to 'Bendlowe's Reports' to confirm that a particular judgment was rendered, while, as already noted, numerous references to the notes of Dyer's colleagues are also found.[125] Unprinted sources were brought to bear when the text of a Yearbook report, statute, patent or other legal instrument was in dispute: thus the manuscript notes of Thomas Gargrave were examined to correct the holding in a case from 17 Edward III.[126] In an argument over the correct words of the Statute of Westminster II, chapter 3, the book of Chief Justice Catlin is cited,[127] and the repeal of another act of parliament, 15 Edward III, chapter 2 (trial of peers), is confirmed by reference to Rastell's collection of statutes 'en libro impresso in Frenche et in libro scripto'.[128] Still another statute (3 Henry VIII, chapter 2, on escheators) is interpreted in virtue of the text found in the book 'of Mr. Gyll, bound in black leather'.[129] Dyer also refers to material cited by his colleague Edward Saunders, who seems to have had access to an extremely valuable collection of legal notebooks.[130] From Saunders' unprinted reports comes a note by Dyer about the conviction of Perkin Warbeck; the source was two 'auncient livers' vouched for by Saunders and purportedly owned in turn by James Hobart and Edward Griffin, Attornies-General under Henry VII and Mary respectively.[131]

Some of these manuscript volumes were well-known and

[124] Ibid. 1a–4a, 41b, 174b, 197b–8a, 285a–6a.

[125] Ibid. 320a; see above, Chap. IV, pp. 141–7.

[126] Sir Thomas Gargrave (1495–1579): no evidence exists of his studying at one of the Inns but he was appointed to the Council of the North in 1539 and was Speaker of the House of Commons in 1559; in the *Common Journal*, i, 53, he is described as 'learned in the laws of this realm'; Dyer, 180b.

[127] Dyer, 298b; Catlin's book is discussed above, Chap. IV, p. 142.

[128] I.T. Petyt MS 511, vol. 13, f. 59.

[129] Dyer 170b; this probably refers to John Gyll, a colleague of the Middle Temple admitted in October 1555 to 'Clerks' Commons'; *Cal. M.T. Recs.* i, 102.

[130] It was Saunders who produced a case reported by Thomas Audley; see above, Chap. II, pp. 49–50.

[131] I.T. Petyt MS 511, vol. 13, f. 54*v*. Hobart held the office of King's Attorney between 1486 and 1507, Griffin from 1552 to 1558.

respected among the profession. One which was cited frequently in Dyer's *Reports* is a Book of Entries compiled by John Jenour, prothonotary of the Common Pleas, to whom reference was made earlier.[132] Others were simply specific pieces of information sought only when the occasion arose: thus Dyer reports that the form of fines established by the statute 4 Henry VII, chapter 24, did not commence for a further two years 'as appears by a search of the fines in the Treasury: ex relatione Bartlame'.[133] A problem concerning the probate and executors of a will was resolved by reference to the notes of Doctor Drury, a judge of the Prerogative Court of Canterbury.[134] From these examples and other evidence it is clear that the rules of citation and precedent in the modern sense were just developing. The principal aim was to ferret out relevant statements of law; opposing counsel might dispute 'whether it was law or no' but would rarely challenge the validity of the source.[135]

Dyer's duties as Chief Justice undoubtedly prevented him from preparing full and fluent reports in the manner of Plowden: it is thus difficult to gauge from a collection such as his the direction in which the common law on a particular subject was moving. Unlike either Coke or Plowden, Dyer seldom took (or perhaps had) the opportunity of 'stepping back' to comment on significant aspects of his craft. Nonetheless, statements produced by way of argument or report contributed to the reshaping process so evident in the sixteenth century. An early instance of this is *Core's Case* (1537), in which the justices of the King's Bench examined in detail the scope of the writs of debt and account.[136] Similarly, *Gilbert's Case* (1538) and *Culpeper v. Bushe* (1554) reviewed in depth the matter of tenures *in capite*,[137] and *Withers v. Isham* (1552) that of prescription.[138] Dyer himself analysed

[132] Dyer, 172a, 189b; see above, Chap. I, p. 21.

[133] Dyer, 256b; the spelling given is that found in the 1585 edition; both Treby (1688) and Vaillant (1794) have miscopied the name as 'Barthalme'; the person in question may have been John Bartlam admitted to the Middle Temple in November 1566 (*Cal. M.T. Recs.* i, 157) and perhaps a 'pupil' of Dyer's.

[134] Dyer, 372a. [135] Turner, p. xv.

[136] Dyer, 20a; *H.E.L.* v, 415. [137] Ibid. 44a, 100b. [138] Ibid. 70a.

current doctrine over a wide spectrum which included the capacity of minors to institute real actions,[139] rights and duties of testamentary executors,[140] pleading of fines,[141] the nature of reversions,[142] and the basis of consideration in the formulation of a binding contract.[143] Equally important are the appearances of new forms of action. Slander began its history in the common law courts as a regular remedy about 1535 and one of the earliest cases is found in Dyer;[144] the writ of trover as a distinct species of case is examined in the leading decision of *Lord Mounteagle v. Countess of Worcester* (1555);[145] and one of the first recorded reports of an action *de ejectione firmae* which included a lease executed for the express purpose of trying title is to be found under Michaelmas term 1580.[146]

If Dyer's office was, in some respects, a hindrance to effective note-taking, it had certain compensating advantages. Professional expertise apart, members of the bench were accorded privileges and granted responsibilities unavailable to their colleagues at the bar. This meant considerably more variety of experience within the vast range of the judicial process. Under the Tudor monarchy judges were employed to help draft legislation and, equally important, advise on its execution:[147] thus on the last day of Michaelmas term in 1563 the justices assembled by order of the Queen to consider how the voluminous legislation of 1563 might best be put into force.[148] Their counsel was also necessary in the operation of many of the new tribunals established under Henry VIII as well as of the Court of Chancery when matters relating to

[139] *Basset's Case* (1556), ibid. 133a.

[140] *Stokes v. Porter* (1559), ibid. 166b.

[141] *Fitzwilliams v. Copley* (1570), ibid. 290a.

[142] *Throckmorton v. Tracy* (1555), ibid. 124b; *Winter's Case* (1572), ibid. 308b.

[143] *Andrew v. Boughey* (1552), *Pecke v. Redman* (1555), *Calthorpe's Case* (1574), *Onely v. Earl of Kent* (1577), ibid. 75a, 113a, 334b, 355b.

[144] *Anon.* (1536), ibid. 19a; Plucknett, *Concise History*, p. 493.

[145] Dyer, 121a; Fifoot, pp. 103–4.

[146] *Gerrarde v. Worseley*, Dyer, 374a.

[147] K. Pickthorn, *Early Tudor Government, Henry VII* (1934), p. 52; Neale, *House of Commons*, pp. 372–3.

[148] Dyer, 236a.

the common law were discussed. The reports of Dyer and his contemporaries abound with examples of this kind of activity.[149]

On a somewhat less exalted level the judiciary was required to perform a wide range of duties which made justice more readily accessible. As of old, judges constituted the core of the circuit system, occupying senior positions and receiving the higher fees.[150] Closer to Westminster, they were commissioned to hear writs of error from cases tried in the courts of the city of London. From the numerous entries on the Patent Rolls this procedure was evidently much in demand. Since the time of Henry VIII such appeals were heard in the Guildhall rather than at St Martin-le-Grand.[151] Typical was a commission to Edward Saunders and Dyer in 1558 to hear an appeal in error in a suit between Thomas Panel and the Mercers' Company which had been instituted originally without the Queen's writ 'according to the custom of the city', before sheriffs and coroner.[152] The special nature and importance of these cases usually merited the appointment of one or both of the Chief Justices to decide them:[153] Dyer himself seldom reports them although he does include a number of items relating to the operation of custom within the city.[154]

The Privy Council seems to have directed an endless stream of disputes for settlement by the two Chief Justices, particularly in Dyer's last years. It is hardly surprising that so many appeals were made for such preferential hearing when the best legal minds in the realm were available. Thus when George Chaworth could no longer afford to continue his suit against Thomas Shipman the Council committed the affair to Dyer and Christo-

[149] Ibid. 260b, 313b, 372a; Plow. 72; B.M. Harl. MS 5141 (Dalison), 1, 10*v*, 19*v*; Harg. MS 8, f. 214; Lansd. MS 1084, f. 136.

[150] A list of Justices of Assize for the summer circuit, 1574, lists eight judges, three serjeants and the Attorney-General; B.M. Harg. MS 405.

[151] The procedure is outlined in *F.N.B.*, tit. 'Error in London', p. 49, see also 2 Leon. 107; a modern explanation is given by A. Pulling, *Laws and Customs of London* (1842), p. 173.

[152] *C.P.R.* 1557–8, p. 453; see above, p. 154.

[153] For example, *C.P.R.* 1563–6, pp. 34, 35.

[154] Dyer, 83a, 229a, 245b, 352b; Petyt MS 511, vol. 13, f. 49*v*.

pher Wray for settlement:[155] they were also called upon to adjudicate a controversy over the liberties of both the Blackfriars and Whitefriars between the Lord Mayor of London and the occupiers of the precincts in question.[156] Another dispute concerned the tenants of Blyborough, Lincolnshire, who sought justice against Henry Askew for enclosing certain of their commons.[157]

Senior legal and other officers were often retained to act as arbitrators over a wide range of public and private controversies. One such, between the Bishop of Ely and the City of London relating to the jurisdiction of Ely Place, was eventually committed to the determination of the Lord Keeper, the Earl of Leicester, Sir Walter Mildmay and the two Chief Justices.[158] 'A great question' on the surrender of a leasehold was submitted for resolution by four arbiters, the Chief Justices, Chief Baron and Anthony Browne.[159] The justices of assize for Huntingdon sought the advice of Dyer 'for their better assistance' in a complaint from the inhabitants of Warboys against Sir Henry Cromwell.[160] Not surprisingly, if powerful litigants asked for redress they generally received it: when the Privy Council was unable to decide rights to a manor between Lord Mountjoy and the Earl of Huntingdon, the dispute was handed over to Dyer and William Periam 'for conclusive decision'.[161] The scope of these adjudications seems unlimited, embracing such subjects as seizure of a felon's property, new customs in London and Norwich, fraudulent conveyances, private quarrels, and forfeiture of entailed land.[162] While Dyer's share of this out-of-court activity arose mainly from his office, some clearly sprang from his reputation as a learned jurist: in this respect he must have been almost the equal of Plowden, with whom he is known to have served as an arbitrator.[163]

155 *A.P.C.* 1577–8, pp. 59–60. 156 Ibid. 429.

157 Ibid. 1581–2, pp. 257–8. 158 Petyt MS 511, vol. 13, f. 51*v*.

159 Dyer, 200b. 160 *A.P.C.* 1575–7, p. 91.

161 *C.S.P. Dom.* 1581–90, p. 58.

162 *A.P.C.* 1578–80, pp. 6, 22, 129–30, 291–2, 359.

163 Dyer, 316a; Holdsworth, *Sources and Literature*, p. 94; cf. *Manxel's Case*, T. 6 Eliz. Plow. 1–15 (separate foliation).

While many of his entries suffer from their brevity and lack of fluency, in its range of subject-matter Dyer's must be regarded as the most useful collection of reports covering the mid-sixteenth century. As one who had access to virtually every branch of judicial organization, he has recorded practically all phases of the decision-making process and in doing so has provided posterity with an invaluable source of social as well as legal history. Of particular interest is the information to be gleaned from Dyer—as well as from his fellow reporters—with respect to judicial procedure as it operated beyond the confines of the common law courts. It is in this regard that the informal, ubiquitous nature of law-reporting proves most rewarding to the historian.

Some observations have already been made on the distinction between the official record and unofficial report of a case.[164] John Reeves, the eighteenth-century legal historian, characterized the difference in this manner:

> a record is a concise entry of all the real and effective steps made in a judicial proceeding, a report is a short note of the progress towards making those steps . . .[165]

Initially, the 'progress' referred to meant arguments advanced at the bar and examined by the bench, but various sixteenth-century reports also provide useful glimpses of the mechanics of decision. By 'mechanics' is meant not so much the logic of pleadings or clash of authorities as the context or forum within which disputes were ultimately resolved. Just as the steps recorded in the plea rolls tell only half the story of a lawsuit, so the report of its hearing in Westminster Hall often fails to explain how it was finally decided. One of the chief virtues of Dyer's reporting is that he takes his readers behind the scenes to where he and the more privileged of his confreres reached their conclusions.[166]

The most important 'unofficial' decision-making body was the Court of Exchequer Chamber. Throughout the later Yearbooks

[164] Above, Introduction, pp. 2–5.

[165] *A History of English Law* (1869), ii, 231.

[166] In many instances, of course, there was no final judgment to report; *H.E.L.* v, 369–70; Plow. 60.

and private reports of the sixteenth and seventeenth centuries 'chequer-chamber cases' are to be found in abundance. Yet this body was never a court of record, although in virtue of various acts of parliament it acquired a quasi-official status in the common law system. Its origins probably date back to the late thirteenth or early fourteenth century when the judges of the Common Pleas and King's Bench met informally to thrash out problems of particular complexity. By Dyer's time (namely 1579) the composition of the court had become fixed; it consisted of the common law justices and any barons of the Exchequer who were also 'of the coif'.[167] While statutory Courts of Exchequer Chamber were empowered after 1585 to hear writs of error from the King's Bench and Exchequer of Pleas, the original tribunal remained as a forum of high-level debate.[168] By the reign of Elizabeth a 'chequer chamber case' had come to mean a dispute of special prominence.[169] Despite the great prestige which attached to the institution there were no formal restrictions as to who could plead there such as existed in the Common Pleas: apprentices and utter-barristers were often reported as arguing on equal terms with judges and serjeants. The decision to refer litigation to the Chamber rested solely with the justices of the trial court, irrespective of the wishes of the parties. Once the issues had been scrutinized and some sort of consensus arrived at, judgment was given in the original tribunal.[170]

It has been estimated that over 200 cases from the Exchequer Chamber are reported in the Yearbooks.[171] The number found in private reports of the sixteenth century is about the same.[172] Dyer himself includes only about a dozen cases argued in the Chamber, but their fewness is deceptive inasmuch as the majority

[167] Originally only the Chief Baron was admitted, but after 1579 any baron who was a serjeant became eligible; Hemmant, i, p. xv; cf. Co. Litt. 155a.

[168] Stat. 27 Eliz. c. 8 (amended 31 Eliz. c. 1, ss. 2, 3); cf. 4 Inst. 110, 119.

[169] Thomas Smith, *De Republica Anglorum* (1906), p. 73; Foxe, vi, 50.

[170] Hemmant, i, p. lxxvi; *H.E.L.* i, 242.

[171] Hemmant, i, p. xxxi.

[172] Jenkins' *Centuries* contains 279 for this period, but includes selections from the Yearbooks.

of extra-judicial hearings had shifted to Serjeants' Inn, Fleet Street. This 'remarkable deviation' was a sixteenth-century phenomenon: the earliest reference to its use comes from Justice John Spelman's notebook in 1523,[173] and the first printed report of a case decided there appears in the Yearbook for Easter 1527.[174] For the next seventy-five years a constant stream of decisions, opinions and recommendations issued from the Fleet Street hostel and to a less extent the neighbouring Inn on Chancery Lane. With the death of Elizabeth there seems to have been a wholesale reversion to the Exchequer Chamber itself.[175]

The assembling of judges outside Westminster Hall for extraordinary purposes took on special significance with the advent of the Tudors. In Michaelmas term 1485 they met at Blackfriars to ponder the implementation of certain acts of parliament:[176] afterwards they proceeded to Whitefriars where the topic of their own wages entered the deliberations.[177] Later in the term the delicate question of attainders left from the previous reign was disposed of.[178] Confusion was bound to occur in the wake of a new regime which was consolidating its power—hence what seems to have been a certain amount of disruption in normal judicial processes. In Henry VIII's reign hearings of this sort, though rare, reflected some of the troubles of the time. One which received the attention of an early private reporter, Serjeant John Carrell, was the debate between Richard Kidderminster and Dr Henry Standish as an aftermath of the Hunne affair in 1515. On three separate occasions, twice at Blackfriars and once at Baynard's Castle, the king himself presided over exchanges which foreshadowed the fate of the church fifteen years later. While technically not a law report, the narrative includes some cogent

173 B.M. Harg. MS 388, ff. *26v*, 30.

174 YB E. 19 Hen. VIII, pl. 5; this entry was copied by Dyer into his own notebook; Dyer, 3a; cf. Hemmant, i, p. xxiii.

175 Hemmant, i, p. xxiv.

176 YB M. 1 Hen. VII, pl. 3; cf. Vinogradoff, p. 273.

177 YB M. 1 Hen. VII, pl. 4; Vinogradoff, p. 273.

178 YB M. 1 Hen. VII, pl. 5.

remarks by Chief Justice Fineux on the jurisdiction of the secular law.[179]

For the greater part of the century, however, extraordinary conferences on subjects of public concern were mainly confined to the Exchequer Chamber or the two Serjeants' Inns. Sometimes discussions shifted from one place to another;[180] evidently the locus of debate was not necessarily indicative of its importance. The use of the Inns was probably a matter of convenience. Two hostels reserved for members of the coif—judges as well as serjeants—were in operation by the early part of Henry VIII's reign, if not before.[181] These houses, unlike the Inns of Court and Chancery, were not part of the legal educational system but were in the nature of clubs for the élite of the profession. One authority, writing at the end of the century, stated that

> In these two Colledges or Innes of Serjeants doe common, lodge, converse, conferre and consult, the chiefe justices of either Bench . . . and the rest of the judges and barons, and also the serjeants at law . . .[182]

In point of prestige the Inns were on an equal footing and cases were argued at both: for some reason, however, Serjeants' Inn, Fleet Street, was employed far more often and became the principal centre for the adjudication of 'Exchequer Chamber' cases.[183] Dyer notes thirty-seven cases so adjudicated, eleven in the Chamber itself, twenty-six at the Fleet Street hostel. Comparison with a sample of other reports, both printed and manuscript, confirms that this ratio of one to two persisted during the course of the century.[184]

The range of subject-matter which came under scrutiny was

[179] Keil. 181–5; Ogle, p. 13. [180] Hemmant, i, p. xxiii.

[181] E. Williams, *Early Holborn* (1927), ii, 1297–1302; H. C. King, *Serjeants' Inn, Fleet Street* (1922), p. 66.

[182] G. Buck, *Third University* (1615), X. 1069; *H.E.L.*, ii, 492, n. 2; Stow, *Survey*, p. 72.

[183] R. Robinson, 'A Briefe Collection of the Queenes . . . Courtes of Recordes', *Camd. Misc.* xx (Camd. 3rd Series, lxxxiii), 15, 18; 3 Co. Rep. Pref. xxv; cf. Plow. 73.

[184] Printed reports of Popham, Savile, Coke and Croke; B.M. Harl. MS 5141, Harg. MS 8.

wide and unrelated to specific forms of action: the prime consideration was whether the issue was one of particular complexity or legal significance, although the social prominence of the parties involved was also a factor. It was Coke's contention that some adjournments were as much for weight as difficulty, and certainly, to judge from the Yearbooks and Dyer, the suits of influential litigants predominated.[185]

Among such litigants the Crown took the lead. Typical of these was 'un grande question' posed by the Chancellor to the judges in Hilary term 1486 relating to a bill 'mis en le Common hous' (1485) confirming Henry Tudor's succession.[186] Did a similar act under Henry IV (7 Henry IV, chapter 2) include the resumption of franchises and liberties? Their lordships' answer was in the negative,[187] and the problem of privileged areas of jurisdiction remained unsolved until 1536. Henry VIII was sufficiently interested in his rights to services attaching to the Constableship of England to receive in person the judgment of Chief Justices Fineux and Rede at Greenwich in 1514: the office had belonged to the ancestors of the Duke of Buckingham, but because it was 'very high and dangerous' the King would not call for the resumption of services.[188] Much later—at the outset of Elizabeth's reign—a series of 'Resolutions' was adopted at Serjeants' Inn which sought to clarify the statute 1 Edward VI, chapter 7, relating to the demise of the Crown.[189] Similar resolutions were agreed upon by the judges in 1569 on the importation of books against the Royal Supremacy,[190] and an anonymous reporter recorded their interpretation of an act passed in 1571 which required the reading of the Articles of Religion by any clerk prior to induction.[191] John Savile reports two conferences at the Fleet Street Inn which reflect the government's constant struggle to protect the Established Church against attacks from both 'right' and 'left': in 1581 it was decided by a full panel of

185 Coke's remarks at the end of *Calvin's Case*, 7 Co. Rep. 28a; cf. Hemmant, i, p. lxxvi.

186 G.R. Elton (ed.), *The Tudor Constitution* (1962), p. 4.

187 YB H. 1 Hen. VII, pl. 25.

188 Keil. 171–2; Dyer, 285b.

189 Dyer, 165a.

190 Ibid. 282a.

191 C.U.L. MS Gg. 2. 5, f. 118.

judges that Campion '& auters Jesuits & Seminaries' were susceptible of prosecution under the new treasons act, and three years later the same act was deemed applicable against Robert Browne for his publication of a book 'conteinant divers seditious matters'.[192] Sometimes a private dispute was turned into a matter of public policy through the intervention of the Crown. An outstanding example is the *Case of the Duchy of Lancaster* (1562) found in the reports of both Dyer and Plowden.[193] The question touched the validity of leases executed by Edward VI of land in the Duchy, and these were upheld on the ground that Edward, though a minor, had made them in his capacity as king rather than as Duke of Lancaster.

It is clear from various sources that Queen Elizabeth took an interest in suits even where they did not directly affect the Crown. This in turn could not help but influence the attitude of the judges. A classic example is *Shelley's Case* (1579),[194] the leading decision on contingent remainders. Fraught as the case was with the most involved points of the law of real property, Elizabeth nevertheless followed the outcome: as a firm advocate of free alienation it was to her interest that full rights of wardship should be retained.[195] Coke mentions an episode in a Chancery case concerning land alienated without authority by the Dean and Chapter of Norwich Cathedral: the Queen, 'greatly offended that she was so deceived', referred the matter to Lord Keeper Egerton and the Chief Justices before whom counsel argued at York House.[196] In *Fermor's Case* (1602), when the plaintiff sought to overturn a fraudulent conveyance by fine based on the statute of 1490, the Lord Keeper, Thomas Egerton, 'considering the great mischiefs which might ensue by such practices', had the case removed out of Chancery and placed before the Chief Justices who in turn referred it to the full judiciary at Serjeants' Inn.[197]

[192] Savile, 3, 49; Poph. 93.
[193] Dyer, 209b, 232a; Plow. 212; see Appendix III, p. 320.
[194] 1 Co. Rep. 88b.
[195] Ibid. 105a; Simpson, *History of Land Law*, p. 95.
[196] 3 Co. Rep. 73b.
[197] Ibid. 77b; the statute in question is 4 Hen. VII, chap. 24.

Few matters on which the government sought legal advice were discussed as fully-fledged 'chequer chamber' cases. The majority were comparatively trivial items—the fate of humble subjects, the seisin of a particular manor, the interpretation of leases and covenants and the like. Thus William Cordell, the Queen's Solicitor, demanded of the Common Bench in 1555 whether Sir Peter Carewe still owed 200 marks to the Crown after his pardon.[198] Six years later a joint committee of jurists was able to satisfy the Keeper of the Great Seal on the power of the J.P.s to grant a writ of restitution in quarter sessions.[199] Was a bastard born of English parents in an English overseas dominion, namely Tournai, a liege subject? Dyer, Catlin and Saunders, the three Chief Justices, informed Bacon that he was.[200] Gilbert Gerrard, the Attorney-General, came into the Common Pleas in 1580 with a query on behalf of the Queen regarding estates of mixed tenure: doubtless she was pleased when the judges decided that the Crown was entitled to the wardship of land held by socage where the tenant in question was also seised of property held of the Queen *in capite*.[201]

Among the various tribunals themselves there was a good deal of unofficial cooperation in the pursuit of justice. In Easter term 1561 the justices of the King's Bench were much in doubt over a challenge to the array by a former sheriff, so Corbet was dispatched to the Court of Common Pleas to seek an opinion.[202] When an action was taken against the ordinary on an intestate's bond, the Bishop of London felt obliged to seek advice from the common law judges at Fleet Street.[203] In an Exchequer case of 1573 it was discovered that one of the jurors was not a hundredor and there were doubts as to his qualifications; 'Baron Birche was sent into the Bench, to know the opinions there'.[204] Whatever the provenance of a legal problem, and in spite of the constant jurisdictional war being waged beneath the surface, members of

[198] Dyer, 124a; not surprisingly, the court decided that he did.
[199] Ibid. 187a. [200] Ibid. 224a.
[201] Ibid. 366b; Simpson, *History of Land Law*, pp. 18–19.
[202] Dyer, 182b. [203] Ibid. 232a. [204] Ibid. 316a.

the bench and bar seemed ready to assist one another to discover the law—if only for the sake of stimulating debate.[205]

Argument was the stuff of every barrister's life. The practice of referring a problem to the courts or to an unofficial body of jurists was not confined to the Crown, it was common at every level of legal process. Today, under stricter rules of procedure, opinions rendered by the court only emerge as a result of the joining of issue between two or more parties.[206] In the sixteenth century this was not necessarily the case. Then as now the adjudication of disputes in the central courts rested in the hands of a select group of judges and advocates, but their success in coping with the increasing mass of litigation depended to a greater degree on mutual trust and cooperation, and this involved the informal exchange of advice between bench and bar. The resulting flow of information is one of the features of law-reporting from the Yearbooks to Coke.

The process of 'putting cases' or 'moving questions' can be ambiguous: it is not always easy to determine whether such items were part of an actual suit or of a hypothetical one designed as an exercise in forensic skill. Wherever lawyers gathered, including the House of Commons, they were in the habit of posing doubtful points to one another in the style of mooting.[207] The following extract from Dyer seems more appropriate to a medieval university than to a Tudor law court:

> It was moved for a question by Beldlowe[s], that if there be a grandmother on the part of the father, a mother and son: and the grandmother have a brother likewise; [and] the son purchase land in fee, and die without issue, Whether the brother of the grandmother, or the brother of the mother shall be heir to him *quaere*.

In fact this conundrum was the crux of a leading case, *Clere v.*

[205] Examples are *Eare v. Snowe* and *Bransby v. Grantham*, Plow. 504 at pp. 515, 525; on a wider front see W.J.Jones, 'Conflict or Collaboration? Chancery Attitudes in the reign of Elizabeth I', *A.J.L.H.* v (1961), 12–54.

[206] A.V.Dicey, *Law of the Constitution* (1960), pp. 195, 203. Such a trend was evident by the mid-seventeenth century; March's *Reports*, 155.

[207] Neale, *House of Commons*, pp. 357, 420; *Proceedings in Parliament 1610*, i, 199–203; ii, 226–48.

Brook, which was begun in the Common Pleas in 1572.[208] Dyer and his fellow-reporters frequently record queries arising from actions pending in court. Thus, in Hilary term 32 Elizabeth, Serjeant Cooper sought the judges' opinion on whether goods might be taken in execution which had been sold by the debtor prior to the service of a writ of *fieri facias*.[209] Again, in Easter term 1600 Serjeant Harris moved a case in the King's Bench which he said was then pending before Sir Richard Lewknor, Justice of Chester, 'who desired their opinion therein'.[210] Enterprising practitioners, it seems, were ready to ask questions at any opportunity, and reporters to record the answers. An unknown writer in Henry VIII's time noted that Humphrey Browne came to the bar and 'demande de Fitzherbert adonque sole en le comen banke' a question regarding false verdict in a writ of right.[211] In Hilary 25 Elizabeth Edmund Plowden is reported as having gone to Lord Burghley and taxed him on a matter concerning land held by a town corporation; the only advice the Lord Treasurer was able to offer was that Plowden should view the relevant records.[212] So far as the judge and serjeants were concerned, the process of question and answer was a reciprocal one. Carrell, for instance, reports a case where Justice Eliot of the Common Bench sought advice from those serjeants at the bar concerning the qualifications of a juror.[213] In Trinity 1544 Judge Shelley asked Serjeants Bromley and Hales their opinion on the validity of an attornment executed jointly by a husband and wife although the lease had originally been made with the wife alone: after much discussion the opinion of the serjeants and Shelley carried despite the objection of Justices Baldwin and Browne.[214]

In whatever way a question reached the judges a certain protocol in its presentation was usually observed—the more momentous the legal implications the greater the formality. Normally the

[208] Dyer, 314a; also reported by Plowden, 442–51, who attempts to clarify the problem by reproducing 'a tree of consanguinity'.

[209] Croke Eliz. 174.

[210] Ibid. 753.

[211] B.M. Harg. MS 388, f. 239.

[212] B.M. Harg. MS 373, f. 212; cf. ibid. f. 223.

[213] Keil. 167b.

[214] Lib. of Congress, Gell MS, f. 41*v*.

salient issues of the case were established by arguments from counsel of the respective parties. For the more important disputes there would be two pleaders on each side, probably serjeants, and in litigation affecting the Crown's interests either the Attorney-General or Solicitor-General would argue, if not both. The speeches, which would doubtless have been carefully prepared beforehand,[215] frequently lasted for days at a time. The process was then repeated by the justices sitting on the case, with whom, of course, the ultimate decision rested. These conventions of presentation seem to have hardened as the century progressed. The *Earl of Arundel's Case*, reported by Dyer in 1575, exemplifies a fully-fledged Exchequer Chamber hearing.[216] Following a presentation of the issues in the Common Pleas the case was adjourned to the Chamber where Serjeants Barham, Fettiplace, Bell and Popham 'argued on three several days *pro* and *contra*'; later at Serjeants' Inn, Fleet Street, the judges 'of both Benches' came to a final decision. The most elaborate examples of pleading come from Coke's reports late in the century. In *Chudleigh's Case* (1589–95) he observes that there was a five-year delay during which the issue was debated many times at the bar before going to the Exchequer Chamber in 1594: here Coke and Francis Bacon—so often matched against one another in and out of court—reviewed the points at issue, after which a total of eleven judges and barons consumed a further six days putting forward their opinions.[217] *Calvin's Case* (1608) was a high point in extended, formal argument. It began as a private suit, but its far-reaching implications—the right of a Scottish subject to sue in an English court—assured its quick removal to the Exchequer Chamber where it was argued 'openly' by pleaders and judges over the course of three terms. During Easter term eight junior members of the bench spent four days in discussing it, and in Trinity the four remaining puisne judges put their views, to be

[215] In *Stowell v. Zouch*, Plow. 375, it is noted that Justice Corbet, who died before delivery of his final argument, 'left a draft of it which was found in his study after he died'; cf. 3 Leon. 271.

[216] Dyer, 342a at p. 343b. [217] 1 Co. Rep. 120a at p. 121a.

followed on two separate days by Coke and Fleming, the Chief Justices, and Lord Ellesmere, the Chancellor—a total of fifteen judges.[218] Ellesmere alone took four hours delivering his judgment although he had earlier feared that age and infirmity would prevent his expounding at length.[219]

Is it surprising that the wheels of justice turned so slowly? Apart from the interminable delays which a resourceful defendant could contrive during the course of a suit, it can be appreciated how sluggish decision-making itself could be. Thomas Starkey had said as much in the fifteen-thirties:

> I see many mennys materys heng in sute ii, iij, or iiij yere and more, and can not be fynyschyd; the wych causys of themselfe be not so obscure but they myght be defynyd in fewar days then they heng yerys . . .[220]

Time and again the reports demonstrate that even causes of legal significance or involving powerful suitors could be held up for years while arguments dragged on from term to term. According to Bendlowes, *Bold v. Molineux* first came before the Common Bench in Easter term 1534;[221] Dyer does not take up his report of the proceedings until the summer of 1536,[222] and it was not until the autumn that judgment was rendered. A writ of assize taken by Thomas Wimbish against Elizabeth Tailbois is first recorded in a manuscript report for Michaelmas 1544 while being debated at Serjeants' Inn, Fleet Street.[223] Despite a series of conferences no decision had been reached by 1547, in which year the plaintiff launched a new action, this time for trespass, which Plowden reports.[224] When this case finally reached open court in 1551 it was argued by four serjeants and the full bench over several days, but in the end no judgment was given.[225] Yet again, in Hilary 6 Edward VI, Wimbish and his wife took to the courts, instituting a second action of assize, the legality of which was

[218] 7 Co. Rep. 2a–2b; *H.E.L.*, v, 163–4.
[219] *H.E.L.* v, 234.
[220] *Dialogue between Pole and Lupset*, p. 118.
[221] Bendl. 13.
[222] Dyer, 14b.
[223] Lib. of Congress Gell MS, ff. 107, 116; cf. Brooke tit. 'Collusion & Covin', no. 46.
[224] Plow. 360–8.
[225] Ibid. 60.

argued in Trinity term at Serjeants' Inn, Chancery Lane. Plowden's report was concerned with the question whether the writ was properly directed; he leaves the case itself still hanging fire in 1552.[226]

Sometimes the span could be measured, not in years, but decades. Dyer has a short entry for 1552 concerning a tenant in ancient demesne;[227] the plea had been commenced, he states, 'in the court of Lewis Pollarde, Justice', so that—as Pollard had died in 1526[228]—it had dragged on for over twenty-five years. Dyer also mentions an action 'that had depended undiscussed thirty years in the Court of Wards', although according to Serjeant Carrell it had been ruled on by the judges in Exchequer Chamber.[229] Some delays were attributable to bureaucratic neglect: the prothonotary of the Common Pleas omitted for five years to enter judgment for one Robert Smith, the plaintiff in a writ of replevin.[230] But *Walsingham's Case* (1579) went undecided for ten years mainly as a result of complex pleadings and what is described in the report as 'mature deliberation'—first in the Exchequer and then in the Exchequer Chamber.[231] According to Popham another case languished in the courts because Saunders, the Chief Baron, would not concur with his colleagues' point of view; it was not until after his death and replacement by John Jeffrey that the matter was resolved.[232] While these examples are exceptional they are not inconceivable in view of the busy calendar which faced magistrates during term and on circuit. Unless a suit was dealt with at one blow, the danger of postponement and cumulative delay increased: this was certainly true in *Butler and Baker's Case*, in Easter 37 Elizabeth, where it was found necessary to argue the issues on twenty-one separate occasions.[233]

One reason why actions of particular weight were frequently

226 Ibid. 73–7. 227 Dyer, 69b.

228 *D.N.B.* xlvi, 60, as corrected in the 'Additions and Corrections' filed at the Institute of Historical Research, University of London.

229 *Coningesby v. Throckmorton*, M. 1 & 2 Eliz., Dyer, 174b; Simpson, *Land Law*, pp. 41–2.

230 Plow. 437. 231 Ibid. 547 at p. 561.

232 B.M. Lansd. MS 1084, ff. 106–6*v*. 233 3 Co. Rep. 35b.

dissected so thoroughly was the urge to attain 'consensus'. The absence of an integrated procedure for appeals meant that a suitor's claim for justice rested with the trial court although writs of error were available in certain circumstances.[234] Coupled with this was the belief that somehow, somewhere, some principle of the common law existed to cover every situation—if only it could be found and applied.[235] The technique of isolation and application lay, it seems, in incessant, though frequently tortuous, oral argument.

Throughout the sixteenth century the more conscientious reporters stressed the efforts of both pleaders and judges to achieve unanimity in their deliberations.[236] This does not mean that the majority principle did not obtain within the courts—it did[237]—and for the mass of ordinary litigation dissenting judgments were common enough. Yet time and again the reports emphasize that a given statement of law was the 'clere opinion' of the court. And when it came to Exchequer Chamber cases, Maitland's dictum certainly applies: 'it is unanimity that is wanted, . . . it is unanimity that is after a sort obtained'.[238] When a problem was adjourned to Serjeants' Inn for discussion by a full panel of justices the verdict was expected to embody the views of all.[239] The therapeutic value of airing opinions openly was extolled by Tudor jurists, as Coke notes in the *Case of Alton Woods* (1600):

> the Lord Keeper said, that although it was sufficient for him to rely upon the opinion of the . . . judges, without whom he could not proceed to judgment, yet it was convenient for every judge openly to shew the reason and cause of his judgment.[240]

In such an atmosphere it is not surprising to find many instances

[234] Plucknett, *Concise History*, pp. 387–8.

[235] Gray, pp. 135–7. [236] Co. Litt. 254a.

[237] Plucknett, *Concise History*, p. 347, citing YB M. I Ric. III pl. 2; cf. Sir Goronwy Edwards, 'The Emergence of Majority Rule', *Trans. R.H.S.* 5th Series xv (1965), 171–87; see also Lib. of Congress, Gell MS f. 94*v*.

[238] F. W. Maitland, *Township and Borough* (1898), p. 35.

[239] See case on impositions, H. 3 Eliz., B.M. Harg. MS 132, f. 67; also the remarks of Saunders in Plow. 560.

[240] 1 Co. Rep. 51b; cf. *De Republica*, p. 56; Edwards, p. 171; Plow. 94–5.

of dissenting judges changing their opinions.[241] An unprinted entry of Dyer's from Hilary term 1562 describes how a case on impositions went from Exchequer to Exchequer Chamber to Serjeants' Inn until Baron Luke finally changed his opinion and accord was reached.[242] A Court of Wards matter was argued in Hilary 1571 at the Fleet Street Inn, but the judges were divided evenly six against six; next term the argument was resumed at William Cecil's lodgings near the Savoy, where after four-and-a-half hours of debate Justice Carus reversed his stand, thus breaking the deadlock and influencing the decision of Cecil himself.[243] This passionate pursuit of consensus sometimes drove litigants to seek a settlement of their own or to go to arbitration rather than to let judicial process run its marathon course.[244]

The emphasis on unanimity becomes more pronounced in the late sixteenth and early seventeenth centuries. The reports of Popham and Coke, among others, seem to reflect this trend as part of a more discriminating attitude towards decided cases.[245] For Coke, unanimous judgments were essential 'for the honour of the law, and for the quiet of the subject in appeasing much diversity of opinions';[246] a case such as *Wimbish v. Tailbois* was of no authority because 'the judges were divided two by two'.[247] At the same time, the sages of the common law were prepared to accept help from any quarter in their quest of agreement: this could include holy writ, philosophical speculation and historical

[241] Such a procedure should not, of course, be confused with the practice instituted by James I of consulting his judges separately prior to judgment in order to influence their decision: Spedding, v. 115–20.

[242] B.M. Harg. MS 132, f. 67.

[243] Dyer, 286b; see also ibid. 157b, 358b; Plow. 95, 297; Croke Eliz. 109.

[244] For example, Dyer, 340a–1a; 1 Leon. 91.

[245] Poph. 5, 42; 1 Co. Rep. 48a; 4 Co. Rep. 93a.

[246] *Slade's Case*, 4 Co. Rep. 92b at p. 93a; *Argumentum ab authoritate est fortissimum in lege*, Co. Litt., 254a.

[247] *Slade v. Drake*, Hobart, 300; Coke again enunciates the rule, 4 Inst. 64, that where the judges were divided equally no decision could be given—*paribus sententiis res absolvitur*. It was found necessary in James I's reign to add one judge to each of the Common Pleas and King's Bench to try to avoid stalemates of this kind; 4 Co. Rep. Pref. xviii.

chronicle.[248] Again, it was Coke, that arch-defender of native English law, who conceded that in matters of difficulty the judges might 'confer with the learned in that art or science, whose resolution is required to the true deciding of the case in question'.[249] Similarly, it had been regular practice at least from the time Dyer began compiling his reports to consult with the doctors of canon and civil law on points of difficulty.[250]

From what has already been said it is clear that many conferences held at Serjeants' Inn were not in the nature of orthodox Exchequer Chamber hearings. An analysis of sixteenth-century law reports reveals that most of these meetings pertained to the ordinary flow of litigation through the courts and involved considerably fewer than the full common law judiciary: indeed, it can be said that a significant proportion, albeit a minority, of the lawsuits which reached Westminster Hall were resolved by means of extra-judicial conferences of one sort or another. Just as the clerical work performed by court officials was largely done outside both the sessions and the precincts of the tribunal concerned,[251] so the lawyers developed and extended the practice of arguing cases and issues beyond the confines of the formal hearing.

From the evidence of practitioner-reporters, especially Dyer, it is clear that the decision-making process was a continuous one bounded only by the absence of the judges on circuit and the patience of litigants. Time and again court proceedings were suspended while the relevant issues were examined in conference at the Inns. Dyer mentions Serjeants' Inn only about a dozen times other than in relation to Exchequer Chamber cases, yet he has at least another hundred entries of an extra-judicial character which probably emanated from discussions held in Fleet Street or Chancery Lane. Their very number indicates that such meetings were a regular feature of the term's activities. Since they

[248] Plow. 110, 129, 305, 369, 444; 3 Co. Rep. 40a.

[249] 3 Co. Rep. Pref. xxb.

[250] Dyer, 59b, 209a; 6 Co. Rep., 22b; Plow. 125; B.M. Lansd. MS 1084, f. 68; Add. MS 25194, ff. 50–3.

[251] Hastings, pp. 39–40; Neale, *House of Commons*, pp. 266–7.

invariably included justices from two or more tribunals they cannot be regarded as a reconvening of the original trial. Unlike the great public-policy cases, these gatherings were unofficial and procedurally informal: but their frequency and their attendance by roughly the same persons suggest some measure of organization.

In 1561 Dyer concludes his report of a short, relatively unimportant suit relating to the custom of borough English by stating that 'all the Board in Serjeants' Inn [held] that the youngest shall have it by descent . . .'.[252] The 'Board' probably comprised those judges and serjeants who lodged or had chambers at Fleet Street and perhaps in Chancery Lane across the road:[253] a later report of this case gives their names as Catlin, Dyer, Saunders, Whiddon, Browne and Bendlowes.[254] Similar entries show certain changes in the make-up of the 'Board', but it invariably included the two Chief Justices and Chief Baron, a circumstance which strengthens the impression that these conferences were organized assemblies. A study of the many extra-judicial hearings noted by William Dalison before 1558 provides additional information:[255] out of a total of 240 entries, 102 consist of arguments staged in the Holborn Inns, a third of these being at Chancery Lane. From the way in which these entries are arranged it appears that the 'Board' dealt at one sitting with a number of actions then being heard in the courts, the points at issue in many of them being resolved so that the rendering of judgment was little more than a formality. Even when reporting arguments presented in open court both Dyer and Dalison sometimes interpose opinions formulated out of court at unofficial meetings.[256] Similar entries appear in later reports such as those of Anderson, Croke, Popham,

[252] Dyer, 179b.

[253] In the previous term Dyer, in *Sir Richard Crumwell's Case* (M. 1 & 2 Eliz.), reported the opinion 'of the greater part of the Judges and Serjeants of both houses'; ibid. 169b.

[254] Jenkins, 220.

[255] B.M. Harl. MS 5141, ff. 1–45; see above Chap. IV, pp. 119–21.

[256] For instance, Dyer, 274b; Harl. MS 5141, ff. 7*v*–8, 14*v*, 30, 40; cf. Dyer, 367b.

Savile and Moore, as well as in numerous manuscript collections, so that the practice must have persisted at least until the end of the century.[257]

The reports also yield evidence of regular meetings of the justices of assize at Serjeants' Inn for the purpose of resolving difficulties encountered on circuit.[258] During Michaelmas term 1560 they met to deal with a series of cases which had arisen during the preceding summer tour; these included the question of reading to prove a man's clergy, rights to wood under a monastic lease and the rendering of two verdicts by the same jury.[259] In the following Hilary term *Stone's Case*, which raised the issue of priority between capital and clergyable offences, was 'well debated at Serjeants' Inn by all the judges of both benches and of assize'.[260] These conferences continued well into James I's reign; Henry Yelverton reports that his father put a question to the judges at Fleet Street which he had encountered during the Oxford Assizes in 1610, and then 'relate lour opinions overtment en Bank le Roy'.[261] Such gatherings might also serve to plan for future circuits by ironing out expected difficulties.[262] On the other hand, the practice of removing cases by writ to Westminster aggravated existing delays,[263] a consequence which prompted one reformer to recommend that no cause should be removed unless 'gentlemen of the shire' were unable to determine it.[264] Yet all too often issues of law could not be determined by local magistrates but required the attention of trained legal minds; and where the stakes were large the litigants were more than willing to take their disputes to the highest level.[265]

While the two Serjeants' Inns were focal points in the decision-making process, there were other locales in London and Westminster where current issues were discussed and interpreted.

[257] 1 And. 110. 162; Croke Eliz. 129; Poph. 50, 107, 121; Moore, 602; Savile, 67; Harl. MS 1696, f. 9*v*; 1722, f. 14; Harg. MS 8, f. 125*v*.

[258] *H.E.L.* i, 276–85. [259] Dyer, 205a, 207a, 209a. [260] Ibid. 214b.

[261] Yelverton's *Reports*, 180–1. [262] For example, Poph. 16, 96.

[263] Plow. 475; Croke Eliz. 12.

[264] *Dialogue between Pole and Lupset*, p. 190.

[265] For example, Lib. of Congress, Gell MS, f. 85.

The Inns of Court and Chancery, while primarily designed for the instruction of students, also served as a forum of discussion for the profession at large. The line between learning and litigation was sometimes a fine one. Points of law were frequently cited from lectures and moots in reports and abridgments.[266] Conversely students and benchers made a practice of debating the merits of judgments and opinions rendered in court; some of these, of a controversial character, established themselves as 'common diversities' in the moots.[267] The reporters apparently attached considerable weight to dicta emanating from these learning exercises, especially when propounded by the benchers or readers.[268] Churches, too, were sometimes used by barristers just as they were by law clerks for secular ends;[269] during the reigns of Henry VII and Henry VIII, at least, judicial conferences were occasionally convened at St Bride's, Fleet Street, no doubt because of its proximity to the Inns of Court.[270]

Somewhat more informal, but no less important to the judicial process, were the numerous discussions which took place in the chambers of the Chief Justices. Thus in 1549 Mountague C.J. is reported as having heard arguments 'en camera' relating to *Lady Latimer's Case* (1545).[271] In the case of *Gate v. Wiseman* (1557) Dyer notes that evidence was taken 'without argument at bar or bench, counsel being heard at Lord Brooke's chambers only': that such procedure was not always accepted gracefully appears from the reporter's addendum that 'Browne, serjeant was very angry with the above judgment'.[272] The refusal of Bishop Bonner to take the oath of supremacy in 1564 was 'much discussed among

[266] Dyer, 4b n. 5; Fitzherbert, tit. 'Accion sur le case', no. 45; B.M. Harg. MS 4, f. 46*v*; C.U.L. MS Gg. 3, 26, f. 126.

[267] Plow. 63; Dal. 110.

[268] For example, B.M. Harl. MS 1691, f. 100*v*, and Harg. 9, f. 179*v*.

[269] Hastings, pp. 38–40

[270] Two such conferences have been reported: YB M. 20 Hen. VII, pl. 20 and Keil. 174.

[271] Dyer, 59b.

[272] Ibid. 140b; cf. Plow., 70.

all the justices at Lord Catlyn's chambers'.[273] Dyer himself, when Chief Justice, must have heard many cases in chambers, although he refers to only two such occasions, one being at his rooms in the Fleet Street hostel:[274] Chief Baron Roger Manwood and Chief Justice Christopher Wray similarly heard arguments in their chambers at Serjeants' Inn.[275]

According to Dr Ives a share of legal business in the late fifteenth century seems to have been carried on in London taverns.[276] Although this may refer to routine meetings between lawyer and client, and not necessarily to litigation, the reports reveal a parallel practice, because judges and serjeants utilized mealtimes at their hostels to debate current issues. 'Table cases' of this sort clearly arose from the practice of mooting which was carried on at the Inns of Court and Chancery in the evenings.[277] Some of those decisions of constitutional importance at the beginning of Henry VII's reign had been taken during or after dinner at Blackfriars; later in the same Yearbook are two cases debated at Chief Justice Hussey's Inn while he was dining with his colleagues of the King's Bench.[278] Such gatherings were often planned in advance; thus in Trinity term 1486, when a problem concerning sanctuary arose, it is recorded that 'touts les justices & serjants le roy furent puis manger le vendredi prochein ensuant . . . & la arguerent touts'.[279] Dyer underscores the breadth of his own reports by referring to certain statements or opinions *ad mensam*: at least five such entries turn up in his notes.[280] Like his references to other forms of extra-judicial procedure these must represent only

[273] Dyer, 234a; the oath was administered under the statute 5 Eliz. chap. 1; R. W. Dixon, *History of the Church of England* (1902), vi, 29–37; see below, Chap. VI, p. 203.

[274] Dyer, 289b, 313b.

[275] Savile, 47; L.I. Mayn. MS 29, ff. 148–51; see also Plow. 212, 220; 1 Leon. 12; B.M. Harl. MS 5141 (Dalison), f. 1.

[276] 'Legal Profession', p. 502.

[277] See above, Chap. I, pp. 32–5; B.M. Harg. MS 373, f. 185*v*; Harl. 1619, f. 109.

[278] YBB H. 1 Hen. VII, pl. 12, 13; M. 2 Hen. VII, pl. 6, 7.

[279] YB T. 1 Hen. VII, pl. 1.

[280] Dyer, 221a, 300b, 329b, 350a; Petyt MS 511, vol. 13, f. 50*v*.

a fraction of the questions reviewed in such informal circumstances. In one such entry Dyer explains that judgment was formulated *per omnes in prandio apud hospitium Justiciariorum* 'in Fleete Streate'.[281] In all probability some of these discussions at the noon meal arose from suits argued at the courts that morning, but many appear to have been the result of casual conversations.[282] The practice seems to have spread to the civilians and canonists as well: in his argument in *Buckley v. Rice Thomas* (1554) Edward Saunders informed the court that he had sought and obtained advice from the Doctors of the Arches at their table.[283]

Advocates of all ranks, it seems, never stopped talking shop; useful snippets of information could be picked up at any time or place, given at least one practitioner wishing to talk and another willing to listen. One diligent reporter noted a comment by Fitzherbert 'veniendo de Westminster'.[284] Dalison refers to an occasion early in 1553 when Gosnold, the King's Solicitor, conveyed some information regarding the Duke of Norfolk's attainder to John Carrell at the gate of Serjeants' Inn, Fleet Street.[285] A few months later Dyer, not to be outdone, recites the words of a patent from the time of Edward III of which he was apprised *ex relatu Episcopi Eliensis redeundi ab aula westmonasterii*.[286]

The reports of the sixteenth century demonstrate how essential extra-judicial proceedings, formal and informal, were to decision-making. In the final analysis the success of such a system, like that of Tudor government on a wider scale, rested on the skill and leadership of a small, but powerful, group of men drawn mainly from the same social class. Living and working together during term and travelling on circuit at other times in the year, the ser-

281 Dyer (1592 edn.), 300b.

282 According to Fortescue, the judges sat in court from 8 to 11 in the morning and having refreshed themselves spent the rest of the day in study and contemplation: *De Laudibus*, p. 129; see also Hastings, p. 35; W. C. Bolland, *Manual of Year Book Studies* (1925), p. 100.

283 Plow. 125; this case is examined more fully below, Chap. VI, pp.223–4.

284 YB M. 27 Hen. VIII, pl. 5.

285 B.M. Harl. MS 5141, f. 12.

286 Dyer, 92b.

jeants and judges of Dyer's day formed a tightly-knit professional community unique in English society: 'they knew that they alone knew the law, they knew each other and how to use each other, in their exchequer chamber assemblies they had a vast potentiality of cooperation.'[287]

[287] Pickthorn, *Henry VII*, p. 58.

CHAPTER VI

Edmund Plowden

'THE two late reporters are Ma. Plowden and Sir James Dyer, who by a severall and distinct kind of discourse, have both laboured to profit posterite.' [1] In any study of sixteenth-century law reporting the names of Dyer and Plowden must inevitably be linked, as indeed they were from the time their work was published. The two men had some things in common. Both flourished in the period immediately following the demise of the Yearbooks; both studied at and began practising from the Middle Temple; and both attained a high reputation for skill and integrity in their chosen field. In other respects, however, their careers exhibit contrast rather than similarity, a fact which is reflected in their reports. Plowden, a steadfast Catholic, forfeited the chance of high office; Dyer was a *politique* who, like William Cecil, saw to it that his religion did not interfere with his career. Any assessment of their respective achievements as reporters relates directly to their professional attainments. Plowden, with time at his disposal, sought out those cases which seemed to pose the nicest legal problems; Dyer, a Chief Justice with a busy round of official duties, limited himself to cases which came within his professional orbit. As has already been observed, Dyer turned this situation to advantage, using it to record a wide sample of legal proceedings, both 'official' and 'unofficial'. With Plowden it was otherwise: for much of his life he was forced to rely on his own ability, and it was by sheer merit that he won the reputation of being at once the ablest and the most honest lawyer of his time.[2] It is in part a corollary of this that his 'exquisite and elaborate' *Commentaries* have come to be regarded as the most accurate and painstaking

[1] Written in 1601: William Fulbecke, *A Parallele*, p. 26.

[2] William Camden, *Annales* (1717), ii, 424; *D.N.B.* xv, 1314–5.

collection of its kind produced in the sixteenth and seventeenth centuries.[3] If Dyer's *Reports* are the product of an eminent judge, Plowden's *Commentaries* are the work of a great advocate.

Despite his later fame, much of Plowden's early life is obscure. He was born in 1518 and before taking up legal studies spent three years at Cambridge.[4] He tells us that he entered the Middle Temple in 1538 at the age of twenty and he is reputed to have studied so assiduously that he never left the precincts of the Temple for three years. The fact that his father had supported Catherine of Aragon may have driven him in upon himself.[5] Plowden's already intensive education was augmented some years later. He apparently spent four years at Oxford in studies which led to his being admitted to practise 'chirurgery and physic' by the University Convocation in 1552.[6] This seemingly incongruous pursuit may also have been prompted by his adherence to Catholicism during the regimes of Somerset and Northumberland when he perhaps felt the need of an alternative profession.[7] Yet it was during Edward VI's reign that he began practising law and already in 1548 he was named as a trustee by John Winchcombe the elder in a family settlement.[8] Plowden began reporting at least as early as 1550. The date of his admission to the bar has not been recorded, but when it did take place he was already a 'plodding and studious man' whose wide range of knowledge shows up in the *Commentaries*, as for example in the *Case of Mines* (1567).[9]

Plowden's uncompromising religious attitude was a decisive factor in his career. There can be little doubt that promotion to the coif and eventually to the bench was open to him on the score of ability, but unlike Bendlowes he could not reconcile himself even to the tepid Protestantism of the Elizabethan Settlement. He

[3] 3 Co. Rep. Pref. ivb; Winfield, pp. 187–8; Holdsworth, *Sources and Literature*, p. 92.

[4] Cooper, *Athenae*, i, 501.

[5] Hist. Parl.; Plow. Pref. iii.

[6] A. A. Wood, *Athenae Oxonienses* (1813), i, 503.

[7] Wallace, p. 145; cf. the life of Dr Thomas Phayer who qualified as a physician in 1558: Wood, i, 316.

[8] Hist. Parl.

[9] Lloyd, *State Worthies*, p. 383; Plow. 310 at p. 338.

refused in 1569 to subscribe to the Act of Uniformity and was bound over for one year;[10] he was one of a group of lawyers known to have heard mass 'at Baron Brown's, Fish Street Hill';[11] and in 1580 articles were exhibited against him before the Council for not attending church since 1569 and for contributing to the Middle Temple's being 'pestered with papists'.[12] It is also reported that he and Nicholas Harpsfield advised Justice Anthony Browne in the preparation of two books written on behalf of Mary Queen of Scots' claim to the English throne.[13] His religious disabilities notwithstanding, Plowden developed a prosperous practice, being described in 1576 as 'very lerned, of good lyvinge'.[14] He purchased land at Burghfield, Berkshire, and Shiplake in Oxfordshire. He was associated with the leading Catholic family of Berkshire, the Englefields, and it was Sir Francis Englefield who entrusted the administration of his Shropshire estates to Plowden. In 1558 he succeeded to his father's property in the same county.[15] Although a life-long Catholic it was characteristic of Plowden that he left legacies to poor parishioners and the Anglican vicars of the parishes in which his properties lay.[16]

In company with several other conservatively-minded lawyers Plowden had enjoyed rapid advancement under Mary. Like Bendlowes and Dalison he had his taste of politics in the parliaments of the 'fifties. He sat in the House of Commons on three occasions, representing Wallingford in October 1553, Reading in November 1554 and Wootton Bassett in 1555.[17] He was one of thirty-nine members of the last Parliament indicted in the King's Bench for unlicensed absence from the Commons: Plowden took

[10] *C.S.P. Dom.* 1547–80, p. 355.

[11] Ibid. Add. 1566–79, p. 550; the 'Baron Brown' in question was second baron of the Exchequer 1550–8.

[12] Ibid. 1547–80, p. 689; cf. Henry Foley (ed.), *Records of the English Province of the Society of Jesus* (1878), iv, 540–1.

[13] *H.M.C. Salisbury*, i, 542; cf. H. W. Woolrych, *Lives of Eminent Serjeants-at-Law* (1869), i, p. 130.

[14] *Cal. I.T. Recs.* i, Appendix iv, 471, printed from State Papers, Domestic, Elizabeth, cxi, no. 27.

[15] Hist. Parl. [16] P.C.C. 54 Brudnell (1585). [17] Hist. Parl.

a traverse pleading his innocence and succeeded in having the indictment withdrawn.[18] In the autumn of 1553 he was appointed a member of the Council of the Marches of Wales; a year later he was made a Justice of the Peace for various Midland counties; and in 1557 he became Deputy Chief Steward for the Duchy of Lancaster.[19] But greater rewards were to elude him. Along with twelve other lawyers Plowden received the Queen's writ in October 1558 to become serjeant the following Easter: but on Mary's death the writs abated and Plowden's name was not among those called by Elizabeth later in the year.[20] In 1579 high office might again have come his way. After Nicholas Bacon's death in February of that year the Queen waited some two months before appointing Thomas Bromley Chancellor in his place.[21] It has been suggested that the post was offered first to Plowden on condition that he conform; an autograph letter from Elizabeth to this effect was reputedly found among some old documents at Plowden Hall but afterwards lost.[22] The episode, if it took place, occurred during the dispute between Burghley and Leicester over the possibility of marriage between Elizabeth and the Duke of Alençon; Leicester was a supporter of Bromley's candidature and seems on this occasion to have scored over Cecil.[23] Plowden himself was acting for the Crown at this time in an important action which he reported: when he refers to the installation of Bromley he gives no hint of any personal involvement.[24] The

[18] 4 Inst. 17–18; Strype, *Memorials*, III, i, 262–4; Hist. Parl.

[19] Hist. Parl.; the exact date of Mary's reorganization of the Council of Wales cannot be determined; Williams, *Council in the Marches of Wales*, p. 37.

[20] *C.P.R.* 1557–8, p. 457; 1558–60, p. 65; Foss, v, 347.

[21] Bacon held the office of Lord Keeper, but Bromley received the title of Lord Chancellor together with its higher salary.

[22] Foley, iv, 539; details of this episode are found in *Records of the Plowden Family* by 'B.M.P.', printed in 1887 for private circulation. A copy of what is claimed as Plowden's reply to the Queen has been reproduced in Woolrych, p. 115. The alleged offer to Plowden is reminiscent of the strategy employed against Edmund Campion shortly after his capture in July 1581: Richard Simpson, *Edmund Campion* (1907), pp. 338–40.

[23] *H.M.C. Tenth Rep.* App. IV, p. 409; Hist. Parl.; E. St. J. Brooks, *Sir Christopher Hatton* (1946), pp. 171–2.

[24] *Walsingham's Case*, E. 21 Eliz., Plow. 547 at p. 565. All references and quota-

fact remains that, apart from his inclusion in the commissions of peace for Berkshire in 1562 and 1564, he held no public office of consequence under Elizabeth.[25]

Plowden achieved distinction in three related capacities: as barrister, treasurer of the Middle Temple, and law reporter. Either because of his intense dedication to study or his sojourn at Oxford little is recorded of his early years at the Temple. It was not until the autumn of 1557 that he was first appointed reader:[26] no indication survives of the subject of this or of his second lecture in 1560, but a shortened version of a reading given at New Inn on Westminster II, chapter 1, exists in manuscript.[27] Plowden's most significant contribution to the Middle Temple came with his long tenure as treasurer between 1561 and 1566: it was during this period and the years following that he superintended the construction of the new hall.[28] Since he never qualified to lodge at one of the Serjeants' Inns he remained as senior apprentice in the Temple and a moving force in its operation until his death in 1585.

As an advocate Plowden was conspicuously successful, but there is little trace of his pleading before 1558. The Yearbooks had already ceased before he was admitted to the bar. The first reference to his arguing a case is in Michaelmas term 1554 in the Court of Wards.[29] One of his first important clients was the Dean of Westminster from whom he received an annual stipend.[30] It is from this time that his name begins to appear with some regularity in contemporary reports.[31] He was, of course, barred from plead-

tions from the *Commentaries* are taken from the English edition of 1816 unless otherwise stated.

[25] *C.P.R.* 1560–3, p. 439; 1563–6, pp. 20, 39, 41.

[26] *Cal. M.T. Recs.* i, 110, 115, 123.

[27] Ibid. 128, 130; Dugdale, *Origines Juridicales* p. 217; his reading at New Inn is preserved in B.M.Harg. MS 89; cf. Cooper, *Athenae* i, 501.

[28] *Cal. M.T. Recs.* i, 131, 144, 158, 183, 199; *M.T. Bench Book*, pp. 7–8.

[29] Lib. of Congress, Gell MS, ff. 129*v*–30.

[30] *H.M.C. Tenth Rep.* App. IV, p. 409; cf. Ives, 'Legal Profession', p. 404.

[31] For example, Dyer, 209b, 274b, 308b, 314b, 316a, 334a, 354b; B.M. Harg. MS 8, f. 339; Harg. 10, f. 4*v*; Harg. 4, ff. 57, 155*v*, 178*v*; Harl. 1696, ff. 13*v*, 14*v*–15.

ing before the Common Bench, but his opinions were noted frequently in Exchequer Chamber cases and conferences at Serjeants' Inn. In his own 'Commentaries' Plowden usually designated himself 'an apprentice of the Middle Temple': it is in this guise that he first appears in a suit before the barons of the Exchequer in 1561.[32]

After Elizabeth's accession he became adept at extricating both himself and his fellow-Catholics from the sanctions of the new Acts of Supremacy and Uniformity.[33] 'The case is altered—no priest, no Mass', is a phrase which became established in legal folklore following an abortive attempt to indict Plowden for attending mass.[34] Yet his standing as an advocate was such that, after assisting Edmund Bonner to escape the obligation to take the oath of Supremacy, he was retained to act on behalf of the Anglican hierarchy as well.[35] In October 1566 he appeared at the bar of the House of Commons as counsel for Gabriel Goodman, Dean of Westminster, to oppose the abolition of sanctuaries for debt: according to Strype, Plowden pleaded 'with great reasons, laws and chronicles' and in the end the bill was defeated.[36] His clients were often drawn from the 'Establishment': by 1567, when he acted as counsel for William, Earl of Pembroke, he was already receiving an annual retainer of £5 from the Earl of Leicester.[37] Twelve years later Plowden's advice probably succeeded in retrieving the rights of certain Cheshire gentlemen to estates originally surrendered by the Dean and Chapter of Chester under Henry VIII.[38] The government itself retained his services in a number of important disputes. He was one of those whose opinion was sought by the Queen in the *Case of the Duchy of Lancaster* (1561),[39] and in 1568 he was consulted, along with the Solicitor-General, Richard Onslow, and Serjeants Wray and

[32] *Stradling v. Morgan*, E. 2 Eliz., Plow. 202. [33] 1 Eliz., chaps. 1 & 2.

[34] Foley, iv, 542.

[35] Woolrych, p. 119; cf. Dyer, 234a.

[36] John Strype, *Annals of the Reformation* (1824), I, ii, 229; Cooper, i, 501.

[37] *Records of the Plowden Family*, p. 20; *H.M.C. Tenth Rep.* App. IV, p. 409.

[38] B.M. Harl. MS 2060, ff. 90–113. [39] Plow. 212.

Manwood, about the patents for battery and calamine stone.[40] He was also one of a number of senior practitioners who examined the evidence in a dispute between Archbishops Grindal and Sandys over demesne land in Battersea.[41] At the instigation of the Privy Council he also undertook to advise humbler subjects such as Francis Tregion, a prisoner in the Marshalsea in 1578.[42] His good offices were sought as an arbitrator as readily as were those of the judges: in 1575, for instance, he helped to mediate in a dispute between the boroughs of Weymouth and Melcombe Regis.[43] Above all, he had the respect of his own profession, and it was Chancellor Bromley for one who praised 'the great discretion, circumspection and honesty of Mr. Plowden'.[44]

It was his reputation as an advocate, no less than as a reporter, which made Plowden one of the few practitioners of the mid-century whose legal pronouncements have been accorded as much respect as those of the judges. His argument in a case from Hilary 1559 regarding the royal prerogative vis-à-vis imposts stands as the basis of the later and more famous decision in *Bate's Case*.[45] Several copies still exist of Plowden's presentation in Easter term 1584 of Sir Thomas Tresham's claims to the manor of Houghton in Northamptonshire,[46] and two lengthy reports dealing with contingent remainders, which were widely reproduced, feature the opposing arguments of Plowden and John Popham, later Chief Justice of the King's Bench and himself a reporter.[47]

[40] *C.S.P. Dom.* 1547–80, p. 307; Plowden reports the trial at length, pp. 313–40; cf. M.B. Donald, *Elizabethan Monopolies* (1961), pp. 91–2.

[41] John Strype, *Edmund Grindal* (1821), p. 366.

[42] *A.P.C.* 1577–8, p. 249.

[43] Ibid. 1575–7, p. 368; cf. Dyer, 111a.

[44] Quoted in Cooper, i, 502.

[45] Virtually identical copies exist in H.M. Harg. MS 27, f. 84–5*v* (cf. f. 92) and Harg. 132, f. 66*v*; see Hall, 'Impositions and the Courts', pp. 207–8; the case is reported in Dyer, 165a.

[46] Among the manuscripts in which this speech is recorded are B.M. Harg. MS 9, ff. 2–14*v*; Lansd. MS 1072, f. 95; Add. MS 35951, f. 26*v*; L.I. Mayn. MS 82, ff. 57*v*–75; Bodl. Rawl. MS C. 85, ff. 55*v*–67*v*; C.U.L. MS Ff. 5, 4, ff. 344–61*v*.

[47] The two cases have, not surprisingly, become entangled over the years, but the earlier of the two is *Calverley's Case* (1577) and is found in the following collections: B.M. Harl. MS 6707, ff. 85–87; C.U.L. MS Ii. 5.20, ff. 7*v*–11; Bodl.

Another example of Plowden's 'grand learning en le ley' has been recorded by William Doddington of the Middle Temple in connection with a claim by the Crown to Hay Wood in Hereford.[48] The best known of Plowden's speeches comes from the case of *Basset v. Manxel* (1563) debated at Serjeants' Inn, Fleet Street, before Chief Justices Dyer and Catlin.[49] The suit, which involved title to some manors in Glamorgan, originated by bill in Chancery; the report, 'made by an uncertain author', mentions that the other pleaders were Bell, Bromley and Wray, but it gives only Plowden's arguments. 'At the request of certain students' the proceedings were printed by Tottel soon after the *Commentaries* themselves and they have been appended to every subsequent edition.[50] The same is true of the *Quaeries*, a series of 376 moot points probably compiled from Plowden's readings and found in various manuscript versions.[51]

Plowden was not always right in his opinions but even his mistakes seem to have been worthy of note. Leonard reports a case in 1578 where Plowden gave bad advice to a sheriff in regard to a writ of extent: Justice Manwood tactfully observed that the return was insufficient—'perhaps Master Plowden did not know' of a certain entry already on the roll which indicated that execution had not taken place?'[52] A more serious error is mentioned by William Hudson in his treatise on the Star Chamber. It seems that Plowden took the view that jurisdiction in the Star Chamber was governed by the statute 3 Henry VII, chapter 1. How much

Rawl. MS C.85, ff. 152*v*–64*v*; Longleat MS 240, ff. 116*v*–20; H.L.S. MS 2079, ff. 57–63; cf. Dyer, 354b. The second case is consistently cited without parties as 'Le opinion de Ed. Plowden de Middle Temple en un case vouchante le toller per lacte del tenant del terre le futur use appoint de surder'; see B.M. Harl. MS 6707, ff. 87*v*–9; Lansd. 1078, ff. 104–6; Harg. 15, ff. 6–9*v*; Harg. 373, ff. 88–97; L.I. Mayn. MS 29, ff. 252–7; Misc. 361, f. 152*v*; it can be tentatively dated as T. 1581.

48 B.M. Lansd. 1133, ff. 135–6*v*.

49 Plow. 1–15 (separate pagination at the end of regular reports).

50 First printed in 1579 (Beale, no. R.-486).

51 Probably first printed in 1620 (*S.T.C.* no. 20048); B.M. Harg. MSS 353, 351, 389; Add. MSS 36078, 36081.

52 *Colshil and Hastings' Case*, 20 Eliz., 2 Leon. 13.

his interpretation governed later practitioners is hard to say but one protégé, Serjeant Lovelace, accepted it and put forward a demurrer based on this point: when challenged with evidence to the contrary he could only answer that since Plowden had first put his hand to the demurrer he assumed he might follow St Augustine in any matter.[53]

Most of the surviving material which relates to Plowden's work at the bar was copied in the early seventeenth century when his reputation as a reporter was firmly established. It was in this capacity that he made his singular contribution to legal literature In practically every respect the *Commentaries* constitutes a break with tradition. It is one of the few sixteenth-century legal works, and the only set of reports, prepared for publication by an author in his own lifetime,[54] and Plowden had the distinction of seeing his own cases cited within a year of their being printed. His own copy of the first part of the *Commentaries*, complete with personal glosses in the margin, is still preserved in the library of his descendants.[55] Most remarkable, in view of the previous history of legal publishing, was the fact that the first volume came out within a few months of the adjudication of the last case.[56]

The immediate reason for this swift transition from notebook to printed page was given by Plowden in his Preface, but it bears re-examination. After he had lent some of his notes to colleagues, he tells us, certain less scrupulous individuals obtained access to them and hastily prepared copies of cases, some of which came into the hands of printers. The dual threat of slovenly transcription and unskilled printing moved the author to undertake an immediate but carefully prepared edition of his own. He

[53] *H.E.L.* i, 513.

[54] Another legal work in this category is Fitzherbert's *Abridgement*; Wallace, p. 144.

[55] The writer is indebted to Mr W. F. G. Plowden for the opportunity of examining this volume at Plowden Hall, Shropshire.

[56] The last case was argued in Trinity 1571 and the reports were brought out in the following October.

had the encouragement of many colleagues on the bench,[57] and with such backing he found a ready collaborator in Richard Tottel, who brought out the book in October 1571. Its reception was such as to lead to several further printings, together with a second collection, during the course of the next twenty-five years.[58] Part I was printed in October 1578 and after Part II had appeared in the following year both volumes were bound and sold together. This composite work also contained tables prepared by William Fleetwood, and the *Manxel Case*.[59] The first English translation did not appear until 1761, after which three further editions were produced, the last in 1816.[60]

It is clear that Plowden edited his notes with great care and endeavoured to elucidate as well as to report the authoritative legal opinions of his day. This accounts for the insertion of a number of personal annotations or glosses within the body of certain reports. It also explains why he took the trouble to inform his readers when he omitted certain arguments: thus he mentions in one case that before his coming Serjeants Morgan and Brooke had argued and that the next day 'I came late, for Saunders had begun his argument . . . and I was disturbed in my place, so I could not well report all that was said that day'.[61] Plowden was aware that reporting the speeches of living colleagues was a delicate art. Whatever his omissions, he took great pains to include any points which he deemed material to the issue while giving equal weight to both sides. 'I have not,' he assured his readers, 'given just cause of offence to any' nor 'of purpose or

57 Plow. Pref. iii, v; cf. Plucknett, 'Ellesmere', p. 245 n. 9; Dyer cited the *Commentaries* as early as 1573; B.M. Harg. MS 373, f. 173.

58 There were further editions in 1578, 1579, 1584, 1588, 1594, 1599; Beale, nos. R.-484, -485, -485a, -487a, -488b, -489, -489a, -490.

59 As in other works he published Tottel also added appropriate references to Brooke's *Abridgment*.

60 The others were brought out in 1779 and 1792; the latter was published in Dublin as a two-volume quarto edition. Plowden's reports were reprinted (with all the printed reports of decisions of the Superior Courts between 1220 and 1865) in the *English Reports* (1907), vol. 75.

61 *Wimbish v. Tailbois*, M. 4 Edw. VI, Plow. 38 at p. 46.

malice disgraced any man in these reports.'[62] Even where certain pleaders were passed over he made a point of listing their names and ranks. In short, while Plowden originally collected material for his own use, he was determined that once out of his hands it should combine utility with fairness to those involved.

Unlike most reporters of the time he began at the beginning—with a full and lucid heading for each case which includes the names of the parties, the date of argument, the tribunal concerned and the term in which the action was instituted. Here again, Plowden was catering for the requirements of colleagues, especially students who were increasingly being encouraged to cite cases with greater precision. In most of his entries he inserted at the beginning a copy of the official record and at the end the final judgment. Occasionally this yields a report spanning several years and including arguments in more than one tribunal. Each entry is a carefully prepared piece of work, complete in itself and independent of the rest of the volume.

Almost as significant as Plowden's decision to publish his own collection was Tottel's to print it. Tottel has been condemned for relying too heavily on the efforts of earlier printers,[63] but he knew how to gauge the market in law books and he must be credited with starting the revival of systematic reporting. He was undoubtedly aware of the increasing number of manuscript reports circulating during the 'sixties and 'seventies. Until he brought out the *Commentaries* there had been no new cases published since Myddleton's Yearbook for 27 Henry VIII.[64] It may have been the response to his reissue of Fitzherbert's *Graunde Abridgement* in 1565 which encouraged Tottel to accept the publication of fresh material to succeed the Yearbooks, albeit in a novel form. With new statutes and forms of action demanding judicial attention, the profession could not continue to rely on the unprinted notes of its members; the very reasons which prompted Plowden to publish demonstrate the weakness of so haphazard an

[62] Plow. Pref. vii–viii. [63] Putnam, pp. 31–2.

[64] Beale, nos. R.-469, -470; cf. Cowley, pp. xlix–l; this Yearbook came out sometime between 1541 and 1547.

arrangement. The appearance of the *Commentaries* not only satisfied a need for fresh decisions but created a continuing demand for them: it also proved that under the right conditions reports could be produced both quickly and accurately.[65]

Despite the fact that Plowden's cases occupy 567 folio-sized pages in the combined edition, there are only sixty-three separate entries, forty-three in Part I, twenty in Part II. Obviously these are, on average, much lengthier than those compiled by his contemporaries. And while the period spanned extends from 1550 to 1580 there is no attempt to cover all the years concerned, although the cases are arranged chronologically. Here again, Plowden took care to explain his motives. Because some actions 'hung in argument eight, ten or twelve terms', it was impossible to reduce them to a single year. At the same time, because a span of several years might intrude between consecutive entries, it was virtually impossible to emulate the Yearbooks and 'preserve an uninterrupted connexion and dependency in time'.[66]

This does not explain, however, why Plowden was content to publish such a comparatively small number of decisions out of a fairly long career: the average is two per year, with five the maximum.[67] It is probable that he had collected considerably more: he mentions in his Preface that he had notes of many other arguments but abandoned them for lack of a final decision.[68] Plowden was prepared to report proceedings at length but only when the issues under examination were resolved: here he differed from both Dyer and Dalison, in many of whose entries no 'sanction of judgment' is found. Of his unprinted cases Plowden gave some to friends, keeping no copies and thus dissociating himself from these inferior specimens. A few scraps of information hint at Plowden's generosity: George Croke notes a report of an Exchequer case in 7 Elizabeth shown him by Coke, 'which he

[65] *H.E.L.* v, 371–3; Plucknett, 'Genesis of Coke's Reports', pp. 191–4.

[66] Plow. Pref. viii; for example, *Walsingham's Case*, 547 at pp. 552, 562; *Wimbish v. Tailbois*, 38 at p. 60; *Smith v. Stapleton*, 426 at pp. 437–8, all of which span several years or terms.

[67] Dyer averages roughly 25 entries per year, Coke 14.

[68] Pref. vii.

said he had from Edmund Plowden',[69] and Coke himself acknowledges the latter's assistance in his own reports.[70] There also survives at least one set of cases strikingly reminiscent of Plowden's style, but without any indication of authorship.[71]

Having restricted his selection of cases for publication to actions upon which judgment had been rendered, Plowden amplified his treatment of them. From the outset of his career he had made notes on points of law at moots and readings and in the courts until

> I became at last disposed to report the arguments and judgments made in the king's courts upon demurrers in law, as abounding more copiously with matter of improvement, and being more capable of perfecting the judgment, than arguments on other occasions.[72]

The break with the Yearbook tradition was complete. With the introduction of written pleadings significant debate came to centre on demurrers or special verdicts, which had to be thoroughly scrutinized by pleaders and judges alike before acceptance or rejection by the court. Thus while Plowden, like the Yearbook reporters, laid great stress on oral argument, he did so for different reasons. The older form of reporting had consisted mainly 'of the sudden sayings of the judges' in response to motions put by pleaders at the bar. This was in the days of verbal pleadings when the art of advocacy was concerned with the framing of the issues of law rather than their resolution. All too often the Yearbook reporters neglect to record the final judgment in a suit because their readers would not have been interested. By the end of the sixteenth century the opposite was true, with many private reporters tending to note court decisions in isolation and with scant regard for the facts or oral arguments.[73]

For Plowden it was 'the arguments of those who were men of

[69] Croke Eliz. 24; the same report occurs in 1 Leon. 331–5.
[70] 3 Co. Rep. 79a.
[71] B.M. Harg. MS 9, ff. 182–271*v*; all the entries come from 1576.
[72] Plow. Pref. iii.
[73] Maitland, *Year Book 3 Edw. II*, p. lxxi; *H.E.L.* v, 371–3; Milsom, pp. 61–6.

5. Edmund Plowden, portrait by an unknown artist. (By permission of W. F. G. Plowden, Esq., Plowden Hall.)

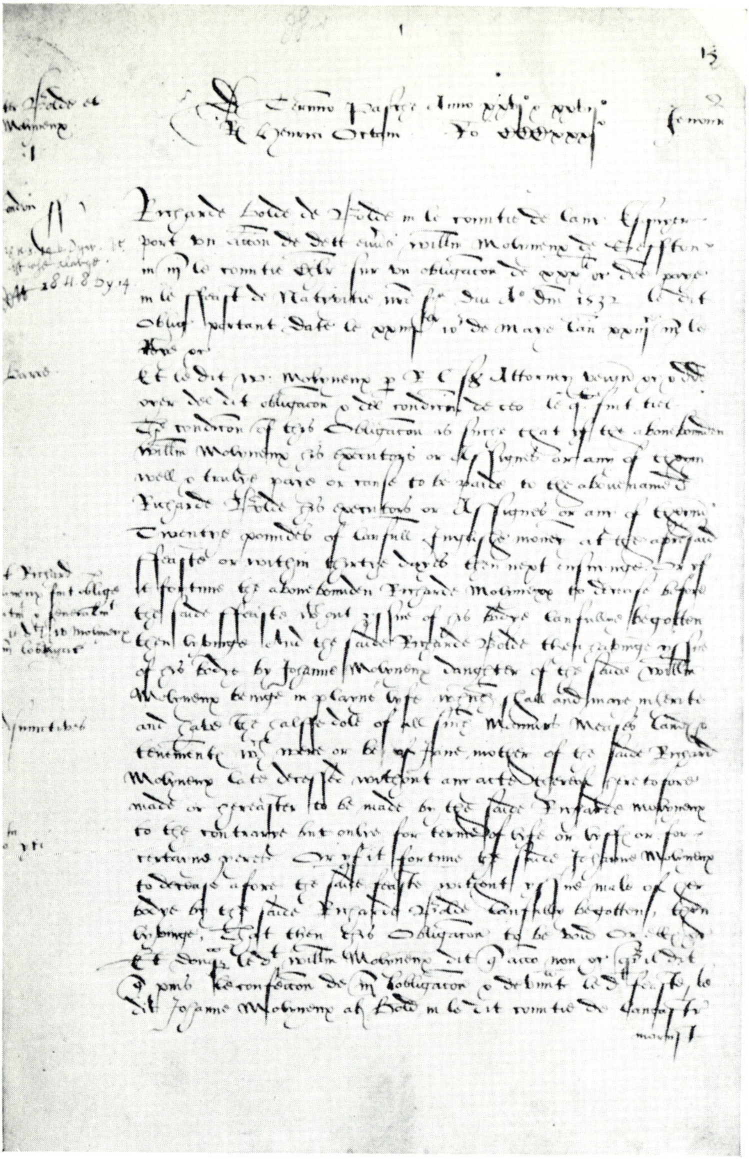

6. The first case reported by William Bendlowes: a folio from the original set of MS reports. (Bodleian Library, Rawlinson MS C. 728, f. 13.)

greatest note and reputation for learning' which merited special attention. Because his own practice lay chiefly in the King's Bench and Exchequer he gave prominence to senior apprentices and utter-barristers as well as to serjeants and justices. His reports were the first to highlight the pleading of the Attorney and Solicitor-General, two legal officers who eventually superseded the King's Serjeants as the Crown's chief advocates.[74] The number of persons who seem to have taken part in notable cases must have taxed Plowden's ingenuity: in one King's Bench action 'many apprentices and . . . all the serjeants' argued at the bar, as well as four judges.[75] But it was above all 'the sages of the law', justices of proven reputation like James Dyer, Anthony Browne, Edward Saunders and Roger Manwood, who are given the place of honour. Despite his not being qualified to plead there Plowden takes more than a third of his reports from the Common Pleas. Notwithstanding its relative decline in popularity among litigants, business was brisk enough and important suits were still being heard there. Like most of his contemporaries, he valued the court's educative function and esteemed its judges; hence he devoted more space to its dicta than to those of the other tribunals. The King's Bench and Exchequer together accounted for another third of his entries, and there are cases from Chancery (1), the Court of Wards (3), Exchequer Chamber (4), Serjeants' Inns (2) and the London Court of Hustings (2), together with assorted notes taken from commissions of assize.

Plowden's method, although more consistent than most reporters', was not rigorously so. Thus a few cases in his collection are comparatively brief. His report of a Chancery suit, *Ross v. Pope* (1551), deals cursorily with the application of common law on the execution of recognizances;[76] a challenge to the jury taken in the Common Pleas is disposed of in a page, although the

[74] For instance, Plow. 3, 7; *H.E.L.* v, 341. The terms 'Solicitor-General' and 'Attorney-General' did not come into vogue until the time of Elizabeth, although as 'King's Solicitor' and 'King's Attorney' they appear as early as 1487; YB E. 2 Hen. VII, pl. 7; Ives, 'Legal Profession', pp. 260–1.

[75] *Fulmerston v. Steward*, E. 6 Edw. VI, Plow. 102.

[76] Plow. 72 Appendix IV, pp. 339–40.

principle involved was of considerable importance;[77] and when the validity of a premature pardon was considered by the King's Bench Plowden, although not present, included a brief résumé.[78]

These exceptions apart, the treatment is fairly uniform, with the written pleadings placed first and followed by the author's summary of the facts and legal issues. Then come the arguments of counsel and/or the bench. While Plowden often characterized an entry as 'a brief report', some of them run to twenty-five or even thirty pages. He describes his method in the Preface:

> I have for the most part reported cases in a summary way, collecting together the substance . . . of all that was said on one side and on the other, and oftentimes of all that was said by the judges themselves, without reciting their arguments verbatim.[79]

Plowden's mastery of this sort of reporting can be traced as it developed in the earlier years. He himself regarded the case of *Throckmorton v. Tracy* (1555) as the dividing line.[80] Although reproduced in a 'summary way', it fills eighteen pages made up chiefly of the arguments of opposing counsel. It is not perhaps typical of Plowden's work, being a 'Serjeants' Case' in which eleven old and new members of the coif participated.[81] Nonetheless, when compared with, say, *Reniger v. Fogassa* (1550), his first case, it exhibits greater signs of selectivity and organization:[82] the debates are more compact, with various exceptions carefully tabulated, and where counsel became repetitious the reporter said so and cut out the offending words. In Plowden's opinion 'there are few arguments so pure as not to have refuse in them': the art of reporting lay in separating the relevant material from the rest, and although on occasion he did insert additional words of his own 'showing the matter more fully', at no time did he depart from 'the sense or intent of the party'.[83] One of the considerations which prompted Plowden to make his work public

[77] *Newdigate v. Earl of Derby*, M. 1 & 2 P. & M., Plow. 117; Appendix IV, pp. 341–2; cf. Dyer, 107b.

[78] *Cole's Case*, M. 13 Eliz., Plow. 401.

[79] Plow. Pref. iv.

[80] Plow. 145–63; Pref. iv.

[81] Dyer, 124b.

[82] Plow. 1–20.

[83] Plow. Pref. iv.

was that most of the unauthorized versions put about lacked the pleadings. The benefit to his readers of their inclusion lay in the fact that his collection then served both as a set of reports and as a book of entries. In its discharge of the second function he considered it 'more sure and safe to be relied upon' than ordinary volumes of that type, for it was only when pleadings could be studied in the context of litigation that they could be relied upon.[84] Both Bendlowes and Coke were to follow Plowden's lead, although in modified form.

The subject-matter of litigation in the 'Commentaries' is of necessity limited, although quite varied. Unlike his reporter-colleagues Plowden was less interested in specific actions than in the enunciation of general principles. In the medieval period, as exemplified in the Yearbooks, pleaders had tended to argue in the scholastic tradition, extracting legal issues from a given set of facts. The sixteenth century saw the real beginning of the inductive process in judicial decision-making which has characterized the common law ever since.[85] And it is Plowden's Reports which best illustrate the process. At a conference held in Serjeants' Inn, Chancery Lane, the question arose whether an original or a judicial writ should be directed to the coroner in the event of a sheriff's default:[86] within the three pages in which the Chancellor's authority to issue common law writs is reviewed, mundane considerations of fact and evidence soon give way to loftier statements of principle:

For every thing that is shewn [in evidence] shall be taken most strongly against the person that shews it.

Our law says that nothing is true but what may be tried, for truth never wants trial.[87]

Again, from a seemingly trivial dispute over the transport of £40 worth of wood there emerged a full-scale discussion of the

[84] Ibid. v–vi.

[85] Allen, *Law in the Making*, pp. 161–2, 201–7 especially p. 203 n. 1.

[86] *Wimbish v. Willoughby*, T. 6 Edw. VI., Plow. 73–6.

[87] Ibid. 75, 76.

basis of consideration as applied to valid contracts.[88] In another entry the Common Bench held that an executor who was also creditor of an estate might retain assets against the claims of subsequent creditors: the judges added—summing up eighteen years of doctrine on the Statute of Wills—that 'testaments are much favoured and the will of the testator is benignly respected by the law'.[89] The interpretation of legal instruments in the light of the maker's intention is indeed one of the most pregnant themes explored by Plowden and it merits special consideration.[90]

Some historians have read significance into Plowden's choice of title for his Reports.[91] He himself adduces two reasons for using the term 'Commentaries': it was a distinctive title which students and practitioners could cite conveniently, and it connoted a 'register or memorial of acts and sayings', a good description of the volume.[92] There is some risk in assuming that the title reflects Plowden's practice of inserting his own remarks in the reports: these are 'commentaries' in the generally accepted meaning and they form an integral part of the collection. But Plowden was careful to divorce his own opinions from those of counsel and court: the object of these glosses was either to elucidate a legal point or to supplement authorities cited, and if, like Coke, Plowden attempted to systematize certain aspects of jurisprudence, there was never any doubt where the words of the court ended and those of the reporter began. Some of Plowden's remarks are merely brief observations on the merits of a judgment, references to relevant acts of parliament, or quotations of legal definitions and maxims. In the later entries, as he gained experience and seniority, the comments become less deferential and more didactic. In the leading decision of *Stowel v. Lord Zouch* (1569) he admits to leaving out several cases cited by Serjeant Bendlowes

[88] *Sharington v. Strotton*, M. 6 & 7 Eliz., ibid. 298 at p. 305.

[89] *Woodward v. Lord Darcy*, T. 4 & 5 P. & M., ibid. 184 at p. 185; cf. YB T. 19 Hen. VIII, pl. 4.

[90] See below, pp. 227–39; cf. S.E. Thorne, Introduction to *A Discourse upon the Exposition and Understanding of the Statutes* (1942), pp. 94–7.

[91] Veeder, p. 9; cf. Plucknett, *Concise History*, p. 280.

[92] Plow. Pref. viii.

because in his opinion the statute to which they related was not germane to the case.[93] Other observations really amounted to instructions to the reader on such matters as proceeding in the Court of Exchequer, obtaining a writ of consultation or bringing forward a bill of intrusion.[94] Occasionally they approximate to minor treatises which had discernible influence on his colleagues and successors, whether reporters like Coke and Popham or luminaries like Christopher Hatton and Thomas Egerton. A good example is Plowden's lengthy statement at the end of *Eyston v. Studd* (1574) which epitomized current doctrine on the interpretation of statutes.[95]

Most law reports of the time, particularly those compiled late in the century, contain cases extracted from others' notebooks which have invariably gone unacknowledged either because the reporter did not envisage a public readership or because the printer did not know or care about their origin. Plowden, by contrast, was scrupulously fair in acknowledging any assistance he received. To fill gaps occasioned by his absence from court he often relied upon 'the credible relation of others'.[96] Usually he submitted a draft of his report to the serjeants and judges who had argued in the case.[97] At one of the assizes held in the Guildhall Brooke's argument 'was immediately reported' to Plowden, possibly by the Chief Justice himself;[98] on another occasion he was able to obtain from Chief Justice Catlin, in whose chamber the meeting took place, a relation of a conference at Serjeants' Inn between the four judges of the King's Bench.[99] In the interests of both learning and reporting Plowden might even petition the bench to elaborate its reasons for rendering a particular judgment.[100] He evidently enjoyed the confidence of Dyer, who on one occasion showed him passages from his notes on a text from Bracton.[101]

93 Plow. 353 at p. 375.

94 Ibid. 383, 471, 561; *F.N.B.* 112, 451.

95 Plow. 459 at pp. 465–8; cf. the treatises on interpretation of statutes attributed to Hatton and Egerton: Thorne, *Discourse*, pp. 58, 60, 140–54.

96 For instance, Plow., 169, 261, 401, 410, 481, 514.

97 Plow. Pref. vii.

98 *Panel v. Moor*, T. 2 & 3 P. & M., Plow. 91 at p. 92.

99 *Chapman v. Dalton*, T. 7 Eliz., ibid. 284 at pp. 291–2.

100 Ibid. 309.

101 Ibid. 159.

On occasion his religion could be an obstacle to Plowden's work: when his presence was noticed at the trial of Edmund Campion he was ordered to leave by one of the judges 'not liking that he should report it, or even witness it'.[102] On the other hand, Edward Saunders was particularly helpful to his friend and fellow Catholic. In the case of *Throckmorton v. Tracy*, he supplied Plowden in advance with the information that Brooke had opted for judgment in favour of the plaintiff.[103] It was Saunders, then Chief Baron, who also supplied much of the material for *Sir Thomas Wroth's Case* (1573) in the Exchequer; Plowden had submitted his report for approval and correction, because judgment had not been pronounced in open court.[104] Similarly, when he submitted his notes on a criminal prosecution at Warwick assizes to the justices for confirmation, Dyer added some observations of his own.[105] Plowden was untiring in his search for accuracy and a clear interpretation of the law: in the decision of *Clere v. Brook* (1573) he put an involved point on consanguinity successively to Manwood, Harper and Mounson, all judges of the Common Bench.[106]

It is widely recognized that Plowden was the most 'scientific' of early reporters. In addition to taking careful notes and seeking the corroboration of his colleagues, he studied the record in advance so that he had a grasp of the issues before they were argued.[107] Yet to some degree the 'commonplace' character so evident in Dyer's reports persists in the *Commentaries*. Plowden made reference to the promotion and death of friends; thus he mentions the passing of Anthony Browne in 1567—'who was a judge of profound learning and great eloquence'—and his replacement by Richard Harper.[108] Even more incongruous in such a purposeful compilation are the Latin verses composed in memory of Browne and two other advocates of note, Thomas

[102] Simpson, *Campion*, p. 434. [103] Plow. 145 at p. 163.
[104] Ibid. 452 at pp. 455–8.
[105] *The Queen v. Saunders*, H. 18 Eliz., ibid. 473, 475.
[106] Ibid. 442 at p. 451. [107] Plow. Pref. vi–vii.
[108] Plow. 356.

Gawdy and Richard Catlin.[109] In the course of other entries the reporter lists the call of new serjeants; with typical thoroughness he includes for the members of one group their Inn and county seat.[110] Extraneous comments are rare, although on one occasion we are told that Justice Humphrey Browne did not argue 'because he was so old that his senses were decayed and his voice could not be heard'.[111]

The impact of Plowden's pioneering effort was not only reflected in the production of further new collections, it was felt by the profession as a whole. Almost from their first appearance in 1571 the *Commentaries* became required reading for students as well as practitioners;[112] by 1585, when Plowden died, the wheel had come full circle. Having begun his own studies when the Yearbooks constituted the only source of current decisions, he succeeded in transmitting to future generations what was still relevant and useful among their entries. William Fleetwood, who compiled a table for the edition of 1578, considered Plowden's reports the best source for learning the elements of common law.[113] Coke also 'reverenced much' the wealth of information found in their lengthy entries although he did not hesitate to point out mistakes which came to light in 'the wisdom of time',[114] while Chief Justice Rolle, himself a reporter of some consequence, ranked Plowden first among the private reporters as worthy of a student's attention.[115] A half-century later Roger North, while stressing the value of Yearbook learning, suggested that beginners should start with Plowden as less abstruse. In the eighteenth century the work was still a recognized text-book, and, like Dyer's, was augmented with a wide range of references and citations in the later editions.

The rapid assimilation of Plowden into the curriculum of

[109] Ibid. 180, 376; but cf. *D.N.B.* vii, 960.

[110] Ibid. 164, 342. [111] Ibid.

[112] For instance, Dyer, 376b; Bendl. 312; B.M. Harl. MS 5141 (Dalison), f. 24; C.U.L. MS Dd. 10.37, f. 165*v*.

[113] Dedication, *Annalium*, p. i. [114] Noted in Spedding, vi, 76–7.

[115] Preface to Rolle's *Abridgment* (1668), p. viii; Henry Rolle was Chief Justice of the Common Pleas 1648–55.

the Inns of Court is demonstrated by the number of surviving summaries of his work in manuscript. Anthony Benne entered the Middle Temple in 1583 and must have begun compiling short notes from Plowden's cases soon after.[116] Similarly, Humphrey Rant prepared a set of extracts and tables shortly after his admission to Gray's Inn in 1614.[117] Thomas Twisden of the Inner Temple employed a different approach; he set out a summary of the issues in each 'commentary' and then rewrote the cases more fully with emphasis on the arguments.[118] Another student whose early notes have survived was Timothy Turner, who entered Gray's Inn in 1607; his first set of cases consisted of an abridgment of Plowden's entries from Part I of his Reports.[119] Several other collections appear to be the work of students or young practitioners: their similarity of arrangement, if not of style, makes it obvious that all were taken from the printed volumes and not from some independent manuscript source.[120] The printers soon recognized the popularity of these condensed versions of Plowden: Thomas Ashe, that indefatigable abridger, prepared a summary in French which was published in 1600 and again in 1607. A set of choice cases—*Critica Juris Ingenioso*—came out in 1661.[121]

Plowden and Dyer may be said to have initiated two branches in the style of subsequent reporting. Dyer's system of recording day-to-day processes was the more widely emulated: those few who count as disciples of Plowden must surely have been conscious of preparing 'reports' rather than mere 'notes of cases'. Both Bendlowes and Coke not only copied certain features of the *Commentaries* but reflected a similar awareness of the profession's requirements. One lasting legacy, common to the bulk of reports

[116] B.M. Harl. MS 4562, ff. 107–21*v*; *M.T. Adm. Reg.* i, 52.

[117] Harl. 924, ff. 1–32*v*; *G.I. Adm. Reg.* p. 140.

[118] H.L.S. MS 2144, ff. 1–57; Twisden entered the Inner Temple in 1617 (*Adm. Reg.* p. 219), later becoming a justice of the King's Bench.

[119] Turner's notebook was lent to the writer by its owner, Sir John Neale; note especially ff. 4–14*v*; *G.I. Adm. Reg.* p. 118.

[120] Other MSS include B.M. Harg. 403; Harl. 996, 1345, 6681; Lansd. 1116–7; Add. 24845; L.I. Mayn. 123; Bodl. Rawl. C.498, 647; Lib. of Congress MS 55.

[121] *S.T.C.* nos. 20037–8, P.2608–10.

from the late-sixteenth century onwards, was the emphasis on fuller and more accurate case headings. This was coincidental with the rise of precedent, itself considerably encouraged by Plowden's accurate citations. By the latter part of the century references to plea rolls, naming of parties and dating by terms had become a regular feature of both printed and unprinted reports.

By their very nature many of Plowden's entries might be termed 'leading cases'. Despite imperfections in the system of reporting, 'consistency of judicial decision' was much in evidence in the sixteenth century. The methods by which it was achieved were sometimes crude but none the less real. Even without the doctrine of *stare decisis* certain notable decisions exercised a *de facto* control over later litigation:[122] to barristers of the time they were 'principal' cases. One judge, in a letter to Cecil, commended to his attention a report of Dyer's which he described as 'long, good and worthy of reading':[123] although the description might better have been applied to much of Plowden's output, it demonstrates that certain decisions transcended the vagaries of individual note-taking. On the other hand, by studying different versions of the same 'principal' case we can gain an insight into the art of reporting as it was practised by lawyers of the sixteenth century.

In view of the selective nature of Plowden's entries it may appear surprising that more of them are not recorded elsewhere. Doubtless this is in part because some of his key disputes arose in the Court of Exchequer: both *Reniger v. Fogassa* and the *Case of Mines*, involving weighty principles of interpretation and occupying a combined total of fifty pages, originated there.[124] Again, the fact that of the nineteen King's Bench suits only two are reported elsewhere[125] is to be explained by the preponderance in these private compilations of cases in the Common Pleas, the court in which their authors chiefly practised or studied. It is

[122] This is particularly true of Exchequer Chamber cases: Hemmant, ii, pp. xviii–xix; cf. Lewis, xlviii, 230–4.

[123] *H.M.C. Salisbury*, xv, 391; cf. Plow. 96. [124] Plow. 1–20, 310–39.

[125] *Fulmerston v. Steward*, E. 6 Edw. VI, ibid. 102–10; Dal. 132; *Bracebridge v. Cook*, T. 14 Eliz., Plow. 416–24; B.M. Harg. MS 10, ff. 40*v*–3; see Appendix III, pp. 316, 324–5.

harder to understand why some of Plowden's own reports from that court are not found in Bendlowes, Dyer or Dalison, especially in view of the part which they and other reporters took in pleading some of these cases.[126] One such is *Willion v. Berkley* (1562), the subject of Plowden's longest entry, which undertakes a penetrating examination of the statute *De Donis* (1285) and the writs of formedon. Both Harper and Bendlowes contributed useful arguments on the nature of entail as it related to the Crown while Dyer as Chief Justice summed up the issues and together with Anthony Browne gave the opinion of the court. Among other points the judges analysed the corporate capacity of the king and his relationship to the body politic.[127]

Roughly one-third of Plowden's cases (19) are reported independently by colleagues, fifteen of them having been argued before the Common Bench. Not unexpectedly, most of these occur in Dyer.[128] Superficially, the main contrast between the two reporters' styles is one of scale: thus in the deliberation on the Duchy of Lancaster leases Dyer disposes of the issues in one page, Plowden takes thirteen.[129] But where two entries are comparable in length and subject-matter the main difference lies in presentation. Thus in *Newdigate v. the Earl of Derby* (1554) each report conveys the cardinal point that a peer of the realm was entitled to challenge any jury which did not contain at least one knight;[130] but Dyer's version, although adequate for professional purposes, is sketchy and disjointed and lacks the polish and structural unity found in Plowden's. Both reporters note the citation from Fitzherbert's Abridgment upon which the decision was based, but Plowden quotes it at length whereas Dyer merely cites it among several cases; on the other hand Dyer, prepared as always for any eventuality, ends by speculating whether a commoner could challenge on the same ground if his opponent were a knight. In short, the two versions exemplify the contrast between

[126] Plow. 272–3, 277, 345, 529.

[127] Ibid. 223 at p. 234; *H.E.L.*, iv. 184.

[128] See Appendix III

[129] Dyer, 209b; Plow. 212–23.

[130] Dyer, 107b; Plow. 117; Appendix IV, pp. 341–2.

an assiduously compiled notebook and a carefully prepared set of reports.

The difference between a reporter who takes part in litigation and one who observes it is seen in the case of *Throckmorton v. Tracy* (1555).[131] Dyer's presentation, although lengthy by his standards (six pages), consists exclusively of his own arguments which he had delivered as a newly-appointed serjeant: true, these constitute a concise, carefully reasoned exposition of reversions, but the opinions of the other ten serjeants and four judges are omitted. Plowden's eighteen-page entry gives a more balanced account. Of particular interest is his report of Dyer's speech which is equal in length and markedly similar in content to its author's version, although not copied from it. It illustrates Plowden's scrupulous technique; he apparently conferred with Dyer and perhaps read his notes, but took most of his information while present at the hearing. Characteristically, he extends his treatment to later terms when the bench argued, thus covering the entire suit.[132]

Despite the care he lavished on them, Plowden's reports were not always superior to Dyer's. In *Kidwelly v. Brand* (1551),[133] an early decision noted by Plowden, the issue concerned the demand for, and payment of, rent 'out of the land'. Proceedings differed from most in that the judges made their decision without open argument by counsel. Plowden was content to take his information from the record, having been absent when the judges discussed the case. Dyer, although still an apprentice, provides a more readable summary of the facts and points out that he was involved in the case; he reports directly the pronouncements of the court and in particular the opinion of Justice Hales. By contrast, Plowden's version supplies a rare instance where he introduced his own views directly into the text of a report.

There are only five cases reported by both Bendlowes and Plowden. No doubt Bendlowes attempted to avoid duplication

[131] Dyer, 124b–6b; Plow. 145–63.

[132] Plowden's report covers Hilary & Easter 1555.

[133] Plow. 69–71; Dyer, 68a–8b; Appendix III, p. 315.

as much as possible particularly since his entries lacked much by comparison. A good illustration is the decision of *Welcden v. Elkington* (1577) which Dyer also notes.[134] An action of trespass was instituted in relation to the demise of a term of years which had given rise to a conflict of interest between the executor and remainderman: this was an issue which came to the courts frequently and attracted the notice of reporters, particularly in the second half of the century.[135] Plowden doubtless chose this particular action for the detail in which the nature of an unexpired term was discussed with particular reference to possessory and proprietory rights. The final judgment upholding executory limitation of a term was noted by all three reporters. Dyer concentrated on the majority view—his own and Manwood's—drawing attention to the testator's original intent; Plowden maintained the balance by including the opposing arguments of Popham and Windham, who distinguished various modes of occupation of property; while Bendlowes, apart from transcribing the pleadings, merely observed that judgment was given on the basis of a beneficiary's consent to the conditions of a legacy.

One last 'principal' decision which may be examined for purposes of comparison is *Fulmerston v. Steward* (1554), one of five cases found in 'Dalison' and noted by the reporter himself.[136] It concerns a leasehold and the effect upon it of Henry VIII's act dissolving the larger religious houses.[137] Here was another matter which was often the object of litigation, but in this instance the problem was complicated by the renewal of the lease a year before the dissolution act of 1536; by upholding the provisions of the second lease the King's Bench established a precedent which held firm in similar cases under Elizabeth.[138] Dalison and Dyer give very similar versions, concentrating on

[134] Plow. 516–25; Bendl. 308–11; Dyer, 358b; see Appendix III, p. 327.

[135] For instance, C.U.L. MS Gg. 3.26, f. 115*v*; B.M. Lansd. MS 1084, f. 68.

[136] Plow. 102–10; Dyer, 102b–3b; B.M. Harl. MS 5141, ff. 23*v*–24; the case is also reported in Harl. MS 1691, ff. 90–90*v*, but this version was probably abridged from Dyer.

[137] 31 Hen. VIII, chap. 13.

[138] For example, B.M. Harg. MS 8, ff. 6, 56*v*, 59*v*, 151.

arguments from the bench, particularly those of Justices Bromley and Portman, but confining their attention to the technicalities of pleading. Plowden's much fuller account adds considerably to the importance of the decision by examining the court's interpretation of the act. The gravity of the case is shown by his statement that it was argued 'by many apprentices and by all the serjeants at the bar'.[139]

Plowden, the 'reporters' reporter', designed his collection solely as a guide for his colleagues in the profession. For the most part, therefore, his work has little to offer the general historian. Among the exceptions to this rule is the case of *Buckley v. Rice Thomas* (1555), which is also noted by Dyer.[140] This is the only suit reported at common law over a disputed election in the sixteenth century, although a number of others impinge on the subject.[141] Dyer disposes of the issues in a page-and-a-half while Plowden in his 'brief' recital covers the same ground in ten pages. Both stress two overriding issues arising from the false return by a sheriff of a Member for a Welsh constituency. Historically, the most significant point relates to the validity of an election 'by the greater number' without indication of the number of electors. Legally, the point deemed of greater weight was whether the statute 27 Henry VIII, chapter 26, uniting England and Wales, governed the sending of representatives from the Welsh shires to Parliament: in the end the Common Bench held the affirmative on both issues. Plowden, still in his early phase of reporting, lavishes perhaps too much attention on the intricacies of debate, particularly the legal implication of the term *licet* in the sheriff's return.[142] As he was absent for the arguments of counsel he concentrates upon the opinions of the four recently-appointed

[139] Plow. 102; the case also appears in B.M. Harl. MS 1691, ff. 90–3.

[140] Plow. 118–31; Dyer lists the case as argued in E. 2 & 3 P. & M.; Dyer, 113b.

[141] *Executors of Skewys v. Chamond*, E. 36 & 37 Hen. VIII, Dyer, 60a–60b; *Bronker's Case*, T. 1 Eliz., Dyer, 168b; *Anon.*, 18 Eliz., B.M. Harg. MS 8, f. 214; *Anon.*, E. 2 & 3 P. & M., Harl. MS 5141, f. 32*v*; see Edwards, xiv (1964), 187–91.

[142] See argument of Saunders J. at 124–5.

judges,[143] of whom Stanford and Brooke make some interesting comments on election procedure. Stanford held that it was enough for the sheriff to state generally that a member had been elected 'by the greater number', whether this was by voice or by show of hands. Brooke concurred, adding that a declaration of election was sufficient without reference to the number of electors involved and citing in support of this view his own experience as a Member of Parliament for London.[144] Without any direct precedents for its guidance the court considered a number of intriguing analogies, the shearing of a flock of sheep, provision of a minor with the necessities of life and theft of property from an inn.[145]

Historically, perhaps the most celebrated report in the *Commentaries* is that of *Hales v. Petit* (1562).[146] Neither the parties to the action nor the 'matters of law' debated are especially memorable in themselves. As Plowden relates it, the case told the familiar story of a widow suing for restitution of property originally held in jointure: what made it different was the identity of the deceased husband and the manner of his death. The involvement of members of the judiciary and their families in litigation was not uncommon in the sixteenth century, as the law reports attest;[147] but the Hales affair, of which there are four different versions, was more than a dispute over the property of a judge.[148] James Hales had been elevated to the Common Bench in 1549 as a distinctly Protestant member of the profession—one of the few who seems to have manifested his religious sentiments during this troubled period. He was an able and highly respected jurist whose opinions were frequently sought in the last years of Edward VI.[149] Despite

143 Anthony Browne, Saunders, Stanford and Brooke.

144 Plow. 128; cf. Edwards, p. 188.

145 Plow. 128; Brooke does cite one precedent from the 'Old Book of Entries', 149b.

146 Plow. 253–64.

147 Among those judges whose litigious exploits are reported are Richard Harper (I.T. Petyt MS 511, vol. 13, f. 43*v*) and Roger Manwood (Bendl. 217).

148 See Appendix III, p. 320.

149 Note particularly the reports of Dalison, above Chap. III, p. 120.

his support of Mary's claim to the throne he soon ran foul of Gardiner, the new Lord Chancellor, by his legitimate but impolitic interpretation of the religious legislation still in force from the previous regime. He was imprisoned and after months of intimidation was made to recant. Soon after his release in 1554 he died by drowning.

Barely a month after Hales's death Dyer reports a case which concerned the franchise of chattels originally leased by Thomas Cranmer.[150] In this context Hales's death was secondary to the attainder of Cranmer but Dyer records the accepted fact that Hales had committed suicide. It was on this question that subsequent litigation turned. An inquest by the coroner *super visum corporis* had rendered a verdict of *felo de se*; the Crown accordingly seized the estate in Kent which the judge had possessed jointly with his wife for a term of years. In 1559 his widow Margaret Hales attempted to recover her jointure by an action of detinue.[151] The writ abated, ostensibly because of a procedural flaw, but in the meantime the plaintiff launched a second action, this time by means of a writ of trespass, when, as Plowden reports, the subject of suicide was examined in excruciating detail.[152] The estate had been granted to one Cyriac Petit of Gray's Inn on the premise that the lease was forfeited, but the question remained whether the forfeiture had taken place in the lifetime of Sir James Hales, for otherwise the plaintiff would be entitled to the property by survivorship. As Anthony Browne phrased the question,

> Sir James Hales was dead, and how came he to his death? It may be answered, by drowning: and who drowned him? Sir James Hales; and when did he drown him? In his life-time.[153]

The court upheld the defendant's title, accepting the view that between the time he threw himself into the river and the moment

[150] *Bishop of Chichester v. Webb*, M. 1 & 2 P. & M., Dyer, 107b–8b.

[151] Reported in B.M. Harg. MS 388, ff. 243*v*–6*v* and Bodl. Rawl. MS C.112, f. 147.

[152] *Hales v. Petit*, M. 4 & 5 Eliz., Plow. 257–64; see particularly the arguments of Carus, Bendlowes et al., 259–60.

[153] Ibid. 262.

of his death Hales committed the felony.[154] The hairsplitting logic and legal sophistry which such an issue evoked prompted Shakespeare, who evidently read Plowden's report, to insert some lines of dialogue into the gravediggers' scene in *Hamlet* bearing a striking, if somewhat ludicrous, similarity to the case.[155] Its historic and literary interest apart, *Hales v. Petit* as reported by Plowden explores in depth the question of forfeiture for felony and the rationale of classifying suicide as a felonious act. It is worth noting that the court firmly excluded the Church from taking advantage of such forfeitures.

Plowden was not guilty of false modesty. He considered his collection superior to any previous set of reports 'in point of credit and authority'.[156] He had chosen cases for publication which he judged would have lasting value, and in doing so he was deliberately attempting to bring order to a disordered world. Reporting in the form of the later Yearbooks or personal notebooks did little more than serve the immediate needs of the working barrister, and conflicting or ill-formulated decisions were all too common in an activity devoid of rules or organization. Plowden saw his work as a means of reconciling diversities of opinion. By recording only judgments decided 'after great and mature deliberation' rather than preserving 'sudden sayings' he hoped—perhaps naïvely—to establish a more rational basis for future reporting.[157] It was to be centuries before this hope was realized, but his claim that the *Commentaries* carried 'the greatest credit and assurance' remains unchallenged. Plowden was groping towards a coherent doctrine of precedent such as that which was also to inspire Coke in his more ambitious, if less reliable, scheme of reports. But Coke also tried to incorporate Dyer's comprehensive technique, providing for his readers an encyclopedia of legal disputes. For Plowden what really mattered

[154] Ibid. 262.

[155] *Hamlet*, Act v, Scene 1; Foss, v, 373; Wallace, pp. 147–53; cf. Arthur Underhill's remarks in *Shakespeare's England* (1962), i, 393.

[156] Plow. Pref. vi.

[157] *Lives of the Norths*, i, 27; Dyer, 324b; Dal. 88.

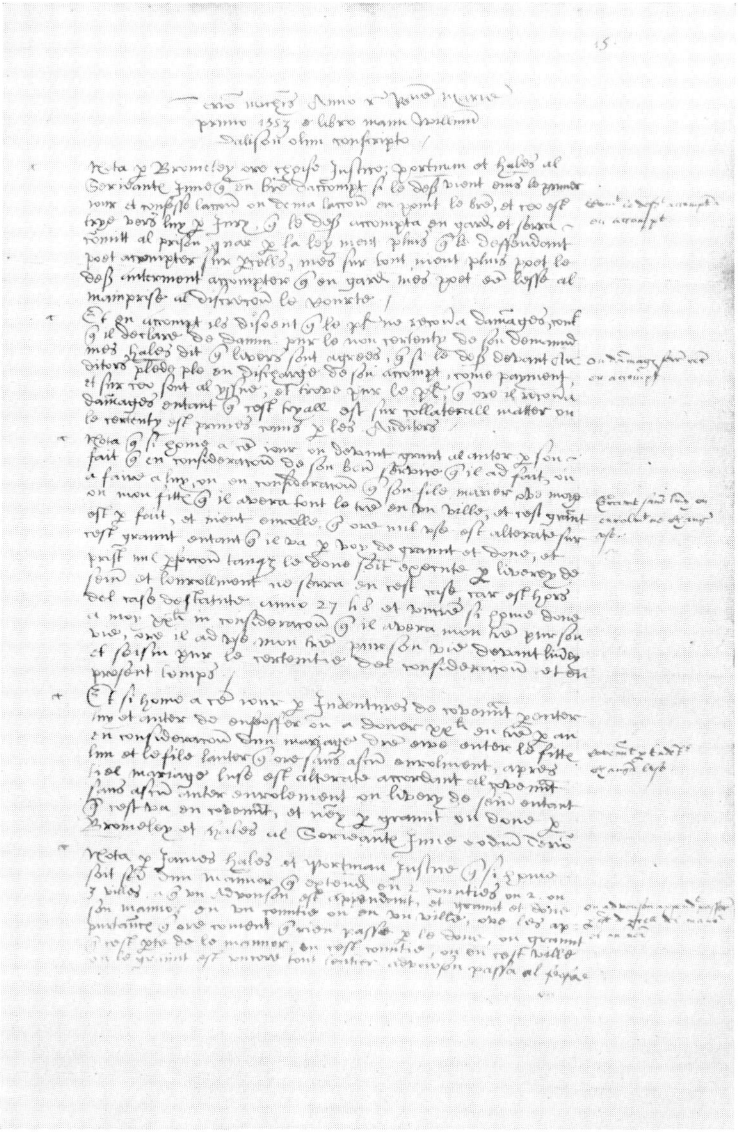

7. The first folio of William Dalison's collection of cases as transcribed by William Lambarde. (B.M. Harl. MS 5141, f. 15; by courtesy of the Trustees of the British Museum.)

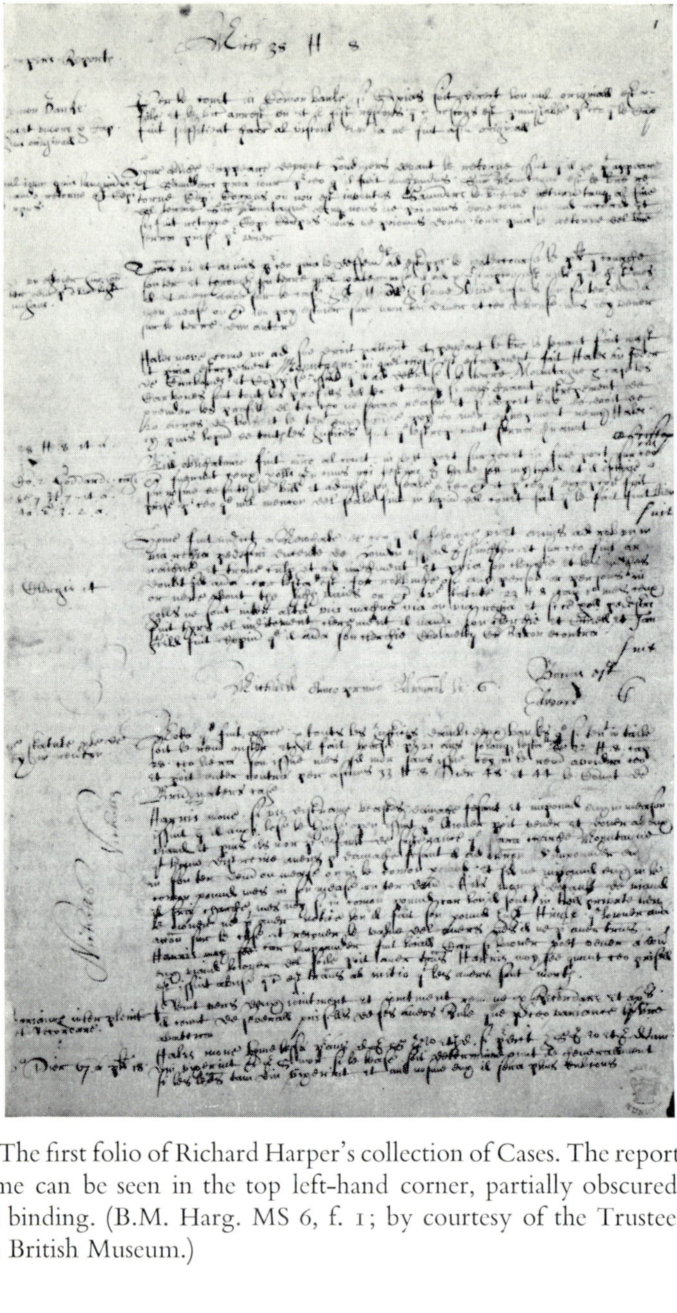

8. The first folio of Richard Harper's collection of Cases. The reporter's name can be seen in the top left-hand corner, partially obscured by the binding. (B.M. Harg. MS 6, f. 1; by courtesy of the Trustees of the British Museum.)

was the development of the principles by which conflicting claims were to be resolved.[158]

In a sense, he shared with Dyer the overriding aim of every lawyer, to bring certainty to the decision-making process. But whereas Dyer was concerned primarily with maintaining intact what he and his colleagues on the bench regarded as a coherent body of law based on 'immemorial custom', Plowden's interest was to ensure that the law provided effective remedies for litigants when their rights had been infringed. If this sometimes meant that the law must be altered to suit the needs of justice, so be it; after all, it was Plowden who on more than one occasion uttered the aphorism, 'blessed be the amending hand'.[159] Dyer, great jurist that he was, typified his age and his profession in regarding the law as existing in a rarified state, above and beyond human needs and aspirations. Plowden was all the greater for being untypical of his time: he never lost sight of the human equation, and in one of his own speeches he cited Aristotle in order to remind his colleagues that 'people are necessary before laws',[160] a truism which merits reaffirmation in every age.

It has been claimed that the history of statutory interpretation begins in the sixteenth century. Before that time the courts had tended to regard statutes as isolated rulings enacted to supplement the common law;[161] now lawyers came increasingly to regard them as the supreme authority. The religious and legal reforms inaugurated under Henry VIII were buttressed by acts of parliament which enhanced the prestige of both legislature and legislation. The very length of the Reformation Parliament (1529–36) did much to transform it from the High Court of Parliament into an integral part of the political system by which England was governed. Once Henry's guiding hand was removed, and as Tudor society and its problems grew more sophisticated, the scope and import of legislation increased. By the middle of Eliza-

[158] Allen, *Law in the Making*, pp. 223–4.

[159] Coke records this in the Epilogue, 4 Inst.

[160] Plow. 303.

[161] Thorne, *Discourse*, pp. 3, 8–10; T.F.T. Plucknett, *Statutes and their Interpretation* (1922), pp. 20–5.

beth's reign the legislators themselves were becoming conscious of their role as law-makers rather than as mere enunciators of governmental policy; when the functions of creation and enforcement of law began to merge Parliament was on the road to supremacy.[162]

The courts were also instrumental in the process by which statutes attained greater recognition; from the compilers of the late Yearbooks down to Coke reporters were purposefully noting the impact of new legislation on the common law and the manner in which judges chose to interpret it, and Coke would himself assert that the prime function of law-reporting was the exposition of acts of parliament enacted since the end of the Yearbooks.[163] By Plowden's time certain canons governing the status of acts of parliament had come to be accepted. It was established, for instance, that a statute of limited application or jurisdiction must be specifically pleaded, while general statutes need not.[164] As a corollary of this, Dyer and Plowden noted in the *Fulmerston Case* that an act did not have to be recited in its entirety when only a part of it was relevant to the pleadings.[165] Although little distinction was made between medieval legislation and that of more recent parliaments, the courts did begin to discriminate between the assizes of Edward I and subsequent acts.[166] The attitude of the judges, however, was neither uniform nor consistent. As early as 1494 Chief Justice Hussey declared that 'un recitall en act parliament est estoppell a touts homes'.[167] Yet in 1551 Mountague C.J. attempted to minimize the application of the Statute of Uses by dismissing parliament as 'nothing but a court',[168] and

[162] Pickthorn, *Henry VIII*, pp. 132–5, A.F. Pollard, *Factors in Modern History* (1960), pp. 96–100; Elton, *Tudor Constitution*, pp. 228–34, 333–6.

[163] 3 Co. Rep. Pref. xvib.

[164] Thorne, *Discourse*, pp. 13–21, 35–9; cf. *Anon.*, M. 36 Hen. VIII, Lib. of Congress Gell MS, ff. 23*v*, 75*v*; Dyer, 119a; Croke Eliz. 267.

[165] Plow. 105; Dyer, 102b; cf. Co. Litt. 98b.

[166] *Jennyson v. Rocke*, M. 38 & 39 Eliz., B.M. Lansd. MS 1084, f. 130; cf. 2 Inst. 99, 585.

[167] Quoted by Dyer in his unpublished notes, I.T. Petyt MS 511, vol. 13, f. 52*v*.

[168] Plow. 59, 398.

a minority of the profession persisted at least until the reign of James I in regarding parliament as simply the top of a pyramid of tribunals. While acknowledging the superiority of statute law Coke was always ready to qualify this principle if he saw sufficient grounds.[169]

However the lawyers viewed an act of parliament in theory, they were faced with the task of applying its provisions to the affairs of their clients. The basis of interpretation, then as now, lay in adjusting the enacted law to particular factual situations as they arose.[170] From the evidence of both printed and manuscript reports it is clear that the courts were increasingly concerned with interpreting legal instruments of all types, and in Plowden's time interpretation as a conscious activity was being systematized. Chief Justice Mountague reiterated the standard rule with regard to the condition of an obligation: where something is susceptible of a double intent, *ad proximum antecedens fiat relatio*.[171] In 1544 Justice Shelley noted that in construing deeds the principle was the same as that for statutes, recourse to the intention of the maker.[172] William Stanford, an authority on interpretation, endorsed the practice of accepting the most beneficial construction of words with respect to a lease,[173] and in 1556 he laid down three rules for the interpretation of a deed which had by then become standard common law doctrine: the instrument was presumed to benefit the party in whose favour it was made, it could not be annulled where the words indicated that a valid agreement was intended, and the words must be construed in accordance with the intent of the parties.[174]

Plowden must have recognized the growing significance of statute law and the need for unambiguous rules of interpretation. Although he makes no reference to the subject in his Preface, more than one-third of the cases he reported are concerned with

[169] *Bonham's Case* (1610), 8 Co. Rep. 107a; 2 Inst. 200, 313, 472.
[170] Thorne, *Discourse*, p. 3.
[171] *Bold v. Molineux*, T. 28 Hen. VIII, Dyer, 14b.
[172] *Reade v. Bullocke*, T. 35 Hen. VIII, ibid. 56b.
[173] *Browning v. Beston*, 6 Edw. VI, Plow. 131 at p. 135.
[174] *Throckmorton v. Tracy*, E. 2 & 3 P. & M., ibid. 160.

acts of parliament and their application. With characteristic flair he focused the arguments of several judges and barristers on the question and added a number of cogent remarks of his own; taken together, these constitute a valuable corpus which not only reflected contemporary thought but summarized doctrines formulated in the Yearbooks, St German's *Doctor and Student* and the treatise on the prerogative by William Stanford.[175] The influence exerted in turn by the *Commentaries* has long been recognized. Professor Thorne points out that Thomas Egerton as a student copied extracts from Plowden into his commonplace book; and whether or not Egerton was the author of the 'Discourse', those manuscript copies of it transcribed after 1571 also contain cases and glosses from Part I of the *Commentaries*.[176] The later, but more superficial, treatise attributed to Sir Christopher Hatton also drew heavily on Plowden,[177] while Coke, as in all his work, shows Plowden's influence when discussing the subject in his *Institutes*.[178]

In one of his last reports Plowden expounded at length the concept of equity as applied to statute law.[179] This, he explained, involved the process whereby 'the internal sense' rather than the strict meaning of the words of an act was sought: 'equity', he went on, 'enlarges or diminishes the letter according to its discretion'. It is this 'correction of the general words' by the courts which occupied so much of Plowden's and his colleagues' attention. Referring to the provisions of the second Statute of Westminster, chapter 3 (1285),[180] Chief Justice Brooke decided that if the words were followed strictly there would result inconvenience through loss of recompense under warranty; the court was obliged in such cases to construe acts of parliament according

[175] *Doctor and Student*, pp. 53–62; William Stanford, *Exposicion of the Kinge's Prerogative*, pp. 272b, 265b, 381b; cf. Thorne, *Discourse*, pp. 78–80, 92–8; Allen, *Law in the Making*, pp. 451–5.

[176] Thorne, *Discourse*, pp. 94–7; Plucknett, 'Ellesmere', p. 245 n. 9.

[177] *A Treatise concerning Statutes* (1677); cf. Thorne, *Discourse*, p. 10 n. 10.

[178] Co. Litt. 24b; 2 Inst. 382, 401; cf. Allen, p. 452, where there is an anachronistic reference by Plowden to Coke.

[179] *Eyston v. Studd*, E.16 Eliz., Plow. 459 at pp. 465–8.

[180] The statute gives 'receipt' for the reversioner on the default of tenant in dower, by courtesy, in tail or for life; Plucknett *Concise History*, p. 411 n. 3.

to equity and reason even though the words did not allow it. Brooke concluded that:

in all statutes there are some private cases excepted out of the general provision by equity of reason, in avoidance of a greater mischief.[181]

Inasmuch as the majority of statutes contained sanctions in the form of penal clauses, the reports tend to concentrate on the process of restriction in order to prevent injustice. Such an attitude was fairly settled by Justice John Spelman's time.[182] Edward Saunders, upon whom Chancellor Hatton relied for some of his views, claimed that judicial discretion in the interpretation of penal statutes was directed towards mitigating 'the violence of the letter'.[183] Earlier, Serjeant John Pollard had summed up the profession's attitude when he stated that such clauses must be taken strictly and never extended against those on whom the penalty was inflicted.[184] He went on to expound four grounds on which a man might be excused a violation of law: avoidance of a greater mischief, necessity, compulsion and involuntary ignorance. In such situations one 'may break the words of the law and yet not break the law itself'.[185]

The reports show clearly that the courts were often obliged to solve difficulties created by the law-makers. Thus after 1535 the Statute of Enrolments began posing problems.[186] Evidently the judges strove to keep its provisions within manageable limits: Harper records in 1565 that a move to have its terms extended to land situated in cities and boroughs was rejected,[187] and in another case Plowden and Bromley took the majority view in claiming that enrolments applied only to bargain and sale, not to a

[181] *Reniger v. Fogassa,* H. 4 Edw. VI, Plow. 1 at p. 13; cf. Co. Litt. 272a, 290a.

[182] B.M. Harg. MS 388, f. 165.

[183] *Stowel v. Lord Zouch,* H. 11 Eliz., Plow. 353 at p. 364.

[184] Ibid. 17; this principle had long been accepted; see YBB E. 5 Hen. VII, pl. 12; H. 21 Hen. VII, pl. 28; *Discourse*, pp. 154–61; *Treatise concerning Statutes*, p. 75.

[185] Plow. 19.

[186] Not to mention the Statute of Uses which exercised the courts for more than a century; Simpson, *History of Land Law*, pp. 173–9.

[187] *Anon.* 7 Eliz., B.M. Harg. MS 4, f. 191*v*; cf. Dyer 229a.

covenant and grant upon consideration.[188] Not surprisingly the common law judges were equally ill-disposed towards enlarging the terms under which the conciliar courts had been erected. The three Chief Justices in 1560 decided that the Court of Wards did not have authority to dispose of lands other than those in the possession of the ward during minority.[189] A strict interpretation of the authority of the Court of Augmentations was urged in the *Earl of Southampton's Case*, although in the same report Serjeant Bromley reminded the court that permissive regulations were to be construed liberally.[190] Similarly, Dalison reports an action which upheld the powers of justices of oyer and terminer, even in penal statutes, where they were not specifically mentioned: here the overriding demand for law and order superseded the tendency to limit penal clauses.[191]

A related subject was that of perjury as governed by the acts 32 Henry VIII, chapter 9, and 5 Elizabeth, chapter 9.[192] At a conference at Serjeants' Inn, Fleet Street, in Michaelmas term 1564 the judges examined the recent act in relation to previous legislation and decided that perjury was not an offence triable in Star Chamber;[193] four years later the Court of King's Bench moved to prevent the removal of interrogation under that act from the purview of the common law. In both cases a strict interpretation of the relevant clauses succeeded in excluding conciliar jurisdiction.

In Plowden's report of *Hill v. Grange* (1556) the Statute of Reversions was scrutinized.[194] Sir Robert Brooke pointed out that parliament's intention had been to remedy a general mischief —the inability of grantees in reversion of monastic estates to take

188 *Sharington v. Strotton*, M. 7 & 8 Eliz., Plow. 307.

189 *Willoughby's Case*, H. 2 Eliz., Dyer, 178b.

190 M. 33 Hen. VIII, Dyer, 50a; B.M. Harl. MS 5141, f. 10*v*.

191 *Anon.*, E. 2 & 3 P. & M., B.M. Harl. MS 5141, f. 31*v*.

192 The first act refers to unlawful maintenance in the King's Courts, including Star Chamber, Chancery, 'or elsewhere', the second recites it and adds penalties for perjury in the courts mentioned.

193 *Onslowe's Case*, M. 7 & 8 Eliz., Dyer, 243a; Croke Eliz. 521.

194 32 Hen. VIII, chap. 34; Plow. 172–9.

action against lessees—and that consequently it was not the intent of the legislature to make a general act for all grantees in reversions.[195] Similarly, in 1560 Plowden himself examined the import of an act passed in Edward VI's last parliament to minimize extortion by crown receivers.[196] In his opinion it had to be presumed that the drafters meant only to punish agents of the king and not those acting for private persons: it had always been the duty of the judges, he contended, to interpret those acts which were general in words 'to be but particular where the intent was particular'.[197]

There were occasions when the application of a statute was circumscribed by the courts despite potential benefits which might have accrued from its extension. In *Partridge v. Strange* (1553) the bench was unanimous in deciding that an act relating to pretended titles should not be enlarged so as to prevent perjury and maintenance: the primary duty of the court, according to Justice William Cook, was to see that penal statutes were not enlarged in scope.[198] Several years later the King's Bench was faced with an indictment under the Enclosure Act of 1563: the court dismissed the prosecution on a procedural technicality notwithstanding the merits of the case.[199]

In the foregoing examples the common law judges purposely took a restrictive view of certain legislation in order to dispense justice or prevent injustice. Invariably the courts were governed by the particular facts before them. The same pragmatic attitude seems to have operated with respect to the opposite trend in doctrine. This is the second rule of equity which Plowden applied to permissive legislation, namely, that 'when the words of a statute enact one thing they enact all other things which are in like degree'.[200] His use of the term 'interpretation' in this context

[195] Plow. 173.
[196] 7 Edw. VI, chap. 1.
[197] *Stradling v. Morgan*, E. 2 Eliz., Plow. 199 at p. 204.
[198] 32 Hen. VIII, chap. 9; Plow. 77 at p. 86.
[199] C.U.L. MS Dd. 10. 37, ff. 169*v*–70.
[200] Plow. 467; see *A Treatise concerning Statutes*, pp. 28–9.

was something of a novelty and is a further indication of the growing authority attaching to acts of parliament.[201]

Signs of a broadening trend were evident in the later years of Henry VIII in the form of exceptions to the penal rule,[202] but for several years it remained a matter of division among the judges. In *Wimbish v. Tailbois*, argued in 1551, two opposing statutes came under scrutiny. Serjeant William Cook, arguing for the traditional policy of restriction, contended that the penal clauses in 11 Henry VII, chapter 20 (recovery by covin) took precedence over the permissive principle in the Statute of Uses.[203] Sir James Hales, taking the view of the court, decided that notwithstanding penal clauses which debarred tenants in tail from binding their issue by recoveries, 'yet it shall be extended by equity, inasmuch as it was made in restraint of liberty which the common law gave to the prejudice of others'.[204] In more general terms, Justice Whiddon contended that it was no longer good law to assume that penal statutes could not be enlarged by equity, unless they abridged the rights of a particular person.[205] Saunders perhaps expressed the new principle most cogently in a dissenting opinion from *Partridge v. Strange* (1553):

> although the statute [32 Henry VIII, chapter 9, on pretended titles] gives a penalty, yet seeing it is very beneficial to the public weal, things which are out of the letter shall be taken within the equity of it.[206]

The motives which sometimes prompted this new line of interpretation were not always so commendable. This was especially so in matters of public policy such as the implementation of treason acts. Here the courts were no doubt influenced by the attitude of the Crown and the enhancement of their own

[201] Thorne, *Discourse*, p. 62; yet even by the end of the century the words of a statute lacked sufficient sanction to force the courts to include coverage of a similar case not provided for; 5 Co. Rep. 37b.

[202] For instance, Y B E. 27 Hen. VIII, pls. 22, 24; Brooke, tit. 'Waste', nos. 3 & 4; B.M. Harg. MS 388, ff. 164*v*–7.

[203] Plow. 43. [204] Plow. 53. [205] Ibid. 46. [206] Ibid. 82.

jurisdiction.[207] Dalison reported a decision from 1553 where it was contended that statutes were presumed affirmative and that negative sanctions must be express ones—but here the matter involved the issuing of letters patent by the Queen.[208] Certain acts designed to reform specific bodies of people such as the clergy were often enlarged by the judges to cover exceptions.[209] In certain circumstances, however, a statute might be construed against the interests of the Crown. In *Willion v. Berkley* (1562) the king was held bound by *De Donis Conditionalibus* though not specifically mentioned, the court presuming that if the monarch ordained a remedy for a particular mischief he did not intend to be at liberty to commit the same himself.[210]

The practical necessity for reappraising the old rule on penal statutes really arose as parliament moved into new fields of legislative activity. The Statute of Artificers, for example, with its precise regulations on work and wages was prone to rigid application: the common law courts were always ready to exert their authority over the justices of the peace and sought justification through 'the words and spirit' of the act to mitigate its effects. Legislation of a controversial nature such as that dealing with usury was also construed to the advantage of borrowers where injustice might otherwise occur, and 'l'equities de le estatute' frequently invoked to assist litigants to circumvent the increasing rigidity of old forms of action.[211]

For the judiciary to enlarge the scope of an act of parliament required considerable skill and not a little ratiocination. With parliament's augmented authority came a formal hardening of its enactments which tended to narrow the courts' freedom to

[207] Dyer, 131b, on stats. 33 Hen. VIII, chap. 23, 35 Hen. VIII, chap. 2, and 1 & 2 P. & M., chap. 10; 2 And. 149; Moore, 669.

[208] Dalison in B.M. Harl. MS 5141, f. 19.

[209] See YB E. 27 Hen. VIII, pl. 24; Dyer, 203b.

[210] Plow. 248; see also Dyer, 52a, 225b; it was already accepted doctrine that this rule related only to the king in a personal sense, and not to his tenants; Vinogradoff, p. 281.

[211] For example, B.M. Harl. MS 5141, f. 25*v*; Harg. 4, f. 191*v*; Harg. 10, f. 4*v*.

interpret them.[212] From mid-century onwards the judges increasingly had recourse to the concept of legislative intent. This was by no means a novel doctrine but Plowden was the first to give it real emphasis.[213] He notes, for instance, the argument of Thomas Bromley in 1554 that judges had sometimes 'expounded the words quite contrary to the text . . . in order to make them agree with reason and equity'—a result always presumed to be intended by parliament.[214] Two years earlier he had referred to the words of his colleague Edward Saunders who contended that penal statutes could be extended by equity 'if the intent of the makers of it may be so perceived'.[215] In fact, equity was frequently invoked to apply statutory provisions to cases similar enough to be presumed intended, although not mentioned.[216]

The means by which jurists were expected to divine the intent of the legislature were usually left undefined. Plowden does, however, apply a helpful test:

> when you peruse a statute, . . . suppose that the lawmaker is present, and that you have asked him the question you want to know touching the equity, then . . . give yourself such an answer as you imagine he would have done, if he had been present.[217]

The lawyers naturally regarded themselves as capable of applying the law in all its forms, including legislative intent. No doubt Coke's later pronouncements on the subject gained inspiration from Plowden's Reports.[218] Certainly the words of Saunders in 1553, when he alluded to the private and 'judicial' knowledge of a statute which every judge was deemed to possess, have a familiar ring:

[212] Thorne, *Discourse*, p. 62.

[213] Ibid. pp. 59–61, and *A Treatise* . . ., pp. 28–9; see an early example in YB T. 4 Hen. VII, pl. 6, per Serj. Jay.

[214] Plow. 109.

[215] Ibid. 82.

[216] See Allen, *Law in the Making*, p. 452; *Discourse*, pp. 151–4.

[217] Plow. 467.

[218] 2 Inst. 25; it was Coke's opinion that statutes were no longer drafted by men capable of understanding the law, hence the proliferation of 'mischiefs and defects'; 2 Co. Rep. Pref. xiii.

of your private knowledge you cannot judge, but may use your discretion . . . But where you have a judicial knowledge, . . . you may give judgment according to it.[219]

It was considered the duty of the profession to employ its particular command of the subject for the public good: this included not only the enlargement of the terms of statutes but a clear exposition of obscure words and passages.[220] Some practitioners also implied that the court had a duty to direct its experience and training towards extension of statutes by equity where they were considered ineffectual.[221] One obvious guide to parliament's intention lay in the preambles which were such a feature of Tudor legislation: these were, in Dyer's words, 'a key to open the minds of the makers of the act',[222] and both Saunders and Plowden held that the true intent of the legislators could be revealed by comparing the preamble with clauses of the act.[223]

The ideal for which both bench and bar professedly strove was justice, and to achieve it they needed to have recourse to reason. Thus Chief Justice Fineux had asserted before 1527 that where the intention of the makers of an act could not be discerned the judges must employ 'comen reson'.[224] Words might well be expounded beyond, if not in a sense contrary to, their normal meaning if this were agreeable to equity and reason,[225] and, conversely, 'the words ought to receive such construction as shall not clash with common reason'.[226] Yet difficulty arises in any attempt to elucidate this doctrine or to determine the criteria by which sixteenth-century judges applied it. The standard text used by the profession was St German's *Doctor and Student*, where an effort was made to list those branches of the law most in need of amendment.[227] Plowden attempted to build around the statutes

[219] Plow. 83; cf. Co. Litt. 98b.
[220] Plow. 53, 82; cf. *Treatise*, p. 30.
[221] Plow. 302.
[222] Ibid. 369; Elton, *Tudor Constitution*, pp. 333–4.
[223] Plow. 82, 205.
[224] B.M. Harg. MS 388, f. 164*v*.
[225] Plow. 109–10; Thorne, *Discourse*, pp. 57, 60, 76–7, 143–4.
[226] Plow. 88; *Discourse*, p. 143; Co. Litt. 272b, 381b.
[227] Allen, pp. 452–3; *Discourse*, p. 79 n. 165.

a system of equity based on a form of 'reason' equivalent to the *sinderesis* of the Chancery, although in this he was not successful.[228]

In the final analysis, however, the basis for extending (or limiting) the scope of a statute must be recognized as expediency. It was the capacity of the law to grapple with new factual situations rather than with abstract theories which brought justice to the litigant. Plowden and his contemporaries could dilate on the rationale behind the expansion or contraction of given legislation, but questions had to be answered both according to the necessity of the matter and according to that which is consonant to reason and good discretion,[229] and it would be unrealistic not to see in necessity and 'extraneous circumstances' the ultimate considerations. Once the process had been rationalized it was projected backwards to an age unaware of the power of statutes let alone their interpretation.[230] Chief Justice Brooke tacitly recognized the essentially pragmatic nature of interpretation when he 'construed the minds of the makers of the statute out of mere necessity to avoid a mischief',[231] and Serjeant John Pollard made the point explicitly in contending that

> necessity shall be a good excuse in all laws and that all laws give place to necessity.[232]

Plowden nevertheless made a signal contribution to the development of interpretation. The very care with which he presented current doctrine focused attention on an essential branch of the advocate's craft. To make the distinctions between general and specific acts, and affirmative and negative ones, and to enlarge equity were necessary first steps in the treatment of parliamentary legislation as public policy as well as private initiative. And if Plowden's own conception of *epichaia*—really the equivalent of equity in its abstract sense—was too broad for practical

[228] Allen, p. 455.
[229] Argued by Plowden in *Stradling v. Morgan*, E. 2 Eliz., Plow. 199 at p. 205.
[230] Thorne, *Discourse*, p. 62; but see Stanford's remarks, Dyer, 130b–1.
[231] Plow. 14. [232] Ibid. 18.

implementation, so that it soon came to be restricted to the maker's intention within the statute itself,[233] what was of lasting influence was his concern to demonstrate the means by which the judges dealt with changing conditions. They were guardians of legal continuity who had both the opportunity and the obligation to adjust acts of parliament 'by the rule and reason of the common law'. Even today the canons of statutory interpretation are not radically different from those set out by Plowden and his immediate successors.

233 Allen, p. 455; Thorne, *Discourse*, pp. 41–2, 54–6; Plowden's only notable disciple was Thomas Ashe, and to a lesser degree Coke; see *Heydon's Case*, 3 Co. Rep. 7a.

CHAPTER VII

Edward Coke and the New Era

BY the time of Plowden's death in 1585 the formative phase of law reporting in England was over. Two editions of each part of the *Commentaries* had been published, while the first edition of Dyer's *Reports* was due in a few months' time. With the profession aware of the need for a steady supply of fresh decisions the practice of collecting cases was firmly reestablished. While barristers tended to cite printed reports in their arguments there is no doubt that they relied on contemporary manuscript material to keep themselves informed of current doctrine. During the last fifteen years of the century a striking increase occurred in the number of practitioner-reporters and the volumes they produced: fully two-thirds of the surviving manuscripts so far discovered which relate to the Tudor period cover the years from 1575 to 1603.[1]

A number of these three hundred and more collections are duplicates, while others were welded together from a variety of second-hand sources. The majority appear to be the work of seventeenth-century compilers or copyists who evidently wished to provide themselves with a store of Elizabethan cases to complement their reports from the reigns of James I and Charles I. Much of this late-sixteenth century material resembles the Year-books in containing no indication of authorship, yet it has been found possible to identify over forty lawyers who can be called reporters as opposed to mere copyists, compilers or owners of collections.[2] The work of most of them remains in manuscript; only twelve sets were ever printed, and none of these—leaving aside Coke's monumental series—stands in the first rank of legal

[1] See Appendix I, pp. 284–305. [2] See Appendix II, pp. 308–13.

literature.[3] Few of the men whose authorship has been established enjoyed recognition in their own lifetime, although many of the reports they prepared began to circulate during the early years of James I, if not before. They stand as a bridge between those reporters who had begun practising at the close of the Yearbook era and those who, like Coke and Croke, were not called to the bar until the fifteen-seventies. In view of the expansion which was then taking place within the common law, in both numbers of litigants and remedies available to them, much of this material deserves more attention than it has hitherto received.

It is understandable, if regrettable, that the majority of legal historians should have restricted themselves to printed sources when tracing the evolution of the common law in the sixteenth century.[4] The combination of poor handwriting and defective (or nonexistent) tabulation which characterizes most manuscript collections has been sufficient to discourage all but the most persevering scholars. There is less justification, however, for the attitude which has traditionally been taken towards the subject of law-reporting itself. A 'linear' view of the growth of reporting in the sixteenth century has been applied not only to the shift from Yearbooks to private reports but also to the conveniently continuous series of decisions running from Dyer and Plowden, on the one hand, to Coke on the other. In respect of both chronology of entries and order of printing such an approach has a superficial logic: Coke's earliest first-hand report, *Shelley's Case* (1581), was one of Dyer's last, and the fourth edition of Plowden's *Commentaries*, Part I, by Wight and Norton in 1599 preceded by a year Wight's publication of the First Part of Coke's Reports.[5] Yet it remains true that two generations of lawyers had come to the bar between the fifteen-thirties and Coke's entry to the Inner Temple in 1572, and that among their number several had begun noting cases and compiling reports well before Dyer was first printed or Coke had begun his reporting career.

[3] Wallace, pp. 122–6, 136–43, 153–220; *H.E.L.* v, 358–63.

[4] Fifoot, Preface, p. vii.

[5] Beale, pp. 107–10, 287; *S.T.C.* nos. 5493–4.

The leading students of sixteenth- and early seventeenth-century reports, Wallace and Holdsworth, largely ignored the existence of manuscript collections,[6] as did Plucknett in his more recent analysis of Coke's work. All three writers were, of course, adhering to the practice adopted by the profession itself from the Restoration. By that time there had accumulated a sizeable stock of printed reports from the reign of Elizabeth which virtually eliminated the further use of decisions preserved only in manuscript. Unfortunately, in the process many poorly-reported cases were absorbed into common law doctrine while valuable collections were neglected by the publishers because the manuscripts were either inaccessible or lost. During the last two hundred and fifty years both lawyers and historians have accepted almost without question the adequacy of printed reports and the interpretation which these have given to many leading decisions.[7] Even the most conscientious of commentators has applied a 'legal' rather than the sounder, if less dogmatic, 'historical' approach to English law.

This limited approach has had serious consequences. It has resulted in the disregard of some important and influential cases, while many of those which were published could well have been reappraised if compared with other manuscript versions. Then again, some volumes have been condemned out-of-hand because of faulty printing without reference to surviving manuscript copies upon which they were based. The quality of Bendlowes' *Reports* in this respect has already been considered. A similar case arises with Moore's *Reports*: the text was not printed until 1663, yet several carefully transcribed copies still survive to indicate that the collection was circulating soon after the author's death in 1621 and was much in use during the next forty years.[8]

[6] Cf. above, pp. 104–10.

[7] Notable exceptions are Prof. Hall's treatment of Lane's *Reports*, especially in connection with *Bate's Case*; 'Impositions and the Courts', pp. 200–18, and 'Bate's Case', pp. 405–27, and J.H. Baker's 'New Light on Slade's Case', C.L.J. xxix (1971), 51–67.

[8] Among the surviving copies are four at the B.M.: Harl. 4585, Lansd. 1059,

The same observation holds true with respect to the work of Anderson, Popham and Savile.[9] The failure of some particularly full and authoritative collections to receive attention from printers may have had a bearing on the manner in which judges of the later seventeenth century interpreted the law: it has certainly influenced legal historians of this century. Reports such as those attributed to Francis Rhodes, Christopher Wray, Peter Warburton and Christopher Yelverton, all judges of considerable standing, still merit careful scrutiny, if not sympathetic editing.

It is clear that reporting in the late-sixteenth century can only be properly considered in relation to the careers and professional standing of the authors in question. The same general observations apply to both printed and unprinted reports. A few, such as the notes of Rhodes, Savile and Warburton, appear to be the product solely of the individuals in question.[10] Others, like the reports of Chief Justices Anderson, Popham and Fleming, as well as those of Francis Windham and Francis Moore, are based mainly on personal observation, with some 'foreign' matter added.[11] Still others, such as the volumes attributed to Nicholas Jordan, Richard Godfrey and Humphrey Ware, are compilations in the strict sense of the word, that is to say, a conflation of other men's work with perhaps some first-hand cases as well.[12]

The reporters themselves are fairly representative of the profession as a whole, although, as might be expected, they are stronger in the upper than in the lower ranks. Of the forty individuals who, on the evidence available, can be designated law reporters in the late Elizabethan period, eighteen were judges, three were serjeants and another half-dozen held the office of sheriff or recorder.[13] Apart from John Gouldesborough and Richard Brownlow, who were prothonotaries of the Court of Common Pleas, the remainder were, for the most part, advocates

and Add. 25191 and 35937; another is at Lincoln's Inn, Barr. 9, and a sixth at Harvard University, H.L.S. 2097.

[9] See Appendix II, pp. 308–9.

[10] Ibid. [11] Ibid. pp. 308–11. [12] Ibid.

[13] This means that all six Chief Justices under Elizabeth collected cases except Anthony Browne whose tenure lasted only two months.

of considerable standing in the courts, generally at the level of senior apprentices, although some, like William Brocke and Edward Hendon, began reporting as students. Richard Lydell, who entered the Middle Temple in 1598, noted at the beginning of his case-book that he started attending the courts in Westminster to make reports in 1601 after which he 'tout solement frequent quotidie le comen banke'.[14] A few authors whose work survives do not seem to have practised or cannot be traced in the records of the Inns,[15] but such men as Eusebius Andrewe, Hugh Cressy or Edmund Escourte, whose careers are somewhat obscure, did achieve distinction within their respective Inns as readers, benchers or in some other capacity.[16] Many reporters, including William Brocke, Nicholas Ducke, Edward Hendon and Humphrey Ware, served in parliament at one time or other.[17] Not surprisingly, the work of noting cases was usually unconnected with religious affiliation. Whereas Richard Godfrey, described in 1579 as 'well practised, riche', was expelled from Gray's Inn in 1582 for persistent backwardness in matters of religion, Christopher Yelverton, a member of the same Inn and also 'very welthie, lerned', was clearly of a Puritan cast of mind: yet both display objectivity in their approach to legal matters.[18]

[14] The reports of these three practitioners commence soon after their admission to the study of law; see Appendix II, pp. 310–13. The inscription in question is found on the flyleaf of a volume, together with his autograph, containing reports for E. 43 Eliz.–H. 15 James I; L.I. Mayn. 66, ff. 136–395.

[15] Three fairly extensive collections have been ascribed respectively to 'Ledyton' (Ladynton, Ledyngton?), Stewell and Francis Barkesdale, but no record of their names appears in the Admission Books of the Inns of Court; B.M. Add. MSS 25198, 25199 and H.L.S. MS 1058.

[16] Andrewe is described in a set of reports attributed to him (B.M. Harl. MS 3209) as a bencher of Lincoln's Inn; *L.I. Adm. Reg.* i, 131; *Black Books*, ii, 110, 169, 247; an entry 'ex libro Andrews' is found in the 1688 edition of Dyer, 350a. Cressy entered Lincoln's Inn in 1598 and acted as treasurer of the House in 1629–30; *Black Books*, ii, 56, 170, 289; his reports survive as B.M. Add. MS 35947. Escourte was also a member of Lincoln's Inn and delivered a reading there in 1618; *Black Books*, ii, 56, 167, 197; cf. B.M. Harl. MS 4552.

[17] *Official Returns*, i, 428, 432, 457, 463, App. p. xli.

[18] *G.I. Pension Book*, i, xxxv, 52; Neale, *Elizabeth I and her Parliaments*, i, 91–2.

The techniques employed in reporting litigation from the latter part of Elizabeth's reign continued to exhibit wide variation. It was a period of experimentation and improvisation without firm guidelines; practitioners took the initiative in determining what points of law were relevant and what were the best means of recording them. The work of Dyer and Plowden exerted considerable influence upon the style of succeeding generations, yet each reporter naturally tailored his notes to suit his own requirements. Members of the bench such as John Popham and Thomas Fleming tended to give particular attention to the opinions and dicta of senior practitioners and fellow judges.[19] A junior practitioner like Nicholas Ducke was apt to try to relate specific factual situations to available legal remedies; in his book these two aspects predominate over the argument of bench and bar.[20] One lawyer, Edward Hendon, while a student, followed Bendlowes' technique of extracting material directly from the plea rolls.[21] On the other hand, many reporters of all ranks, typified by Edmund Escourte, Richard Lydell, John Savile and Thomas Owen, were content to make brief abstracts of disputes, the remedy sought and the court's resolutions.[22]

The most notable development in reporting during the last quarter of the century was a clearer demarcation between tribunals. Even the larger collections such as those attributed to George Croke and Christopher Wray contain entries from the King's Bench and Common Pleas grouped under separate terms and years. The upsurge of business in the King's Bench is reflected in the increased number of volumes devoted exclusively to its decisions. Approximately thirty-five separate collections emanate from this court, of which nine can be ascribed to identifiable reporters:[23] practitioners such as Hugh Cressy, Thomas Fleming

[19] Popham, who was Chief Justice of the King's Bench (1592–1607), was succeeded by Fleming (1607–13); see Appendix II, pp. 308–9.

[20] B.M. Harg. MS 51.

[21] B.M. Harl. MS 1331, ff. 1–54; L.I. Misc. MS 791, ff. 112–67*v*.

[22] The reports of Savile and Owen are in print; see Appendix II, pp. 308–9.

[23] Ibid. pp. 308–12.

William Daniel, Thomas Harris and Edmund Escourte come into this category with cases taken from the years 1585 to 1601.[24] To a less extent, the same trend is observable in the Court of Exchequer where a number of barons, notably Laurence Tanfield, John Savile and John Walter, collected material which in later years found its way into the notebooks of colleagues.[25] Reports devoted exclusively to the Courts of Chancery and Star Chamber were also being prepared in the same period. The majority of common lawyers, however, adhered to the traditional procedure of including notes from conciliar courts only when these impinged upon their own sphere of interest.[26] Thus the printed reports of Coke, Popham, Croke and Moore, as well as the less familiar collection of John Stevens and various other manuscript volumes, contain a wide selection of cases decided both inside and outside Westminster Hall.[27] Despite a trend towards specialization which was to become more marked in the seventeenth century, the majority of Elizabethan reporters went on pursuing worthwhile legal issues irrespective of forum. As long as the decision-making process continued to transcend courts and jurisdictions the reports were bound to follow suit.

It would not be fitting to conclude this survey of sixteenth-century reporting without some reference to Sir Edward Coke. While both his life and writings have been examined in some detail by legal historians,[28] there remains much to be said about Coke's role as a reporter.[29] The remarks which follow will, however, be mainly confined to an appraisal of Coke's amply-

[24] Ibid. pp. 308–11.

[25] The cases of Savile have been printed (1675); those of Walter are found in B.M. Harg. MS 5; but of Tanfield only a few remnants survive; Herts R.O. Gorhambury MS XII. A.6.A, ff. 16–18*v*.

[26] *H.E.L.* v, 162–3, 276–7; cf. Jones, *Court of Chancery*, pp. 3–4.

[27] The work of Stevens is found in B.M. Harg. MS 26, ff. 17–68.

[28] *H.E.L.* v, 425–93; Wallace, pp. 165–96; Foss, vi, 108–28; Plucknett, 'Genesis of Coke's Reports', pp. 190–213; Thorne, *Sir Edward Coke, 1552–1952* (Selden Society Lecture 17 March 1952); M.D. Bowen, *The Lion and the Throne* (1957).

[29] It is the writer's intention to pursue the study of Coke's reports together with those of his contemporaries and immediate successors.

stated methodology in this field. Whatever his faults Coke could never be accused of approaching anything by half-measures. His own credentials were impressive. By the time he came to publish his first volume of reports in 1600 his library contained virtually every Yearbook and 'private' set of reports then in print and many of those in manuscript, a circumstance which explains why he is so often the source of information on earlier reporters. Thus his library catalogue includes, among other useful volumes, an interleaved and annotated copy of Littleton's *Tenures* containing the core of his first Institute as well as the earliest-known selection of Bendlowes' reports and an anonymous collection of cases from the years 1579 to 1589.[30] Among his other manuscripts were the original note-books of Dyer, part of Justice Spelman's reports and a complete set of Bendlowes' cases, together with assorted material from the later years of Elizabeth.[31] His own storehouse of decisions appears to have been far in excess of those which went into print; he cites a number of contemporary cases which he must have picked up at random during his first twenty years of practice.[32] If it is true, as is often asserted, that Coke's encyclopaedic knowledge of English law was not matched by an equally critical use of the material he amassed, the fact remains that no lawyer of his or any other age has come so well schooled to the task of reporting cases in court.

From the time of his call to the bar in 1578 Coke recognized the value of reporting, not only for its utility, but as an aid to learning. He started making notes systematically in 1579 and held that the recording of notable decisions was the most perspicuous form of self-teaching.[33] It is generally assumed that Coke, like most of his colleagues, collected cases for his personal use alone: on the con-

[30] *Catalogue of the Library of Sir Edward Coke*, no. 369; this volume is now B.M. Harl. MS 6687.

[31] *Catalogue* nos. 293, 302, 328, 330, 336; no. 293 is now B.M. Harl. MS 6686, no. 330 probably B.M. Add. MS 25189.

[32] Plucknett, 'Genesis of Coke's Reports', pp. 203–4.

[33] 1 Co. Rep. Pref. iv–v; 6 Co. Rep. Pref. ixa. All references to Coke's *Reports* are taken from the English edition of 1738.

trary, certain ritual protestations to this effect notwithstanding,[34] he was probably the first reporter who from the outset worked for the profession as much as for himself. His report of *Shelley's Case* was written at the end of 1581 and presented in the following January to his patron and fellow Inner Templar Thomas Sackville, Lord Buckhurst, together with a letter of dedication.[35] Already by this time Coke was formulating with some clarity his creed concerning 'the lief and the light of trewth'. He lamented the neglect of methodical reporting and reliance on a series of 'running reportes' which failed to convey the right reason and rule of the case: he also cautioned students against dependence on memory when citing cases in court, both for the sake of their reputations and in the interests of their clients, who might receive a favourable judgment on one occasion but lose on another because the grounds of judgment were not adequately recorded.[36]

It is impossible to trace the sources of all Coke's material. Most of his important decisions from the reign of Elizabeth appear to have been taken at first hand while he was successively Solicitor-General and Attorney-General. His earliest report, *Vernon's Case* (1572), was based on Dyer's version, with additional references and comments which he inserted some years later.[37] Many of the shorter entries found in Parts IV to VII may have been borrowed from other practitioners, but nothing was ever incorporated into his notes verbatim. Every case was adapted to serve a purpose and was invariably brought up to date by the addition of contemporary citations. The reports in Parts VIII to XI were, for the most part, the product of Coke's ten years on the bench when he was deliberately compiling cases for publication. His supply of material exceeded the work put into print during his lifetime and

[34] 4 Co. Rep. Pref. xii, 7 Co. Rep. Pref. iib.

[35] Several copies of both the report and dedication survive; *H.M.C. Ninth Rep.* App., 361; L.I. Misc. MS 361, ff. 1–11; Mayn. 29, ff. 207, 267*v*–75*v*; B.M. Harl. MS 443, ff. 1–9*v*; Add. 35953, ff. 13*v*–21.

[36] Dedication to Lord Buckhurst, L.I. Misc. MS 361, f. 1*v*.

[37] 4 Co. Rep. 1a at 3b; cf. Dyer, 317b; another report, *Case of Market Overt*, 5 Co. Rep. 83b, may have originally been reported by Anderson; cf. 1 And. 344–5.

some of the loose ends appear in two inferior posthumous volumes.[38]

In his dedication to Lord Buckhurst Coke points to Plowden as the 'one learned & grave man' who first revived the art of reporting. With the answer no doubt in mind, he ponders whether there is within the profession another prepared to note the resolutions of bench and bar. It is clear that as early as 1582 Coke regarded himself as Plowden's successor and entertained thoughts of emulating the great work. When Coke began practising Plowden's was the only 'modern' volume of reports in print, and by the time his own cases began to come out the sole addition had been Dyer's collection. Coke's first eleven volumes were published between 1600 and 1615 and from then onwards they held the field as a prime source of current decisions.[39] The influence of Plowden is immediately apparent: at one point Coke even described his collection as 'in the nature of Commentaries'.[40] Many of the entries from Parts I, II and III include a copy of the pleadings, because Coke considered their insertion necessary as much for the instruction of students in arguing cases as for the clearer understanding of his reports.[41] As a general rule he advised aspiring law reporters to check their work against the official record: taking by ear that which was spoken in court was, to his mind, 'a dangerous kind of reporting'.[42] In later volumes, where the entries are shorter and grouped under specific headings, or when he was anxious to issue decisions while they were fresh in the minds of his colleagues, Coke omitted the pleadings, although he seems to have followed his own advice and always to have verified his notes by reference to the plea rolls.[43]

[38] Parts XII and XIII, though taken from Coke's own notes, were probably cases which Coke had deemed unfit for publication; see the Preface to Bulstrode's *Reports*.

[39] The eleven first-hand volumes were published in 1600, 1602 (Parts 2 & 3), 1604, 1605, 1607, 1608, 1611, 1613, 1614 and 1615.

[40] 3 Co. Rep. Pref. xviia.

[41] 1 Co. Rep. Pref. vii.

[42] Co. Litt. 293b; 4 Inst. 17.

[43] For example, *Rigeway's Case* (1594), 3 Co. Rep. 52a at p. 52b.

In other respects the influence of Plowden may appear less evident. Coke's entries do not follow any sort of chronological sequence, there is no attempt to present a cross-section of arguments, and it is often difficult to disentangle Coke's glosses from the words of the pleaders. Yet in the first three volumes, those printed during Elizabeth's time and containing cases exclusively from her reign, there is an unmistakable affinity with Plowden. Coke had probably planned a two-part work containing leading cases concerned primarily with property and conveyancing; it was only at a late stage, so it seems, that he found it necessary to divide the second volume into two sections, both of which were published in 1602.[44]

Although Plowden had set out his entries in chronological order, he saw no particular significance in this and gave up any pretence of 'continuation or dependence of term or time'. Coke merely took the process one step further and presented his entries in order of merit—and merit as he saw it was the relevance of a case to current doctrine and its probable influence on later decisions. Coke's technique of combining the arguments of two or more advocates in one exposition, as well as his habit of digesting the issues under arbitrary headings, was again taken from his precursor.[45] Plowden reported his cases 'in a summary way', gathering the substance of the arguments from both sides of a dispute: Coke employs almost the same language in *Chudleigh's Case* (1589) when he declares that it is not his aim to report the arguments at large, 'but to make such a summary collection of the effect and substance of them all'.[46] Just as Plowden had named the pleaders whose speeches he omitted as well as those he included, so Coke in his more important cases usually listed the names of the barristers and judges whose arguments he reported. Sometimes he would supplement his notes by means of the 'credible relation

[44] 1 Co. Rep. Pref. vi; Plucknett, 'Genesis of Coke's Reports', pp. 204–6.

[45] It was Plowden who first evolved the practice of presenting a summary of arguments under numbered groups; for example, *Bracebridge v. Cook* (1572), Plow. 416 at p. 418.

[46] 1 Co. Rep. 120a at p. 132a.

of others', a phrase again reminiscent of Plowden;[47] at others he undertook to confer with his more senior colleagues in order to substantiate (or discredit) a controversial judgment or opinion. The difference between the Elizabethan reports of Coke and those of Plowden is really a matter of degree: both reporters reserved the right to alter particular arguments so long as the 'sense and intent' were retained.[48]

Coke frequently omitted the speeches of counsel altogether and concentrated on opinions from the bench, especially if the dispute moved to the Exchequer Chamber or Serjeants' Inn.[49] He professed a high regard for the judges and saw in their pronouncements the heart of the common law; as he was accustomed to say, they were *lex loquens*.[50] One of the motives he gave for publishing his reports was to preserve the more memorable resolutions propounded by the sages of the law, and he reflected nostalgically on his early career when 'the courts of justice were furnished with men of excellent judgment, gravity and wisdom' like Bacon, Wray, Dyer and Saunders. It is typical of Coke that he could equate personal character with legal acumen: thus he could assert that no man of 'a loose and lawless life' ever gained a sound knowledge of the law, while all who did achieve such proficiency were invariably 'honest, faithful and virtuous'. Only someone of Coke's single-minded devotion to the law could translate its practice into a crude version of the Protestant ethic.[51]

Throughout his reports and their prefaces Coke enunciated some ideals on the method and purpose of law-reporting which were not always reflected in his own work or that of his colleagues. Many have accused Coke of taking liberties with both the facts and the law; yet most of the charges levelled against him can be refuted by comparing his reports with their counterparts in

47 *Chudleigh's Case*, ibid.

48 *Calvin's Case*, 7 Co. Rep. 1a at p. 4a; cf. Plow. Pref. iv.

49 1 Co. Rep. 42a, 53a, 53b; 2 Co. Rep. 70b.

50 Co. Litt. 130a; 7 Co. Rep. 4a.

51 4 Co. Rep. Pref. xiii; 1 Co. Rep. Pref. vi: 2 Co. Rep. Pref. iv; Co. Litt. Pref. xxix–xxx.

such collections as Moore, Croke, Leonard and Anderson, and in the more extensive manuscript volumes.[52] Undoubtedly he was guilty at times of 'exhorbitant and extravagant opinions' and of 'scattering or sowing his own conceits', but since the cases complained of were usually ones in which he took part such censures apply more to Coke's conduct as an advocate than to his role as a reporter. Much of the criticism has been levelled by later commentators, while that voiced by his contemporaries—notably Bacon and Egerton—sprang from professional or political rivalry rather than from considerations of method, style or accuracy.[53]

Only a man of Coke's supreme self-confidence, not to say arrogance, could have deemed it possible to bring order and logic to the chaos which still prevailed in English land law. It was in his efforts to clarify complex issues and to resolve divergent opinions that he tended to oversimplify the arguments of colleagues and hence incur mistrust. His belief that he could bring greater certainty to the law was not shaken in 1616 when he was ordered by the Privy Council to revise his Reports: after devoting (as he claimed) several months to this task Coke could only discover four trivial errors out of five hundred cases—fewer than in the sixty-four entries in Plowden![54] During the sixteen years in which he was engaged in compiling his Reports for publication Coke frequently noted how he was able to settle doubtful points and give proper direction for similar disputes in the future.[55] In his earliest printed report, *Lord Buckhurst's Case* (1598), he quotes Egerton as declaring that the question under consideration (warranty of title) 'was now well explained and all books upon good and solid reason reconciled';[56] referring to *Dive v. Maningham* (1550) and related cases in Plowden, he is satisfied that all

[52] Thus in B.M. Lansd. MS 1084, ff. 98, 136, there are independent reports of *Butler and Bakers Case* (1591) and *Lord Buckhurst's Case* (1598); cf. 3 Co. Rep. 25a and 1 Co. Rep. 1a.

[53] Wallace, pp. 175–83; *H.E.L.* v, 430 nn. 2 & 3, p. 464 n. 6.

[54] This extraordinary episode is fully documented by Spedding, vi, 76.

[55] 3 Co. Rep. Pref. xvib; 7 Co. Rep. Pref. iia.

[56] 1 Co. Rep. 1a–2a.

points of conflict are now reconciled by the action he is reporting;[57] and his analysis of *Slade's Case* (1602) ends with the not unjustified comment that 'a doubt in our books [is] well resolved'.[58] Yet he sometimes depicts a more resolute posture than that adopted by the court simply by omitting those issues in a dispute upon which the judges could not agree.[59]

It is symptomatic of the growing importance attached to individual decisions that Coke used his reports to amplify topics of particular interest to the profession. He was, perhaps, the first reporter to appreciate fully the emergence of 'case-law' in its modern sense. In earlier volumes he tended to follow Plowden by inserting short asides usually in the form of advice to his readers: thus in *Lane's Case* (1586) he concludes his report by suggesting that leases were better executed under the Great Seal than under the Exchequer Seal,[60] and in *Butler and Baker's Case* (1597) he warns landowners against bequeathing their property by testament without the aid of legal counsel while listing eight rules to be followed where this is not possible.[61] Later, his reporting style became characterized by fuller treatment of some relevant branch of the law. The classic example is *Caudry's Case* (1591), which in effect expounded current and past ecclesiastical doctrine in a juridical defence of the Royal Supremacy.[62] When Queen Elizabeth died the problem of discontinuance of legal process necessitated a conference of judges on whose deliberations Coke based a short history of the subject.[63] In *Twyne's Case* (1602) the subject of fraudulent gifts came before the Star Chamber: its deliberations were assisted by Chief Justices Popham and Anderson who, according to Coke, cited at length a number of recent common law decisions which attempted to reconcile the court's position with that of the governing statute, 13 Elizabeth, chapter

[57] *Whelpdale's Case* (1604), 5 Co. Rep. 119a at p. 119b.

[58] 4 Co. Rep. 91a at p. 95b.

[59] For example, *Corbet's Case* (1599), 1 Co. Rep. 83b–8a; Simpson, *History of Land Law*, p. 198 n. 1.

[60] 2 Co. Rep. 16b at p. 17b.

[61] 3 Co. Rep. 25a at pp. 36a–6b.

[62] 5 Co. Rep. i–xli.

[63] 7 Co. Rep. 29b–31b; cf. Dyer, 165a.

5.[64] Thus, in addition to summarizing the medieval common law, Coke had a talent for bringing it into line with Elizabethan legislation.

In pursuit of his purpose Coke was prone to devour historical sources with what Maitland called 'uncritical voracity':[65] a counterfeit treatise like the *Mirror of Justices*, because it confirmed his own preconceived notions on Anglo-Saxon codes, he accepted whole-heartedly. It is also incontestible that in his vigorous approach to advocacy he would contradict himself over the years: his dicta in *Bonham's Case* (1610) and the *Case of Non Obstante* (1582) on the authority of statute law and the royal prerogative were inconsistent with earlier statements on these subjects and led to his difficulties with the Privy Council when he was compelled to revise his more controversial reports.[66] His attitude towards Parliament was ambivalent. He attributed the revival of law-reporting itself to the need for an exposition of statutes enacted since the accession of Henry VIII.[67] In *Butler and Baker's Case* he examined at length the two Statutes of Wills, while in the *Case of Fines* (1602) he reported on the effect of that Henrician act upon the common law.[68] His deep concern with legislation is also apparent in the Preface to Part III of the Reports where he surveys many of the cases in his previous two volumes and the acts to which they related, including that 'broad spreading statute of 27 H. 8, c. 10 of uses'.[69] Yet, as expounded by Coke, the canons of interpretation employed at the turn of the century were no further advanced than those formulated by Plowden, while in *Bonham's Case* he is found using language which closely resembles that of the later Yearbooks. As with his predecessors on the bench Coke's final recourse in interpreting statutes was 'common droit & reason', although his authorities were becoming valueless in the face of fresh problems. Similarly, he followed Plowden's rules on

[64] 3 Co. Rep. 80b at pp. 82a–83b.
[65] Introduction, *Mirror of Justices* (S.S.), pp. ix–x.
[66] 8 Co. Rep. 107a at p. 118a; 12 Co. Rep. 18; *H.E.L.* v, 475.
[67] 3 Co. Rep. Pref. xvib.
[68] Ibid. 27a–8a, 30a–5a, 84a–91b.
[69] Ibid. Pref. xviia.

the equity of statute although he employed the concept sparingly.[70]

Bacon's famous tribute to the Reports, uttered in spite of strong mutual reservations and personal animosity, provides a clue to Coke's outstanding achievement. Without the Reports, conceded Bacon, the law was like a ship without ballast, 'for that the cases of modern experience are fled from those that are adjudged and ruled in former times'.[71] What Bacon neglected to add was that it was Coke's impressive mastery of those decisions of former times which marked a watershed in sixteenth-century reporting. The modern doctrine of precedent, with its well-established gradation of judicial authority and the binding force of decided cases 'on all fours', was still centuries away when Coke completed his Reports,[72] but his coupling of comprehensive citation with an attempt to bring some measure of uniformity to the mass of conflicting decisions did much to clear the ground in which the doctrine of *stare decisis* could take root.

Among the numerous paradoxes in Coke's personality was his penchant for urging high ideals upon his colleagues while he pursued his own ends with callous determination. He could enlist the aid of 'infinite precedents in all ages' to impress his point of view[73] and also blandly ignore this vast repository if it suited his purpose, as when he argued against monopolies and gild regulations.[74] Yet in both disputes—as in so many others—he helped the common law to advance towards its dual, if conflicting, ends of stability and change. If his impulses are sometimes suspect the principles involved are no less valid today than they were four hundred years ago. Practitioners, as well as historians of the law, would do well to recall this famous exhortation:

Let all professors of the law give to these books that justice which these

[70] Thorne, *Discourse*, pp. 64–5, 96–9; one of Coke's early cases on statutory interpretation is *Heydon's Case* (1584); 3 Co. Rep. 7a–9a; cf. Co. Litt. 272b, 381b.

[71] Spedding, vi, 65. [72] Allen, p. 203 n. 1. [73] 3 Co. Rep. Pref. iiib, 95a.

[74] *Darcy v. Allein* (1602), 11 Co. Rep. 84b; *Ipswich Tailor's Case* (1614), 11 Co. Rep. 53a; Thorne, *Coke*, pp. 10–12; cf. D. O. Wagner, 'Coke and the Rise of Economic Liberalism,' *Econ. Hist. Rev.* vi (1935–6), 30–44.

books have in them, that is, to give to every book and case, his own true understanding: and not by wresting or racking, or inference of wit to draw them (no not for approving a truth) from their proper and natural sense.[75]

[75] 3 Co. Rep. Pref. xviib.

APPENDIX I

Manuscript Reports for the Tudor Period

The reports are arranged by content (not by date of transcription) in the following order:

A. Henry VII; B. Henry VII–Henry VIII; C. Henry VII–Philip & Mary;
D. Henry VII–Elizabeth;
E. Henry VIII; F. Henry VIII–Philip & Mary; G. Henry VIII–Elizabeth;
H. Edward VI–Philip & Mary; I. Edward VI–Elizabeth;
J. Philip & Mary–Elizabeth;
K. Elizabeth

A. HENRY VII

(1) *Bodl. Lat. misc. C.55:* 180 fols., three late-15th cent. hands:
(i) ff. 1–94*v* contain reports from the Yearbooks 6–10 Edw. IV (1466–71), 49 Hen. VI (1470–1), 11–15 Edw. IV (1471–6), 20–1 Edw. IV (1480–2) and 1 Hen. VII (1485–6);
(ii) ff. 57–94*v* consist of Yearbook 35 Hen. VI (1456–7). This entire section comprising ff. 1–94*v* was apparently owned by Robert Constable serjeant-at-law 1494–1501.
(iii) ff. 95–179*v* consist of Yearbooks 36, 37 & 39 Hen. VI (1457–9, 1460–1).

(2) *B.M. Harg. 105:* 238 fols., two early-16th cent. hands representing two distinct collections:
(i) Yearbooks East. 22 Edw. IV–2 Rich. III (1482–5) (ff. 1–88*v*);
(ii) Yearbooks 1–8, 10, 13, 20 & 21 Hen. VII (1485–93, 1494–5, 1497–8, 1504–6) (ff. 91–238). One of the later possessors of this MS was John Byrom of Gray's Inn (adm. 1676).

(3) *H.L.S. 8:* 66 fols., late 16th cent.; consists of a fragment of a larger collection of Yearbook reports with cases for 5–8, 12 Hen. VII (1489–93, 1496–7) translated into English.

B. HENRY VII–HENRY VIII

(1) *C.U.L. Mm.4.3:* 128 fols., written in a hand of the first half of the 16th cent. Ff. 58–94*v* consist of short notes from the Yearbooks of Hen. VIII, ff. 96–125 the Yearbooks of Hen. VII: in effect a small abridgment or commonplace book.

C. HENRY VII–PHILIP & MARY

(1) *B.M. Add. 35938:* 224 fols., late 16th cent.; a collection of Yearbook reports for the reign of Hen. VII together with sixteen cases reported for the period 24 Hen. VIII–2 & 3 Phil. & Mary (1532–56) dealing with the subject of uses. The Yearbook cases are patterned on the printed version although somewhat condensed and heavily annotated.

D. HENRY VII–ELIZABETH

(1) *C.U.L. Gg. 3.26:* 365 fols., various 16th & 17th-cent. hands. Ff. 97–109 contain reports for 1–23 Hen. VII (1485–1508) entitled 'ex libro Roberti Kiloway [Keilwey]' but in reality the work of John Carrell Sr. Ff. 109–34 comprise reports for 22–9 Eliz. (1579–87) but these are not connected with either Carrell or Keilwey but may originate in the Inner Temple.

(2) *I.T. Petyt 511, vol. 12:* 413 fols., various hands of the late 16th and early 17th cents. Ff. 1–8*v* consist of random entries from the Yearbooks and 'Keilwey' covering the period between 1 Edw. III and 13 Hen. VII (1327 & 1498). Ff. 9–337 form a distinct collection consisting of extracts from the Yearbooks 18 Hen. VI–27 Hen. VIII together with reports from various 'private' sources extending from Edw. VI to Eliz. (up to 1581). This section is a conflation of the work of several reporters including Dalison, Harper and Bendlowes. The remainder of the volume (ff. 338–413) is made up of random reports from the later years of Elizabeth ascribed to James Altham, a baron of the Exchequer (1606–17).

(3) *B.M. Harl. 1345:* 262 fols., late 16th cent. Extracts from the Yearbooks Edw. IV–Hen. VIII together with material from Plowden's *Commentaries*, Parts I & II.

(4) *B.M. Harl. 1624:* 328 fols., various 17th-cent. hands. Ff. 1–33*v* contain entries from 4, 5 & 6 Hen. VII (1488–91) some of which are attributable to John Carrell Sr. Ff. 33*v*–55 include cases from 1, 6, 9 & 11 Henry VIII (1509–10, 1514–15, 1517–18 and 1519–20) most of which are printed in Keilwey's *Reports* and also attributable to John Carrell Sr. Ff. 55*v*–85 contain material taken from another collection covering the years 1557–63 and ascribed to the Elizabethan judge Richard Harper. A further set of Elizabethan reports (1562–73), transcribed in a different hand, is found at ff. 87–129 while ff. 130–328 form yet another collection consisting principally of cases from 31–8 Eliz. (1588–96). The authors of the last two have not been determined.

(5) *L.I. Mayn. 86:* 111 fols., late 16th cent. Reports for 4, 5, & 6 Hen. VII (1488–91), 1, 6, 7, 9 & 11 Hen. VIII (1509–10, 1514–15, 1517–18 and 1519–20), 4 & 5 Phil. & Mary, 1, 2 & 5 Eliz. (1557–63); virtually identical with the corresponding material in D (4) above.

(6) *B.M. Harl. 1691:* 210 fols., probably copied from various sources in the second half of the 16th cent. Consists of material emanating from the Inner Temple including readings, moot cases and reports. The reports consist of the following:

(i) cases 'ex libro Magistri Carelle', 4–11 Hen. VII (ff. 66–89*v*) originally collected by John Carrell Sr. Some of these entries are also found in D (4) & (5) above.

(ii) a series of cases reported for the years 1554–60 (ff. 90–8) not specifically connected with the Carrell family. Some of these entries are also found in G (37) below.

(iii) a further group of cases ascribed to Master 'John Caryll' (the son of John Carrell Sr.) consisting of reports covering the years 1529–37 (ff. 98–112);

(iv) reports from 1, 31 & 33 Hen. VIII (1509–10, 1539–40,

1541–2). One entry, the case of *Conyngsby v. Mallom* (1509), appears in the printed 'Keilwey' (ff. 113–21);

(v) ff. 123–33 contain a distinct set of cases taken from the years 1532–4 & 1536–7, a few of which turn up in Dyer's *Reports*;

(vi) ff. 140–4*v* contain a selection of reports covering the years 1527–45;

(vii) a report of unknown origin of the case of *Wimbish v. Tailbois* (1545) (ff. 167–70*v*) closely akin to the version found in G (35) below (ff. 107–11).

E. HENRY VIII

(1) *Bodl. Rawl. C.705:* a set of moot cases compiled by John Daniel of Gray's Inn and taken, for the most part, from the Inns of Chancery during the reign of Hen. VIII. This collection also includes material from moots and readings in Gray's Inn including a reading delivered by Justice John Spelman (1514, 1519 or 1521).

(2) *H.L.S. 125:* 79 fols., mid-16th cent. A series of 172 numbered moot cases argued in the Middle Temple before 1550.

F. HENRY VIII–PHILIP AND MARY

(1) *B.M. Harg. 2:* 91 fols., early 17th cent. A series of short case notes taken from the reigns of Hen. VIII, Edw. VI & Mary. The anonymous compiler has extracted a series of entries from Brooke's Abridgment and arranged them in chronological sequence giving appropriate references to the source in each instance.

G. HENRY VIII–ELIZABETH

(1) *B.M. Harg. 388:* 255 fols., late 16th cent. A collection of reports and other legal material taken from the reigns of Hen. VIII, Edw. VI, Mary and Eliz. consisting of four distinct segments:

(i) case reports 1–32 Hen. VIII (1509–41) ascribed to Justice John Spelman of the King's Bench (ff. 1–207);

(ii) a notebook comprising cases, extracts of moots and readings, comments on the law and descriptions of related events—also attributable to Spelman (ff. 208–216);

(iii) cases taken 'en temps H. 8' generally within the years 1527–35, but not associated with Spelman (ff. 217–55); this section follows closely ff. 140–56 of G (14) below;
(iv) reports taken from Phil. & Mary and Eliz. extending to 1564; virtually identical with ff. 24–32 of G (14) (ff. 241–55).

(2) *C.U.L. Gg.2.5:* 553 fols., mid-17th cent. Cases taken chiefly from Eliz. and Jas. I but including a group of reports extending back to Hen. VIII. The volume contains, among other items, the following:
(i) ff. 1–23*v*: a section headed 'Les Reports de Gulielme Benloe serjeant al Ley' containing 233 numbered entries abridged from Bendlowes' Reports, Trin. 31 Hen. VIII–East. 20 Eliz. (1539–78);
(ii) ff. 24–8*v*: a series of miscellaneous cases taken from the early years of Eliz.; author unknown;
(iii) ff. 29–35*v*: 'certaine cases in temps H. 8 reporte per Spilman'; consist of twenty-two numbered entries attributed to John Spelman a justice of the King's Bench, 1532–44;
(iv) ff. 36–44: reports for 4 & 5 Phil. & Mary (1557–8); many entries attributable to Harper;
(v) ff. 47–186: a series of reports covering the reign of Eliz. taken from several sources including Dyer, Harper and Bendlowes.
(vi) ff. 189–245: an autonomous volume of reports for Hil. 28 Hen. VIII–East. 24 Eliz. (1537–82), also compiled from various separate collections.
(vii) ff. 266–540: a selection of cases taken, for the most part, from the later years of Eliz. but interspersed with a few entries extending from the reign of Edw. VI to Chas. I; much of the material corresponds to the printed reports of George Croke.

(3) *B.M. Lansd. 1072:* 228 fols., 17th cent. A wide-ranging collection of notes and case reports, Hen. VIII–Eliz. Ff. 4–55 contain material closely aligned to that found in G (1) above (ff. 156–254*v*). The remainder of the MS covers the reign of Eliz. generally drawing on such sources as Bendlowes, Harper and Coke.

(4) *C.U.L. Ii.5.20:* 63 fols., mid-17th cent. A varied selection of cases Mich. 1 Hen. VIII–7 Jas. I (1509–1610) including material from Dyer, Keilwey, Moore and Croke.

(5) *B.M. Lansd. 1084:* 145 fols., late 16th-early 17th cents. A volume consisting of two distinct collections:

(i) ff. 1–36 are copied in a 16th-cent. court hand and comprise a series of short entries chiefly from the reign of Eliz. but including case-notes extending back as far as 1510; some of the material can be ascribed to John Carrell Sr. & Jr., Nicholas Hare, James Dyer and Richard Harper.

(ii) ff. 36*v*–145*v* contain a series of reports covering most of Elizabeth's reign and erroneously ascribed to Christopher Wray. The reports at ff. 37–42*v* (1581–6) were probably prepared by Francis Windham. This section as a whole was probably transcribed in the early 17th cent. and may have belonged to Endymion Porter (1587–1649) a frequent emissary to Spain under Chas. I who studied at Gray's Inn in 1620.

(6) *H.L.S. 1058:* 109 fols., 17th cent. A set of reports for 25 Eliz.–5 Jas. I (1582–1608) signed at the end by one Francis Barkesdale and dated 1634. Barkesdale was probably the scribe as there was no one of that name studying at the Inns of Court in this period. Preceding the main body of reports is a series of short notes on decisions, Hen. VIII–Eliz., ascribed to such prominent practitioners as John Carrell Sr. and Nicholas Hare (ff. 1–6) (cf. G (5) above).

(7) *Bodl. Rawl. 728:* 292 fols., late 16th cent. The original version of Bendlowes' Reports belonging to the author and covering the years 1511–79; probably compiled between 1573 and 1584.

(8) *B.M. Add. 25189:* 159 fols., late 16th cent. Another copy of Bendlowes' Reports comprising cases for the period 1511–79. This MS may have belonged to Edward Coke.

(9) *B.M. Add. 25190:* 31 fols., late 16th cent. abridgment of Bendlowes' Reports as found in G (8) above and containing 288 numbered entries together with an exhaustive table of subject matter at the back.

(10) *B.M. Harl. 5142:* 182 fols., late 16th cent. A fairly complete version of Bendlowes' Reports 3 Hen. VIII–East. 20 Eliz. (1511–78).

(11) *Lib. of Congress 26:* 291 fols., late 16th cent. Another complete collection of Bendlowes' Reports together with a greatly condensed version of Plowden's *Commentaries*, Part I. One 17th-century owner of the MS appears to have been Edward Goldynge.

(12) *H.L.S. 16:* 488 fols., late 16th cent. Two separate sets of reports originally owned by John Savile, a baron of the Exchequer under Eliz. and Jas. I and himself a law reporter. Ff. 5–224 constitute a full set of Bendlowes' Reports; ff. 225–448 contain a series of cases principally from the reign of Eliz. for the years 1583–90 but including a few entries extending as far back as 1509 (ff. 448*v*–52); those found at ff. 303–460 may be the work of Christopher Wray.

(13) *B.M. Harl. 355:* 163 fols., late 16th–early 17th cents. Another selection from Bendlowes' Reports with entries from the years 1511–79.

(14) *B.M. Harg. 3:* 158 fols., early 17th cent. A miscellaneous selection of material taken from the reigns of Hen. VIII, Edw. VI, Mary and Eliz. Ff. 1–23*v* consist of 'diverse titles of law' taken from Hen. VIII; ff. 24–5 consist of reports 'en temps Phillip et Mary'; ff. 26–32 contain cases for 1–6 Eliz. (1558–64) including a condensed version of *Hales v. Petit* (f. 26); ff. 33–137 comprise seventy-eight full-length entries from Bendlowes' Reports for the period Mich. 3 Hen. VIII–East. 10 Eliz. (1511–68); ff. 140–56 include a series of reports of varying length described as

'en temps H. 8', most of the entries being for 19–26 Hen. VIII (1527–35); cf. G (1) above.

(15) *B.M. Add. 25001:* 250 fols., late 16th or early 17th cent. A complete collection of Bendlowes' Reports corresponding to the original MS (G (7) above) with cases for Mich. 3 Hen. VIII–Hil. 21 Eliz. (1511–79). In addition the volume contains a few cases from the years 1600–3 together with miscellaneous notes on practice and pleading in the Court of Chancery.

(16) *B.M. Add. 35940:* 322 fols., 17th cent. A consolidation of various case collections covering the years 1511–73. The volume includes the work of Bendlowes, Dalison, Harper, Moore and Anderson, though mostly in an abridged form.

(17) *B.M. Add. 25200:* 223 fols., 17th cent. A collection consisting principally of cases from the Court of King's Bench 31–42 Eliz. (1588–1600) but also including (at ff. 202–21*v*) twenty-six entries from Bendlowes' Reports, 1511–62.

(18) *B.M. Add. 21068:* 333 fols., 17th cent.; consists of an incomplete set of reports attributable to William Bendlowes. The series runs from Mich. 3 Hen. VIII to Mich. 8 & 9 Eliz. (1511–66).

(19) *C.U.L. Dd.13.24:* 102 fols., late 16th cent. A miscellaneous collection of pleadings, moot cases and reports. Ff. 81–98*v* comprises law cases extracted from Bendlowes' Reports, chiefly Hen. VIII and Eliz.; ff. 99–102*v* contain a number of precedents of pleadings and deeds together with a few undated reports.

(20) *B.M. Add. 25191:* 392 fols., 17th cent. A copy of the reports compiled by Francis Moore and purportedly taken from the reporter's original notebook. The material, which includes cases originally prepared by William Bendlowes, runs from 3 Hen. VIII–44 Eliz. (1511–1602).

(21) *B.M. Add. 25192:* 103 fols., 17th cent. An abridgment of the material in G (20) above.

(22) *B.M. Add. 35937:* 397 fols., 17th cent. Another copy of Moore's Reports including both first-hand material and cases extracted from Bendlowes. This volume belonged to Nicholas Lechmere, baron of the Exchequer 1689–1700.

(23) *B.M. Harl. 4585:* 453 fols., early 17th cent. Another copy of Moore's Reports allegedly *scripto propria manu ipsius.* Cases reported extend from 1511 to 1602; owned at one time by Robert Paynell of Gray's Inn (circa 1620).

(24) *H.L.S. 2097:* 219 fols., 17th cent. Another copy of Moore's Reports with cases extending from 1512 to 1595.

(25) *B.M. Lansd. 1059:* 397 fols., 17th cent. Another copy of Moore's Reports supposedly transcribed from his own MS and covering the period 1511–1602. This copy appears to have belonged at one point to Henry Powle, Speaker of the Convention Parliament of 1689.

(26) *I.T. Barr. 9:* 535 fols., 17th cent. Ff. 74–535 contain a set of Moore's Reports purportedly taken from the author's original MS; the material extends from 3 Hen. VIII to 44 Eliz. (1511–1602). The first 73 leaves comprise a commonplace book with entries from 'Abatement' to 'Wreck'.

(27) *I.T. Barr. 19:* 881 fols., 17th cent. A small quarto volume containing another set of Moore's Reports; in addition, at ff. 830–81, there is a set of reports of unknown origin taken from the Exchequer Chamber and Court of Wards.

(28) *Trinity College Dublin 720:* 392 fols., various 17th-cent. hands. Another set of Moore's Reports purportedly copied from the original MS and covering the period 1511–1602; bequeathed by an Irish judge, Jerome Alexander (d. 1670), to Trinity College.

(29) *C.U.L. Ee.6.12:* 116 fols., early 17th cent. A collection compiled from the work of various practitioners: ff. 1–85 contain material from 3 Hen. VIII–44 Eliz. (1511–1602) extracted from Bendlowes, Moore and John Walter; ff. 95–116 contain a separate set of cases taken from the reports of Richard Lydell of the Middle Temple (adm. 1598).

(30) *C.U.L. Ll.3.8–10:* three volumes of reports running from 1534 to 1603 compiled in the 17th cent. Ll.3.8 (481 fols.) contain material taken from Bendlowes, Moore, Harper and Dyer; Ll.3.9 & 10 (516 & 180 fols.) deal with the later years of Eliz. (1589–1603) and contain a large number of entries found in Croke Eliz.

(31) *B.M. Stowe 421:* 209 fols., early 18th cent. A copy of legal notes, originally compiled by Christopher Yelverton, in the hand of John Anstis (circa 1717–31), in English and French; included at ff. 136*v*–8 are notes taken from 6, 7 & 10 Hen. VIII. At ff. 63–5, 92*v*–102*v* are Elizabethan cases as found in Yelverton's book of reports (cf. K (90) below).

(32) *Longleat 240:* 190 fols., 17th cent. A conflation of several collections covering most of the reign of Eliz., with a few cases extending back to Hen. VIII. Some sections are designated, such as those taken from a book 'desouth le mayne de Fenner Justice' but which, in fact, are early reports out of Bendlowes (ff. 187–90). At f. 189*v* is a series of excerpts, Mich. 7–Trin. 21 Hen. VIII (1515–29) initially prepared by Justice John Spelman and reproduced by Fenner.

(33) *B.M. Add. 36080:* 199 fols., late 16th cent. Sixty-seven numbered cases extracted from Bendlowes' Reports for the years 1518–78.

(34) *C.U.L. Dd.10.37:* 170 fols., late 16th cent. A diverse collection including:

(i) another selection of cases from Bendlowes' Reports, 10 Hen. VIII–Mich. 16 & 17 Eliz. (1518–74) (ff. 154–63);
(ii) reports of untraceable origin covering the latter years of Eliz. (ff. 163*v*–70).

(35) *Lib. of Congress Gell MS:* 146 fols., mid-late 16th cent. A set of reports extending from Mich. 18 Hen. VIII to Mich. 14 & 15 Eliz. (1526–72) taken from various sources:
(i) the cases for 18, 26–7 Hen. VIII constitute the Yearbook cases for this period although slight variations exist in relation to the printed editions (ff. 1–55);
(ii) the majority of reports cover the years 33–5, 36, 38 Hen. VIII, 1–4, 7 Edw. VI, 1 Mary and 1 & 2 Phil. & Mary (1541–5, 1547–50, 1553–5); the source of this material cannot be determined although certain entries turn up in other collections such as D(6) above and reports ascribed to Dyer, Plowden and Harper (ff. 57–137);
(iii) a single entry for Hil. 1 Eliz. (1559) (f. 137) extracted from Plowden's *Commentaries* (187–99) and two final cases for 1571 of unknown origin but clearly of later vintage than the bulk of the collection (ff. 138–46*v*).

(36) *Herts. R.O. Gorhambury XII.A.6.*A–E*:* five small quarto volumes prepared in the late 16th and early 17th cents., probably by George Croke; later edited by Harbottle Grimston and forming the basis of Croke's three printed volumes of reports covering the reigns of Eliz., Jas. I and Chas. I. The MSS can be analysed as follows:
(A) 185 fols; notes and cases 27 Hen. VIII–Mich. 29 & 30 Eliz. (1535–87). This volume comprises material drawn from a wide cross-section of 16th cent. reporting, including the work of Bendlowes, Spelman, Harper, Dyer, Coke, Tanfield, Lewis, Clayton and Chamberlain;
(B–E) these four volumes contain, respectively, 184, 187, 186 and 235 fols. Collectively the material covers the period East. 6 Eliz.–Mich. 8 Chas. I (1564–1632). In addition to supplying

material for the printed editions of Croke's *Reports* the MS provides useful information on many of the sources employed by the reporter. These include cases initially noted by such fellow Templars as Edmund Prideaux, John Walter, William Brocke and William Clayton.

(37) *I.T. Petyt 511, vol. 13:* a volume of miscellaneous legal material compiled in the latter part of Elizabeth's reign and including the following:

(i) cases taken from the years 1529–37 attributed to John Carrell Jr. (ff. 1–14). These reports correspond closely to material found in D (6) above (ff. 98–112);

(ii) reports for the years 1554–60 (ff. 15–18) also similar to material in D (6) (ff. 90–8);

(iii) cases and notes collected by James Dyer on circuit, 1 Mary–23 Eliz. (1553–81) (ff. 19–48*v*);

(iv) further notes and cases compiled by Dyer 'which for some private reasons hee thought not fitt to make them vulgarr', 1–17 Eliz. (1558–75) (ff. 49–70*v*);

(v) a series of miscellaneous reports, some of which are found in the printed Dyer, covering the period 1559–70 (ff. 94–101).

(38) *B.M. Lansd. 1077:* 64 fols., mid-17th cent. A broad selection of cases prepared for Timothy and Richard Levinge of the Inner Temple. The selection is centred on Elizabethan material but includes entries extending from 1529 to 1629.

(39) *B.M. Harg. 5:* 112 fols., early 17th cent. A collection of reports taken mainly from the later years of Eliz. (1579–92) but including entries extending back to Hil. 21 Hen. VIII (1530) (f. 106). Included in this volume is a report of *Winter's Case* (1572) as found in various other collections (cf. App. III, p. 323).

(40) *B.M. Harg. 33:* 233 fols., early 17th cent. Miscellaneous legal material which includes extracts from Bendlowes' Reports

(ff. 99–110) for the period Mich. 24 Hen. VIII–Trin. 17 Eliz. (1532–75).

(41) *B.M. Harg. 373:* 229 fols., late 16th cent. A valuable collection of reports compiled by Nicholas Jordan of the Inner Temple (adm. 1588) from the material of such fellow Inner Templars as Richard Harper, John Carrell Jr., Thomas Otley, Thomas Gawdy, Francis Beaumont, Edward Coke and John Bullocke. The collection embraces the period Mich. 2 & 3–East. 35 Eliz. (1560–93) together with one entry from East. 26 Hen. VIII (*Lord Dacre's Case*).

(42) *B.M. Harl. 925:* 86 fols., 17th cent. A small (8to) student's notebook containing cases taken from the years 1534–79. Ff. 1–8*v* consist of Yearbook reports for Trin. 26–Mich. 27 Hen. VIII (1534–5); ff. 9–86*v* contain extracts out of Plowden's printed *Commentaries*, Parts I & II.

(43) *B.M. Harl. 4817:* 243 fols., 17th cent. Three separate collections of reports from the reign of Eliz.:

(i) a series of short case notes, 3—Mich. 33 & 34 Eliz. (1560–91) of unknown origin (ff. 1–4);

(ii) a complete set of Anderson's Reports, East. 26 & 27 Hen. VIII–Hil. 45 Eliz. (1535–1603) (ff. 5–149);

(iii) a collection of reports attributed to Justice Peter Warburton, Trin. 36 Eliz.–Hil. 13 Jas. I (1594–1616) plus a single entry for Hil. 7 Chas. I (ff. 150–238).

This last collection was put together by Robert Paynell of Gray's Inn who claims to have copied it from Serjeant (Edmund ?) Reeve also of Gray's Inn (adm. 1607).

(44) *Trinity College Dublin 704:* 21 fols., 17th cent. 'Cases and reports' extracted from the Reports of William Bendlowes, 1535–60.

(45) *B.M. Harl. 785:* 198 fols., 16th and 17th cents. A diverse collection of legal and historical material in various hands and

languages. Ff. 104–98 comprise a series of notes and case reports which appear to be the work of John Birche, a baron of the Exchequer under Eliz. This material includes extracts of cases 29–32 Hen. VIII (1537–41), Edw. VI, Phil. & Mary and 11–15 Eliz. (1568–73).

(46) *B.M. Harg. 6:* 79 fols., late 16th cent. Reports 38 Hen. VIII–Mich. 26 & 27 Eliz. (1546–84), attributed to Richard Harper and originally owned by William Nichols of the Middle Temple (adm. 1582).

(47) *B.M. Add. 25188:* 100 fols., late 16th cent. Reports taken from the Court of Common Pleas for 38 Hen. VIII–21 Eliz. (1546–79). The material covering the years 1546–65 is associated with the work of Richard Harper.

(48) *B.M. Harg. 8:* 227 fols., early 17th cent. Another collection of reports, 38 Hen. VIII–Mich. 26 & 27 Eliz. (1546–84), ascribed to Justice Harper and evidently sharing a common source with G (46) above.

(49) *Longleat 221:* 102 fols., late 16th-early 17th cents. Reports 38 Hen. VIII–9 Eliz. (1546–67), similar in content to the material found in G (53) below ascribed to Harper.

(50) *C.U.L. Ll.3.14:* 285 fols., early 17th cent. Reports 38 Hen. VIII–Trin. 27 Eliz. (1546–85); a volume of cases very similar in content to G (48) above ascribed to Richard Harper.

(51) *L.I. Misc. 791:* 199 fols., early 17th cent. A volume of reports and miscellaneous notes prepared by a professional scribe but annotated by successive owners. In 1658 the MS was owned by Richard Levinge of the Inner Temple. The volume is made up of the following material:

(i) a series of cases described as 'Justice Harpers Reports' 1546–84 (ff. 1–14);

(ii) a copy of Anderson's Reports (ff. 15–67*v*);
(iii) reports for the years 1593–9 ascribed to Humphrey Ware of the Inner Temple (adm. 1588) (ff. 71–110);
(iv) reports for 1584–97 prepared by Edward Hendon of Gray's Inn (adm. 1586) (ff. 110*v*–67*v*);
(v) a selection of entries out of Bendlowes' Reports, 1535–78 (ff. 168–97).

(52) *Bodl. Rawl. C.112:* 271 fols., late 16th cent. A set of reports covering the years 1546–79 entitled 'Dalisons Reports' but in fact related to work ascribed to Richard Harper. This volume was probably first prepared for Henry Powle father of the Speaker of the 1689 Convention parliament.

(53) *B.M. Harg. 4:* 342 fols., early 17th cent. A two-part volume of reports taken from the reigns of Hen. VIII, Edw. VI, Mary and Eliz. Ff. 4–96, entitled, 'notes collecte en temps del Roigne Elizabeth', include cases for the years 1572–82 for which no author can be suggested, although it appears that the material was prepared by or for one practitioner. Ff. 97–331 contain reports ascribed to Richard Harper extending from 38 Hen. VIII to East. 29 Eliz. (1546–87). Ff. 332–42 contain miscellaneous legal notes including a report of *Whetstone's Case* concerning the Chantries Act of 1547.

(54) *L.I. Hill 123:* 98 fols., early 17th cent. Ff. 1–66 contain a collection of cases for the period Mich. 38 Hen. VIII–Trin. 6 Eliz. (1546–64) attributable to William Dalison and Richard Harper. Ff. 69–98 (also in the same hand) consist of a series of reports for the years 1588–90.

(55) *B.M. Add. 24845:* 519 fols., early 17th cent. Reports Mich. 38 Hen. VIII–41 Eliz. (1546–99). Ff. 1–111 consist of cases ascribed to Dalison and Harper and closely aligned to the printed version of Dalison's *Reports* (1689). The residue of the volume contains a selective cross-section of mid- and late-16th

century reporting including the work of Dyer, Plowden and Coke.

(56) *B.M. Add. 25198:* 308 fols., various early 17th-cent. hands. This MS consists principally of cases for East. 37–Mich. 39 & 40 Eliz. (ff. 1–283), but included as well are some abridged reports for Mich. 38 Hen. VIII–Hil. 9 Eliz. (1546–67) connected with the work of Harper (ff. 283*v*–97). Affixed to the cover of the MS is a vellum fragment with the inscription, 'Legyton his Reports'. The Catalogue cites the name as Ledyton, neither name can be traced in the records of the Inns.

(57) *B.M. Lansd. 1121:* 121 fols., early 17th cent. A collection of readings presented by Coke, Egerton and Shuttleworth together with some random reports. Ff. 67–79 contain cases associated with Richard Harper for the years 1546–63; ff. 80–120 cover the years 1577–95, including Francis Bacon's argument in *Chudleigh's Case* (1589).

(58) *B.M. Harg. 12:* 261 fols., 17th cent. A collection of cases adjudicated in the King's Bench and Common Pleas during the reigns of Eliz. and Jas. I together with a few entries taken from Hen. VIII. This volume was prepared in part by a Master Godfrey, possibly Richard Godfrey of Gray's Inn (circa 1580).

(59) *B.M. Harg. 403:* 261 fols., 17th cent. A four-part collection consisting of:
(i) reports mainly from the reign of Elizabeth (ff. 1–153*v*);
(ii) an abridgment of Coke's *Reports*, Parts 1–3 (ff. 154–215);
(iii) an abridgment of Owen's *Reports* (ff. 216–25);
(iv) an abridgment of Coke's *Reports*, Part 4 (ff. 226–61).
Section (i) contains selected cases out of Plowden (ff. 5–61*v*), sixty-seven short, numbered reports (ff. 62–7*v*), a series of cases taken from various reporters including Dyer, Harper and the Yearbooks extending back to temp Hen. VIII (ff. 68–122), forty-seven short notes from the reign of Eliz. (ff. 122*v*–5), a series of

reports labelled 'Pophams Reports' and emanating mainly from the King's Bench for the years 1587–97 (ff. 125*v*–47), and a series of undated entries entitled 'Dier hors de print' which contains material similar to other collections ascribed to James Dyer (ff. 147*v*–53*v*).

H. EDWARD VI–PHILIP AND MARY

(1) *B.M. Harl. 5141:* a collection of legal material and character sketches of prominent Elizabethans prepared at various times in the late 16th and 17th cents. Ff. 1–45 consist of reports for Mich. 6 Edw. VI–Trin. 4 & 5 Phil. & Mary (1553–8) compiled by William Dalison, a justice of the King's Bench (1556–9). This particular volume belonged to William Lambarde who married the widow of Dalison's son and apparently had the reports copied directly from the judge's own notebook.

I. EDWARD VI–ELIZABETH

(1) *B.M. Harl. 4814:* 286 fols., 17th cent. A mixed collection of late 16th–early 17th-cent. cases. Ff. 1–264*v* consist of various reports extending from 1547 to the reign of Chas. I; ff. 34–42 consist of material purportedly collected by Francis Moore; ff. 42–53*v* contain cases relating to prohibitions; ff. 157–65 include reports 1 Edw. VI–Trin. 16 Eliz. (1547–74) of mixed origin; ff. 165–217*v* contain cases for the years 1594–6. A smaller, separate collection is found at ff. 265–299 consisting of reports scattered between Mich. 28 & 29 and 40 Eliz. (1586–98), apparently the property of one John Adams of Lincoln's Inn (adm. 1559, 1579 or 1637).

(2) *B.M. Lansd. 1095:* 141 fols., late 16th & mid 17th cents. Reports taken from the King's Bench and Common Pleas for the reign of Eliz. together with a few cases from 2 Edw. VI (1548) and 4 Chas. I (1628, added later). The reporter, whose identity is not revealed, was evidently in practice around 1588 (see ff. 18, 45).

(3) *B.M. Lansd. 1106:* 127 fols., late 16th cent. A conflation of several collections including:

(i) reports Mich. 4 Edw. VI–Mich. 10 & 11 Eliz. (1551–68) (ff. 25–33); (ii) a collection covering the years 1564–72, 1595–6 (ff. 38–57). This is a prime example of a set of reports put together from diverse sources without regard to chronology or origin; owned by Robert Paynell in the early 17th cent.

(4) *MS belonging to Sir John Neale:* 153 fols., early 17th cent. A student's notebook prepared by Timothy Turner of Gray's Inn (circa 1612–13). Starting at the back of the volume is a series of moots and court cases including eight leaves of reports abridged from Plowden's *Commentaries*, Part I.

(5) *Bodl. Rawl. C.498:* 130 fols., 17th cent. An octavo volume containing brief summaries of cases from Plowden, Parts I & II.

(6) *B.M. Harl. 6681:* 81 fols., 17th cent. Another selection of extracts out of Parts I & II of Plowden's *Commentaries* together with a table of subject-matter.

(7) *Lib. of Congress 55:* 255 fols., late 16th cent. A small octavo volume containing a condensation of Plowden. Each 'commentary' is summarized, but without inclusion of the pleadings. There is a heading for each entry which includes a reference to the printed original. The name of 'Townsende' is inscribed at the top of ff. 59 & 60.

(8) *H.L.S. 2144:* 63 fols., early 17th cent. A complete set of cases from Plowden's reports but without pleadings. These are preceded by 9 leaves setting out the salient issues in each of Plowden's cases in Part I of the *Commentaries*. This volume belonged to Thomas Twisden of the Inner Temple (adm. 1617) who became justice of the King's Bench in 1660.

(9) *H.L.S. 1051:* 397 fols., 17th cent. A set of Anderson's Reports, 1535–1603, preceded by a group of short miscellaneous cases for Hil. 5 & 6 Edw. VI–Mich. 33 & 34 Eliz. (1552–91).

(10) *B.M. Harl. 1699:* 168 fols., 17th cent. 'Notes collecte in tempes dell raigne la Roigne Elizabethe': a collection of cases consisting of 605 numbered entries which in fact run from 6 Edw. VI to 20 Eliz. (1552–78). This volume appears to be a consolidation of several collections the sources of which have not been identified.

(11) *C.U.L. Dd.5.50:* 70 fols., early 17th cent. This volume is mainly composed of 17th-century readings but ff. 59–70*v* contain a series of cases for Edw. VI and Eliz. The former are closely related to material attributable to Richard Harper.

J. PHILIP AND MARY–ELIZABETH

(1) *B.M. Lansd. 1119:* 125 fols., 17th cent. A volume of readings and reports. At ff. 61–100 are found random cases for 4 & 5 Phil. & Mary–Hil. 38 Eliz. (1557–96) interspersed with readings such as those of Dyer (ff. 78–85) and Bromley (ff. 86–94), among others. Included as well are cases extracted from the Yearbooks of Hen. VI (ff. 4–18). Beginning at the back of the volume (ff. 124–100) is another series of reports 24–7 Eliz. (1581–5). At ff. 74–7 are 'ascuns cases hors del liver de More' consisting of 25 entries covering the years 1566, 1576 & 1583.

(2) *I.T. Barr. 13:* 220 fols., two or three 17th-cent. hands. This MS comprises, for the most part, cases for the period 1589–1622, but includes a few entries dating back to East. 4 & 5 Phil. & Mary (1558).

K. ELIZABETH

(1) *L.I. Mayn. 87:* 347 fols., 17th cent. Two separate volumes bound together:

(i) reports, Mich. 1–Mich. 20 & 21 Eliz. (1558–78); several collections combined together representing such reporters as Bendlowes, Harper and Dyer (ff. 1–246);
(ii) reports, Mich. 42 & 43 Eliz.–Trin. 1 Jas. I (1600–3) taken from the Common Pleas (ff. 247–347).

(2) *L.I. Hale 134:* 198 fols., late 16th cent. Reports 1558–94 with particular emphasis on the period 1586–94. This collection is compiled from numerous sources including the work of George Croke.

(2a) *L.I. Misc. 487:* 365 fols., neat scribal hand of late 16th cent., on the vellum cover is the inscription: 'My Fathers Reports Temps Eliz', and on the last leaf the name Jeffrey Snignell(?). The volume comprises a wide selection of Elizabethan reports, 1559–90 including such cases as *Dauncy v. Southwell* (1560, ff. 175*v*–9), *Andrews v. Blunt* (1572, ff. 269*v*–326*v*) and *Vernon v. Vernon* (1572, ff. 349*v*–54*v*).

(3) *H.L.S. 2071:* 88 fols., late 16th–early 17th cents. A diverse collection of Elizabethan cases covering the years 1559–82. Many of the entries can also be found in Nicholas Jordan's 'Collectanea' (G (41) above).

(4) *MS belonging to Professor S.E. Thorne:* 45 fols., later 16th cent. A collection of case reports extending from Mich. 1 & 2–Trin. 7 Eliz. (1559–65) which originally belonged to Chief Justice Edmund Anderson. The entries in this volume appear to be taken from the reports of James Dyer for the years in question and represent what is probably the only pre-publication collection of Dyer's work surviving.

(5) *Longleat 224:* 167 fols., 17th cent. Reports, 1559–99 with the main emphasis on 1595–9. Some cases appear to be the work of Edmund Escourte of Lincoln's Inn (see f. 17; cf. K (125) below).

(6) *B.M. Harg. 27:* 148 fols., 17th cent. A volume of legal material once belonging to Robert Hyde, Chief Justice of the King's Bench under Charles II. Included is a collection of cases attributed to John Popham, Mich. 34 & 35–East. 39 Eliz. (1592–7) (ff. 8–83*v*) and a leading decision from the MS reports of Dyer, 'Case of the Town of Southampton touchinge Impositions', Trin. 1 Eliz. (f. 92).

(7) *B.M. Harg. 132:* 77 fols., 17th cent. Another body of legal matter, largely from the 17th century, belonging to Chief Justice Hyde and including the Southampton impositions case (1559) extracted from Dyer's original MS (ff. 66*v*–7).

(8) *B.M. Add. 35941:* 292 fols., late 16th–early 17th cents. A volume composed of several sets of reports bound together and extending over the reigns of Eliz. and Jas. I. Ff. 19–68 contain entries for Mich. 1 & 2–Hil. 26 Eliz. (1559–84) some of which can be ascribed to Bendlowes and Harper; ff. 69–72 contain reports for the years 1590–5, ff. 73–190 reports for Hil. 26 Eliz.–12 Jas. I (1584–1615) and ff. 206–92 a lawyer's commonplace book interspersed with King's Bench reports for the years 1589–91.

(9) *B.M. Harg. 10:* 72 fols., late 16th–early 17th cents. A set of select reports ascribed to Richard Harper, Hil. 2–Mich. 15 & 16 Eliz. (1560–73). Ff. 62–6*v* contain a treatise in English on ownership of 'sea lands and salt shores'.

(10) *B.M. Lansd. 1086:* 144 fols., early 17th cent. Reports and readings from the reign of Eliz. Ff. 97*v*–127*v* contain cases which can be ascribed to Richard Harper, Mich. 2 & 3–Mich. 6 & 7 Eliz. (1560–4).

(11) *B.M. Harg. 37:* 184 fols., early 17th cent. Reports and tracts from Eliz. and Jas. I concerned mainly with the courts of Exchequer Chamber, King's Bench and Common Pleas. This volume was the property of Henry Calthorpe. One series of entries

extends from Mich. 2 & 3 to Hil. 7 Eliz. (1560–5) many of which are found in Harg. MSS 4 & 8 and ascribed to Richard Harper (ff. 119*v*–48). Another series of cases covers the years 1583–90 (ff. 3–174*v*).

(12) *B.M. Harg. 374:* 169 fols., 17th cent. Reports Mich. 2 & 3–Mich. 17 & 18 Eliz. (1560–75) attributable, for the most part, to Richard Harper but including material ascribed to Francis Rhodes (ff. 84*v*, 173–5), Thomas Fleming (f. 62*v*) and Thomas Bedingfield (ff. 5–7, 78).

(13) *H.L.S. 2079:* 170 fols., early 17th cent. Reports 3–28 Eliz. (1560–86). Ff. 3–24*v* contain entries attributable to Richard Harper covering the years 1559–65.

(14) *B.M. Add. 25197:* 51 fols., 17th cent. A mixture of several sets of reports embracing the period 3–40 Eliz. (1560–98). There is no indication of the reporters or owners concerned.

(15) *B.M. Harl. 1059:* 143 fols., 17th cent. A consolidation of several separate collections of reports together with other legal material principally from the 17th century. Ff. 112*v*–39 contain cases for Trin. 3–Trin. 38 Eliz. (1561–96) including excerpts from Bendlowes, Plowden and Brownlow (ff. 109, 117, 126). At ff. 87–93 is found 'un informacion pur intrusion exhibita in curia wardorum vs Sir Edward Coke' (n.d.).

(16) *B.M. Harl. 1696:* 22 fols., 17th cent. A small but well-prepared set of reports taken from the common law courts and Court of Wards, 1562–88. The cases appear to have been extracted from various 16th-cent. collections by a single, unidentified compiler. The work of Dyer, Bendlowes and Harper is represented.

(17) *B.M. Lansd. 1062:* 424 fols., 17th cent. A large conflation of several sets of reports, Trin. 4 Eliz.–17 Jas. I (1562–1620), in

possession of Humphrey(?) Rant of Lincoln's Inn adm. 1597(?). Edward Umfreville believed that the collection was initially put together by Serj. Edmund Reeve (adm. G.I. 1607).

(18) *B.M. Harl. 5143:* 238 fols., late 16th–early 17th cents. A set of Bendlowes' Reports confined to 5–21 Eliz. (1562–79). In addition, ff. 223–30*v* contain excerpts of a reading delivered by Edmund Dudley in 1496; ff. 231–4 include a series of random decisions temp. Eliz.

(19) *C.U.L. Ii.5.38:* 271 fols., late 16th cent. A miscellaneous selection of Elizabethan cases including:
(i) 5–28 Eliz. (ff. 1–37*v*) and
(ii) Trin. 24–Trin. 30 Eliz. (ff. 38–260).

(20) *B.M. Lansd. 1133:* 161 fols., 17th cent. A selection of readings, leading cases and second-hand reports:
(i) readings by Thomas Bromley and Thomas Marowe (ff. 31, 56) together with Fitzherbert's preface to his treatise on Justices of the Peace (ff. 96–101);
(ii) a number of mid-Elizabethan leading cases (ff. 128–37) and a series of decisions relating to copyholders (137–9);
(iii) a series of short reports covering roughly the years 1563–70 many of which the anonymous compiler attributes to contemporary practitioners, generally of the Middle Temple, such as Christopher Crowe (adm. 1557), Matthew Ewens (adm. 1568), Robert Giles (adm. 1524–50), Edmund Store (adm. 1524–50), George Fettiplace (adm. 1552) and Thomas Ashe (adm. 1563) among others.

(21) *C.U.L. Hh.2.9:* 440 fols. (many blank), various 17th-cent. hands. Reports from the King's Bench, Common Pleas and Court of Wards, Mich. 6 & 7–Trin. 30 Eliz. (1564–88). These cases are compiled from various sources; the later entries also appear in Croke.

(22) *I.T. Barr. 17:* 249 fols., 17th cent. A collection of general notes and case reports. Ff. 1–247 contain cases for East. 25–Mich. 37 & 38 Eliz. (1583–95), but inserted amongst these (ff. 14*v*–17) is a series of entries taken 'ex libro Harper' 1564–74 and another series (ff. 19*v*–20) 'ex libro Edm. Prideaux' (called to the bar in 1584).

(23) *MS belonging to Sir John Neale:* 183 fols., first half 17th cent. A volume of reports from the period Eliz.–Chas. I interspersed with commonplace entries. Ff. 26–35 contain a selection of 'Justice Harpers Reports', 1564–70, which appear to have been part of a larger collection compiled by Robert or William Tipper of Gray's Inn (both adm. 1607). Ff. 36–95 contain a collection for Mich. 37 & 38–Trin. 38 Eliz. (1595–6) the source of which cannot be determined. The entire volume was put together and owned by Timothy Turner of Gray's Inn (adm. 1607) who evidently benefited from the notes taken by several colleagues. In addition to Tipper he has transcribed notes initially prepared by Elias Brantingham and Thomas Chamberlain, both admitted to Gray's Inn in 1578. (See I (4) above.)

(24) *H.L.S. 1192:* 130 fols., late 16th–early 17th cents. A consolidation of several collections embracing the period 1564–1603.

(25) *B.M. Harl. 6707:* 118 fols., early 17th cent. A miscellaneous group of Elizabethan reports compiled by a lawyer of the early 17th century. The volume consists in large measure of leading decisions from the period East. 7–East. 32 Eliz. (1565–90), mainly taken from the King's Bench and Court of Exchequer.

(26) *B.M. Lansd. 1067:* 240 fols., various 17th-cent. hands. Two distinct sets of reports:
(i) 9–15 Eliz. (1566–73) including a series of cases at assize 'taken out of the reports of Mr. Kempe', 1566–8, possibly Richard Kempe of Gray's Inn (adm. 1556) who was practising as late as 1599 (ff. 3–41);

(ii) reports of undetermined origin, Mich. 28 & 29–Hil. 43 Eliz. (1586–1601) (ff. 42–240).

(27) *B.M. Add. 25211:* 233 fols., 17th cent. A series of reports copied in a single hand, 9 Eliz.–12 Jas. I (1566–1615) but following no strict chronological sequence. The Elizabethan material is found mainly between ff. 140 and 225 and emanates from the King's Bench and Common Pleas. There is no indication of authorship.

(28) *L.I. Mayn. 77:* 200 fols., early 17th cent. A set of reports prepared by Justice Francis Rhodes concerned with cases adjudicated in the Court of Common Pleas between 1567 and 1575.

(29) *B.M. Lansd. 1145:* 131 fols., various 17th-cent. hands. A wide selection of Elizabethan reports with particular emphasis on the years 1568–75. A number of entries are also found in MSS attributed to Richard Harper.

(30) *B.M. Add. 35953:* 64 fols., early 17th cent. Reports taken from the years 1569–91 and 1603 (Mich. 1 Jas. I). The Elizabethan cases include a number emanating from Coke, including his report of *Shelley's Case* together with a dedicatory letter to Lord Buckhurst (ff. 13*v*–14). At f. 29 is a report of *Vernon v. Vernon* (1572) prepared by Justice Robert Mounson 'come fuit escrye desouth sa mayne'.

(31) *C.U.L. Mm.4.31:* 127 fols., late 16th–early 17th cents. Reports from the reigns of Eliz. and Jas. I:
(i) ff. 3–23 contain cases from the early years of Eliz.;
(ii) ff. 53–62: errors in Exchequer Chamber, 1586–1600;
(iii) ff. 62–7: arguments out of the Common Pleas, 1594–6.

(32) *I.T. Petyt 516 vol. 6:* 143 fols., 17th cent. A selection of leading cases, 1570–80 (ff. 1–98) together with later entries from the reigns of Jas. I and Chas. I (ff. 99–141).

(33) *C.U.L. Ii.5.12:* 102 fols. A volume of reports compiled originally about 1600 but embracing material ranging from 1571 to the reign of Chas. I. The bulk of reports come from the King's Bench and Common Pleas for the years 1588–96.

(34) *B.M. Harl. 2036:* 156 fols., two 17th-cent. hands. Reports Mich. 13 & 14–36 Eliz. (1571–94). Ff. 2–50*v* contain a selection of King's Bench decisions copied in a neat scrivener's hand, 1589–91; ff. 51–156 appear to be the work of a practitioner and contain cases for 1570–94.

(34a) *John Rylands Library, Fr.118:* 295 fols., early 17th cent. Various hands and collections of reports 1572–1625. The main group of Elizabethan cases is found at ff. 15–226.

(35) *C.U.L. Gg.3.3:* 44 fols., early 17th cent. A series of six leading cases taken from the years 1572–5 and generally ascribed to the reports of Richard Harper; one entry, *Sheldon v. Gilbert* (1574), is described as being taken 'ex reports Will Watson de Interiori Templo'. (Possibly the William Watson admitted in 1557.)

(36) *B.M. Harl. 4552:* 176 fols., 17th cent. Two collections covering 15–41 Eliz. (1572–99). Included are a large number of cases concerned with copyhold (ff. 5*v*–30). Much of the more general material can be found in the printed Reports of Croke.

(36a) *University College London; Ogden 29:* 285 fols., early 17th cent. (circa 1633). A collection of cases compiled by Timothy Turner of Gray's Inn which includes extracts from Coke's *Reports*, Parts 1, 2, 5, 10 & 11 (ff. 1–58), reports from various sources for Trin. 40–Trin. 42 Eliz. (1598–1600) (ff. 76–212), extracts from Coke's *Reports*, Part 4 (ff. 217–19) and reports for East. 4–East. 12 Jas. I (1606–15) (ff. 220–85). At f. 76 Turner has written, 'I received this reporte of my cosin Thomas Waller in

Lent 7 & 8 Car.'; at f. 129 he notes a case, Mich. 40 & 41 Eliz. ex libro Ed. Hall'.

(36b) *Eaton Hall* (Duke of Westminster): 120 fols., 17th cent. Two collections of cases, the first beginning with *Vernon's Case* (1572), the second with *Clayton's Case* (1595).

(37) *I.T. Barr. 76.* (Two volumes):
(i) 230 fols., 17th cent. Reports Trin. 14–Trin. 40 Eliz. (1572–98). Some entries appear in printed form in Leonard's and Croke's Reports;
(ii) 431 fols., same 17th-cent. hand. Reports taken principally from the years 1593–1600 together with a few earlier leading cases (ff. 1–17). A number of cases seem to have originated with Coke and other printed collections.

(38) *L.I. Mayn. 82:* 146 fols., 17th cent. A mixed collection of reports, Mich. 14 & 15 Eliz.–Hil. 17 Jas. I (1572–1620). Ff. 1–63 contain 17th century material; at the other end of the MS are 83 leaves of Elizabethan cases.

(39) *C.U.L. Ff.5.16:* 92 fols., 17th cent. A general legal notebook which includes at ff. 63–82 a series of reports for the years 1573–92 together with some miscellaneous items in English brought before the Court of Wards or the two chief justices.

(40) *B.M. Add. 25193:* 93 fols., 17th cent. Reports from the reigns of Eliz. and Chas. I. Ff. 1–78 consist of cases prepared by Chief Justice Anderson between 1573 and 1603.

(41) *B.M. Lansd. 1103:* 60 fols., early 17th cent. A short selection of leading cases, Hil. 15–Hil. 41 Eliz. (1573–99) extracted from, among others, Harper and Coke.

(42) *M.T. 6.B:* 388 fols., 17th cent., French and English. Four collections bound together in one volume covering the

years 1573–1627. Ff. 1–35 contain reports for Hil. 15–East. 41 Eliz. (1573–99). At f. 4*v* is a copy of Plowden's argument in *Brent v. Lord Pawlett* (1575) on contingent remainders. Ff. 45–71 contain reports for 1590–7 some of which are taken from Coke and John Walter. This volume may have been the property of William Norman of Norfolk.

(43) *B.M. Lansd. 1057:* 285 fols., early 17th cent. A large collection of leading decisions and pleadings prepared by two or more copyists over a lengthy period of time. The law reports proper encompass the later years of Eliz. but some cases begin as early as 1561. No evidence of authorship or ownership of this MS is to be found but some of the material is similar to that ascribed to Richard Harper in other collections. At f. 17*v* are some notes written in English 'out of Hales Book' (James Hales, justice of the court of Common Pleas, 1553–4?). Ff. 188–276 contain a series of lengthy, well-organized reports for the years 1574–7 which are strongly reminiscent of Plowden's style although there is no actual evidence of his authorship.

(44) *B.M. Harg. 9:* 280 fols., 16th & 17th cents. Reports taken from various years of Eliz. with emphasis on the years 1574–6 (ff. 182–271*v*). Many entries are similar in style to Plowden's mode of reporting.

(45) *Longleat 241:* 29 fols., 17th cent. Notes of cases in the King's Bench 17–32 Eliz. The majority of entries come from the years 1585–9.

(46) *B.M. Add. 16169:* 477 fols., late 16th cent. A combination of readings, reports and miscellaneous legal matter prepared by an unidentified law student of the Middle Temple between 1575 and 1588. The reports include the *Serjeants' Case* of 1579 but generally emanate from the courts of King's Bench and Exchequer rather than Common Pleas.

(47) *Bodl. Rawl. C.341:* 98 fols., late 16th–early 17th cents. Two separate collections in one volume:
(i) reports Mich. 31 & 32–Hil. 33 Eliz. (1589–91) collected by John Walter (ff. 1–43);
(ii) reports Trin. 17–Trin. 22 Eliz. (1575–91) of mixed origin (ff. 44–98).

(48) *B.M. Harl. 4998:* 309 fols., 17th cent. A wide selection of cases, Hil. 19 Eliz.–East. 10 Jas. I (1577–1612), including reports out of the Exchequer Chamber, 1586–98 (ff. 277–83).

(49) *B.M. Harg. 11:* 201 fols., various early 17th-cent. hands. Reports Hil. 19–Trin. 31 Eliz. (1577–89). This volume appears to have been the property of the Sheffield family, various members of which attended the Inns of Court between 1577 and 1663.

(49a) *L.I. Misc. 488:* 177 fols., early 17th cent. Two collections:
(i) ff. 1–122: Mich. 19 & 20–East. 30 Eliz. (1577–88), with additional entries up to 1605;
(ii) ff. 123–177 (running from back to front): cases from the reign of James I.
The volume contains the bookplate of Sir John Richardson.

(50) *B.M. Add. 35942:* 121 fols., early 17th cent. Reports 1578–1592. This collection includes a number of long and informative cases taken from the three common law courts. Among these is an argument presented by Plowden (ff. 33–7), an early appearance by Thomas Egerton (f. 4), a report by Dr. Lloyd, 'doctor de Arches' (ff. 5*v*–6) and an early appearance by Thomas Owen, a law reporter in later years (f. 25).

(51) *B.M. Lansd. 1101:* 81 fols., early 17th cent. A collection of general legal matter including:
(i) reports attributed to John Savile, a baron of the Exchequer (1598–1607). The cases in question cover the years 1578–82 and do

not appear in Savile's printed collection although they emanate from the Court of Exchequer (ff. 1–26);

(ii) another set of Elizabethan reports (1572–86) many of which do appear in the printed Savile, albeit in a somewhat garbled form (ff. 38–76).

(52) *B.M. Add. 35949–52:* four volumes of reports taken principally from the common law courts together with a few decisions from the Star Chamber and Court of Wards. The series extends from 1579 to 1622 and apparently is the product of a single, unidentified practitioner—probably attached to the Middle Temple. The MSS may be described as follows:

(i) *35949:* 202 fols., Mich. 21 & 22–Trin. 34 Eliz. (1579–92). The reporter makes numerous personal interjections and refers to opinions and cases contributed by colleagues such as 'Towse del Inner Temple' (f. 156*v*) and 'Popham Chief Justice dangliter' (f. 178). The name Nicholas Bouker appears on f. 3 but no such individual appears in the records of the Inns.

(ii) *35950:* 199 fols.; Mich. 35 & 36–Hil. 40 Eliz. (1593–8). At f. 15 the author records that this is the second volume 'del reports des casses queux ieo collect . . . a les courts al Westminster'. Included is material contributed by Thomas Stephens of the Middle Temple (adm. 1578) and by (Rowland) Royle, also of the Middle Temple (adm. 1591).

(iii) *35951:* 199 fols.; East. 40–Hil. 44 Eliz. (1598–1602). Before his regular series of cases the reporter has inserted (ff. 1–12) a report of *Winter's Case* (1572) which is similar to the 'Harper' version in K (9) above. Ff. 13–26 contain notes on a reading delivered by Blanchard at the Middle Temple in 1571.

(iv) *35952:* 212 fols.; Trin. 44 Eliz.–20 Jas. I (1602–1623). At f. 162*v* the reporter has inserted an extract from Edmund Dudley's reading at Gray's Inn in 1496. There is a report of *Bate's Case* (1606) at ff. 78*v*–80*v*, and, at various points, there are descriptions of the creation of judges and serjeants (ff. 32, 78, 102*v*).

(53) *B.M. Harl. 1693:* 227 fols., three early 17th-cent. hands.

Reports taken, for the most part, from the Court of Common Pleas, 1580–99. The name of George Homeston appears on the fly-leaf. At ff. 11–12*v* appears a report of *Shelley's Case* and commentary thereon.

(54) *B.M. Harl. 1588:* 198 fols., 17th cent. A collection of reports and commentaries consisting mainly of cases for 1580–95 (ff. 2–170), reports from the Court of Wards in the reign of Eliz. (ff. 171–7) and the decision in *Buckhurst v. Fenner* together with other cases for the years 1582–1594 (ff. 178–94). At ff. 194–8 is a treatise on the statute 32 Hen. VIII, c. 28 (leases).

(55) *I.T. Barr. 10:* 126 fols., 17th cent. Short notes of cases Hil. 23 Eliz.–Trin. 6 Jas. I (1581–1608) taken at second hand from several sources.

(56) *L.I. Mayn. 63:* this MS could not be found in the Library of Lincoln's Inn; it is catalogued as containing King's Bench reports, 1581–1601.

(57) *B.M. Lansd. 1087:* 278 fols., early 17th cent. Reports taken out of the three common law courts for 24–37 Eliz. (1581–95) apparently taken at first hand by a practitioner of the time (see f. 136).

(58) *B.M. Harl. 4556:* 217 fols., 17th cent. A miscellaneous collection of readings, reports and precedents. The reports constitute part of a larger collection extending from Trin. 23–34 Eliz. (1581–92) of which only the entries for 1590–1 remain (ff. 34–52).

(59) *B.M. Lansd. 1076:* 189 fols., 17th cent. Reports extracted from various collections and transcribed by various hands dealing with the years 1582–1600; emanating from the King's Bench and Common Pleas.

(60) *B.M. Add. 25196:* 385 fols., 17th cent. Reports 26–42 Eliz. (1583–1600) from the King's Bench and Common Pleas. The name of Paul Sidnor(?) is inscribed on the flyleaf.

(61) *B.M. Add. 35943:* 330 fols., transcribed in 1598. A collection of cases taken from the Court of Common Pleas for Mich. 25 & 26–Mich. 36 & 37 Eliz. (1583–94) with some later additions from Jas. I. The lawyer-compiler evidently gathered material from various contemporary notebooks.

(62) *L.I. Mayn. 29:* 285 fols., late 16th cent. Reports East. 25–East. 33 Eliz. (1583–91), including Coke's report of *Shelley's Case* and the arguments of Plowden and Popham on contingent remainders (ff. 207, 267*v*–75*v*, 252–7).

(63) *B.M. Add. 25208:* 107 fols., 17th cent. Reports from the reigns of Eliz. and Jas. I: ff. 1–13*v* contain a series of 77 numbered entries, 26–37 Eliz. (1583–95), in the illegible hand of a busy practitioner; apparently part of a more extensive collection.

(64) *L.I. Mayn. 66:* 395 fols., 17th cent. Two sets of reports:
(i) ff. 3–135*v*: East. 26–Trin. 36 Eliz. (1584–94), in various hands and order, including a series of decisions concerning copyholders (ff. 37–40*v*);
(ii) ff. 136–395: East. 42 Eliz.–Hil. 14 Jas. I (1600–17). This collection was prepared by Richard Lydell of the Middle Temple (adm. 1598), who took notes personally while attending proceedings of the Court of Common Pleas.

(65) *B.M. Harl. 443:* 201 fols., various 17th-cent. hands. A volume of miscellaneous legal matter including a copy of *Shelley's Case* (1579) with Coke's dedicatory letter (ff. 1–9*v*), a series of copyhold cases (ff. 82–91) and various sets of reports for the period 1584–94.

(66) *B.M. Harl. 4562:* 121 fols., early 17th cent. Ff. 1–106*v* contain anonymous reports, Hil. 26–Mich. 31 & 32 Eliz. (1584–9); ff. 107–21*v* consist of a series of short notes of decisions taken from the early years of Eliz. collected by Anthony Benne of the Middle Temple (adm. 1583). Some of the entries are extracted from Plowden (ff. 107–11*v*).

(67) *H.L.S. 9:* 40 fols., late 16th cent. A series of entries, circa 1584–6, some of which report cases at length while others consist merely of short (undated) opinions.

(68) *C.U.L. Ii.5.26:* 200 fols., 17th cent. Reports, chiefly out of the King's Bench, for Eliz. and Jas. I. Ff. 91*v*–222*v* contain cases for Mich. 27 & 28–Hil. 44 Eliz. (1585–1602).

(69) *B.M. Lansd. 1061:* 65 fols., 17th cent. Reports 28 Eliz.–11 Jas. I (1585–1614), taken for the most part from the Common Pleas during the years 1587–97.

(70) *B.M. Harl. 3209:* 112 fols., 17th cent. A concisely written volume of entries, 28 Eliz.–10 Jas. I (1585–1613) taken from proceedings in the King's Bench and Court of Chancery. These reports appear to be the work of Eusebius Andrewe, a bencher of Lincoln's Inn in the early 17th century.

(71) *B.M. Harl. 1331:* 82 fols., late 16th–early 17th cents. A legal notebook containing, at ff. 1–54, a series of reports, Trin. 27–Trin. 30 Eliz. (1585–8). These reports appear to be the work of Edward Hendon while an inner barrister at Gray's Inn (adm. 1586).

(72) *C.U.L. Dd.11.64:* 185 fols., late 16th–early 17th cents. Reports taken chiefly out of the King's Bench. Some of the material was prepared by Thomas Harris (appointed serjeant in 1589). Ff. 2–8 include cases for 1591–3, probably in Harris' own handwriting. The main collection covers the period 1585–8

(ff. 10–159). A subsequent series (ff. 175*v*–184) runs as late as 1591. (A commonplace book catalogued as C.U.L. Ll.2.11, may also be the work of Harris.)

(73) *B.M. Harl. 1722:* 42 fols., 17th cent. A carefully compiled set of reports for Trin. 27–Hil. 29 Eliz. (1585–7); largely concerned with personal actions, especially debt and detinue.

(74) *B.M. Add. 25195:* 99 fols., early 17th cent. A collection of readings, reports and legal treatises. Included is Coke's lecture at New Inn (ff. 7–9*v*), John Glanville's at Lincoln's Inn (1588) and Thomas Fleming's at Lincoln's Inn (1570). Ff. 23*v*–90 contain cases for 1586–96 from the common law tribunals and the Court of Wards.

(75) *B.M. Add. 35944:* 70 fols., late 16th cent. Decisions from the Common Pleas East. 28–East. 33 Eliz. (1586–91) reported by William Brocke of the Inner Temple.

(76) *H.L.S. 1057:* 293 fols., early 17th cent. Reports East. 28–Trin. 36 Eliz. (1586–94) prepared by William Brocke.

(77) *B.M. Lansd. 1073:* 162 fols., 17th cent. Reports Mich. the 28 & 29–Mich. 36 & 37 Eliz. (1586–94) taken mainly out of Common Pleas.

(78) *H.L.S. 110:* 289 fols., early 17th cent. Reports Hil. 29–East. 36 Eliz. (1587–94) collected at second hand by Arthur Turner around 1619; many entries turn up in Croke Eliz.

(79) *C.U.L. Mm.6.58:* 306 fols., various hands, 15th–17th cents. This MS includes the Autumn reading of Thomas Frowyck in 1495 at the Inner Temple (ff. 1–8), a series of moot cases (ff. 33–85) and proceedings in the Court of Arches in 1613 between *Glover and Roan* (ff. 208–20). Ff. 114–52 contain reports 30–35 Eliz. (1587–93) which appear to come out of a larger collection. The

volume appears to have belonged, at one time, to one R. Powell of the Inner Temple. (Cf. G (52) above and K (181) below.)

(80) *B.M. Harl. 1633:* 188 fols., 17th cent. An anonymous collection of King's Bench reports, 1587–91.

(81) *B.M. Harl. 4812:* 90 fols., 17th cent. Reports, East. 29–East. 33 Eliz. (1587–91). Inscribed on the vellum cover are the initials 'R.H.' (Richard Hutton?) and 'F.R.' (Francis Rhodes?).

(82) *B.M. Add. 25194:* 66 fols., late 16th–early 17th cents. A volume consisting of 115 numbered reports taken out of the King's Bench and Common Pleas for Hil. 29–Hil. 32 Eliz. (1587–90); not arranged in chronological order.

(83) *L.I. Misc. 361:* 205 fols., 17th cent. A collection containing a number of 16th-century items. The volume is prefaced by a copy of Coke's dedication to Lord Buckhurst and his version of *Shelley's Case* (ff. 1–11). Among other reporters whose work is utilized are Bendlowes (f. 12), Humphrey Ware (f. 178), Thomas Owen (ff. 184–97) and Harper (ff. 189–205). Interspersed throughout the MS are other cases from the reign of Eliz. attributable to Harper and Coke, among others. The largest single group of cases is found at ff. 100–52 covering the years 1587–9.

(84) *C.U.L. Mm.6.58:* 152 fols., 17th cent. Reports East. 30–Hil. 35 Eliz. (1588–93), extracted from a larger collection. The MS also includes readings on statutes from Hen. VII and after.

(85) *B.M. Add. 35945:* 325 fols., 17th cent. Reports Hil. 30–Mich. 34 & 35 Eliz. (1588–92) taken from the King's Bench and Common Pleas. A number of entries can be traced to the printed reports of Croke and Moore.

(86) *Longleat 222:* 83 fols., 17th cent. Reports Hil. 30–Mich. 31 & 32 Eliz. (1588–9) largely based on the Reports of Croke.

(87) *L.I. Mayn. 55:* 305 fols., 17th cent. Two sets of King's Bench reports:
(i) Hil. 31–Mich. 39 & 40 Eliz. (1589–97) (ff. 1–249);
(ii) East. & Trin. 30 Eliz. (1588) together with a number of undated entries (ff. 254–305).

(88) *C.U.L. Mm.4.35:* 226 fols., 17th cent. A MS entitled 'Godfryes Reports The First Part'. The cases run indiscriminately from 1575 to 1615 but are mainly concentrated in the period 1589–93. This material appears to be drawn to a large extent from various existing reports. For Richard Godfrey see G (58) above.

(89) *C.U.L. Ff.5.26:* 181 fols., late 16th–early 17th cents. Various collections of Elizabethan cases:
(i) rough case-notes 34–35 Eliz. (1591) (ff. 1–2*v*);
(ii) reports, 1588–9 (ff. 3–51*v*);
(iii) a full report of *Ayleworth's Case* (1589) in English and French (ff. 52–84*v*, 112–24);
(iv) *Englefield's Case* (Exchequer, 1590) (ff. 85–111*v*);
(v) personal notes by a practitioner of cases pleaded 1593–1601 (ff. 125–68*v*, 171–81);
(vi) six cases reported while the courts sat at St. Albans in 1593 (ff. 169–70*v*). (Cf. K (130) below.)

(90) *B.M. Harg. 17:* 221 fols., late 16th–early 17th cents. A collection of reports Hil. 32 Eliz.–Trin. 9 Jas. I (1590–1612) which appears to be the first-hand work of Christopher Yelverton.

(91) *B.M. Harl. 6686:* 700 fols., late 16th–early 17th cents. A thick octavo-sized notebook containing brief case notes and precedents for the years 1590–1608. This volume was compiled by Sir Edward Coke and belonged to his library. (See Hassall, *Catalogue of the Library of Sir Edward Coke*, no. 293.)

(92) *B.M. Add. 25201:* 183 fols., 17th cent. Reports prepared, for the most part, by a practitioner of the period and covering the

years 1590–1601. The concluding case, *Strode v. Horsey*, is undated and written in a neat scrivener's hand.

(93) *B.M. Add. 35946:* 272 fols., early 17th cent. Reports Mich. 32 & 33–Trin. 42 Eliz. (1590–1600). There is no indication of the reporter's identity although at f. 121 he labels some entries 'Hill 35 Eliz in Com Banco ex collectione mea propria'.

(94) *C.U.L. Gg.4.9:* 299 fols., early 17th cent. Various collections of reports from Eliz. and Jas. I; ff. 73–90*v* contain entries for Mich. 32 & 33–East. 37 Eliz. (1590–5).

(95) *C.U.L. Ii.5.16:* 265 fols., early 17th cent. Reports Mich. 32 & 33–Hil. 36 Eliz. (1590–4) transcribed in various hands from a number of sources including Coke and Croke.

(96) *Longleat 223:* 137 fols., 17th cent. Reports Mich. 32 & 33–Mich. 33 & 34 Eliz. (1590–1); many cases found in Croke's *Reports*.

(97) *C.U.L. Ff.5.20:* 66 fols., late 16th cent. Sixty-seven numbered reports taken out of the King's Bench for Mich. 32 & 33 Eliz. (1590); many appear in Croke's *Reports*.

(98) *Bodl. Rawl. C.756:* 75 fols., 17th cent. Notes of law cases abridged by 'Tho. C[——]', 1591–1632.

(99) *C.U.L. Ee.3.2:* 109 fols., late 16th cent. An incomplete collection of reports, 1591–6, taken from the Common Pleas and King's Bench; many entries are found in Croke Eliz.

(99a) *Alnwick Papers 516* (Duke of Northumberland): 1,111 fols., early 17th cent. A large collection of cases covering consecutive terms from East. 33 to Hil. 45 Eliz. (1591–1603) taken from the King's Bench and Common Pleas.

(100) *L.I. Mayn. 32:* 32 fols. (18 used), early 17th cent. A summary of the reading delivered by Matthew Ewens in 1591 on the stat. 32 Hen. VIII, chap. 28 (leases) together with a few short reports from the same period.

(100a) *C.U.L. Ee.6.17:* 262 fols., 17th cent. A two-part MS consisting of:
(i) reports from the three common law courts East. 36–Trin. 40 Eliz. (1594–8) (ff. 1–120);
(ii) King's Bench reports East. 34–Mich. 38 & 39 Eliz. (1592–6). Most of the entries are extracted from the *Reports* of Coke and Croke.

(101) *C.U.L. Dd.10.51:* 211 fols., 17th cent. Reports from the King's Bench and Common Pleas, East. 34 Eliz.–Trin. 14 Jas. I (1592–1616). Many of the cases appear in Croke's *Reports.*

(102) *B.M. Harg. 50:* 272 fols., early 17th cent. Reports East. 34–Hil. 39 Eliz. (1592–7) out of King's Bench and Exchequer. This volume was presented by Serj. Arthur Turner to Serjeant Calthorpe in 1618 in exchange for other law books. (Cf. K (131) below.)

(103) *B.M. Harl. 6745:* 216 fols., early 17th cent. Cases principally out of the King's Bench, 1592–6, compiled personally by an unnamed Jacobean practitioner. A few entries emanate from the Exchequer Chamber (e.g. f. 56). At f. 179 is an Exchequer Chamber case 'ex libro W.C.'. (See also K (109) below.)

(104) *B.M. Harg. 88:* 155 fols., late 16th–early 17th cents. A collection of readings (ff. 1–92) and reports (ff. 95–155) purportedly in the hand of Chief Justice Popham (see f. 93). The cases in question cover the period Mich. 34 & 35–Mich. 38 & 39 Eliz. (1592–6) and are similar in organization and content to Popham's *Reports.*

(105) *Longleat 225:* 128 fols., 17th cent. Reports Hil. 34–Hil. 36 Eliz. (1592–4); many entries appear in Croke Eliz.

(106) *Longleat 226:* 33 fols., 17th cent. Reports East. 34–Hil. 35 Eliz. (1592–3) taken primarily out of the King's Bench and closely related to the appropriate sections in Croke.

(107) *H.L.S. 1080:* 94 fols., early 17th cent. Reports Mich. 35 & 36 Eliz.–Trin. 13 Jas. I (1593–1615). A large number of these decisions were adjudicated in the Court of Common Pleas while sitting at St. Albans. A few entries are taken from the King's Bench 'ex reportes W [Pennyman?] de interiori templo'.

(108) *C.U.L. Ii.5.24:* 188 fols., early 17th cent. Reports of cases argued in the King's Bench and Common Pleas 1593–6, many of which appear in Croke.

(109) *B.M. Lansd. 1071:* 332 fols., 17th cent. Three Elizabethan collections:

(i) reports taken principally from the years 1597–1603 of undetermined origin (ff. 6–158*v*);

(ii) reports, Mich. 38 & 39–Trin. 39 Eliz. (1596–7); a collection purportedly owned by Chief Justice Anderson. As all the entries emanate from the King's Bench they cannot be the first-hand work of Anderson, but possibly were prepared for him (ff. 165–242*v*);

(iii) cases copied in two or three 17th-cent. hands, Mich. 35 & 36–Trin. 36 Eliz. (1593–4). These reports are taken from the King's Bench and Common Pleas 'ex collectione W.C.' (ff. 254–330). (Cf. K (103) above.)

(110) *B.M. Lansd. 1102:* 93 fols., early 17th cent. Reports from the King's Bench and Common Pleas, Mich. 35 & 36–Trin. 36 Eliz. (1593–4); similar in content to the equivalent section in Croke's *Reports*.

(111) *C.U.L. Ii.5.25:* 234 fols., 17th cent. Reports Trin. 36 Eliz.–17 Jas. I (1594–1620) copied out of the casebook of John Bridgman but originally reported by Justice Peter Warburton.

(112) *H.L.S. 2070:* 80 fols., 17th cent. Reports Mich. 36 & 37 and Hil.–Trin. 42 Eliz. (1594, 1600), taken from the King's Bench.

(113) *B.M. Harg.* 7 (2 vols.): 214 fols., 17th cent. Reports Trin. 36–Trin. 41 Eliz. (1594–9) extracted from the work of several reporters. Much of the material (Trin. 36–Trin. 38 Eliz.) was brought together by Humphrey Ware, Lent Reader at the Inner Temple in 1613. There is also some indication that certain of the cases were originally reported by John Waterhouse and John Bridgman (ff. 68–74).

(114) *C.U.L. Gg.6.29:* 152 fols., early 17th cent. Reports Mich. 36 & 37–East. 40 Eliz. (1594–8).

(115) *C.U.L. Ii.5.13:* 129 fols., early 17th cent. Reports East. 36–Mich. 40 & 41 Eliz. (1594–8), largely appearing in Croke Eliz.

(116) *B.M. Harl. 1697:* 189 fols., early 17th cent. A collection of King's Bench reports 1594–8. Hil. term, 39 Eliz. is missing and stated to be in another volume (see f. 127).

(117) *L.I. Misc. 489–90:* two volumes bound together: (i) 418 fols., (ii) 372 fols. Both in the same 17th cent. hand. Together the two volumes cover the years 1594–8 and in large measure are identical with the relevant cases in Croke Eliz.

(118) *L.I. Misc. 491:* 328 fols., 17th cent. Cases from the Common Pleas Trin. 36–Trin. 40 Eliz. (1594–8).

(119) *B.M. Harl. 1631:* 417 fols., 17th cent. Reports from various sources extending from 1594 to 1634. Ff. 1–286 contain

cases for the period East. 36–Mich. 39 & 40 Eliz. (1594–7); no indication of the compiler concerned.

(120) *B.M. Harg. 14:* 125 fols., same hand as Harg. 13. Reports, Trin. 36–Hil. 38 Eliz. (1594–6) taken from the Courts of King's Bench and Common Pleas.

(121) *B.M. Lansd. 1068:* 187 fols., 17th cent. Reports from various years of Eliz. The material found at ff. 157*v*–86*v* is described by Umfreville as being 'copied from the original MS of I Were' (Humphrey Ware of the Inner Temple—cf. K (113) above, and runs from Mich. 36 & 37 to Mich. 37 & 38 Eliz. (1594–5).

(122) *Longleat 228:* 104 fols., 17th cent. Reports ascribed to Master 'Sydnie' (several attended Gray's and Lincoln's Inn in the late 16th century) dealing with the period 1595–1602.

(123) *B.M. Harl. 1575:* 142 fols., 17th cent. Reports Eliz. and Jas. I. Ff. 1–62 contain entries for Mich. 37 & 38–Trin. 43 Eliz. (1595–1601). No indication of authorship is evident.

(124) *C.U.L. Mm.6.70:* 220 fols., 17th cent. A collection of legal tracts and reports from the 16th and 17th centuries relating in large measure to the subject of tithes. Ff. 111–17 contain cases for Mich. 37 & 38–East. 43 Eliz. (1595–1601).

(125) *I.T. Petyt 516 vol. 5:* 375 fols., 17th cent. A large collection of Elizabethan cases in several hands. Ff. 1–300 contain reports for 1595–1600 followed by some random notes (ff. 347–68*v*). At various points in the MS is found the note 'per Thos Payne' (ff. 158*v*, 188, 299)—probably referring to the scribe concerned. The collection may have been prepared under the direction of Edmund Escourte of Lincoln's Inn (called to the bar in 1598); (cf. K (5) and (36) above). This particular volume was also owned at one time by John Barnesley.

(126) *B.M. Add. 35947:* 242 fols., early 17th cent. Reports taken from the King's Bench 1595–1600. At ff. 81 & 89 is found the note 'per Cressye', possibly Hugh Cressy, a student of Furnival's Inn (adm. 1590).

(127) *Longleat 242:* 214 fols., 17th cent. Reports taken principally out of King's Bench for the period 1595–8; largely duplicated in Croke Eliz.

(128) *Longleat 227:* 270 fols., 17th cent. Various hands and collections, including cases reported for Hil. 37–East. 39 Eliz. (1595–7) from the Common Pleas. In addition there is a report in English of *Zangis v. Whyskard* (1595) concerning the right of boatmen on navigable rivers (cf. K (134) below).

(129) *B.M. Harg. 51:* 178 fols., early 17th cent. Reports of cases argued in the Court of Common Pleas 1595–7 prepared by Nicholas Ducke of Lincoln's Inn (adm. 1589).

(130) *C.U.L. Gg.3.25:* 194 fols., late 16th cent. Reports, East. 37–Hil. 39 Eliz. (1595–7) many of which appear in Croke Eliz. Running backwards from the end of the MS (ff. 172–94) is another copy of *Ayleworth's Case* (1589). Cf. K (89) above.

(131) *B.M. Harg. 356:* 237 fols., early–mid 17th cent. King's Bench reports 1595–7 together with a few entries in a later hand for Trin. 18 Jas. I (1620). This MS was owned by Serj. Turner and includes material cited from the earlier reports of Harper, Rhodes and Dyer.

(132) *H.L.S. 1082:* 207 fols., 17th cent. Reports from the Court of Common Pleas East. 37–Trin. 38 Eliz. (1595–6).

(133) *C.U.L. Gg.5.3:* 161 fols., 17th cent. A book of notes and reports: ff. 90–153 contain cases for Mich. 37 & 38–East. 38 Eliz. (1595–6) many of which appear in Croke Eliz.

(134) *B.M. Harg. 29:* 139 fols., 17th cent. Reports for the reign of Jas. I taken from the Common Pleas and Court of Wards. One case, *Zangis v. Whyskard* (1595), however, is reported from Eliz., probably originating with Christopher Yelverton but translated into English.

(135) *B.M. Add. 25199:* 80 fols., early 17th cent. A collection of court and moot cases: ff. 2–37*v* contain 339 entries reported for the years 1596–8; f. 38 has 10 entries from the same period above which is inscribed the phrase 'ma reportes demaine'. A fragment of vellum on the front cover contains the words 'Stewell his reports' (Stowell?).

(136) *I.T. Petyt 516 vol. 4:* 95 fols., 17th cent. Reports Hil. 39–Mich. 42 & 43 Eliz. (1597–1600) principally out of King's Bench. This material seems to have been put together from various standard collections then in circulation including Croke, Moore and Anderson; the MS belonged to John Barnesley.

(137) *Longleat 229:* 95 fols., 17th cent. Reports taken from the Court of Common Pleas Mich. 39 & 40–East. 42 Eliz. (1597–1600).

(138) *B.M. Harl. 4558:* 150 fols., 17th cent. Two autonomous collections in one volume both of which belonged to Robert Paynell, of Gray's Inn. The two sections deal with Hil.–Mich. 39 & 40 Eliz. and Hil. 15 & 16 Jas. I, respectively (1597 and 1618). The Elizabethan material is found within ff. 1–78*v*.

(139) *C.U.L. Dd.8.48:* 85 fols., early 17th cent. Ff. 1–67 contain cases out of King's Bench, Exchequer Chamber, and Star Chamber for 1597–9 (the Star Chamber cases are reported in Latin). The last 17 leaves of the MS contain two leading cases of note: *Earl of Bedford's Case* (1590) and *Moulton v. Coveney* (1576) adjudicated in the Court of Wards and King's Bench respectively.

(140) *B.M. Lansd. 1074:* 437 fols., various 17th-cent. hands. A volume of mixed legal material including a list of serjeants and judges created in the 16th century (ff. 119*v*–20*v*) and three sets of reports:

(i) King's Bench Hil. 39–Mich. 39 & 40 Eliz. (ff. 1–90);
(ii) Common Pleas 40 Eliz.–1 Jas. I (ff. 121–282);
(iii) Mich. 40 & 41–Hil. 45 Eliz. (ff. 282–426).

Many of the entries concerned are to be found in Croke Eliz.

(141) *C.U.L. Ff.2.14:* 70 fols., early 17th cent. Reports East. 39–Trin. 40 Eliz. (1597–8), for the most part, from Croke Eliz.

(142) *B.M. Lansd. 1099:* 131 fols., late 16th cent. A set of King's Bench reports for the year 1597 prepared by Thomas Fleming, Chief Justice of the court under Jas. I.

(143) *B.M. Add: 25203:* 625 fols., 17th cent. A large collection of reports Mich. 40 & 41 Eliz.–Trin. 1 Jas. I (1598–1603) taken from the Court of King's Bench; evidently copied from one or more sources by a professional scribe.

(144) *B.M. Harl. 1679:* 237 fols., 17th cent. Reports 1598–1600 and 1603–13. The cases for Eliz. are found at ff. 1–28.

(145) *B.M. Stowe 398:* 18 fols., late 16th cent. Report of a case tried in the King's Bench in Mich. 40 & 41 Eliz. (1598).

(146) *B.M. Add. 25202:* 140 fols. (100 blank), early 17th cent. Reports from the King's Bench and Common Pleas for East. 41–East. 44 Eliz. (1599–1602). At f. 12 is found the inscription, 'Rep Tho: Coventry B.R. H. 42 El.', beneath which are 16 short case notes.

(147) *B.M. Harg. 213:* 131 fols., 17th cent. A set of reports of unknown authorship taken from the King's Bench 1599–1601.

(148) *B.M. Lansd. 1065:* 78 fols., two 17th-cent. hands. Reports taken from the Common Pleas for Hil. 41–Mich. 43 & 44 Eliz. (1599–1601); no indication of owner or reporter.

(149) *Bodl. Rawl. C.720:* 83 fols., early 17th cent. Reports East. 41–Hil. 44 Eliz., extracted from the Court of Common Pleas; follows closely the material in Croke Eliz.

(150) *B.M. Add. 25212:* 317 fols., 17th cent. The bulk of the material deals with the first fifteen years of Jas. I, but ff. 1–72 contain cases for Mich. 42 & 43–Hil. 45 Eliz. (1600–3). All the cases have been translated into English.

(151) *Lansd. 1113:* 152 fols., 17th cent. Reports 43 Eliz.–1 Jas. I (1600–3) supposedly in the handwriting of Robert Siderfin whose printed reports cover the years 1657–70.

(152) *L.I. Mayn. 62:* this MS could not be found in the Library of Lincoln's Inn; it is catalogued as reports out of the King's Bench and Common Pleas, 1600–12.

(153) *Longleat 230:* 139 fols., 17th cent. Reports Trin. 42–Hil. 45 Eliz., East. 1 Jas. I (1600–3); many entries appear in Croke.

(154) *Longleat 243:* 99 fols., 17th cent. Reports Hil. 42–Hil. 44 Eliz. (1600–2), together with a few random entries from Jas. I. These reports emanate mainly from the Court of Exchequer, with a few from Star Chamber.

(154a) *L.I. Misc. 492:* 550 fols., two 17th cent. hands. Reports from the King's Bench Mich. 42 & 43 Eliz.–Mich. 2 Jas. I (1600–4).

(155) *B.M. Harg. 13:* 102 fols., 17th cent. Reports Mich. 42 & 43–Trin. 43 Eliz. (1600–1); over half the entries are from the Mich. term. There is no indication of the author or owner concerned.

(156) *I.T. Barr. 6:* 189 fols., 17th cent. 'Reportes de certaine cases', East. 42–Trin. 43 Eliz. (1600–1) taken from the Common Pleas. In addition there is a selection of short notes from late Eliz. and Jas. I (ff. 178–89).

(157) *B.M. Lansd. 1088:* 85 fols., early 17th cent. King's Bench reports for 1600–1 prepared in the same hand as K (57) above.

(158) *I.T. Barr. 30:* 68 fols., early 17th cent. Reports Hil., East., and Trin. 42 Eliz. (1600) taken from the common law courts and Exchequer Chamber; many entries are found in Croke Eliz.

(159) *B.M. Add. 9844:* 313 fols., early 17th cent. Reports from the Court of Common Pleas East. 43 Eliz.–Mich. 9 Jas. I (1601–11). The volume comprises two separate collections with ff. 1–125 containing the Elizabethan material. There is no indication of the reporter or compiler involved although a few cases have been traced to Coke (see for example f. 313*v*).

(160) *B.M. Lansd. 1058:* 59 fols., early 17th cent. Reports East. 43–Hil. 45 Eliz. (1601–3) from the Court of Common Pleas.

(161) *B.M. Add. 25213:* 293 fols., 17th cent. A collection of reports running consecutively from Hil. 43 Eliz. to 20 Jas. I. Composed mainly of short notes, all written in the same hand.

(162) *M.T. 8 E (Treby):* 114 fols., 17th cent. Reports, Trin. 43 Eliz.–Mich. 10 Jas. I (1601–12). Ff. 1–23 contain the material for 1601–3. The name of J. Glynne is written at the end of the volume.

(163) *Bodl. Rawl. G.382:* 85 fols., 17th cent. A selection of cases argued before the King's Bench East. 44 Eliz.–Hil. 13 Jas. I (1602–16). Many are duplicated in Croke Eliz. and Jac.

(164) *I.T. Barr. 7:* 219 fols., 17th cent. Primarily a set of reports covering the reign of Jas. I, but at ff. 1–31 is a series of cases

entitled 'error in Camera Scacarii apud Westminster' from the later years of Eliz.

(165) *B.M. Add. 25233:* 290 fols., 17th cent. A legal note and commonplace book containing extracts of readings (ff. 1, 113, 194), notes on copyhold (ff. 154–76), moot cases taken from Clement's Inn (f. 76) and a selection of court decisions from Elizabeth's reign (ff. 56–113*v*) including an abridged version in English of *Shelley's Case.* The remainder of the MS consists of undated case which probably come from the later years of the 16th century.

(166) *B.M. Harg. 15:* 281 fols., late 16th–early 17th cents. A wide selection of cases from Eliz. and Jas. I. Francis Hargrave believed that Christopher and Henry Yelverton reported some of these cases, but the evidence would seem to indicate that, while Christopher Yelverton was the owner, the material was largely extracted at second hand from a variety of sources.

(167) *Bodl. Rawl. C.647:* 256 fols., late 16th–early 17th cents. A series of abridged cases taken from various collections including those of Plowden, Dyer, Coke, Bendlowes and Popham. This MS was apparently compiled by Richard Powle of Lincoln's Inn, registrar of the Court of Chancery under Eliz. and great-uncle of Henry Powle, speaker of the Convention Parliament of 1689. Included are some Chancery cases for 1599 (ff. 62–5), various anonymous reports (ff. 119, 169) and some material for 1601 ascribed to Master Newbury (ff. 171–5) possibly Humphrey Newbury of Lincoln's Inn (adm. 1595).

(168) *B.M. Harg. 26:* 190 fols., 17th cent. A varied collection of legal material comprising readings (ff. 6–15), reports for East 33–Trin. 39 Eliz. (1591–7) attributed to John Stevens of Lincoln's Inn (ff. 17–68) and a selection of cases taken from the MS reports of James Dyer (ff. 166–74).

(169) *Herts. R.O. Gorhambury XII.A.4:* 26 fols., late 16th–early 17th cents. Notes and reports Eliz. and Jas. I. Included are excerpts out of Dyer's original MS (cf. G (37) above).

(170) *C.U.L. Ff.5.4:* 356 fols., 17th cent. A collection of pleadings and reports. The MS includes material from the earlier years of Eliz. some of which is attributable to Richard Harper (ff. 134–6) and a section concerning copyholders (ff. 156–7).

(171) *C.U.L. Gg.4.14:* 166 fols., early 17th cent. A lawyer's notebook containing, among other items, an abridgment of Dyer's Reports and a copy of Plowden's and Popham's arguments in *Calverley's Case* (1577).

(172) *Bodl. Rawl. C.85:* 210 fols., late 16th cent. Readings and reports including miscellaneous cases from Eliz. (ff. 44–55), various arguments delivered in court by Edmund Plowden (ff. 55*v*–67*v*, 152*v*–72*v*) and a series of leading decisions prepared in law-French and English together with moots and readings (ff. 135–210): these include 'cases collecte hors del premier lecture magistri Snygge' (f. 198) (Thomas Snagge of the Middle Temple; created serjeant-at-law 1580).

(173) *B.M. Harl. 996:* 47 fols., 17th cent. Small octavo notebook containing extracts from the work of various reporters, notably Plowden and Coke; compiled around 1632–3.

(174) *B.M. Harg. 34:* 159 fols., 17th cent. A mixed collection of reports and law treatises from Eliz. and Jas. I including selections from Coke's *Reports*, Part 12 (ff. 108–27*v*) and cases taken out of Exchequer Chamber (ff. 131–40).

(175) *B.M. Lansd. 582:* 99 fols., 17th cent. A small (24to) notebook containing short extracts of cases for Eliz. and Jas. I taken from Coke's *Reports*.

(176) *C.U.L. Dd.14.18:* 150 fols. (100 blank), early 17th cent. A selection of cases abridged from Coke's *Reports*, Parts 1–5.

(177) *B.M. Lansd. 576:* 229 fols., 17th cent. A volume containing various legal matter including an abridgment of Dyer's Reports (ff. 2–65), a treatise on statutory interpretation (ff. 66–72) and a series of extracts from Coke's *Reports* and Coke on Littleton (ff. 73–229).

(178) *B.M. Lansd. 601:* 276 fols., 17th cent. A volume of reports made up principally of cases from Coke's *Reports*, Part 12, together with some unprinted cases ascribed to him from the reign of Jas. I. The MS was owned at one time by Sir Matthew Hale.

(179) *B.M. Add. 25232:* 146 fols., 17th cent. A miscellaneous collection of legal material including notes on practice and procedure prepared by John Gouldesborough, a prothonotary of the Common Pleas (ff. 59–95*v*), short treatises on duelling, judicial combat and pleading (ff. 3, 27–58) and a short set of anonymous reports.

(180) *B.M. Lansd. 1060:* 182 fols., late 16th cent. A number of separate collections consolidated in one volume and ascribed to such practitioners as Richard Harper, John Savile, Matthew Ewens and John Walter. The cases concerned cover most of Elizabeth's reign. An early owner of the MS was Richard(?) Powle.

(181) *B.M. Lansd. 1078:* 132 fols., early 17th cent. A collection of King's Bench reports from the time of Eliz. which belonged to Henry Powle, a Master of the Rolls and Speaker of the Convention Parliament of 1689. At f. 52 the copyist has designated one entry as taken from 'Mr Lysters reports'.

APPENDIX II

Sixteenth-Century Reporters

Name	*Inn and Date of Admission*	*Professional Attainment*	*Period covered by Reports*
John Carrell Sr.	I.T. 1490 ?	King's Serjeant. (1514)	1485–1519
John Spelman	G.I. 1500 ?	Justice K.B. (1532)	1509–1540
John Pollard	M.T. 1515	Justice of Chester and Flint (1557)	1529–1534
John Carrell Jr.	I.T. 1522 ?	Atty.-Gen. Duchy of Lancaster (1544)	[1526–1553]
Robert Brooke	M.T. 1530 ?	Chief Justice C.P. (1554)	1512–1558
William Bendlowes	L.I. 1534	Serjeant (1555)	1511–1579
William Dalison	G.I. 1534	Justice K.B. (1556)	1552–1558
James Dyer	M.T. 1535 ?	Chief Justice C.P. (1559)	1512–1581
Richard Harper	I.T. 1537	Justice C.P. (1567)	1546–1577
Edmund Plowden	M.T. 1538	Treasurer M.T. (1561)	1550–1579

Date of First Publication (where applicable)	*Courts in which Cases are reported*	*Relevant Manuscript Collections*
1602 (as Keilwey's *Reports*)	C.P., judicial conferences	B.M. Harl. 1624, 1691 B.M. Lansd. 1084 H.L.S. 1058 L.I. Mayn. 86
—	K.B., C.P., Exch. E.C., S.I., Comms. of Oyer & Terminer	B.M. Harg. 388 C.U.L. Gg. 11.5 Longleat 240 Herts. R.O. Gorhambury XII.A.6A
—	C.P., K.B.	B.M. Harg. 388
—	C.P., K.B.	B.M. Harl. 1691 I.T. Petyt 511, vol. 13
1573 (as part of his Abridgment)	C.P., K.B., Exch., conferences at S.I.	B.M. Harg. 2, 5 Bold. Rawl. C.644
1609	C.P.	Bodl. Rawl. C.728 B.M. Add. 25189 and many others
1609	C.P., K.B., S.I.	B.M. Harl. 5141 B.M. Add. 24845 L.I. Hill 123
1585	C.P., K.B., Wards, E.C., S.C., jud. conferences, S.I.	I.T. Petyt 511, vol. 13 B.M. Harg. 26, 132 Herts. R.O. Gorhambury XII.A.6A
1609 (as Dalison's *Reports*)	C.P., K.B., S.C., Wards	B.M. Harg. 6, 8 and many others
1571 (Part I) 1579 (Part II)	C.P., K.B. Exch. E.C., Wards, S.I.	H.L.S. 2144 B.M. Harl. 6681 Bodl. Rawl. C.498 and others

Name	*Inn and Date of Admission*	*Professional Attainment*	*Period covered by Reports*
Christopher Wray	L.I. 1545	Chief Justice, K.B. (1572)	1583–1591
Anthony Gell	I.T. 1547	Autumn Reader I.T. (1563)	1541–1572
Francis Rhodes	G.I. 1549	Justice C.P. (1585)	1567–1576
Francis Windham	L.I. 1550 ?	Justice C.P. (1579)	1582–1586
John Popham	M.T. 1550 ?	Chief Justice K.B. (1592)	1592–1597
Edmund Anderson	M.T. 1550	Chief Justice C.P. (1582)	1534–1604
Christopher Yelverton	G.I. 1552	Justice K.B. (1602)	1590–1612
Richard Kempe	G.I. 1556	Reader G.I. (1577 & 1589)	1567–1569
William Daniel	G.I. 1556	Justice C.P. (1603)	1589–1592
Richard Godfrey	G.I. 1560 ?	Ancient of G.I. (1568)	1577–1593
Thomas Owen	L.I. 1562	Justice C.P. (1594)	1558–1614
Peter Warburton	L.I. 1562	Justice C.P. (1600)	1594–1619
John Savile	M.T. 1565	Baron Exch. (1598)	1578–1595
Thomas Harris	M.T. 1566	Serjeant (1589)	1585–1588
Thomas Fleming	L.I. 1567	Chief Justice K.B. (1607)	1571, 1596–1598
Matthew Ewens	M.T. 1568	Baron Exch. (1594)	[1568–1594]
Laurence Tanfield	I.T. 1569	Chief Baron Exch. (1607)	1573–1577
Edward Coke	I.T. 1572	Chief Justice K.B. (1613)	1572–1616
James Altham	G.I. 1575	Baron Exch. (1607)	1585–1591
George Croke	I.T. 1575	Justice K.B. (1628)	1581–1641

Date of First Publication (where applicable)	*Courts in which Cases are reported*	*Relevant Manuscript Collections*
—	C.P., K.B.	H.L.S. 16
—	C.P., K.B., S.I.	Lib. of Congress Gell MS
—	C.P.	L.I. Mayn. 77 B.M. Harg. 374
—	C.P.	B.M. Lansd. 1084
1656	K.B., C.P., E.C., Wards, S.I.	B.M. Harg. 27, 88, 403
1664	C.P., Wards K.B. judicial conferences	L.I. Misc. 791 B.M. Harl. 4817 B.M. Lansd. 1071 B.M. Add. 25193
—	C.P., K.B.	B.M. Harg. 17
—	Assizes	B.M. Lansd. 1067
—	K.B.	Longleat 223
—	C.P., K.B.	B.M. Harg. 12 C.U.L. Mm. 4.35
1656	C.P., K.B.	—
—	C.P., K.B.	B.M. Harl. 4817 C.U.L. Ii.5.25
1675	K.B., C.P., Exch.	B.M. Lansd. 1101
—	K.B.	C.U.L. Dd.11.64
—	K.B.	B.M. Lansd. 1099 B.M. Harg. 374
—	C.P., K.B.	B.M. Lansd. 1060, 1133
—	C.P., K.B.	Herts. R.O. Gorhambury XII.A.6A
1600–1615 (Parts I–XI) 1656 (Part XII) 1659 (Part XIII)	C.P., K.B., Exch., E.C. Chan., judicial conferences, S.I. et al.	L.I. Misc. 361
—	C.P., K.B., Exch., Wards, judicial conferences	L.T. Petyt 511, vol. 12
Croke Car. 1657 Croke Jac. 1658 Croke Eliz. 1661	C.P., K.B., Exch., E.C., Wards	Herts. R.O. Gorhambury XII.A.6A-E

Name	*Inn and Date of Admission*	*Professional Attainment*	*Period covered by Reports*
Edmund Prideaux	I.T. 1575 ?	Treasurer I.T. (1609)	1581–1585
William Leonard	G.I. 1577	Reader Staple Inn (1593)	1540–1615
Henry Yelverton	G.I. 1579	Attorney-General (1617)	1602–1612
Francis Moore	M.T. 1580	Serjeant (1614)	1511–1620
John Stevens	L.I. 1581	Called to the Bar 1589	1591–1597
John Walter	I.T. 1582	Chief Baron Exch. (1625)	1585–1601
Anthony Benne	M.T. 1583	Reader M.T. (1611)	1558–1594
Richard Brownlow	I.T. 1583	Chief Prothonotary C.P. (1591)	1569–1625
William Brocke	I.T. 1584	Autumn Reader I.T. (1608)	1586–1594
John Gouldesborough	M.T. 1584 ?	Prothonotary C.P. (1613)	1586–1601
Edward Hendon	G.I. 1586	Baron Exch. (1639)	1585–1597
Nicholas Jordan	I.T. 1588	Called to the Bar (1597)	1530–1593
Humphrey Ware	I.T. 1588	Bencher I.T. (1612)	1584–1599
Nicholas Ducke	L.I. 1589	Bencher L.I. (1614)	1595–1597
Edmund Escourte	L.I. 1590	Treasurer L.I. (1628)	1595–1598
Hugh Cressy	L.I. 1590	Treasurer L.I. (1629)	1595–1600
John Bridgman	I.T. 1590	Serjeant (1623)	1595

Date of First Publication (where applicable)	*Courts in which Cases are reported*	*Relevant Manuscript Collections*
—	C.P., K.B.	Herts. R.O. Gorhambury XII.A.6B
1658 (Part I) 1659 (Part II) 1663 (Part III) 1675 (Part IV)	C.P., K.B., Exch., E.C., Chan., Wards, S.C.	—
1661	K.B.	—
1663	C.P., K.B., S.C., Chan., Exch., Wards	B.M. Add. 25191 B.M. Harl. 4585 H.L.S. 2097 and many others
—	C.P., K.B., S.C.	B.M. Harg. 26
—	K.B., Exch., S.I.	B.M. Harg. 5, 8 Bodl. Rawl. C.341 C.U.L. Ee.6.12
—	C.P., K.B.	B.M. Harl. 4562
1651 (Part I in conjunction with Gouldesborough) 1652 (Part II)	C.P.	—
—	C.P.	B.M. Add. 35944 H.L.S. 1057
1651 (with Brownlow) 1652 (separate volume)	K.B., C.P., Chan.	—
—	K.B., C.P.	B.M. Harl. 1331 L.I. Misc. 791
—	C.P., K.B., Wards, extra-judicial opinions	B.M. Harg. 373
—	C.P., K.B.	B.M. Harg. 7 B.M. Lansd. 1068 L.I. Misc. 791
—	C.P.	B.M. Harg. 51
—	K.B.	I.T. Petyt 516, vol. 5 Longleat 224
—	K.B.	B.M. Add. 35947 Longleat 224
—	C.P.	B.M. Harg. 7 C.U.L. Ii.5.25

Name	*Inn and Date of Admission*	*Professional Attainment*	*Period covered by Reports*
Humphrey Newbury	L.I. 1595	Called to the Bar (1603)	1601
Richard Lydell	M.T. 1598	Called to the Bar (1603)	1583–1617
Eusebius Andrewe	I.T. 1600	Bencher I.T. (1620 ?)	1585–1613

Date of First Publication (where applicable)	*Courts in which Cases are reported*	*Relevant Manuscript Collections*
—	K.B.	Bodl. Rawl. C.647
—	C.P., K.B.	L.I. Mayn. 66
		C.U.L. Ee.6.12
—	K.B., Chan.	B.M. Harl. 3209

APPENDIX III

Selected Leading Cases Reported between 1535 and 1580

1. *Lord Dacre's Case* East. 26 Hen. VIII; Court of the Lord High Steward.

Peer accused of treason—attempt to waive trial by peers in favour of trial 'per le pays'—denied by committee of judges.

(1) B.M. Harg. MS 388, f. 88*v*;
(2) B.M. Harg. MS 373, ff. 134–5;
(3) I.T. Petyt MS 511, vol. 13, f. 58*v*;
(4) B.M. Add. MS 35953, f. 52.

2. *Levet v. Lewkenor* (i) Mich. 27 Hen. VIII (ii) Hil. 28 Hen. VIII; C.P.

Testament—action of debt taken by executor—executor dies intestate before execution—scire facias taken by administrator—recovery held invalid—new action in debt held necessary. (Unique example of a Yearbook case continued on in a 'private' report.)

(i) YB Mich. 27 Hen. VIII, pl. 7;
(ii) Bendl., 18.

3. *Bold v. Molineux* Trin. 28 Hen. VIII; C.P.

Debt—condition of obligation—date of repayment—interpretation of the words 'then living'—venue.

(1) Dyer, 14b;
(2) Bendl., 13.

4. *Abbot of Bury v. Bokenham* (i) Hil. 28 Hen. VIII (ii) Trin. 28 Hen. VIII; C.P.

Action in wardship—heir of cestuique use in fee—wardships granted.

(i) Dyer, 7b;
(ii) Bendl., 16.

5. *Hollis v. Fuliambe* Trin. 31 Hen. VIII; C.P.
Quare impedit—advowson granted jointly and severally—presentment made by defendant alone—held valid against grantee by fine.
(1) Bendl., 24;
(2) B.M. Harl. MS 1961, ff. 113–15.

6. *Wimbish v. Tailbois* (i) Mich. 36 Hen. VIII, Mich. 1 Edw. VI (ii) Mich. 4 Edw. VI (iii) Trin. 6 Edw. VI; C.P.
Statute of Uses—execution of use—vesting in cestuique use.
(i) Lib. of Congress, Gell MS, ff. 107–11*v*, 112, 116–20*v*; Brooke, tit. 'Collusion', no. 46;
(ii) Plow., 38–60;
(iii) Plow., 73–7 (held here that a writ directed to the coroner in default of sheriff is valid).

7. *Kidwelly v. Brand* Hil. 4 & 5 Edw. VI; C.P.
Lease of abbey lands—default in payment of rent—king's reversioners may enter per stat. 32 Hen. VIII, chap. 34 without further demand.
(1) Plow., 69–71;
(2) Dyer, 68a.

8. *Fulmerston v. Steward* East. 6 Edw. VI; K.B.
Trespass—lease made by college for fifty years, one year before stat. 31 Hen. VIII, chap. 13—first lease *in esse*—second lease valid for twenty-five years.
(1) Plow., 102–10;
(2) B.M. Harl. MS 5141, ff. 23*v*–4*v* (Dalison);
(3) Dyer, 102b–3b;
(4) B.M. Harl. MS 1691, ff. 90–90*v*.

9. *Partridge v. Strange* Mich. 6, Hil. 6 & 7 Edw. VI: C.P.
Debt—action upon stat. 32 Hen. VIII, chap. 9 (pretended titles)—lease for years held to be within its provisions.
(1) Plow., 77–89;
(2) Dyer, 74b;

(3) B.M. Harl. MS 5141 f. 4*v* (Dalison);
(4) Brooke, tit. 'Maintenance', no. 38.

10. *Newdigate v. Earl of Derby* Mich. 1 & 2 Phil. & Mary; C.P.
Writ of assize—challenge to the array—no knight returned—challenge upheld.
(1) Plow., 117;
(2) Lib. of Congress Gell MS, f. 131*v*;
(3) Dyer, 107b.

11. *Buckley v. Rice Thomas* Trin. 1 & 2 Phil. & Mary, East. 2 & 3 Phil. & Mary; C.P.
Debt—held that stat. 23 Hen. VI, chap. 15 (concerning election of burgesses and knights to Parliament) extends to Wales—election 'per majorem numerum' is generally valid for election without the need of showing a specific number.
(1) Plow., 118–30;
(2) Dyer, 113b–14b.

12. *Ward v. Anderson* (i) Mich. 1 & 2 Phil. & Mary (ii) East. 1 & 2 Phil. & Mary; K.B.
Praecipe quod reddat—recovery—error in K.B.—plea of nonage—recovery against infant by default may be reversed.
(i) Dyer, 104a–b;
(ii) B.M. Harl. MS 5141, f. 29*v* (Dalison).

13. *Throckmorton v. Tracy* Mich. 2 & 3 Phil. & Mary; C.P.
Second deliverance—lease by abbot for life—reversion for 21 years at end of lease—death of life tenant before attornment does not invalidate reversion.
(1) Plow., 145–63;
(2) Dyer, 124b–6b;
(3) Brooke, tit. 'Attornment', no. 61.

14. *Lord Mounteagle v. Countess of Worcester* (i) Trin. 1 & 2 Phil. & Mary (ii) Mich. 2 & 3 Phil. & Mary; C.P.

Trover—title to gold chain—writ held to be valid as an alternative to detinue.

(i) Bendl., 41;
(ii) (1) Dyer, 121a–2a;
(2) B.M. Harl. 1691, f. 94.

(See Fifoot, *History and Sources of Common Law*, pp. 103–4.)

15. *Hill v. Grange* (i) Mich. 2 & 3 Phil. & Mary (ii) East. 2 & 3 Phil. & Mary (iii) Mich. 3 & 4 Phil. & Mary; C.P.
Trespass—land not strictly *appurtenant* to a messuage—held that intention of parties may be construed to mean such—grantee of a reversion may enter upon breaking of conditions per stat. 32 Hen. VIII, chap. 34—demand or tender of rent at last moment of day is valid.

(i) B.M. Harl. MS 1691, f. 97;
(ii) (1) B.M. Harl. MS 5141, ff. 33–33*v* (Dalison);
(2) Dyer, 130b–1a;
(iii) (1) Plow., 164–79;
(2) Brooke, tit. 'Entre congeable', no. 139, 'Leases', no. 65. (A 'Serjeants' Case'.)

16. *Sherley's Case* East. 2 & 3 Phil. & Mary; K.B.
Treason committed by a Frenchman or other alien against terms of allegiance is indictable—no right to jury *per medietatem linguae*.

(1) Dyer, 144a–b;
(2) Dal., 22 (B.M. Harl. MS 5141, f. 38*v*).

17. *Villiers v. Beaumont* East. 3 & 4 Phil. & Mary; assize held at Lincoln before James Dyer and Ralph Rokeby.
Novel disseisin—special verdict—bargain and sale—remainder to vendor and heirs in tail—recovery suffered in consideration of marriage—second marriage—issue of first falls within definition of 'an ancestor of the husband' per stat. 11 Hen. VII, chap. 20.

(1) Dyer, 146a–8b;
(2) Bendl., 39–41.

18. *Hyde v. Umpton* (i) Trin. 3 & 4 Phil. & Mary (ii) Mich. 3 & 4 Eliz.; C.P.
Writ of partition—testament drafted in interim between stats. 32 Hen. VIII, chap. 1 (wills) and 34 & 35 Hen. VIII, chap. 5 (elaboration of Stat. of Wills)—devise of manor held by knight-service—valid for two-thirds of property, invalid as regards other one-third.
(i) (1) Bend., 49–50;
(2) Dyer, 150b;
(3) Brooke, tit. 'Testament', no. 26;
(ii) B.M. Harg. MS 4, ff. 161*v*–8.

19. *Bilota v. Poyntel* East. 4 & 5 Phil. & Mary; C.P.
Action on the case taken in response to vexatious suit instituted by defendant and another in Court of Admiralty—only one of two original plaintiffs impleaded—whether action lies per stat. 2 Hen. iv, chap. 11—whether declaration is valid if contract not alleged to be made within the country (dispute settled out of court).
(1) B.M. Harl. MS 1624, ff. 60–2;
(2) Dyer, 159b–60a;
(3) Bendl., 58, 64–5.

20. *Brown v. Sackville* East. 4 & 5 Phil. & Mary; C.P.
Testament drafted at testator's dictation—held that the will was valid notwithstanding it had not been signed or read back to testator before his death.
(1) Bend., 61;
(2) Dyer, 72a.

21. *Tuck v. Frencham* Mich. 1 Eliz.; C.P.
Replevin—lands held in socage—devise to cousin and 'heirs male of his body'—no heirs—held that collatoral can hold only an estate in special tail.
(1) Bendl., 68–72;
(2) Dyer, 171a;
(3) B.M. Harg. MS 388, f. 249.

22. *Skrogges v. Coleshill* Mich. 1 & 2 Eliz.; K.B.
Office in dispute—held that office of exigenter is in the gift of the Chief Justice of the Common Pleas, not the Crown.
(1) B.M. Harg. MS 9, ff. 15–27*v*;
(2) Dyer, 175a–b.

23. *Wrottesley v. Adams* (i) Trin. 1, Mich. 1 & 2, Hil. 2 Eliz. (ii) Hil. 2 Eliz.; C.P.
Ejectio firmae—lease of farm by prior to husband and wife for term of years—husband dies and wife remarries—prior leases reversion of farm to plaintiff upon expiration of first term—reversion subsequently granted to Crown in 1534—held that plaintiff may enter as if first lease had expired 'by the effluxion of time'.
(i) (1) Plow., 187–99;
(2) Lib. of Congress Gell MS, ff. 138–46*v*;
(ii) Dyer, 177b–8b.

24. *Butler v. Lady Bray* (i) Mich. 2 & 3 Eliz. (ii) Hil. 3 Eliz.; C.P.
Writ of entry on disseisin—father granted uses to land to son and future wife—held that the grant of marriage attaches to the person of the father and cannot be granted to others.
(i) (1) Dyer, 189b–91b;
(2) Bendl., 82–4;
(3) B.M. Harg. MS 4, ff. 168–72;
(ii) B.M. Harg. MS 4, ff. 168–72.

25. *Kempe v. Makewilliams* Hil. 3 Eliz.; C.P.
Replevin—two patents issued for custody of Colchester Castle—held that surrender of office is void if misrecited notwithstanding stat. 4 & 5 Phil. & Mary, chap. 1.
(1) B.M. Harg. MS 8, ff. 28*v*–29;
(2) Dyer, 195a;
(3) B.M. Harg. MS 9, f. 145*v*.

26. *Ayer v. Orme* East. 5 Eliz.; C.P.
Replevin—lease of lands in Battersea by Archbishop of York—proviso that when see vacant rent payable to chapter *ut in jure suo*—held invalid upon entry of bailiff to execute for non-payment.
(1) B.M. Harg. MS 4, ff. 186*v*–7;
(2) Dal., 53–6;
(3) Dyer, 221b–2b;
(4) Bendl., 129–30.

27. *Case of the Duchy of Lancaster* (i) (1 Edw. VI?) (ii) temp. Mary (Mich. 4 & 5 Phil. & Mary?) (Duchy Chamber) (iii) Mich. 2 & 3 Eliz. (Serjs'. Inn & Spooner's Inn) (iv) Mich. 3 & 4 Eliz. (Serjs'. Inn) (v) East. Trin., 4 Eliz., Mich. 4 & 5 Eliz. (Court of the Duchy of Lancaster).
Leases executed by Edward VI while a minor are not voidable by reason of non-age.
(i) Brooke, tit. 'Age', no. 52;
(ii) B.M. Harg. MS 4, f. 128;
(iii) Plow., 212–22;
(iv) (1) Plow., 212–33;
(2) Dyer, 209b.
(v) Plow., 222. (Cf. Somerville, i, xiii, 139–40.)

28. *Hales v. Petit* (i) Mich. 1 & 2 Eliz. (ii) Mich. 4 & 5 Eliz.; C.P.
Husband and wife joint-tenants of term for years—husband commits suicide—held that Crown entitled to residue of term notwithstanding wife's rights of survivorship.
(i) (1) B.M. Harg. MS 388, ff. 243*v*–6*v*;
(2) B.M. Harg. MS 4, f. 184*v* (detinue);
(ii) Plow., 253–64 (trespass).

29. *Harrison v. Worley* (i) Trin. 2 Eliz. (ii) Mich. 6 & 7 Eliz. (iii) Hil. 7 Eliz.; C.P.

Audita querela—minor bound by statute staple—action in audita querela must be brought before reaching age of majority.

(i) Bendl., 80;
(ii) Dyer, 232b;
(iii) B.M. Harg. MS 8, ff. 69*v*–72

30. *Bullock v. Burdett* (i) Trin. 7 Eliz. (ii) Mich. 10 & 11 Eliz. (iii) 12 Eliz.; C.P.
Replevin—feoffment of woodland without deed or specific description and at election of feoffees held to be void—freehold cannot be in abeyance.

(i) Bendl., 148–9;
(ii) Dyer, 281a;
(iii) Neale MS, ff. 33–5.

31. *Ap-Richard v. Jones* East. 8 Eliz.; C.P.
Held that writs of error upon judgments in assize cannot be taken before justices of the Court of Common Pleas.

(1) Dyer, 250a–b;
(2) Bendl., 153.

32. *Sir John Savage's Case* (i) Hil. 9 Eliz. (ii) East. 9 Eliz.; C.P.
Office of steward of a manor is not grantable as a reversion save by the Crown.

(i) B.M. Harg. MS 10, f. 15;
(ii) Dyer, 259.

33. *Lady Arundel v. Earl of Pembroke* (i) East. 9 Eliz. (ii) Trin. 9 Eliz.; C.P.
Action in dower—commission out of Court of Augmentations assigned third part of lands to widow of attainted person—held that such assignment did not include rents, notwithstanding confirmation of Crown—the King cannot make good that which was void.

(i) B.M. Harg. MS 10, f. 17;
(ii) Dyer, 263b.

34. *Horneby v. Clifton* Trin. 9 Eliz.; C.P.
Ejectio firmae—lease of premises excepting certain portions—held to be valid only as long as lessor lives—no rights of survivorship.
(1) B.M. Harg. MS 6, f. 41;
(2) Bendl., 181;
(3) Dyer, 264b.

35. *Stephen v. Wall* East. 11 Eliz.; C.P.
Quare impedit—advowson of manor formerly granted to Henry, Lord Stafford—grant of present avoidance of a church held to be a chose in action—grantable by Crown but not subects.
(1) C.U.L. MS Ii.5.20, ff. 5–7*v*;
(2) Bendl., 192–3;
(3) Dyer, 282b.

36. *Pleyer v. Crouch* (i) Hil. 12 Eliz. (ii) East. 12 Eliz. (iii) Trin. 12 Eliz.; C.P.
Assize of novel disseisin—land in Somerset, trial in Gloucestershire—no recovery allowed on verdict—trial must be brought in county where land is situate notwithstanding consent of the parties.
(i) B.M. Harg. MS 373, ff. 114–20*v*;
(ii) (1) Dyer, 283b;
(2) Bendl., 189–92.
(iii) Dyer, 284a.

37. *Newes v. Larke* Mich. 12 & 14 Eliz.; C.P.
Assize of novel disseisin—testament—clause in will excluding any remaindermen from benefit of estate—held that said clause does not require reentry but dissolves estate entirely as against the parties in question.
(1) Plow., 403–15;
(2) Bendl., 196–8;
(3) I.T. Petyt MS 511, vol. 13, ff. 53*v*–4 (Dyer).

38. *Lowe et al. v. Paramore* Trin. 13 Eliz.; C.P.
Writ of right—choice of trial by battle by tenant—demandants default—final judgment in favour of tenant.
(1) Dyer, 301a–2a;
(2) Bendl., 199–201.
(Describes in detail ceremony attending trial by battle.)

39. *Winter's Case* (i) East. 14 Eliz. (ii) Mich. 14 & 15 Eliz.; C.P.
Second deliverance—lease for term of years of three manors—non-payment of rent on any one renders all three liable to re-entry by lessor—reversion sold to third party—held that a bargainee of a reversion is a grantee per stat. 32 Hen. VIII, chap. 34.
(i) Dyer, 308b–9a;
(ii) (1) B.M. Harg. MS 15, ff. 30–7;
(2) B.M. Lansd. MS 1072, ff. 69–88*v*;
(3) B.M. Harg. MS 10, ff. 26–38.

40. *Andrews v. Blunt* (i) East. 14 Eliz. (ii) Mich. 15 & 16, Eliz.; C.P.
Quare impedit—bargain and sale of manor with advowson appendant in fee to the use of purchaser and heirs—recovery of uses and levy of fine rendering rent to vendor—proviso added to grant advowson to vendor for life by deed—purchaser dies seised but before granting advowson—held that proviso constitutes a valid condition—not extinguished by fine—an averment in writing held to constitute a valid use against fine and implies a consideration and use—further held that performance of condition might occur during any point in purchaser's lifetime unless specifically requested.
(i) (1) Dyer, 311a–12a;
(2) Bendl., 201–3;
(3) 2 Co. Rep. 79a (cf. Co. Litt. 222a);
(4) Co. Litt. 222b;

(ii) (1) C.U.L. MS Gg.3.3., ff. 36*v*–45*v*;
(2) B.M. Harg. MS 373, ff. 123*c*–8*v*;
(3) B.M. Add. 24845, ff. 114–17*v*.

41. *Cranmer's Case* (i) East. 14 Eliz. (ii) Mich. 14 & 15 Eliz.; C.P.

Ejectio firmae—Cranmer, Archbishop of Canterbury made feoffment of land in Yorkshire to the use of himself for life and, on decease, to executors for twenty years—attainted for treason and dies intestate—held that the Crown is not entitled to residue of term. (Cf. *H.E.L.* iii, 330.)

(i) Bodl. Rawl. MS C.112, ff. 411–36;
(2) Dyer, 309a–10a;
(3) Bendl., 207–8.
(ii) (1) H.L.S. MS 2079, ff. 3024;
(2) B.M. Harg. MS 374, ff. 77*v*–81;
(3) 2 Leon. 5–7;
(4) B.M. Harg. MS 15, ff. 27–8*v*.

42. *Vernon v. Vernon* (i) Mich. 14 & 15 Eliz. (ii) East. 15 Eliz.; C.P.

Dower—life estate in remainder constitutes as valid jointure and bar to action in dower per Stat. of Uses.

(i) (1) Dyer, 317a–b;
(2) 4 Co. Rep. 1a–5a;
(3) Bendl., 210–2;
(4) B.M. Lansd. MS 1145, ff. 87–100;
(ii) (1) Bodl. Rawl. MS C.112, ff. 226–31*v*;
(2) B.M. Harg. MS 10, ff. 47–9*v*;
(3) B.M. Add. MS 35953, f. 29.

43. *Bracebridge's Case* (i) Trin. 14 Eliz.; K.B. (ii) Hil. 15 Eliz.; C.P. (iii) East. 18 Eliz.; K.B.

(i) Bill of ejectio firmae, *Bracebridge v. Cook*—lease for term of years—lessee grants term to wife of lessor and third party—held that third party entitled to whole estate by survivorship on death of husband and wife.

(1) Plow., 416–20.

(ii) Replevin, *Barwell v. Lucas*—lease of part of demesne for life—held that the reversion remains part of manor, but such reversion does not pass without attornment by lesee.

(1) Bodl. Rawl. MS C.112, ff. 391–8;
(2) 2 Leon. 221–2;
(3) Bendl., 208–10;
(4) I.T. Petyt MS 511, vol. 13, ff. 58–58*v*, 60*v*–1 (Dyer).

(iii) Ejectio firmae, *Bracebridge v. Clowse*—lease of land for 40 years—lessor later re-leases land for 70 years without deed—held that second lease is valid for as many years as remain after the first term.

(1) Plow., 420–4.

44. *Vernon v. Stanley and Manners.*
(i) Trin. 12, Mich. 13 & 14 Eliz.;
(ii) Hil. 13 Eliz.;
(iii) Mich. 14 & 15 Eliz.;
(iv) Hil. 15 Eliz.;
(v) East. 17 Eliz.; C.P.

Formedon in remainder against husband and wife—held that wife may defend action in her own capacity and vouch another to warranty—challenge to the array—held that cousinage of sheriff to ninth degree a valid challenge.

(i) Bendl. 198–9;
(ii) Dyer, 298a;
(iii) (1) Plow., 425;
(2) Dyer, 315b, 319a;
(iv) (1) Dal., 107–10;
(2) B.M. Lansd. MS 1077, ff. 27–30;
(v) (1) Bendl., 204–6;
(2) Dyer, 341a.

45. *Taverner's Case* (i) 14 Eliz. (ii) Hil. 15 Eliz. (iii) East. 15 Eliz.; Court of Star Chamber.

Forgery of memorial rolls by copyholder—complaint in Star Chamber—applicability of stat. 5 Eliz., chap. 14—Crown held competent to pardon corporal punishment—execution for double costs effected by English writ.

(i) B.M. Harg. MS 374, ff. 128*v*–36*v* (English report of Star Chamber proceedings);
(ii) B.M. Harg. MS 10, f. 55 (conference at Serjeants' Inn);
(iii) (1) Dyer, 322b–3a (cf. Elton, *Tudor Constitution*, pp. 258, 270);
(2) B.M. Lansd. MS 1077, ff. 26*v*–7.

46. *Eyston v. Studd* East. 16 Eliz.; C.P.

Ejectio firmae—unmarried woman seised of land in tail, marries and levies jointly fine in fee—conusee renders property back in tail, remainder to heirs of wife in fee—son born of marriage—husband dies, wife remarries and levies jointly another fine—son of first marriage enters land claiming forfeiture per stat. 11 Hen. VII, chap. 20—held that entry is unlawful and that forfeiture in such case was against reason and the true intent of the statute.

(1) Plow., 459–68;
(2) B.M. Harg. MS 373, ff. 167–8;
(3) Bendl. 238.

(Plowden's report is especially noteworthy for his exposition of the interpretation of statutes, 465–8.)

47. *Manwood v. Nyme* East. 16 Eliz.; C.P.

Action of waste instituted by Justice Manwood against tenant of property at Herne Hill—unjustified use of timber.

(1) B.M. Lansd. MS 1057, ff. 277–81;
(2) Dyer, 332b;
(3) Bendl., 217–19. (Cf. *Manwood v. Burston*, Hil. 29 Eliz. 2 Leon., 203.)

48. *Brent's Case* Hil. 17 Eliz.; C.P.
Ejectio firmae—Brent seised of lands in fee made feoffment (after passage of Stat. of Uses) to use of himself and wife for life and, if he survive, to the use of himself and second wife; remainder to third party—feoffment made by Brent and other feoffees to strangers—fine levied—Brent took second wife and died—second wife claimed entry to estates after statutory five years—*scintilla juris*—held that if estate of foeffees be destroyed by alienation before come into being, no use can subsequently arise.
(1) 2 Leon. 14–20;
(2) B.M. Harg. MS 6, ff. 215–27*v*;
(3) Dyer, 339b–41a; (cf. Plucknett, *Concise History*, pp. 592–3).

49. *Welcden v. Elkington* Trin. 19, Hil., East. 20 Eliz.; C.P.
Trespass—termor devises occupation of land to wife 'for as many years as she will live' and remainder of term to son—wife made sole executrix and upon husband's death enters—held that per terms of will widow cannot dispose of term absolutely against son.
(1) Plow., 516–24;
(2) Dyer, 358b–9a;
(3) Bendl., 308–11 (see Simpson, *History of Land Law*, pp. 206–7).

50. '*The Serjeants' Case*' Hil., East. 21 Eliz.; C.P.
Action in replevin—ostensibly concerned with four horses on four acres of land—defendant justified his initial seizure in virtue of four separate avowals—case argued on the basis of four legal issues by the new serjeants (Popham, Rhodes, Gawdy, Fenner, Shute, Windham, Anderson and Baber)—homage & fealty, uses, common recovery and copyhold.
(1) B.M. Lansd. MS 1145, ff. 105–27*v*;
(2) Bodl. Rawl. MS C.112, ff. 3–21;
(3) B.M. Lansd. MS 1072, ff. 126–34;
(4) B.M. Lansd. MS 1133, ff. 123*v*–7;
(5) B.M. Add. MS 16169, ff. 102*v*–5*v*;
(6) B.M. Lansd. 1095, f. 121.

APPENDIX IV

Illustrative Extracts from the Reports of Bendlowes, Dalison, Harper, Dyer and Plowden

The text of the following extracts is that of the printed or MS source cited save where an emendation or addition seems to be called for, the word in question being then placed within square brackets. In the translations square brackets are used for explanatory additions.

BENDLOWES

1. Bendl. 21; Hil. 28 Hen. VIII (1536)

Nota que si home espouse un feme inherite de terres &c. & ad issue per luy, le quel issue est nee in vie & baptize & puis mesme le issue morust & ceo ne fuit unques oye crye ou que si cest issue fuit nee in vie & nient baptize ne oye crie uncore in ceux cases le dit baron apres le mort son feme serra tenant per le courtesie des dits terres. Et les Justices del Common Bank & les Serjeants teigne ceo pur ley.

Note that if a man takes a wife having inheritance of lands etc. and has issue by her, and the said child is born alive and baptized but then dies without once being heard to cry, or else born alive but never baptized nor heard to cry—in both cases the said husband will yet become tenant of the said lands by courtesy upon the death of his wife. And the judges of the Common Bench and the serjeants hold this to be law.

2. Bendl. 42; Trin. 2 & 3 Phil. & Mary (1555)

Thomas Lukyn executor del testament del Thomas Lukyn port un bref de dett envers Thomas Choppin de Alta [Roding] in mesme le Countie. Et counta sur un obligation de 20 l. fait per le dit defendant al dit testator in September lan 31 le Roy H. 8 &c. Et le defendant demand oyer del dit obligation & del condition de ceo le quel fuit in *haec verba*: The condition of this obligation is such that if the within bounden Thomas Choppin at any time within the space of four years from the feast of St. Michael the Archangel next coming &c. do pay &c. to the within named Thomas Lukyn, his executors or assignes nine pounds sterling before hand paid to the said Thomas Choppin by the hands of the said Thomas Lukyn for a bargain and sale of a croft of land called Broadfeilde &c. and a parcell of land lying in Heirs feilde. So that the said Thomas Choppin do not alien, sell, bargain, nor mortgage, the said land to any other person or persons at any time, but onely to the said Thomas Lukyn or his heirs. That then this obligation to be void, or else &c.

Les Justices teigne que ceux parolls ss. So that &c. be as much as if that. Et issint [fuerent pristes] & ne [fessoient] un condition pur ceo que il fault cest paroll And devant les dittz parolls So that &c. issint que le dit defendant ne fuit oblige per cest obligation de payer le dits [ix] lyvers sil nad alien &c. mesme le terre &c. Le author de cest liver fuit [del] counsell ove le [dit] defendant.

Thomas Lukyn, executor of the will of Thomas Lukyn, brought a writ of debt against Thomas Choppin of High Roding in the same county [Essex]. And he relied on an obligation in respect of £20 executed by the said defendant to the said testator in September of the year 31 Hen. VIII [1539] etc. And the defendant asked to hear this obligation and its condition, which was in these words: 'The condition of this obligation is such that if the within bounden Thomas Choppin at any time within the space of four years from the feast of St. Michael the Archangel next coming etc. do pay etc. to the within named Thomas Lukyn, his executors or assigns nine pounds sterling before hand paid to the said Thomas Choppin by the hands of the said Thomas Lukyn for the bargain and sale of a croft of land called Broadfield etc. and a parcel of land lying in Heirs field. So that the said Thomas Choppin do not alien, sell, bargain, nor mortgage the said land to any other person or persons at any time, but only to the said Thomas Lukyn or his heirs. That then this obligation to be void, or else, etc'.

The judges held that these words following: 'So that' etc. be as much as [i.e. amounted to] 'If that'. And they were so taken and did not form a condition, because the word 'And' is lacking before the said words 'So that' etc. Thus the defendant was not obliged under this obligation to pay the said £9 if he had not alienated etc. the land in question etc. The author of this book was counsel for the said defendant.

3. Bendl. 215; Trin. 14 Eliz. (1572). Action on the case taken by Sir William More vs. Agnes Brown for diversion of water being carried by conduit from Clerkenwell; pleadings omitted.

Et apres un nisi prius sur ceo fuit agarde in London. Et le plaintiff done en evidence que le defendant causa un quill de plumbe destre fait hors de un graund pipe del dit conduit a issuer ou conveyer per un cocke a son messuage in le dit parish de Saint [Sepulchres], part del dit ewe, et que le dit defendant per le dit quill & cocke prist & diverte part del dit ewe hors del dit graund pipe la, le fesaunce de quel James Dyer Cheveler doncques chiefe justice del dit nisi prius dit al les jurors la, que ceo fuit le dit trespass, per que le defendant fuit trove culpable. Et le plaintiff aver son judgment & ses damages. Et le author de cest liver fuit del counsell ove [le] dit defendant.

And afterwards a nisi prius on this matter was awarded in London. And the plaintiff declared in evidence that the defendant had a small lead pipe connected to the large pipe of the said conduit to draw and convey part of the said water by means of a tap to her messuage in the parish of St. Sepulchre, and that the defendant by means of the said pipe and tap took and diverted part of the said water out of the said large pipe, the doing of which Sir James Dyer then the presiding justice of the said nisi prius told the jurors constituted the said trespass, wherefore the defendant was found guilty. And the plaintiff was to have his judgment and damages. And the author of this book was counsel for the said defendant.

4. Bendl. 293; Trin. 18 Eliz. (1576). Quare impedit sued against the Bishop of Lincoln by Roger Grendon; pleadings omitted.

Et cest matter fuit argue per les serjeants & justices & iii de les justices fuerent encontre le plaintiff & James Dyer le chief justice argue pur le plaintiff. Et nul judgment done mes [apres] ils eux accorde pur un some dargent agard al plaintiff. Et lauthor de cest liver fuit del counsell ove le dit plaintiff.

And this matter was argued by the serjeants and judges and three of the justices were against the plaintiff, and James Dyer the Chief Justice argued for the plaintiff. No judgment was rendered but afterwards they agreed on a sum of money to be awarded to the plaintiff. And the author of this book was counsel for the plaintiff.

DALISON

5. B.M. Harl. MS 5141, f. 15

Termino Michaelis Anno Regni Reginae Mariae primo 1553
ex libro manu William Dalison olim conscripto

(*a*) Nota per Bromley ore Cheife Justice Portman et Hales al Serieants Inne que en bref daccompt si le deffendant vient eins le primer iour et confesse laccion ou denia laccion en point le bref et ceo est [trove] vers luy per jury que le deffendant [accomptera] en gard et serra committ al prison quar per la ley nient pluis que le deffendant poet accompter sur parcells mes sur tout nient pluis poet le deffendant auterment accompter que en gard mes poet este lesse al mainprise al discrecion le courte

(*b*) Et en accompt ils disoent que le plaintiff ne recovera dammages contre que il declare de dammages pur le non certenty de son demaund mes Hales dit que livers sont agrees que si le deffendant devant auditors plede ple en discharge de son accompt come payment et sur ceo sont al yssue et trove pur le plaintiff que ore il recovera dammages entant que cest tryall est sur collaterall matter ou le certenty est primes conus per les auditors (*c*) Nota que si home a cest iour ou devant grant al auter per son fait que en consideration de son bon service que il ad fait ou a faire a luy ou en consideration que son file marier ove moye ou mon fitts que il avera tout le terre en un ville et cest graunt est par fait et nient enrolle que ore nul use est alterate sur cest graunt entant que il va per voy de graunt et done et prist nul perfeccion tanque le done soit execute per liverey de seisin et lenrollment ne serra en cest case car est hors del case destatute anno 27 H 8 et uncore si home done a moy xx livers in consideration que il avera mon terre pur son vie ore il ad use mon terre pur son vie devant liverey et seisin pur le certeintie del consideracion et en present temps

(*d*) Et si home a cest iour per identures de covenant parenter luy et auter de enfeoffer ou a doner xx livers en terre per an en consideracion dun marriage doncque ewe enter le fitts lun le file lauter que ore sans ascun enrolment apres tiel mariage luse est alterate accordant al covenant sans ascun auter enrolment ou livery de seisin entant que cest va en covenant et nemy per graunt ou done per Bromeley et Hales al Serieants Inne eodem termino

Michaelmas 1 Mary (1553) from the book written in the hand of William Dalison

(*a*) Note per Bromley now Chief Justice, Portman and Hales at Serjeants' Inn that in a writ of account if the defendant comes before the first day and confesses to the action or denies the action on the writ and this is found against him by jury, that the defendant will account in custody and be committed to prison; for, just as by law the defendant may not account by portions but upon the whole, so the defendant may not account otherwise than in custody though he may be allowed mainprize at the discretion of the court.

(*b*) And in an action of account they said that the plaintiff will not recover damages against whom he claims damages because of the non-certainty of his demand; but Hales said that the books are agreed that if the defendant makes a plea before the auditors to discharge himself of his account—as for example, payment—and on this [the parties] are at issue and judgment is found for the plaintiff, that now he will recover damages insofar as this trial is upon collateral matter where the certainty is initially recognized by the auditors.

(*c*) Note that if a man at this day or before grants to another by his deed that in consideration of the good service which he has done or will do for him, or in consideration that his daughter marry me or my son, he shall have all the land in a vill, and this grant is by deed and not enrolled; that now no use is changed on this grant inasmuch as it goes by way of grant and gift and takes no perfection until the gift is executed by livery of seisin and there will be no enrolment in this case as it is outside the terms of the statute 27 Hen. VIII [chap. 16]. And further, if a man gives to me £20 in consideration that he will have my land for his life he has the use of my land for life before livery and seisin by reason of the certainty of consideration and at the present time.

(*d*) And if a man at this day by indentures of covenant between him and another agree to enfeoff or to give £20 in land per year in consideration of a marriage then had between the son of one and the daughter of the other that now without any enrolment after such marriage the use is changed according to the covenant without any other enrolment or livery of seisin seeing that this is effected by covenant and not by grant or gift; by Bromley and Hales at Serjeants' Inn in the same term.

6. Dal. 14; 1 Mary (1553–4)

Nota per Bromeley Chief Justice & Portman & auters clerement agree que si plusors enter se conspire a faire commotion ou a levier guerre encountre le Roigne [en] son Realme pur alter & change religion [ou la ley], si nul act insue ceo nest treason per lestatute de anno 25 E. 3 mes si un de eux apres leve le guerre per reason de cest conspiracy, & les auters seont in lour measons sans auter act fair ilz sont touts traitours per le dit statute car per ceo ilz sont adherents & aidants al traitours, & in treason touts sont principals, & ceo fuit agree per eux mesme lan & terme al arraignement de Sir James Crofts en le Guildhall [in London] per estre adherent a Wiat, quod nota.

Note by Bromley Chief Justice and Portman and others it was clearly agreed that if several enter into conspiracy to make a commotion or to levy war against the Queen in her realm in order to alter and change religion or the law, if no act ensues upon the conspiracy it is not treason under the statute 25 Edw. III [Chap. 2]; but if one of them afterwards wages war by reason of this conspiracy, and the others are in their houses without committing any other act, they are all traitors by the said statute; for by this they are adherents and aiders to traitors; and in treason all are principals and this was agreed by them [the judges] the same year and term at the arraignment of Sir James Crofts at the Guildhall in London for being an adherent to Wyat, note this.

HARPER

7. B.M. Harg. MS 6, f. 1*v*; Mich. 1 Edw. VI (1547)

(*a*) Brooke monstre que un ad port bref dentrie en nature dassise de terre et ad purchase bref de transgressione retornable a mesme le iour et prie que le bref [de transgressione] abateroit Curia il ne abatera

(*b*) Nota per le Signior Mountague si un complaine al un Justice de Peace que J.S. ad fait felony et que il ad emble certaine choses et le Justice luy de liver al prochein Sessions de doner in evidence vers [le felon] pur que il est indicte de ceo et acquit uncore ne le Justice nec le partie soit chargeable in conspiracie

(*a*) Brooke shows that one has brought a writ of entry in the nature of assize of land and has purchased a writ of trespass returnable on the same day and prays that the writ of trespass shall abate. The court: it will not abate.

(*b*) Note by Lord Mountague that if one complains to a justice of the peace that J.S. has committed felony and has stolen certain things, and the justice delivers him to the next sessions to give evidence against the felon upon which he is indicted of this and acquitted; yet neither the justice nor the party is chargeable in conspiracy.

8. B.M. Harg. MS 6, f. 14; East. 3 Eliz. (1561)

Nota per Seriant Cholmeley et Plowden et divers auters in le case de le President del Corpus Christi Colledge en Oxon que si le President ou Maistre dun Colledge devise terre al Colledge ceo est void car al temps quant le devise prenderoit effect le corporacion est sans teste et sans lour teste ne poient ils receave al use lour meason pur ceo que le corporacion est donque imperfect

Note by Serjeant Cholmeley and Plowden and divers others in the case of the President of Corpus Christi College in Oxford that if the President or Master of a College devise land to the College this is void, for at the time when the bequest would take effect the corporation is without its head and without its head cannot receive to the use of its house because the corporation is then imperfect.

9. B.M. Harg. MS 6, ff. 32–32*v*; Trin. 8 Eliz. (1566)

(*a*) Nota per Dier et touts ses companions que si lessee pur ans graunt ouster son estate per indenture rendant rent uncore le grauntee serra attendant al primer lessor et il avera vers luy accion de wast

(*b*) Nota per Dier si gavelkind terre vient al roy per attainder de treason durant le possession le roy le custome est suspend mes sil graunt ceo ouster al estre in fee donque le custome est revive et si terre tenus dun comon person escheate al roy per treason et il graunt le terre de tener de chefe Signioris de fee ore le [tenure] est revive et le grauntee tiendra des signioris sicome il tenoit devant del roy et ceo fuit in bref [de] particion inter Lambert et Lambert

(*a*) Note by Dyer and all his companions that if a lessee for years grants over his estate [to another] by indenture yielding rent, the grantee will yet be answerable to the first lessor who will have action of waste against him.

(*b*) Note by Dyer. If gavelkind land comes to the king through attainder for treason, during the king's possession the custom is suspended but if he grant this over to be in fee then the custom is revived; and if land held of a common person escheat to the king by treason and he grant the land to be held in chief of the lord of the fee the tenure is now revived and the grantee will hold of the lord as he held before of the king, and this was in a writ of partition between Lambert and Lambert.

10. Dal. 63; 6 Eliz. (1563–4)

Action sur le case de ceo que le defendant appelle le pier le plaintiff bastard & ceo fuit trye a Warwicke & le plaintiff avoit judgment de recover, & en mesme le manner Dyer dit lou il appelle le plaintiff mesme bastard, mes Browne dubitavit quia ils ne poient trier le bastardy in le party mes destre [heire?] est auterment, auxi il dit que est auxy reasonable daver action sur le cas lou home appelle le bastard eigne loyal [fits] car per ceo le puisne fits est disable daver inheritance, issint per luy action bien gist sur ceo. Et issint semble loppinion del court que action sur le cas fuit bien mainteinable sur ceux parolx knave mungerel half a Guysian, and no meer Englishman quia a cel temps le Duke de Guyse fuit [reputed comme] enemy al realme & issint en lindictment de Poole, il fuit nosme maximus inimicus Dominae Reginae & Regno inimicus & issint dappeller un auter alien il duist aver action sur le cas, car il est de perder per ceo divers liberties & franchises, quel il duist aver per la ley del terre.

Action on the case where the defendant called the father of the plaintiff a bastard, and this was tried at Warwick and the plaintiff had judgment to recover, and in the same way, Dyer said, as if he had called the plaintiff himself a bastard; but Browne doubted whether they could try bastardy in the party, but if he were an heir it was a different matter; also he said it is just as reasonable to have action on the case where a man calls the bastard 'elder lawful son' for thereby the younger son is disabled from having inheritance. So according to him [i.e. Browne] action certainly lies on those grounds. And it thus seemed to be the view of the court that action on the case was certainly maintainable on the words 'knave mongrel half a Guisian, and no mere Englishman' because at that time the Duke of Guise was reputed a common enemy of the realm and thus in the indictment of Poole he was named *maximus inimicus Dominae Reginae et Regno inimicus*, and thus to call another 'alien' must give him action on the case for he stands to lose by this various liberties and franchises to which he is entitled by the law of the land.

11. Dal. 116; Mich. 15 & 16 Eliz. (1573)

Home est oblige de payer a un auter 20 s. per annum durant 20 ans toward the education of his son, per Mounson ceux parols towards the education of his son sont idle parols & le payment endurera si le fits devie, quaere.

A man is obliged to pay another 20*s.* per annum for twenty years towards the education of his son; Mounson holds that these words 'towards the education of his son' are casual words and that the payment will endure if the son dies; query.

12. Dyer, 93a; *Duke of Norfolk's Case*, Mich. 1 Mary (1553)

Note that in the last parliament of King Henry VIII a bill of petition was exhibited to the king by the lords and commons, for the attainder of the Duke of Norfolk of high treason, which passed through the two houses with the consent of the lords first, and [was] endorsed, 'Soit baille aux commons'; and then, with the assent of the commons, endorsed, 'Les commons sont assentus.' And when it was passed, the king, by his letters patent, bearing date 27 January in the 38th year of his reign, reciting the bill made in the form of an act and concluded and assented unto by the lords and commons, thought proper to grant and give his royal assent and consent to the said bill, and everything therein specified by these words: 'Know ye therefore, &c. that he had given power and authority to four of the lords, or three, to give assent and consent in his name, ratifying what they should do therein'. And the letters patent bore the sign manual of the king, s. Henricus Rex; and had also the great seal [affixed] to them. And this commission was annexed to the said bill, and the bill was also endorsed with these words, 'Soit fait come est desiré'. And it was much debated among the judges whether this was a complete act or not. And they who had purchased the lands which were the duke's of the king, procured a *certiorari* directed to two of the clerks of the parliament, to certify the tenour of an act of parliament made in such a year concerning the attainder of the said duke. And one of the clerks only made a certificate of the naked bill, without the circumstances, &c. And it was questioned whether this was good, because there was no warrant for only one of them to certify. And because the purchasers had procured a *certiorari* for the tenour of the act, without mentioning the commission to have been exemplified in chancery, the duke procured the very original record of the act to be brought by Spilman, the clerk of the parliament, before the judges at Serjeants' Inn. And note that by great probability and strong presumption, the king had not put his sign manual. First, inasmuch as it was written beneath the *teste* of the patent, whereas he was used to putting it above the head. Secondly, the writing was so perfect, that it could never have been written by a man so ill and near his death as the king was, for he died the same night, &c. And some further said, that it was a stamp. And see for this assent the statute 33 Hen. VIII, c. 21. And afterwards, the said act of attainder was declared by the parliament to be null and void. Quaere the act itself [37 Hen. VIII, c. 8].

13. Dyer, 179b; East. 2 Eliz. (1560)

A man seised in fee of lands in borough English after the statute 27 Hen. VIII [c. 10] made a feoffment to divers persons in fee to the use of himself and to his heirs male of his body begotten, according to the course of common law; and afterwards died seised accordingly, having issue two sons: the eldest entered, and held out the youngest. Quaere. And all the Board in Serjeants' Inn thought that the youngest shall have it by descent, notwithstanding the words aforesaid.

14. Dyer, 300b; East. 13 Eliz. (1571)

A feoffment is made in consideration of a marriage to be had, to the use of the feoffor for the term of his life, and after his decease to the wife by name that he was to marry for, during, and until any son that the feoffor should beget of the body of the said wife shall accomplish the age of twenty-one years; and after such time as the said son should arrive at the said age, then to the use of the said wife for and during the time that she should live sole, &c. And afterwards they intermarried, and the husband died without any issue begotten upon the wife, and she entered immediately, and continued sole, &c. Whether her entry be lawful or not, was the question upon a special verdict in *ejectione firmae*. And by the opinion of Weston, Harper and Dyer, her entry is lawful, and the estate and the remainder of the use good, although that he never had such son. And so they gave judgment without any argument; for if a feoffment be made to one and his heirs, *donec et quousque*, I.S. shall pay to the feoffor or to his heirs one thousand pounds; I.S. before any payment is made dies, the feoffor and his heirs shall retain the land absolutely *in perpetuum*; by all, at dinner in the judges' inn in Fleet Street. And yet afterwards in Michaelmas term, in the fifteenth year of the present queen, a writ of error was brought upon this judgment.

15. Plowden, 72; *Ross v. Pope*, 4 Edw. VI (1551)

A Report of a Judgment given in the Chancery, by deliberate Advice, upon an Argument in Easter Term, in the Fifth Year of the Reign of King Edward the Sixth, in a Writ of Audita Querela brought by Robert Ross, of Ingemanthorp, in the County of York,

Esquire, Plantiff, against Sir Thomas Pope, Knight, Defendant.

It appears amongst the rolls remaining in the Court of Chancery *de Termino Anno regni Regis nunc*, that the said Ross entered into a recognizance of 500 marks to the said Pope, and one Robert Curson, Esquire, according to the form of the statute 23 H. 8. cap. 6. And afterwards the same Ross and his wife, by fine, gave to the said conusees the fifth part of the manor of Burton Constable, and other lands in the said county of York, in fee. Afterwards the said Pope, as survivor, sued execution of the said recognizance in London against the said Ross, and his body was taken, and the said Ross, supposing that the said fine of the lands aforesaid discharged the said recognizance, sued the said writ of audita querela comprehending the whole matter, which writ bore date the second day of November last past, and was returned into Chancery on the octave of St. Hilary last passed, at which day the said Sir Thomas Pope appeared: and upon the said writ and declaration he demurred in judgment. And in this present Easter term, 4 Edw. 6, the matter was moved and touched many times. And now the Lord Rich, Chancellor of England, sent for Portman, one of the justices of the King's Bench, and Hales, one of the justices of the Common Bench, to have their advice, what the common law was in this case. For he ought to adjudge in this case according to the course of the common law, inasmuch as the matter came before him by original writ; but upon matters depending before him by bill, he may adjudge according to conscience, but here according to common law. And the said judges came into the Chancery, and sat there with the Chancellor, where the matter was spoke to, and the opinion of the Chancellor, and of the said justices, and of the whole Court of Chancery was, that the audita querela did not lie, because the land, which the conusees took from the conusor and his wife by the fine, was not the debtor, but the body of the conusor remained the debtor, and the land was liable only in respect that it was in the hands of the conusor at the time of the recognizance or after. . . .

16. Plowden, 117; *Newdigate v. the Earl of Derby*, Mich. 1 & 2 Phil. & Mary (1554); pleadings omitted.

> A Report of a Challenge taken in the Common Bench, in the Term of St. Michael in the first and second Years of the Reign of King Philip and Queen Mary, by the Earl of Derby, in an Assize brought before the Justices of the same Bench by John Newdigate, Plaintiff, against him and John Ansell, for Lands in the County of Middlesex. The Parties were at Issue, and the Assize was awarded, and the Jury appeared, and the Challenge was taken as hereafter follows. And it appears in the Rolls of the said Term, viz. Rot. 1454.

Upon this demurrer the court took good advice, for the case was a rare case, and none of the justices or serjeants could remember it to have been ever put in practice in their time, but that it was devised and determined to be put in practice in the assize brought by Wimbush against the Lord Willoughby, but it did not go forwards. And no book or case was found except one, which was in Mich. 13 Ed. 3 where the case appears to be as follows, viz. 'In a quare impedit against the Bishop of Exeter and others, upon the plea of the bishop the inquest was taken at the bar. Stouford: you see how that the writ requires that he should cause knights and other good men, to come, and he has not returned a knight, for which reason we apprehend you will not take this inquest, especially seeing a peer of the realm is party. Gayneford: the words of every *venire facias* are so, and yet a man shall take the inquest, although no knight be returned. Stonore: we have great regard to their coming the first day, and also when a peer of the realm is party, the law is otherwise than between other persons, wherefore since no knight is returned, we award that the whole inquest go without day'.—These are the words of the case, but in some books the case is differently expressed, though the substance and effect of it is the same in all the books that I have seen. And the justices considered well the said book, and the usual words in the writ of *venire facias*, which is, *we command you that you cause to come before*, &c. 12 *as well knights, as other free and lawful men*, &c. which words, viz. (*as well knights*) were not (as it was said) first put in the writ to no purpose. And they thought it well to take good deliberation upon the matter, it being a rare case, lest they should otherwise give judgment contrary to law, or should deny the peers of the realm that privilege which the common law gives them.

[The court ruled that the challenge was valid and quashed the panel.]

SELECT BIBLIOGRAPHY

Note: only those MSS which are not listed in Appendix I are given below. All printed material has been published in London unless otherwise stated.

A. PRIMARY SOURCES

I. MANUSCRIPT

Bodleian Library:	MS e. Mus. 17
British Museum:	Cotton MSS Faustina C.II, Vespasian C.XIV
	Hargrave MS 87
	Harleian MSS 760, 924, 5153–4, 6687
	Royal MSS 17E.VI, 18A.I
Cambridge University:	MSS Gg.11.5, Hh. 4.4–5
Inner Temple:	Barrington MS 56
Kent County Record Office:	Dalison MS E.1, 1/2
Library of Congress:	MS Ac. 1093–4
Lincoln's Inn:	Maynard MS 27
London Guildhall Library:	The Common Paper of the Company of Scriveners
Longleat (Marquess of Bath):	Thynne Papers, vol. II
Public Record Office (Prerogative Court of Canterbury):	Probate registers

II. PRINTED

1. Official Documents

Acts of the Privy Council of England, edited by J.R. Dasent, 32 vols. (1890–1907).

Calendar of Close Rolls, Henry VII, 2 vols. (1955–63).

Calendar of Letters and Papers, Foreign and Domestic, of the Reign of Henry VIII, 1509–47, edited by J.S. Brewer (vols. i–iv); by James Gairdner (vols. v–xiii; with R.H. Brodie, vols. xiv–xxi), 21 vols. (1862–1910). Vol. i edited by R.H. Brodie in 3 parts, 1920; Addenda, vol. i, pts. i, ii (1929–32).

Calendar of Patent Rolls, Henry VII, 2 vols. (1914–16); *Edward VI*, 5 vols. (1924–9); *Philip and Mary*, 4 vols. (1936–9); *Elizabeth*, 5 vols. (1558–72), (1939–66).

Calendar of State Papers, Domestic, edited by Robert Lemon (vols. i & ii, 1547–90); by M.A.E. Green (vols. iii–viii, 1591–1610 and addenda) (1856–72).

Journals of the House of Commons, vol. i (1547–1628).

Return of the Name of Every Member of the Lower House of the Parliaments of England, Scotland and Ireland . . . 1213–1874, 3 vols. Parl. papers (1878), lxii, pts. i–iii.

Statutes of the Realm, edited by A. Luders, T. E. Tomlins, J. Raithby *et al.*, vols. ii–iv (1817–19).

Tudor Royal Proclamations, edited by P. L. Hughes and J. F. Larkin, 3 vols. (New Haven and London, 1964–69).

2. Printed Reports, Abridgments and related Legal Works

ANDERSON, EDMUND, *Les Reports . . . Des Mults Principals Cases Argues & Adjuges . . . en le Common-Bank.*

ASHE, THOMAS, *Promptuary: et Table Generall a les Annales del Ley . . .* (1609).

BENDLOWES, WILLIAM, *Les Reports . . . des divers Resolutions et Judgments Donne . . . en le Temps del Raigne de Roys et Roignes Hen. VIII. Edw. VI. Phil. et Mary, et Elizab.* (1661).

—, *Les Reports . . . des divers Pleadings et Cases en le Court Comen-Bank* (1689).

BROOKE, ROBERT, *Ascuns Nouel cases des les ans et temps le Roy H.8, Ed.6, et la Roygne Mary* (1578).

—, *La Graunde Abridgement* (1573).

BROWNLOW, RICHARD, *Reports (A Second Part) of Diverse Famous Cases in Law* (1652).

—, and GOULDESBOROUGH, JOHN, *Reports of Diverse Choice Cases in Law* (1651).

BULSTRODE, EDWARD, *The Reports*, 3 parts (1688).

COKE, EDWARD, *Institutes of the Laws of England*, 4 parts. Pt. 1: 15th edition, 3 vols. (1794). Pt. 2: 6th edition (1691). Pt. 3: 6th edition (1680). Pt. 4: 5th edition (1671).

—, *The Reports of Sir Edward Coke Kt. in English in Thirteen Parts Compleat . . .* 7 vols. (1738).

A Complete Collection of State Trials . . ., edited by William Cobbett, T. B. Howell *et al.*, vol. i (1816).

CROKE, GEORGE, *The Reports*, 3 parts: Elizabeth (1661); James I (1659); Charles I (1657).

DALISON, WILLIAM, *Les Reports des divers special Cases Adjudge en le Court del Common Bank en les Reignes de . . . Hen. VIII. Edw. VI. Et les Reignes Mar. & Eliz.* (1689).

DYER, JAMES, *Reports of cases in the Reigns of Hen. VIII, Edw. VI, Q. Mary and Q. Eliz.* Translated and edited by John Valliant with additional references and bibliography of the reporter (1794). In addition to this standard English edition reference has been made to two earlier editions:

(i) *Cy ensuont ascun novels cases, collectes per . . . Jasques Dyer.* 1st edition (1585).
(ii) *Les Reports des divers select Matters . . .*, edited by George Treby (1688).

FLEETWOOD, WILLIAM, *Annalium tam Regum Edwardi quinti, Richard tertii, & Henrici septimi, quam Henrici octavi Titulorum . . . Elenchus*, as found in the Maynard edition of the Yearbooks (1679).

FITZHERBERT, ANTHONY, *La Graunde Abridgement* (1516).

—, *La Novel Natura Brevium*, edited and translated by W. Windham with commentary by Sir Matthew Hale (1682).

GOULDESBOROUGH, JOHN, *Reports of . . . choice cases . . . agitated in all the Courts at Westminster . . .* (1653).

HAWARDE, JOHN, *Les Reportes del Cases in Camera Stella, 1593–1609*, edited by W. P. Baildon (1894).

HOBART, HENRY, *The Reports* (1641).

JENKINS, DAVID, *Eight Centuries of Reports* (1734).

KEBLE, JOSEPH, *Reports in the King's Bench*, 3 parts (1685).

KEILWEY, ROBERT, *Relationes quorundam Casuum selectorum ex Libris Roberti Keilwey* (1602).

LANE, RICHARD, *Reports in the Court of Exchequer* (1657).

LEONARD, WILLIAM, *Reports and Cases at Law*, 4 parts (1658–75).

MOORE, FRANCIS, *Cases Collect & Report* (1663).

OWEN, THOMAS, *The Reports* (1656).

PALMER, GEOFFREY, *Les Reports* (1678).

PLOWDEN, EDMUND, *The Commentaries or Reports*, 2 parts (1816). Reference has also been made to Plowden's own copy of the 1st edition of Part 1 (1571).

POPHAM, JOHN, *Reports and Cases* (1656).

RASTELL, JOHN, *Le Liver des Assises & Plees del Coronne* (1516).

RASTELL, WILLIAM, *A Colleccion of Entrees of Declaracions, Barres, . . . and divers other Matters* (1566).

ROLLE, HENRY, *Un Abridgement Des Plusieurs Cases et Resolutions del Common Ley*, 2 vols. (1668).

—, *Les Reports*, 2 vols. (1675–6).

SAVILE, JOHN, *Les Reports* (1675).

WINCH, HUMPHREY, *Reports* (1657).

YEARBOOKS, *Les Reports des Cases en les Ans des Roys Edward V, Richard III, Henrie VII & Henrie VIII Touts qui par cy devant ont este Publies*, edited by John Maynard (1679). For reference purposes this is the most convenient edition, but the following editions were consulted for purposes of dating and textual comparison;
(i) Yearbooks 1–8 Henry VII, published by Richard Pynson [1500–10?].
(ii) Yearbooks 1–8 Henry VII, published by Robert Redmond [1530?].

(iii) Yearbooks 1–16, 20 & 21 Henry VIII, published by Richard Tottel (1555).
(iv) Yearbooks 12–13 Henry VIII, published by Robert Redmond [1535?].
(v) Yearbook 14 Henry VIII, published by Richard Pynson [1523–8?].
(vi) Yearbook 14 Henry VIII, published by Robert Redmond (1540).
(vii) Yearbooks 18–19, 26 & 27 Henry VIII, published by William Myddelton [1545?].

YELVERTON, HENRY, *Les Reports* (1674).

3. Contemporary or near-Contemporary Legal Treatises, Chronicles and other Writings

BUCK, GEORGE, *The Third University of England* (1615). Published at the end of Stow's *Annals*, ed. 1615.

CAMDEN, WILLIAM, *Annales Rerum Anglicarum et Hibernicarum Regnante Elizabetha*, edited by Thomas Hearne, 3 vols. (1717).

EGERTON, THOMAS, *A Discourse upon the Exposition and Understanding of the Statutes*, edited by S.E. Thorne with introduction (San Marino, U.S.A., 1942).

ELYOT, THOMAS, *The Boke named the Governour*, edited by H.H.S. Croft, 2 vols. (1883).

FABYAN, ROBERT, *The New Chronicles of England and France, in Two Parts . . .*, edited by H. Ellis (1811).

FORTESCUE, JOHN, *De Laudibus Legum Angliae*, translated and edited with introduction and notes by S.B. Chrimes (Cambridge, 1942).

FRAUNCE, A., *The Lawyer's Logike . . .* (1588).

FULBECKE, WILLIAM, *A Direction or Preparative to the Study of the Law* (1600).

—, *A Parallele or Conference of the Civil Law, the Canon Law, and the Common Law, of this Realme of England . . .* (1601–2).

HALL, EDWARD, *The Union of the Two Noble and Illustre Families York and Lancaster . . .*, edited by Henry Ellis (1809).

HATTON, CHRISTOPHER, *A Treatise concerning Statutes, or Acts of Parliament: and the Exposition thereof* (1677).

HERBERT, EDWARD, LORD, *The Life and Raigne of King Henry the Eighth* (1672).

HOLINSHED, RAPHAEL, *Chronicles of England, Scotland, and Ireland*, edited by Henry Ellis, 6 vols. (1807–8).

LAMBARDE, WILLIAM, *A Perambulation of Kent* (1576).

NORTH, ROGER, *The Lives of the Right Hon. Francis North, Baron Guilford . . . Sir Dudley North . . . and Rev. Dr. John North*, 3 vols. (1826).

Praxis utriusque Banci. The Antient and Modern Practice of the Two Superior Courts at Westminster (1674).

ROBINSON, RICHARD, 'A Briefe Collection of the Queene Majesties Most High and Most Honourable Courtes of Recordes', edited by R. L. Rickard, *Camd. Misc.* xx (Camd. 3rd Series lxxxiii).

SAINT GERMAN, CHRISTOPHER, *Doctor and Student; or Dialogues between a Doctor of Divinity and a Student of the Laws of England . . .* (1721).

STANFORD, WILLIAM, *Exposicion of the Kinge's Prerogative* (1567).

STARKEY, THOMAS, *A Dialogue between Cardinal Pole and Thomas Lupset*, edited by J. M. Cowper, Early English Text Society, Extra Series, xii (1871).

STOW, JOHN, *The Annals of England . . . from the First Inhabitation untill this Present Yeare 1592* (1631).

WILSON, THOMAS, 'The State of England Anno. Dom. 1600', edited by F. J. Fisher, *Camd. Misc.* xvi (Camd. 3rd Series lii).

4. Other Printed Material

British Borough Charters, 1307–1660, edited by Martin Weinbaum, (Cambridge, 1943).

A Calendar of the Inner Temple Records, edited by F. A. Inderwick, 5 vols. (1896–1937).

A Calendar of Middle Temple Records, edited by C. H. Hopwood (1902).

Catalogue of Notable Middle Templars, edited by John Hutchison (1902).

Early Records of Furnival's Inn, edited by D. S. Bland with introduction (Newcastle-upon-Tyne, 1957).

Historical Manuscripts Commission: First–Fourth, Seventh, Ninth and Tenth Reports with appendices (1870–85).

Historical Manuscripts Commission: Calendar of the Manuscripts of the . . . Marquess of Salisbury . . . preserved at Hatfield House, Hertfordshire, vols. 1 & 15 (1883–1930).

Materials for a History of the Reign of Henry VII, edited by William Campbell, 2 vols., R.S. (1873).

The Middle Temple Bench Book . . ., edited by A. R. Ingpen, 2nd edition (1937).

Middle Temple Records: Minutes of Parliament, 1501–1703, edited by C. T. Martin, 4 vols. (1904–5).

Pension Book of Clement's Inn, edited by Cecil Carr with introduction, S.S. lxxviii (1960).

The Pension Book of Gray's Inn, 1569–1800, edited by R. J. Fletcher, 2 vols. (1901–10).

Proceedings in Parliament, 1610, edited by E. R. Foster, 2 vols. (New Haven, 1966).

Records and Documents concerning Serjeants' Inn Fleet Street, edited by H. C. King (1922).

Records of the English Province of the Society of Jesus, edited by Henry Foley, vol. IV (1877).

The Records of the Honourable Society of Lincoln's Inn: Admissions, 1420–1893, and Chapel Registers, 2 vols. (1896).

The Records of the Honourable Society of Lincoln's Inn: the Black Books, 1422–1845, edited by J.D. Walker and W.P. Baildon, 4 vols. (1897–1902).

A Register of Admissions to Gray's Inn, 1521–1881, edited by Joseph Foster, 2 vols. (1881–5).

Register of Admissions to the Honourable Society of the Middle Temple, from the Fifteenth Century to . . . 1944, edited by H.A.C. Sturgess, 3 vols. (1949).

Students Admitted to the Inner Temple 1547–1660, edited by W.H. Cooke (1878).

Three Learned Readings (1648).

The Tudor Constitution: Documents and Commentary, edited by G.R. Elton (Cambridge, 1962).

WILLIS, BROWNE, *Notitia Parliamentaria, or an History of the Countries, Cities and Boroughs in England and Wales . . .*, vol. i (1730).

B. SECONDARY SOURCES

1. Reference Works

BEALE, J.H., *A Bibliography of Early English Law Books* (Cambridge, USA, 1926); supplement by J.A. Anderson (1943).

BLAND, D.S., *A Bibliography of the Inns of Court and Chancery*, S.S. (1965).

COWLEY, J.D., *A Bibliography of Abridgments, Digests, Dictionaries and Indexes of English Law to . . . 1800*, S.S. (1932).

HASSALL, W.O. (ed.), *A Catalogue of the Library of Sir Edward Coke* (New Haven, 1950).

HOLDSWORTH, W.S., *Sources and Literature of English Law* (1925).

MARVIN, J.G., *Legal Bibliography* (Philadelphia, 1847).

MAXWELL, W.H. and MAXWELL, L.F., *English Law to 1800 . . .*, vol. i of *A Legal Bibliography of the British Commonwealth of Nations* (1955).

MAXWELL, W.H. and BROWN, C.R. *A Complete List of British and Colonial Law Reports and Legal Periodicals* (1937).

NICHOLSON, JENNIFER, *A Register of Manuscripts and Printed Year Books Extant*, S.S. (1956).

SOULE, C.C., 'Year Book Bibliography', *H.L.R.* xiv (1901), 556–87.

WINFIELD, P.H., *The Chief Sources of English Legal History* (Cambridge, USA, 1925).

2. Histories of Law and Legal Institutions

ALLEN, C.K., *Law in the Making*, 7th edition (Oxford, 1964).

BAKER, J.H., *An Introduction to English Legal History* (1971).

BLATCHER, MAJORIE, 'Touching the Writ of Latitat: an Act "of no great moment"', *Elizabethan Government and Society. Essays presented to Sir John Neale*, edited by S.T. Bindoff, J. Hurstfield and C.H. Williams (1961).

FIFOOT, C.H.S., *History and Sources of the Common Law: Tort and Contract* (1949).

GRAY, C.M., *Copyhold, Equity and the Common Law* (Cambridge, USA, 1963).

HALE, MATTHEW, *The History of the Common Law of England*, 3rd edition (1739).

HALL, G.D.G., 'Impositions and the Courts', *L.Q.R.* lxix (1953), 200–18.

HASTINGS, MARGARET, *The Court of Common Pleas in Fifteenth Century England* (Ithaca, 1947).

HEMMANT, M., 'Introduction', *Select Cases in the Exchequer Chamber*, 2 vols., S.S. li, lxiv (1938–48).

HOLDSWORTH, W.S., *Essays in Law and History*, edited by A.L. Goodhart and H.G. Hanbury (Oxford, 1946).

—, *A History of English Law*, 13 vols. (1922–52).

JONES, W.J., *The Elizabethan Court of Chancery* (Oxford, 1967).

LEWIS, T. ELLIS, 'The History of Judicial Precedent', *L.Q.R.* xlvi, xlvii, xlviii (1930–2), 207–24 and 341–60, 411–27, 230–47.

MAITLAND, F.W., *English Law and the Renaissance* (Cambridge, 1901).

—, *Forms of Action at Common Law*, edited by A.H. Chaytor and W.J. Whittaker (Cambridge, 1954).

MILSOM, S.F.C., *Historical Foundations of the Common Law* (1969).

PLUCKNETT, T.F.T., *A Concise History of the Common Law*, 5th edition (1956).

—, 'Ellesmere on Statutes', *L.Q.R.* lx (1944), 242–9.

—, *Statutes and their Interpretation in the First Half of the Fourteenth Century* (Cambridge, 1922).

PUTNAM, B.H., *Early Treatises on the Practice of the Justices of the Peace in the Fifteenth and Sixteenth Centuries*, vol. vii of *Oxford Studies in Social and Legal History* (Oxford, 1926).

RADCLIFFE, G.R.Y. and CROSS, GEOFFREY, *The English Legal System*, 3rd edition (1954).

REEVES, JOHN, *A History of English Law*, edited by W.F. Finlason, 3 vols. (1869).

SIMPSON, A.W.B., *Introduction to the History of the Land Law* (Oxford, 1961).

3. Works concerned with the History of Law-Reporting

BOLLAND, W.C., 'Introduction', *Year Book of the Eyre of Kent, 6 & 7 Edward II*, vol. iii, S.S. xxix (Year Book Series, vol. viii) (1913).

—, *The Year Books* (Cambridge, 1921).

HALL, G. D. G., 'Bate's Case and "Lane's" Reports', *Bul. John Rylands Lib.* xxxv (1952–3), 405–27.

HOLDSWORTH, W. S., 'The Year Books', *L.Q.R.* xxii (1906), 360–82.

MAITLAND, F. W., 'Introduction', *Year Books 1 & 2 Edward II*, S.S. xvii (Year Book Series, vol. i) (1903).

PIKE, L. O., 'Introduction', *Year Book 20 Edward III*, vol. ii, R.S. xxxi (1911).

PLUCKNETT, T. F. T., *Early English Legal Literature* (Cambridge, 1958).

—, 'The Genesis of Coke's Reports', *Cornell Law Quarterly*, xxvii (1942), 190–213.

—, 'Introduction', *Year Book 13 Richard II*, A.S. (1929).

ROGERS, R. V., 'Introduction', *Year Books 9–10 Henry V* (Wurzburg, 1948).

SIMPSON, A. W. B., 'The Circulation of the Yearbooks in the Fifteenth Century', *L.Q.R.* lxxiii (1957), 492–505.

—, 'Keilwey's Reports, Temp. Henry VII and Henry VIII', *L.Q.R.* lxxiii (1957), 89–105.

—, 'The Reports of John Spelman', *L.Q.R.* lxxii (1956), 334–8.

—, 'The Source and Function of the Later Year Books', *L.Q.R.* lxxxvii (1971), 94–118.

TURNER, G. J., 'Introduction', *Year Book 4 Edward II*, S.S. xxvi (Year Book Series, vol. vi) (1911).

VEEDER, V. V., 'The English Reports, 1292–1865', *H.L.R.* xv (1901), 1–21, 109–57.

VINOGRADOFF, PAUL, 'Constitutional History and the Year Books', *L.Q.R.* xxix (1913), 273–84.

WALLACE, J. W., *The Reporters Arranged and Characterized* . . ., 4th edition by F. F. Heard (Boston, 1882).

4. Works relating to the Legal Profession, Individual Practitioners and the Inns of Court

'Autobiography of Baron Savile', edited by J. W. Clay and John Lister, *Yorks. Arch. Jour.* xv (1900), 421–7.

BOWEN, C. D., *The Lion and the Throne: the Life and Times of Sir Edward Coke, 1552–1634* (Boston, 1957).

CAMPBELL, J., *The Lives of the Chief Justices of England*, 3 vols. (1849–57),

COOPER, C. H. and COOPER, T., *Athenae Cantabrigienses*, 2 vols. (Cambridge, 1858–61).

COVERNTON, J. G., 'Some Local Memorials of and References to the Family of Bendlowes in Great Barfield, Finchingfield and Neighbourhood' (Finchingfield, 1934). Unpublished essay, Essex County Record Office—T/G 98.

D'EWES, SIMONDS, *The Autobiography and Correspondence of Sir Simonds D'Ewes*, edited by J. O. Halliwell, 2 vols. (1845).

DUGDALE, WILLIAM, *Origines Juridicales*, 1671.

FOSS, EDWARD, *Judges of England . . . 1066–1864*, 9 vols. (1848–64).
History of Parliament Trust. Biographies in typescript of members of parliament in the reigns of Henry VII, Henry VIII, Edward VI, Philip & Mary and Elizabeth.
IVES, E. W., 'Promotion in the Legal Profession', *L.Q.R.* lxxv (1959), 348–63.
—, 'Some Aspects of the Legal Profession in the Late Fifteenth and Early Sixteenth Centuries', unpublished Ph.D. Thesis (London, 1955).
LLOYD, DAVID, *The Statesmen and Favourites of England since the Reformation* (1665).
MANNING, JAMES, *Serviens ad Legem* (1840).
PLUCKNETT, T. F. T., 'The Place of the Legal Profession in the History of English Law', *L.Q.R.* xlviii (1932), 328–40.
PUGH, CHARLES, 'Origin and Progress of Barnard's Inn', *Notes & Queries*, 7th series (1887), iii, 83–4, 202–4.
Records of the Plowden Family, prepared by 'B.M.P.', printed in 1887 for private circulation.
SPEDDING, JAMES, *The Letters and Life of Francis Bacon*, 7 vols. (1861–72).
THORNE, S. E., 'Introduction', *Readings and Moots at the Inns of Court*, vol. i, S.S. lxxi (1955).
—, *Sir Edward Coke, 1552–1952* (S.S. lecture, 1952) (1957).
WATERHOUSE, EDWARD, *Fortescutus Illustratus* (1663).
WHETSTONE, GEORGE, 'A Rembraunce of the Precious Vertues of . . . Sir J. Dier . . .', *Frondes Caducae*, vol. i (1816).
WILLIAMS, ELIJAH, *Early Holborn and the Legal Quarter of London*, 2 vols. (1927).
WOOD, A. A., *Athenae Oxonienses*, edited by Philip Bliss, 4 vols. (1813–20).
WOOLRYCH, H. W., *Lives of Eminent Serjeants-at-Law of the English Bar*, 2 vols. (1869).
WOTTON, THOMAS, *The Baronetage of England*, 3 vols. (1771).

5. MISCELLANEOUS

BENNETT, H. S., *English Books and Readers*, vols. 1 & 2 (Cambridge, 1952–65).
COBBETT, WILLIAM, *Parliamentary History of England from the Norman Conquest in 1066 to the Year 1803*, vol. i (1806).
CREIGHTON, CHARLES, *A History of Epidemics in Britain from A.D. 664 to the Extinction of the Plague*, 2 vols., 2nd edition (1965).
EDWARDS, J. GORONWY, 'The Emergence of Majority Rule in English Parliamentary Elections', *Trans. R.H.S.*, 5th series, xiv (1964), 175–96.
—, 'The Emergence of Majority Rule in the Procedure of the House of Commons', *Trans. R.H.S.*, 5th series, xv (1965), 165–87.
ELTON, G. R., *England under the Tudors* (1960).
—, *The Tudor Revolution in Government* (Cambridge, 1953).

JENKINSON, HILARY, *The Later Court Hands in England: from the Fifteenth to the Seventeenth Century* (Cambridge, 1927).

—, 'The Teaching and Practice of Handwriting in England', *History*, xi (1926–7), 130–8.

MCKISACK, MAY, *The Parliamentary Representation of the English Boroughs during the Middle Ages* (1932).

NEALE, J. E., *Elizabeth I and her Parliaments, 1559–81* (1953); *1584–1603* (1957).

—, *The Elizabethan House of Commons* (1949).

OGLE, ARTHUR, *The Tragedy of the Lollards' Tower* (Oxford, 1949).

PICKTHORN, K. W. M., *Early Tudor Government*, 2 vols. vol. i, *Henry VII*; vol. ii, *Henry VIII* (Cambridge, 1934).

SOMERVILLE, ROBERT, *History of the Duchy of Lancaster*, vol. i (1953).

STUBBS, WILLIAM, *Seventeen Lectures on Medieval and Modern History* (Oxford, 1886, 1887).

INDEX